I Glory in My Jesus

Brigham Young University
COME, FOLLOW ME SYMPOSIUM
in Honor of Sidney B. Sperry

I Glory in My Jesus

Understanding Christ in the Book of Mormon

Edited by John Hilton III, Nicholas J. Frederick,
Mark D. Ogletree, and Krystal V. L. Pierce

Published by the Religious Studies Center, Brigham Young University, Provo, Utah, in cooperation with Deseret Book Company, Salt Lake City, Utah.

© 2023 by Brigham Young University. All rights reserved.

Printed in the United States of America by Sheridan Books, Inc.

DESERET BOOK is a registered trademark of Deseret Book Company. Visit us at DeseretBook.com.

Any uses of this material beyond those allowed by the exemptions in US copyright law, such as section 107, "Fair Use," and section 108, "Library Copying," require the written permission of the publisher, Religious Studies Center, 185 HGB, Brigham Young University, Provo, UT 84602. The views expressed herein are the responsibility of the authors and do not necessarily represent the position of The Church of Jesus Christ of Latter-day Saints, Brigham Young University, or the Religious Studies Center.

Cover and interior design by Carmen Durland Cole.

ISBN 978-1-9503-0445-5

Library of Congress Cataloging-in-Publication Data
Names: Sperry Symposium (52nd : 2023 : Brigham Young University), author. | Hilton, John, III, editor. | Frederick, Nicholas J., editor. | Ogletree, Mark, 1962– editor. | Pierce, Krystal V. L., editor.
Title: I glory in my Jesus : understanding Christ in the Book of Mormon / edited by John Hilton III, Nicholas J. Frederick, Mark D. Ogletree, and Krystal V. L. Pierce.
Description: Provo, Utah : Religious Studies Center, Brigham Young University : Salt Lake City, Utah : Deseret Book, [2023] | Includes index. | Summary: "Jesus Christ is the central figure in the Book of Mormon. Ancient prophets in the western hemisphere consistently pointed to his life and atoning sacrifice. For example, Nephi wrote, "I glory in my Jesus, for he hath redeemed my soul from hell" (2 Nephi 33:6). After his resurrection, Jesus Christ personally ministered to the Nephites and taught them. This volume shares important reminders about how to focus on Jesus Christ in the Book of Mormon"—Provided by publisher.
Identifiers: LCCN 2023015725 | ISBN 9781950304455 (hardback)
Subjects: LCSH: Jesus Christ—In the Book of Mormon. | Church of Jesus Christ of Latter-day Saints—Doctrines. | Book of Mormon—Criticism, interpretation, etc. | Mormon Church—Doctrines.
Classification: LCC BX8627 .S7765 2023 | DDC 289.3/22—dc23/eng/20230607
LC record available at https://lccn.loc.gov/2023015725

Contents

VII
Introduction

1
1. The Book of Mormon's Relevance for Us:
Promises for Our Time
Reyna I. Aburto

19
2. Jesus Christ and the Gathering of Israel:
A Book of Mormon Perspective
Robert L. Millet

37
3. Coming to Know Christ through the "I Am"
Statements in the Book of Mormon
Joshua M. Matson

63
4. Remember Him: The Christ-Centered Focus
of *Remembering* in the Book of Mormon
Michael David Ricks

87
5. The Brazen Serpent as a Symbol of Jesus Christ:
A Dichotomy of Benevolence and Admonition
Krystal V. L. Pierce

107
6. "That They May Bear Testimony of Him": Jesus Christ's
Communication to and about Prophets in the Book of Mormon
Stephanie Dibb Sorensen

125
7. According to Their Faith: Alma and Amulek
Typify Jesus in Overcoming Evil
Stephan D. Taeger

145
8. "I Am the Law": Jesus Christ and the Law
of Moses in the Book of Mormon
Thora Florence Shannon and Avram R. Shannon

169
9. The Redeemer: Taking upon Him the Sins of the World
Jennifer C. Lane

187
10. Book of Mormon "Trinitarianism" and the Nature
of Jesus Christ: Old and New World Contexts
Stephen O. Smoot and Kerry Hull

211
11. "That Ye Might Feel and See": Touch in
the First Day of Christ's Ministry
Daniel L. Belnap

235
12. Mentoring in the Savior's Way: Learning from
Jesus Christ's Example in 3 Nephi
Camey L. Andersen

249
13. Jesus Christ as a Revealer of Ordinances in the Book of Mormon
David Calabro

259
14. The Way, the Truth, and the Way to Truth:
Harmony in Pursuit of Orthodoxy
Jared M. Halverson

293
15. Ascended into Heaven: The Book of Mormon's
Witness of Jesus Christ's Ascension
William Perez

311
Index

Introduction

At the beginning of the Book of Mormon, Nephi tells us the main reason he is writing: "The fulness of mine intent is that I may *persuade* men to *come unto the God of Abraham, and the God of Isaac, and the God of Jacob*, and be saved" (1 Nephi 6:4).[1] As Nephi passes the plates to Jacob, this emphasis continues. Jacob records, "[Nephi] gave me, Jacob, a commandment that I should write upon these plates a few of the things which I considered to be most precious.... We labored diligently among our people, that we might *persuade* them to come unto *Christ*" (Jacob 1:2, 7).

The small plates were passed from one author to another, finally coming into the possession of Amaleki, who finished the small plates by writing, "I would that ye should *come unto Christ*, who is the Holy One of Israel, ... and offer your whole souls as an offering unto him" (Omni 1:26). Throughout the remainder of the Book of Mormon, there is a consistent focus on Jesus Christ. Consider just a few examples:

- King Benjamin taught, "There shall be no other name given nor any other way nor means whereby salvation can come unto the

children of men, only in and through the name of Christ, the Lord Omnipotent" (Mosiah 3:17).
- Abinadi declared, "Christ . . . is the light and the life of the world; yea, a light that is endless, that can never be darkened; yea, and also a life which is endless, that there can be no more death" (Mosiah 16:8–9).
- Alma the Younger testified, "I know that Jesus Christ shall come, yea, the Son, the Only Begotten of the Father, full of grace, and mercy, and truth. And behold, it is he that cometh to take away the sins of the world, yea, the sins of every [person] who steadfastly believeth on his name" (Alma 5:48).

The pinnacle of the Book of Mormon occurred in 3 Nephi when Jesus Christ personally ministered to the Nephites and Lamanites. He directly told them, "Arise and *come forth unto me*, that ye may thrust your hands into my side, and also that ye may feel the prints of the nails in my hands and in my feet, that ye may know that I am the God of Israel" (3 Nephi 11:14).

The final writers of the Book of Mormon end where Nephi began. Mormon says, "I write unto you, . . . that ye may believe the gospel of Jesus Christ. . . . And I would that I could persuade all ye ends of the earth to repent and prepare to stand before the judgment-seat of Christ" (Mormon 3:20–22), and Moroni concludes his record with one final plea to "come unto Christ" (Moroni 10:32).

Clearly the central purpose of those writing on the plates was to invite and persuade each of us to come unto Jesus Christ. He is the central individual in the Book of Mormon. In 1978 Susan Ward Easton published a landmark article, numerically demonstrating this fact by showing that Christ was mentioned by name or title 3,925 times in the Book of Mormon, which averages out to be once every 1.7 verses.[2]

This valuable study highlights the centrality of Christ in the Book of Mormon; however, it significantly *undercounts* the frequency with which Christ is mentioned by excluding pronouns that refer to him. Consider how the following verse emphasizes the Savior through pronouns: "Begin to believe in the *Son of God*, that *he* will come to redeem *his* people, and that *he* shall suffer and die to atone for their sins; and that *he* shall rise again from the dead, which shall bring to pass the resurrection, that all men shall stand before *him*, to be judged at the last and judgment day, according to their works" (Alma 33:22).

In Dr. Easton's original study, this verse would have counted as one reference to Christ from the title "Son of God." However, the Savior is mentioned five additional times. This verse emphasizes that Jesus Christ is not only the Son of God but is also the one to redeem us through his everlasting atonement and resurrection.

Ultimately the number of references to Jesus Christ is not the most important detail to learn from the Book of Mormon; however, each reference to Christ can teach us about his divine nature and mission. When all mentions of Christ, including titles and pronouns are included, his name appears 7,452 times in the Book of Mormon—an average of more than one reference per verse.[3]

The Book of Mormon has much to teach us about Jesus Christ; indeed, as President Ezra Taft Benson taught, it "is the keystone in our witness of Jesus Christ."[4] In this volume, you will find fifteen carefully crafted essays that examine the life, teachings and nature of Jesus Christ as described in the Book of Mormon. We hope that this exploration of our Savior in the Book of Mormon will help you both "glory in" and "seek" Jesus Christ (2 Nephi 33:6; Ether 12:41).

Finally, we are grateful for the good work of the Religious Studies Center team: Jared W. Ludlow, Devan Jensen, Brent Nordgren, Carmen Cole, and Adi Marshall.

John Hilton III
Nicholas J. Frederick
Mark D. Ogletree
Krystal V. L. Pierce
Brent R. Nordgren
Beverly Yellowhorse
Symposium Committee

Notes

Since 1973 the BYU Sidney B. Sperry Symposium has become one of the premier venues for Latter-day Saint religious studies. The symposium originated to encourage faith-based religious scholarship on Latter-day Saint topics. Beginning in January 2024, the Sperry Symposium will be renamed the *Come, Follow Me* Symposium in Honor of Sidney B. Sperry. The dates changed from October to January to connect the symposium more closely to the *Come, Follow Me* schedule.

1. All emphasis in this introduction is added.
2. Susan Ward Easton, "Names of Christ in the Book of Mormon," *Ensign*, July 1978, 60–61.
3. Some verses contain multiple references to Christ, while others have none. On average there is one reference to Christ for every .88 verses in the Book of Mormon. The counting of these references was done by John Hilton III and Madison Sinclair.
4. Ezra Taft Benson, "The Book of Mormon—Keystone of Our Religion," *Ensign*, November 1986, 5.

1

The Book of Mormon's Relevance for Us

Promises for Our Time

Reyna I. Aburto

We live in a world similar to the one in which Joseph Smith lived in 1820, a world filled with "stir and division amongst the people," "great confusion and bad feeling," "a strife of words," "a contest about opinions," a "war of words," and a "tumult of opinions."[1] We could even compare the current commotion in the world with the environment surrounding Lehi and Sariah's family in Jerusalem, as well as the Nephites and Lamanites in the American continent during the centuries before Christ visited them. There was disobedience to God's commandments, wickedness, abominations, secret combinations, conflicts, wars, and divisiveness, among other things. "Knowing the calamity which should come upon the inhabitants of the earth, [the Lord] called upon [his] servant Joseph Smith, Jun., and spake unto him from heaven, and gave him commandments; and also gave commandments to others, that they should proclaim these things unto the world; and all this that it might be fulfilled, which was written by the prophets."[2]

In His infinite wisdom and mercy, God provided a way for a record to be kept by many prophets, preserved by valiant hands, brought to light by divine means and translated into English by the gift and power of God. The Book of Mormon is another testament of Jesus Christ written for our day and full of promises about Him and from Him that have significant relevancy for us in our time.

President Russell M. Nelson has said, "Prophets have foreseen our day, when there would be wars and rumors of wars and when the whole earth would be in commotion.... [The] gospel of Jesus Christ has never been needed more than it is today.... I love the Lord Jesus Christ and testify that His gospel is the only enduring solution for peace. His gospel is a gospel of peace."[3]

Because the Book of Mormon "contains the fulness of the everlasting gospel,"[4] it can be a constant source of peace for us, the peace that only Jesus Christ can give through His redeeming atonement. President Nelson has also proclaimed, "When I think of the Book of Mormon, I think of the word *power*. The truths of the Book of Mormon have the *power* to heal, comfort, restore, succor, strengthen, console, and cheer our souls."[5]

As we embark together in studying the Book of Mormon, we can find relevance and solace in the promises it contains about and from Jesus Christ, particularly in the promises concerning our day, and, together with Nephi, we can say, "I glory in my Jesus, for he hath redeemed my soul from hell."[6]

We Are All Gospel Teachers

As covenant members of the Church, we all have opportunities to be gospel teachers everywhere we go, from our homes to our Church callings and gatherings, our schools, our jobs, our circles of friends and our communities. One of the beauties of being a gospel teacher is that as we invite others to get closer to Christ by studying and searching the Book of Mormon individually, with their families, with their friends, and in Church gatherings, we can also take that learning journey with them. Together we can express our feelings, our longings, our questions, our hope, our faith, and our testimony of the gospel of Jesus Christ to encourage, comfort, and inspire each other as we all come to our

Savior to receive of His redeeming grace. Together we can realize how relevant the truths and promises taught and given by Jesus Christ and His disciples are for our salvation in our day and how we can apply them in our daily life. The Book of Mormon is full of those relevant truths and promises through which we can receive the Lord's strength to endure the vicissitudes of this world with joy.

Having the Desire to Know

After hearing the things that his father had seen, Nephi "desired to know" them, and he believed "that the Lord was able to make them known unto [him]."[7] Similarly, Enos's "soul hungered" because "the words which [he] had often heard [his] father speak concerning eternal life, and the joy of the saints, sunk deep into [his] heart."[8]

As we prepare to teach the Book of Mormon, we can ask ourselves this question, "What can I do to inspire my learners to have the desire to know the things concerning eternal life in a way that is relevant to them and their soul hungers?"

A key part of sparking desire in learners is to help them see the relevance of what we are teaching to their lives. As one researcher wrote, "Making lessons meaningful for learners is one of the key elements of successful learning, and relevance is a vital contributor to learner engagement. If we feel that what we are learning is relevant to our lives, we become emotionally invested in the lesson and the content, and are more motivated to engage."[9]

Similarly, a document prepared by Brigham Young University says, "Students are more likely to engage when they perceive the value of what they are learning for their personal growth, professional growth, and for the people, communities, and causes they care about."[10]

As gospel teachers we can pray for revelation on how to prepare lessons that are relevant to our learners and help them receive the divine guidance they need in their lives.

How Relevant Is the Book of Mormon in Our Day?

Years ago a group of Brigham Young University students embarked in what was called the Book of Mormon Experiment. "Piggybacking on a round-the-globe field study experience already in the works, the group set up displays [in several cities of the world], and asked passersby to participate in an experiment: read a single page from a Christian book and highlight mentions of deity. The students then asked participants for their impressions."[11]

This is how they described that effort: "One of the most criticized texts in religion history often by people who have not read a single page. The Book of Mormon is another testament of Jesus Christ, but instead of having us tell you that, we asked the world in London, Chicago, Cape Town, Sydney, Las Vegas, Atlanta, Honolulu. We gave all 531 pages of the Book of Mormon to 531 non-members [of The Church of Jesus Christ of Latter-day Saints]. We asked them to look for references of God and Jesus Christ. As they read, they saw a lot, they each became a witness that their individual page testifies of Christ."[12]

Here are some of the reflections they received from the people who participated in the experiment:

"It was one of the first pages of scripture I have ever read. And I think that a book like this one can help people find answers in their life when they feel like they are in darkness. I'm so grateful to have been part of this experiment. I've been in the dark and needed a little more light in my life." —Kate, Australian, nonreligious, read page 184.

"This is the first time that I have ever read a page of Christian scripture. I think the page was good; it's definitely good. It shows that God is a God of miracles, not a God of punishment. He's merciful, He does miracles, and He wants to help us. I believe that God is that way—He wants to help us. Reading this book has helped me. I love it!" —Rafi, United Kingdom, Muslim, read page 430.[13]

If the Book of Mormon had such a powerful and inspiring impact on people who have not heard of it or read it before, as gospel teachers we can pray for ways to help our learners discover and rediscover the truths from this divine book every time they read it.

How Can We Find Relevance in the Book of Mormon?

One thing that we can do is to realize that each of us can find answers to questions of the soul in the Book of Mormon and that the truths it contains are relevant to us.

As we help our family and class members this year, we can follow Jesus Christ's example of teaching in a way that is relevant to them. What did He do to help His followers learn about truths in a relevant way? He used parables, He asked questions, He beheld people, He listened to them, He prophesied and showed how some prophecies had already been fulfilled, and He extended promises. As we try to follow Jesus Christ's example, we can, like Nephi, "liken all scriptures unto us, that it might be for our profit and learning."[14] We can invite each other to find promises about and from Jesus Christ for us in these latter days. We can help each other discover how relevant those promises are for us. And we can encourage each other to find ourselves in the scriptures so that we understand who we are and what our purpose is in our Father's divine plan of salvation.

I asked some young adult friends to share with me how relevant the Book of Mormon is for them. This is what they said:

Toshi: "The Book of Mormon is a short amount of relief from the chaos of my life. Even when I haven't read the book in a long time (many months), I'll still have relief given to me. Even though I don't always feel worthy or feel like it's been too long, as soon as I read it, I'm given the promised blessings from the Book of Mormon."

Mike: "I was a missionary striving for greater faith and testimony of Christ. I prayed and studied God's words as intentionally and intensively as ever. But I didn't feel like I was growing. Definitely not as much as I wanted to. I was reading in Mosiah 26:15–16, which impacted me. It reads, 'Blessed art thou, Alma, and blessed are they who were baptized in the waters of Mormon. Thou art blessed because of thy exceeding faith in the words alone of my servant Abinadi. And blessed are they because of their exceeding faith in the words alone which thou hast spoken unto them.' . . . It felt like those two verses were just for me. God was telling me that I was blessed for my faith. While I still didn't grow in the ways I had wanted to, it was the first time the scriptures felt personalized just to me. Like God was talking to me specifically with those verses."

Brooke: "I've been rereading First Nephi this week and I kind of feel like we all have to go through the wilderness at some point and for some of us dating is that wilderness. We need to hold on even when the bow breaks. I honestly really feel like God has been guiding my life this far, so why do I lose faith in this one aspect of life? I've got to stay positive and hold on. The Book of Mormon had endless examples of this. Times where the wilderness or trial seems to have no end. But we learn that God is still with us in those times and that if we hold on, He always fulfills His promises."

Glen: "One of the ways the Book of Mormon has been relevant in my personal life is that I can feel connected to the people in it, and that helps me feel less alone. For example, Nephi in 1 Nephi 4 spends a whole verse describing how Laban's sword is cool. Jacob, before telling everyone off is basically like, 'Ugh, I wish you all were better and I didn't have to tell you all to shape up.' Nephi (son of Helaman) in Helaman 7 wishes he could have lived in the days of First Nephi. Mormon wishes his people would repent but realizes he has no control over them and is able to find some joy despite living in horrible times. Basically, they all express feelings that I've felt (and probably lots of people) and that helps me feel connected to them."

Elena: "As a missionary, we had a district meeting where we were asked to come with a question in mind—a question about something we were struggling with personally. At the meeting, together we read a chapter from the Book of Mormon. We decided to read the chapter on Lehi's vision. It was incredible to see how every one of us could testify that our personal questions were answered in reading that chapter. The Book of Mormon is more meaningful to me when I turn to it with something specific in mind, whether it's a problem I'm dealing with or a question of how I can help someone else specifically or even just, 'What does God want me to hear today?' When I turn to the Book of Mormon sincerely seeking revelation and application to my personal life, I always find it. No matter what stage of my life I am in, there is always a way to relate the Book of Mormon to my personal life."[15]

These examples show that the truths found in the Book of Mormon can speak to our souls and bring comfort to us. The Book of Mormon is certainly another testament of Jesus Christ. This book was "written by the hand of Mormon upon plates taken from the plates of Nephi," brought "forth by the gift and power of God" and translated by Joseph Smith "by the gift of God." We have received the promise that through the Book of Mormon we can know the "great things the Lord [has] done for [our] fathers" and "the covenants of the Lord," that we can also be convinced "that Jesus is the Christ, the Eternal God, manifesting himself unto all nations."[16]

The Book of Mormon Was Written for Our Day and for Us

From beginning to end, this sacred book of scripture testifies of Jesus Christ and of His divine mission. It was written for us and for our time, and in it we find guidance specific for the latter days. President Ezra Taft Benson explained that one

> great reason why we must make the Book of Mormon a center focus of study is that it was written for our day. The Nephites never had the book; neither did the Lamanites of ancient times. It was meant for us. Mormon wrote near the end of the Nephite civilization. Under the inspiration of God, who sees all things from the beginning, he abridged centuries of records, choosing the stories, speeches, and events that would be most helpful to us.
>
> Each of the major writers of the Book of Mormon testified that he wrote for future generations. Nephi said, "The Lord God promised unto me that these things which I write shall be kept and preserved, and handed down unto my seed, from generation to generation" (2 Ne. 25:21). His brother Jacob, who succeeded him, wrote similar words: "For [Nephi] said that the history of his people should be engraven upon his other plates, and that I should preserve these plates and hand them down unto my seed, from generation to generation" (Jacob 1:3). Enos and Jarom both indicated that they too were writing not for their own peoples but for future generations (see Enos 1:15–16, Jarom 1:2).
>
> Mormon himself said, "Yea, I speak unto you, ye remnant of the house of Israel" (Mormon 7:1). And Moroni, the last of the inspired writers, actually saw our day and time. "Behold," he said, "the Lord hath shown unto me great and marvelous things concerning that which must shortly come, at that day when these things shall come forth among you.

"Behold, I speak unto you as if ye were present, and yet ye are not. But behold, Jesus Christ hath shown you unto me, and I know your doing (Mormon 8:34–35)."[17]

As I read the Book of Mormon, I love finding those passages that are written specifically for each of us. I like to call them "parentheses" because they are parenthetical reflections made by the writers on what they learned from the accounts they chose to write about and the relevance that they would have for us in the latter days.

For example, from the very beginning, in the first chapter of the First Book of Nephi, in the last verse of that chapter, Nephi wrote, "But behold, I, Nephi, will show unto *you* that the tender mercies of the Lord are over all those whom he hath chosen, because of their faith, to make them mighty even unto the power of deliverance."[18] When he says, "I . . . will show unto you," whom is he speaking to? To you! To me! That is how personal the Book of Mormon is. That is how personal the scriptures are. That is how personal the gospel of Jesus Christ is. It is for you! It is for me! It is for each of us! It is for each of our learners!

Mormon uses similar wording when he says, "And I will show unto *you* hereafter that this record is true."[19] Moroni also proclaimed, "I will show unto you a God of miracles, even the God of Abraham, and the God of Isaac, and the God of Jacob; and it is that same God who created the heavens and the earth, and all things that in them are."[20]

And, yes, it is true! As we read the Book of Mormon, we can see, we can feel, and we can know for ourselves that the tender mercies of the Lord are over all of those whom He has chosen, because of their faith, to make them mighty, even unto the power of deliverance. We can acknowledge the miracles that we have witnessed in our lives and in the lives of others. We can see how those promises have been manifest in our life. We can look back and realize how blessed we have been because of our faith. We can know for ourselves the truthfulness of these sacred records and have a closer relationship with our Heavenly Father and Jesus Christ.

The Book of Mormon prophets saw our day and saw us. Nephi testified, "And it came to pass that I, Nephi, beheld the power of the Lamb of God, that it descended upon the saints of the church of the Lamb, and upon the covenant people of the Lord, who were scattered upon all the face of the earth; and they were armed with righteousness and with the power of God in great glory."[21] Nephi saw in a vision that in our day, we would be making covenants with Heavenly Father through Jesus Christ, and that through those covenants and our righteousness in keeping them, we would be "endowed with power from on high."[22] The blessings of that divine power that we can receive include guidance for our lives; inspiration to know how to serve family members and others; strength to endure and overcome challenges; gifts of the Spirit to magnify our abilities; revelation to know how to fulfill the work we are ordained, set apart, or assigned to do; and help and strength to become more like Jesus Christ and Heavenly Father.[23]

The Scriptures Were Written in Retrospective

The scriptural records we have, including the Book of Mormon, were written in retrospective. Often the events depicted in them were written years after the facts happened, as the writers reflected on their experiences and on what they learned from them.

The same thing can happen to us. Even though it may be hard to stop and think about the lessons we are learning as we are in the middle of our trials, we can try to pause and reflect on what we have learned up to that point and who we are becoming because of that learning. We can even go further back and remember the tender mercies we have received from the Lord in the past and that can give us comfort, hope, and strength as we endure our current circumstances.

Also, we may not see the answers to our prayers immediately, but the answers come. As we look back, we can see how our prayers have been answered in miraculous ways, even though we may not have noticed them at the moment. We can see how the Lord has been our light and how He has prepared the way before us all along.[24]

Promises of Prosperity

I joined The Church of Jesus Christ of Latter-day Saints when I was twenty-six years old after "having seen many afflictions in the course of my days,"[25] like Nephi. I was going through a difficult period in my life. I had just separated from my first husband, had a three-year-old son, and was hungry for peace and comfort. When I followed the missionaries' invitation to start reading the Book of Mormon, a recurrent promise found in the book stood out to me: "And inasmuch as ye shall keep my commandments, ye shall prosper, and shall be led to a land of promise."[26] I had never heard that concept before in my life! I thought, "What a beautiful promise!"

I highlighted those words, and as I kept reading, I found that same promise again and highlighted it again. Soon I realized that it was found all over the book and stopped highlighting it. Now I know that maybe it was a mistake from my part. However, with my limited knowledge of the gospel of Jesus Christ, I hung on to that promise. I clung to it, I believed it, and it made a big difference in my life. Somehow I knew that it did not necessarily mean that I would become wealthy. I felt that it had to do with blessings that were more eternal and significant. The Lord is assuring us that if we are obedient to His commandments, we will be blessed and prosper, both temporally and eternally.

Elder Quentin L. Cook taught, "Prospering and being wealthy are not necessarily synonymous. A much better gospel definition of prospering in the land is having sufficient for our needs while having the abundant blessing of the Spirit in our lives. When we provide for our families and love and serve the Savior, we will enjoy the reward of having the Spirit and prospering in the land."[27]

We can continually ask ourselves these questions: "How have I seen the promises of prosperity come true in my life?" and "How can I help my learners look back into their life and reflect on the holistic prosperity they have received because of their honest efforts to keep God's commandments?" As we do that, we could all say, "I glory in my Jesus, for he hath redeemed my soul from hell."[28]

Promises of Knowledge of the Gospel of Jesus Christ

For me, having found the gospel of Jesus Christ at a dark moment of my life is a fulfilling of the prophecy and promise found in 1 Nephi 15:14, "And at that day shall the remnant of our seed know that they are of the house of Israel, and that they are the covenant people of the Lord; and then shall they know and come to the knowledge of their forefathers, and also to the knowledge of the gospel of their Redeemer, which was ministered unto their fathers by him; wherefore, they shall come to the knowledge of their Redeemer and the very points of his doctrine, that they may know how to come unto him and be saved."

A similar promise was given by Jesus Christ Himself when He visited the Nephites on the American continent. He said, "Behold, because of their belief in me, saith the Father, and because of the unbelief of you, O house of Israel, in the latter day shall the truth come unto the Gentiles, that the fulness of these things shall be made known unto them. . . . And then will I remember my covenant which I have made unto my people, O house of Israel, and I will bring my gospel unto them. I will remember my covenant unto you, O house of Israel, and ye shall come unto the knowledge of the fulness of my gospel."[29]

The Savior also gave this promise: "And verily, verily, I say unto you, that when [the words of Isaiah] shall be fulfilled then is the fulfilling of the covenant which the Father hath made unto his people, O house of Israel. And then shall the remnants, which shall be scattered abroad upon the face of the earth, be gathered in from the east and from the west, and from the south and from the north; and they shall be brought to the knowledge of the Lord their God, who hath redeemed them."[30]

I came to the knowledge of the gospel of my Redeemer and of His doctrine when I needed it most. I was shown the iron rod that would lead me to the tree of life that represents the love of God. Because of that, I have tasted of that fruit that is the most desirable, and I can certainly declare that "I glory in my Jesus, for he hath redeemed my soul from hell."[31]

Promises of Redemption through Jesus Christ's Atonement

I know personally that the truths found in the Book of Mormon have the power to change us, the power to draw us closer to Jesus Christ, the power to help us overcome the tribulations we may face in our lives, and the power to bring joy to us as we obey divine laws.

When he was nine years old, my husband Carlos joined The Church of Jesus Christ of Latter-day Saints in Mexico, together with his family. Due to various circumstances, most of his family did not remain active in the Church. However, Carlos did not forget how he felt when the missionaries visited his childhood home and taught him and his family about Jesus Christ and His gospel.

Years later at age twenty-three, he moved to the United States and lived with his brother. They were occasionally visited by members and missionaries, and they kept in their apartment a copy of the Book of Mormon, which, for a long time, basically just gathered dust.

When Carlos was twenty-seven years old, he broke up with a girlfriend and felt devastated. He then remembered how he had felt in his childhood when the Holy Ghost testified of the truth of the gospel of Jesus Christ to his young heart. He finally reached up to the Book of Mormon and opened it. As he started reading, something amazing happened: he could not stop. Back then, he had two jobs and not much spare time, but instead of eating during his breaks, he continued reading the Book of Mormon.

An interesting detail about Carlos's story is that all of this happened when the soccer extravaganza of the 1990 FIFA World Cup was going on. Those who know my husband well know how much he loves and enjoys soccer and how important this every-four-year event is to him. Nevertheless, he completely ignored the World Cup because he was captivated by the Book of Mormon so much that he finished reading it in two weeks with the little spare time he had.

Carlos has described his feelings this way: "As I started reading about Nephi and his family, I immediately related to him because I always tried to be the peacemaker in my family whenever there were conflicts (which, by the way, happen in every family). Nephi had a sincere desire to know the things that his father had seen, and he believed that the Lord was able to make them known to him. Because of that honest desire, Nephi received his own witness of the reality of the Lord Jesus Christ and saw a vision that prepared him for what lay ahead. Somehow, I knew that the same thing could happen to me."

Carlos continued, "I felt that every invitation to repent was given to me personally. The words of Nephi, Jacob, King Benjamin, Mosiah, Abinadi, and all the prophets in the Book of Mormon, and their witness of the divine mission of Jesus Christ, touched my heart in a profound way. As I read how Alma the Younger described his anguish as he remembered his sins, I felt the same way. My soul was tormented with pain. Similarly, when I read of the joy that Alma felt as he remembered 'to have heard [his] father prophesy unto the people concerning the coming of one Jesus Christ, a Son of God, to atone for the sins of the world' (Alma 36:17), I was overwhelmed with joy and the hope that I could also be forgiven."

As Carlos read the Book of Mormon, he had a change of heart and became a new man. He came back to church every Sunday, again renewing the covenant he had made in his childhood. By that simple act of faith of reaching up to the Savior by reading the Book of Mormon, he discovered a whole universe of truth and light in his life.

A Declaration of Our Divine Identity

After being a member of the Church for a few years and realizing the wonderful blessings I was receiving because of the covenants I had made with God, many times I would feel that I did not deserve the overflowing amount of goodness I was enjoying. Many times, I would think that there was a reason beyond my knowledge that allowed me to be so greatly blessed.

When I finally read the Book of Mormon from cover to cover for the first time, I received a personal witness about the implications that our righteousness may have in future generations as I read the account of the Anti-Nephi-Lehies. They made a covenant with God that they would not shed the blood of their brethren and buried their weapons of war deep in the earth as a testimony of their covenant.[32] When I read the passage in Alma 24:20–22, where these faithful covenant keepers did not show any resistance and prostrated themselves before their enemies, who slayed thousands of them, an overwhelming feeling came upon me. At that moment, I felt that someone in that group of brave, humble, and peaceful men was my ancestor. I then understood that it was because of his righteousness in keeping his covenants, so much that he preferred to die rather than break his promise to God, that I have been a recipient of the fulfilling of the promises given by Jesus Christ to the covenant children of God.

In the Book of Mormon, we learn of our true identity. Explaining who we are, Jesus Christ said,

> And behold, ye are the children of the prophets; and ye are of the house of Israel; and ye are of the covenant which the Father made with your fathers, saying unto Abraham: And in thy seed shall all the kindreds of the earth be blessed.
>
> The Father having raised me up unto you first, and sent me to bless you in turning away every one of you from his iniquities; and this because ye are the children of the covenant....
>
> And I will remember the covenant which I have made with my people; and I have covenanted with them that I would gather them together in mine own due time, that I would give unto them again the land of their fathers for their inheritance, which is the land of Jerusalem, which is the promised land unto them forever, saith the Father.
>
> And it shall come to pass that the time cometh, when the fulness of my gospel shall be preached unto them;
>
> And they shall believe in me, that I am Jesus Christ, the Son of God, and shall pray unto the Father in my name."[33]

We are witnessing the fulfilling of the Savior's promises as He continues to gather us in these latter days. As we study the Book of Mormon, we can see how the Lord "suit[s] his mercies according to the conditions of the children of men [and women].[34] We can also see how simple and powerful the gospel of Jesus Christ is and echo the words of Nephi, when he said, "For my soul delighteth in plainness; for after this manner doth the Lord God work among the children of men. For the Lord God giveth light unto the understanding; for he speaketh unto men according to their language, unto their understanding."[35] We can also see how relevant the promises about and from Jesus Christ contained in the Book of Mormon are for us, in our day.

The Fulfillment of the Father's Covenant

The coming forth of the Book of Mormon is a sign that the Father is fulfilling His covenant with the house of Israel, as explained by Jesus Christ:

> And when these things come to pass that thy seed shall begin to know these things—it shall be a sign unto them, that they may know that the work of the Father hath already commenced unto the fulfilling of the covenant which he hath made unto the people who are of the house of Israel. . . .
>
> For in that day, for my sake shall the Father work a work, which shall be a great and a marvelous work among them; and there shall be among them those who will not believe it, although a man shall declare it unto them.[36]

He also gave a warning and a promise:

> For it shall come to pass, saith the Father, that at that day whosoever will not repent and come unto my Beloved Son, them will I cut off from among my people, O house of Israel;
>
> And I will execute vengeance and fury upon them, even as upon the heathen, such as they have not heard.
>
> But if they will repent and hearken unto my words, and harden not their hearts, I will establish my church among them, and they shall come in unto the covenant and be numbered among this the remnant of Jacob, unto whom I have given this land for their inheritance; . . .
>
> And then shall they assist my people that they may be gathered in, who are scattered upon all the face of the land, in unto the New Jerusalem.
>
> And then shall the power of heaven come down among them; and I also will be in the midst.[37]

I conclude with Nephi's words:

> And now, my beloved brethren, and also Jew, and all ye ends of the earth, hearken unto these words and believe in Christ; and if ye believe not in these words believe in Christ. And if ye shall believe in Christ ye will believe in these words, for they are the words of Christ, and he hath given them unto me; and they teach all men that they should do good.
>
> And if they are not the words of Christ, judge ye—for Christ will show unto you, with power and great glory, that they are his words, at the last day; and you and I shall stand face to face before his bar; and ye shall know that I have been commanded of him to write these things, notwithstanding my weakness.[38]

Reyna I. Aburto *is a former second counselor in the Relief Society General Presidency.*

Notes

1. Joseph Smith—History 1:5–6, 10.
2. Doctrine and Covenants 1:17–18.
3. Russell M. Nelson, "Preaching the Gospel of Peace," *Liahona*, May 2022, 6.
4. Book of Mormon introduction.
5. Russell M. Nelson, "The Book of Mormon: What Would Your Life Be Like without It?," *Ensign*, November 2017, 62; emphasis in original.
6. 2 Nephi 33:6.
7. 1 Nephi 11:1.
8. Enos 1:3–4.
9. Jade Blue, "What's It Got to Do with Me? The Role of Relevance in Learner Engagement," cambridge.org/elt/blog/2022/02/10/role-relevance-learner-engagement.
10. "Relevance, Teach Anywhere," teachanywhere.byu.edu/teaching-method/relevance.
11. "An Experiment upon the Word," *BYU Magazine*, Spring 2018, magazine.byu.edu/article/an-experiment-upon-the-word.
12. *Book of Mormon Experiment* video, churchofjesuschrist.org/comeuntochrist/believe/book-of-mormon/book-of-mormon-experiment.
13. *Book of Mormon Experiment* video.
14. 1 Nephi 19:23.
15. These quotations come from personal correspondence.
16. Book of Mormon title page.
17. Ezra Taft Benson, "The Book of Mormon—Keystone of Our Religion," *Ensign*, October 2011, 55–56.
18. 1 Nephi 1:20; emphasis added.
19. 3 Nephi 18:37; emphasis added.
20. Mormon 9:11; emphasis added.
21. 1 Nephi 14:14.
22. Doctrine and Covenants 38:32.
23. See *General Handbook: Serving in The Church of Jesus Christ of Latter-day Saints*, 3.5.
24. See 1 Nephi 17:13.
25. 1 Nephi 1:1.
26. For example, 1 Nephi 2:20.
27. Quentin L. Cook, "Reaping the Rewards of Righteousness" (Brigham Young University Women's Conference, May 2, 2014).
28. 2 Nephi 33:6.
29. 3 Nephi 16: 7, 11–12.
30. 3 Nephi 20:12–13.
31. 2 Nephi 33:6.

32. See Alma 24:17–19.
33. 3 Nephi 20:25–26, 29–31; see also 3 Nephi 29.
34. Doctrine and Covenants 46:15.
35. 2 Nephi 31:3.
36. 3 Nephi 21:7, 9.
37. 3 Nephi 21:20–22, 24–25.
38. 2 Nephi 33:10–11.

2

Jesus Christ and the Gathering of Israel
A Book of Mormon Perspective

ROBERT L. MILLET

In November 1835 Joseph Smith the Prophet described a vital principle of the gospel. "It is a principle I esteem to be of the greatest importance to those who are looking for salvation in this generation," he explained, "or in these that may be called, 'the latter times.' *All that the prophets that have written*, from the days of righteous Abel, down to the last man that has left any testimony on record for our consideration, *in speaking of the salvation of Israel in the last days, goes directly to show that it consists in the work of gathering*."[1]

Few matters have been given more attention in recent years within The Church of Jesus Christ of Latter-day Saints than the gathering of Israel. It has become a topic that President Russell M. Nelson has addressed and emphasized repeatedly to the membership of the Church. In this presentation, we will search and study what the Book of Mormon teaches us about such matters as (1) God's covenant with Israel; (2) why and how Israel is scattered; (3) why and how Israel is gathered; and (4) the Savior's teachings in the Book of Mormon about the gathering. In addition, we will look carefully at what a modern prophet has taught about the work of gathering.

After Adam and Eve were required to leave the Garden of Eden, they were commanded to "offer the firstlings of their flocks, for an offering unto the Lord." They did so in the spirit of obedience, not fully understanding why they were so commanded. "After many days," an angel appeared and explained that these sacrifices were in similitude of the great and last sacrifice that would be offered by the Son of God in a future day. "Wherefore," the angel directed our first parents, "*thou shalt do all that thou doest in the name of the Son*, and thou shalt repent and call upon God in the name of the Son forevermore" (see Moses 5:4–8; emphasis added). In that spirit, the message of this presentation is that we can only grasp the purpose and thrust of the gathering of Israel when we understand the central, saving role of Jesus Christ in that divinely ordained endeavor—an overriding message found throughout the Book of Mormon. We will discover that people are gathered, not just to lands and locations, not just to *a place*, but to *a Person*—namely, the Lord Jesus Christ.

God's Covenant with Abraham

Covenants are two-way promises, sacred arrangements and assurances between Deity and his people. Covenants are initiated by God, and the terms and conditions of the covenant are specified by him. And while a covenant is a spiritual arrangement intended to establish expectations and foster resolve and dedication on the part of mortals, it is far more than an arrangement, much more than a transaction between two parties. A covenant, in the gospel sense, is a means by which our infinite and eternal Father in Heaven links himself with his finite, mortal children. Covenants bind the participants together. Covenants are thus more about *relationship* than the realization of some end, even a righteous end. The making and keeping of sacred covenants is all about linking an individual and a people to the Father and the Son through the power of the Holy Ghost.

Jehovah, who would come to earth as Jesus Christ the Redeemer, entered a covenant with Abraham. The fulness of the gospel covenant which the Lord made with the father of the faithful is so spelled out, so detailed in the book of Genesis (Genesis 13: 14–17; 15:1–10; 17:1–8), that we have come to know it as the Abrahamic covenant. The clearest statement of this covenant, however, is found in the Book of Abraham (2:8–11) in the Pearl of Great Price. By combining what is stated in Genesis with the Book of Abraham, we read that God promised Abraham the following: (1) through him would come a great nation; (2) God would make Abraham's name great among all nations; (3) the blessings of the gospel and the priesthood would come through the descendants of Abraham; (4) those who received the gospel would be known as the seed of Abraham; (5) the Lord would bless those who blessed Abraham's posterity and curse those who cursed the family of Abraham; (6) the descendants of Abraham would be entitled to a land inheritance; (7) through the literal seed of Abraham, all the families of the earth would be blessed; and (8) descendants of Abraham, whether lineal or adopted, would, through obedience and faithfulness, eventually receive exaltation, which entails the continuation of the family unit into eternity.[2]

Jehovah expected Abraham's descendants to choose him as their God, to forsake or avoid the false beliefs and corrupt practices of the surrounding nations, and to keep the commandments of God. The covenant was continued through Isaac (Genesis 26:1–5), Jacob (Genesis 28:10–15), and all the faithful descendants of the great patriarchs.

Because Lehi was of the tribe of Manasseh (Alma 10:3), the son of Joseph, the promises that God had made to Father Abraham continued through Lehi's descendants. Nephi reminded his wayward brothers that their father Lehi had declared that in the latter days the gospel of Jesus Christ would come to his descendants through the Gentiles. "Wherefore, our father hath not spoken of our seed alone, but also of *all the house of Israel, pointing to the covenant which should be fulfilled in the latter days; which covenant the Lord made to our father Abraham, saying: In thy seed shall all the kindreds of the earth be blessed*" (1 Nephi 15:18; emphasis added).

Following the deaths of Jesus Christ and the meridian apostles in Israel and the subsequent loss of the keys of the priesthood, the gospel covenant was no longer in effect in the Old World. Isaiah had described such a time: "The earth also is defiled under the inhabitants thereof; because they have transgressed the laws, changed the ordinance, broken the everlasting covenant" (Isaiah 24:5). Thus, Joseph Smith, the "choice seer" (2 Nephi 3:6–7) who was charged to oversee the Restoration, was assigned to restore plain and precious truths *and many covenants of the Lord* that had been lost from the Bible through the centuries of its transmission (see 1 Nephi 13:26; see also verses 28, 35–36).

In a letter to newspaper editor Noah C. Saxton, the Prophet Joseph declared, "The time has at last arrived when the God of Abraham, of Isaac, and of Jacob, has set His hand again the second time to recover the remnants of his people." The Prophet then called upon the inhabitants of the earth to "repent of all your sins, and be baptized in water for the remission of them, in the name of the Father, and of the Son, and of the Holy Ghost, and receive the ordinance of the laying on of the hands. . . . These are the requirements of the new covenant, or first principles of the Gospel of Christ."[3]

The Scattering of Israel

Moses warned ancient Israel that if they should reject their God they would be scattered among the nations, dispersed among the Gentiles. "If thou wilt not hearken unto the voice of the Lord thy God," he said, "to observe to do all his commandments and his statutes which I command thee this day . . . [you will be] removed into all the kingdoms of the earth. . . . And the Lord shall scatter thee among all people, from the one end of the earth even unto the other; and there thou shalt serve other gods, which neither thou nor thy fathers have known" (Deuteronomy 28:15, 25, 64). The Lord spoke in a similar vein through Jeremiah some eight centuries later (see Jeremiah 16:11–13).

Because of their wandering ways, the people of God became scattered—alienated from Jehovah, from the people of the covenant and the ways of righteousness, lost as to their identity as covenant representatives, and displaced from the lands set aside for their inheritance. Israel was scattered because of apostasy, because they strayed from the ordinances and broke the everlasting covenant (compare Doctrine and Covenants 1:15). In offering his own commentary on what we know as Isaiah 49, Nephi pointed out that the work of gathering pertains to "things both temporal and spiritual; for it appears that the house of Israel, sooner or later, will be scattered upon all the face of the earth, and also among all nations." And then, in speaking specifically of the ten northern or "lost" tribes of Israel, he said, "Behold, there are *many who are already lost from* . . . *those who are at Jerusalem*. Yea, *the more part of all the tribes have been led away*; and *they are scattered to and fro* upon the isles of the sea; and whither they are none of us knoweth, save that we know that they have been led away" (1 Nephi 22:3–4; emphasis added).

In writing of the Jews, who represent all the house of Israel (see 1 Nephi 15:17, 20; 3 Nephi 29:8; Mormon 5:14), Jacob taught that "after [the Lord] should manifest himself they should scourge him and crucify him. . . . And after they have hardened their hearts and stiffened their necks against the Holy One of Israel, . . . they [will be] driven to and fro." In short, they "shall be scattered, and smitten, and hated" (2 Nephi 6:9–11; compare 10:5–6).

Nephi son of Helaman delivered a scathing rebuke: "O repent ye, repent ye! Why will you die? Turn ye, turn ye unto the Lord your God. Why has he forsaken you? It is because you have hardened your hearts; yea, ye will not hearken unto the voice of the good shepherd." Now notice the following simple expression: "And behold, *instead of gathering you, except ye will repent, behold, he shall scatter you forth*" (Helaman 7:17–19; emphasis added).

Although Israel is almost always scattered because of her apostasy or wandering ways, there are times when the Lord scatters or leads away certain branches of his chosen people to various parts of the earth to accomplish his purposes—to spread the blood and influence of Abraham throughout the globe. Sometimes God will lead away groups of people from among the wicked in a sinful world (see 1 Nephi 21:1). This was certainly the case with the Lehite colony, a branch of Joseph who were led away from their Palestinian homeland to another hemisphere because of wickedness in Jerusalem. It was also true of those who followed Mulek, the son of Zedekiah, to the promised land at about the same time (Mosiah 25:2; Helaman 6:8, 21).

Nephi taught, "Behold, the Lord hath created the earth that it should be inhabited; and he hath created his children that they should possess it. And he raiseth up a righteous nation, and destroyeth the nations of the wicked. And *he leadeth away the righteous into precious lands*, and the wicked he destroyeth, and curseth the land unto them for their sakes" (1 Nephi 17:36–38; emphasis added). Or even more plainly, Jacob explained,

> And now, my beloved brethren, seeing that our merciful God has given us so great knowledge . . . , let us remember him, and lay aside our sins, and not hang down our heads, for we are not cast off; nevertheless, we have been driven out of the land of our inheritance; but we have been led to a better land. . . .
>
> For behold, *the Lord God has led away* [groups of people] *from time to time from the house of Israel, according to his will and pleasure*. And now behold, the Lord remembereth all them who have been broken off, wherefore he remembereth us also. (2 Nephi 10:20, 22; compare 2 Nephi 1:5)

The Gathering of Israel

Just as the scattering comes because of transgression, the gathering of Israel is accomplished through turning to the Lord, repenting of sin, and accepting his gospel.[4] Individuals were gathered in ancient days when they aligned themselves with the people of God, with those who practiced the religion of Jehovah and received the ordinances of salvation. They were gathered when they gained a sense of tribal identity, when they came to know who they are and whose they are. They were gathered when they congregated in those places set apart as sacred sites for people of promise.

"Ye shall be gathered one by one, O ye children of Israel," Isaiah declared (Isaiah 27:12; see also 43:1–6). The call to the dispersed of Israel has been and ever will be the same (Jeremiah 3:14; compare Ezekiel 11:17, 19–20; 28:25–26; 36:24–28). That is, gathering is accomplished through individual conversion— through faith, repentance, baptism, confirmation, and then through continued faithfulness.

The Book of Mormon is even more specific in clarifying this principle of gathering: the people of Israel will be gathered again to the degree that they return to Christ, his doctrine, and his Church (1 Nephi 15:14; 2 Nephi 9:2) and become formally associated with the Saints of God. As we mentioned earlier, people are gathered, not just to lands and locations, not just to *a place*, but to *a Person*. Nephi wrote that "after the house of Israel should be scattered they should be gathered together again; or, in fine, after the Gentiles had *received the fulness of the Gospel* the natural branches of the olive-tree, or the remnants of the house of Israel, should be grafted in, or *come to the knowledge of the true Messiah*" (1 Nephi 10:14; emphasis added).

Nephi later explained to his rebellious brothers some of their father's words concerning Israel's destiny:

> And now, the thing which our father meaneth concerning the grafting in of the natural branches through the fulness of the Gentiles, is, that in the latter days, when our seed shall have dwindled in unbelief, yea, for the space of many years, and many generations after the Messiah shall be manifested in body unto the children of men, *then shall the fulness of the gospel of the Messiah come unto the Gentiles, and from the Gentiles unto the remnant of our seed—*
>
> And at that day shall the remnant of our seed know that they are of the house of Israel, and that they are the covenant people of the Lord; and then shall they know and come to the knowledge of their forefathers, and also to *the knowledge of the gospel of their Redeemer*, which was ministered unto their fathers by him; wherefore, they shall come to *the knowledge of their Redeemer and the very points of his doctrine, that they may know how to come unto him and be saved*. (1 Nephi 15:13–14, emphasis added; compare 2 Nephi 30:5)

Nephi taught that after his posterity had been scattered, the Lord would "proceed to do a marvelous work among the Gentiles." And then in speaking of what we know as the restoration of the fulness of the gospel, Nephi added, "The Lord God will proceed to make bare his arm in the eyes of all the nations, in *bringing about his covenants and his gospel unto those who are of the house of Israel. Wherefore, he will bring them again out of captivity, and they shall be gathered together to the lands of their inheritance; and they shall be brought out of obscurity and out of darkness* [see Doctrine and Covenants 1:30; 109:73]; and *they shall know that the Lord is their Savior and their Redeemer*, the Mighty One of Israel" (1 Nephi 22:8, 11–12; emphasis added).

Jacob, son of Lehi, reminded his people that the Lord God "has spoken unto the Jews, by the mouth of his holy prophets, even from the beginning down, from generation to generation, until the time comes that they [the Jews, or the house of Israel] shall be *restored to the true church and fold of God*; when they shall be gathered home to the lands of their inheritance, and shall be established in all their lands of promise" (2 Nephi 9:2; emphasis added). After Jacob had taught that the people of Jerusalem who reject the Savior will be "scattered among all nations," the Savior himself added, "*The day cometh that they shall believe in me, that I am Christ, then have I covenanted with their fathers that they shall be restored in the flesh, upon the earth, unto the lands of their inheritance*" (2 Nephi 10:6–7; emphasis added). Notice the specificity of this last quotation: the Jews are to be restored to the "true church and fold of God." Once again, the gathering in these last days is not just about returning to lands of inheritance; it consists of believing that Jesus is the Christ, coming into the fold (joining the true Church), and gathering with the Saints into their congregations, their branches and wards, districts and stakes where they reside.

Among some of his last words to those who would one day read his writings, Mormon, the great prophet-editor of the Nephite record, spoke words of power and plainness to future generations: "I speak unto you, ye remnant of the house of Israel; and these are the words which I speak: *Know ye that ye are of the house of Israel*. Know ye that *ye must come unto repentance*, or ye cannot be saved. . . . Know ye that ye must come to the knowledge of your fathers, and repent of all your sins and iniquities, and *believe in Jesus Christ, that he is the Son of God*, and that he was slain by the Jews, and by the power of the Father he hath risen again, whereby he hath gained the victory over the grave" (Mormon 7:1–3, 5–6; emphasis added).

These teachings in the Book of Mormon help clarify a matter that is frequently misunderstood by members of the restored Church. The physical gathering of Jews from all over the world to the Holy Land—Zionism—is not the prophesied gathering of Judah. "Judah will gather to old Jerusalem in due course; of this there is no doubt," Elder Bruce R. McConkie wrote. "But *this gathering will consist of accepting Christ, joining the Church, and receiving anew the Abrahamic covenant as it is administered in holy places*. The present assembling of people of Jewish ancestry into the Palestinian nation of Israel is not the scriptural gathering of Israel or of Judah. It may be prelude thereto, and some of the people so assembled may in due course be gathered into the true church and kingdom of God on earth, and they may then assist in building the temple that is destined to grace Jerusalem's soil. But *a political gathering is not a spiritual gathering*, and the Lord's kingdom is not of this world."[1] When the scriptures thus speak of a day when the Jews "begin to believe in Christ" (2 Nephi 30:7), they are teaching that some Jews will begin to be converted to The Church of Jesus Christ of Latter-day Saints before the Second Coming in glory. A remnant of such converts to the Church will thereby be in place for the grand events associated with the Savior's return (see Doctrine and Covenants 45:43).

The prophet Mormon referred to a future day when the message of the Book of Mormon would go to "the unbelieving of the Jews: and for this intent shall they go—*that they may be persuaded that Jesus is the Christ, the Son of the living God*; that the Father may bring about, through his most Beloved [Son], his great and eternal purpose, in restoring the Jews, or all the house of Israel, to the land of their inheritance, which the Lord their God hath given them, unto the fulfilling of his covenant" (Mormon 5:14; emphasis added).

The resurrected Savior spoke to the assembled Nephites of the establishment of the New Jerusalem: "And then shall they [the Gentiles] assist my people that they may be gathered in, who are scattered upon all the face of the land, in unto the New Jerusalem." The Lord then spoke words that seem to apply to life in the Millennium: "And *then shall the power of heaven come down among them; and I also will be in the midst*. And then shall the work of the Father commence at that day, even when this gospel shall be preached among the remnant of this people. Verily I say unto you, at that day shall the work of the Father commence among *all the dispersed of my people, yea, even the tribes which have been lost, which the Father hath led away out of Jerusalem*" (3 Nephi 21:24–26; emphasis added). The great work of gathering in that millennial day will *commence* in the sense that it will be of such magnitude that it will cause all former gatherings to pale in significance.

As Nephi, the son of Lehi, was about to close his first book, he wrote of the great millennial day and the gathering to take place during those thousand years of peace: "And the time cometh speedily that the righteous must be led up as calves of the stall, and the Holy One of Israel must reign in dominion, and might, and power, and great glory. And *he gathereth his children from the four quarters of the earth*; and he numbereth his sheep, and they know him; and *there shall be one fold and one shepherd*; and he shall feed his sheep, and in him they shall find pasture. And *because of the righteousness of his people, Satan has no power; wherefore, he cannot be loosed for the space of many years*" (1 Nephi 22:24–26; emphasis added).

Moroni inserted himself into the record of the Jaredites and spoke of the latter day building up of Jerusalem and the establishment of the New Jerusalem. "And then cometh the New Jerusalem; and blessed are they who dwell therein, for it is they whose garments are white through the blood of the Lamb; and they are they who are numbered among the remnant of the seed of Joseph, who were of the house of Israel." Then in referring to the Jews of a future time, as well as the ten lost tribes: "And then also cometh the Jerusalem of old; and the inhabitants thereof, blessed are they, for *they have been washed in the blood of the Lamb*; and they are they who were *scattered and gathered in from the four quarters of the earth, and from the north countries,* and are partakers of the fulfilling of the covenant which God made with their father, Abraham" (Ether 13:10–11; emphasis added). People are "washed in the blood of the Lamb" through acceptance of the first principles and ordinances of the gospel (see 3 Nephi 27:19–21).

The rather complex but amazing allegory of Zenos, either read or quoted by Jacob, is a long and winding narrative that dramatizes how endlessly patient God is with his chosen people. It seems to take us through Israel's history, such as from the destruction of Jerusalem to the time of the Restoration to the great Millennium. It is Jacob's way of reconciling the fact that the Jews will, on the one hand, stumble and thereby "reject the stone upon which they might build and have safe foundation"—Jesus Christ—and yet that Christ will somehow "become the great, and the last, and the only sure foundation, upon which the Jews can build" (Jacob 4:15–16). Jacob then unfolds this "mystery" to the readers of the Book of Mormon by presenting the allegory.

And what is the mystery? It is how wandering groups of Israelites, who move through periods of faithfulness and wickedness, can ever become "a chosen generation, a royal priesthood, an holy nation, a peculiar people" (1 Peter 2:9). It is the love of God, the fact that despite our tendency to stray and at times be disloyal to the royal within us, he is ever willing to forgive and gather his sheep into the sheepfold.

The Risen Lord Speaks of the Gathering

During his mortal ministry, the Lord Jesus declared, "I am the good shepherd: the good shepherd giveth his life for the sheep. . . . I am the good shepherd, and know my sheep, and am known of mine. As the Father knoweth me, even so know I the Father: and I lay down my life for the sheep. And other sheep I have, which are not of this fold: them also I must bring, and they shall hear my voice; and there shall be one fold and one shepherd" (John 10:11, 14–16).

Following his resurrection and appearance to the American Hebrews, he taught those who had gathered near the temple in Bountiful. He explained to this American branch of Israel, descendants of Joseph of old, "This is the land of your inheritance; and the Father hath given it unto you. And not at any time hath the Father given me commandment that I should tell . . . unto them concerning the other tribes of the house of Israel, whom the Father hath led away out of the land. This much did the Father command me, that I should tell unto them" concerning his "other sheep." He went on to explain that Lehi's people had been "separated from among them [those in Israel] because of their iniquity; therefore, it is because of their iniquity that they know not of you," nor of the lost tribes who also were separated from them, as well. He then declared, "Ye are they of whom I said: Other sheep I have which are not of this fold. . . . And they understood me not, for they supposed it had been the Gentiles; for they understood not that the Gentiles should be converted," not by the Lord's actual appearance but rather "the Gentiles should be converted through their preaching" (3 Nephi 15:13–17, 19–23).

The Savior instructed the Nephites to write the things he had just taught them concerning the fact that they and the lost tribes of Israel were the "other sheep" of which he had spoken in the Old World. Through his ministry, teaching, organization, and performance of covenants and ordinances, Jesus Christ gathered the Lehites and the ten tribes in their respective lands of inheritance. The Lord counseled the Nephites to make a record of what they had been taught about the other sheep because a day would come when the Gentiles would be "scattered forth upon the face of the earth because of their unbelief."

The fulness of the gospel would be taken from among the Gentiles because they had rejected it. This day is what is known as "the fulness of the Gentiles" or the fulness of the times of the Gentiles. "And then will I remember my covenant which I have made unto my people, O house of Israel, and I will bring my gospel unto them" (3 Nephi 16:10–11). In summary, the Redeemer taught the Nephites that because of the sinfulness of the Gentiles in the last days, they would be scattered. He would then begin to gather his people, the house of Israel, and bring the fulness of the gospel to them.

Jesus counseled the Nephites to search the words of Isaiah regarding the destiny of Israel. He spoke of a time when the covenant that God had made with scattered Israel would begin to be fulfilled. "And then shall the remnants [of Israel], which shall be scattered abroad upon the face of the earth, be *gathered in from the east and from the west, and from the south and from the north; and they shall be brought to the knowledge of the Lord their God, who hath redeemed them*" (3 Nephi 20:13; emphasis added).

Jesus later declared, "Ye are the children of the prophets; and ye are of the house of Israel; and ye are of the covenant which the Father made with your fathers, saying unto Abraham: And in thy seed shall all the kindreds of the earth be blessed. The Father having raised me up unto you first, and sent me to bless you in turning away every one of you from his iniquities; and this *because ye are the children of the covenant*" (3 Nephi 20:25–26; emphasis added).

In teaching those gathered near the temple at Bountiful, the risen Lord spoke of the gathering: "And I will remember the covenant which I made with my people [the Jews]; and I have covenanted with them that *I would gather them together in mine own due time*, that I would give unto them the land of their fathers for their inheritance, which is the land of Jerusalem, which is the promised land unto them forever, saith the Father." Now note what follows: "And it shall come to pass that the time cometh, when *the fulness of my gospel shall be preached unto them*; and *they shall believe in me, that I am Jesus Christ, the Son of God*, and shall pray unto the Father in my name" (3 Nephi 20:29–31; emphasis added).

The Final Phase of Gathering

So is it the case that once a person has been taught the gospel, accepts the message of the Restoration, and been baptized and confirmed by those holding proper authority that the gathering has come to an end for that individual? Isn't this the process by which a woman or a man qualifies for salvation or eternal life (see Doctrine and Covenants 6:13; 14:7)?

"While salvation is an individual matter," President Nelson explained, "exaltation is a family matter. Only those who are married in the temple and whose marriage is sealed by the Holy Spirit of Promise will continue as spouses after death and receive the highest degree of celestial glory, or exaltation.... To be saved—or to gain salvation—means to be saved from spiritual and physical death." President Nelson taught further, "To be exalted—or to gain exaltation—refers to the highest state of happiness and glory in the celestial realm. These blessings can come to us after we leave this frail and mortal existence. The time to prepare for our eventual salvation and exaltation is now."[6]

It is in light of these grand principles that we can appreciate more fully the words of the Prophet Joseph Smith, delivered on June 11, 1843: "What was the object of gathering the Jews, or the people of God, in any age of the world? ... The main object was *to build unto the Lord a house whereby He could reveal unto His people the ordinances of His house and the glories of His kingdom, and teach the people the way of salvation*; for there are certain ordinances and principles that, when they are taught and practiced, must be done in a place or house built for that purpose.... It is for the same purpose that God gathers together His people in the last days, to build unto the Lord a house to prepare them for the ordinances and endowments, washings and anointings, etc."[7] Thus the final phase of the gathering of the members of the house of Israel is the gathering to holy temples or, as Isaiah expressed it, to "the mountain of the Lord's house" (Isaiah 2:2; 2 Nephi 12:2). President Boyd K. Packer put it simply when he stated, "The ultimate end of all we do in the Church is to see that parents and children are happy at home and sealed together in the temple."[8]

A Modern Prophet Speaks of the Gathering

In recent years, no senior Church leader has said more about God's covenant with Abraham and his posterity, as well as the gathering of the house of Israel, than President Nelson. In November 1988, Elder Nelson delivered an address to Brigham Young University students entitled "Thanks for the Covenant," in which he explained such matters as who we are, how we are descendants of Abraham, Isaac, and Jacob, God's covenant with Abraham, and how we are entitled to those same blessings as we receive and are faithful to our temple covenants.

In April 1995 Elder Nelson delivered a message in general conference entitled "Children of the Covenant." He taught, "The Master appeared in these latter days to renew the Abrahamic covenant.... *We are ... children of the covenant.* We have received, as did they of old, the holy priesthood and the everlasting gospel. *Abraham, Isaac, and Jacob are our ancestors. We are of Israel. We have the right to receive the gospel, blessings of the priesthood, and eternal life. Nations of the earth will be blessed by our efforts and by the labors of our posterity.* The literal seed of Abraham and those who are gathered into his family by adoption receive these promised blessings—predicated upon acceptance of the Lord and obedience to his commandments.... Rewards for obedience to the commandments are almost beyond mortal comprehension."[9]

More recently (June 2018), in a very significant message to the youth of the Church entitled "Hope of Israel," President Nelson extended an invitation and delivered a charge: "Now, we would like to talk with you about *the greatest* challenge, *the greatest* cause, and *the greatest work on earth.* And we want to invite *you* to be part of it! My dear young brothers and sisters, these surely *are* the latter days, and the Lord is hastening His work to gather Israel. *That gathering is the most important thing taking place on earth today. Nothing else compares in magnitude, nothing else compares in importance, nothing else compares in majesty.* And if you choose to, if you want to, you can be a big part of it."

President Nelson went on to teach a simple truth that has enormous implications: "*Anytime you do anything that helps anyone—on either side of the veil—take a step toward making covenants with God and receiving their essential baptismal and temple ordinances, you are helping to gather Israel.* It is as simple as that."[10]

In February 2022 President Nelson spoke to some 750,000 Latter-day Saints in California about these same principles. "Many of your friends are seeking to understand *why* they are here on earth," he said. "They want to know if life has any meaning. They want to make a difference in the world but they don't know who they can trust. Do you realize that you have the answers your friends are seeking? . . . This gathering [of Israel] is all about giving every human soul the chance to hear and accept the gospel of Jesus Christ. It is all about saving souls."[11]

Finally, in an address to the members of the Church in India, he said, "This is the Church of Jesus Christ, restored in these latter days so that the families of scattered Israel can be gathered into the fold of the Lord. They don't have to be gathered physically into any one place. The gathering place for the people of India is *India*. The gathering place for the people of Sri Lanka is *Sri Lanka*. The gathering place for the people of Nepal is *Nepal*. The gathering place for the people of China is *China*. Our job is to be gathered into the fold of Christ—wherever that is—and to live by His precepts from now on."[12]

Conclusion

Concerning the gathering of Israel, Elder McConkie wrote, "The biblical prophets, in profuse abundance, tell of the scattering and gathering of the house of Israel. They set forth the sins and evils that caused the scattering and prescribe the righteousness and good works that underlie the gathering." Now note what follows: "But they do not use the words *gospel* and *church* and *Messiah* and *Zion* and *covenant* as clearly and plainly and with the same full meaning that those words have in the Nephite account. As with almost all the doctrines of the gospel, the Book of Mormon adds a perspective and gives a view of eternal truth that can be received in no other way."[13]

President Nelson explained, "This doctrine of the gathering is one of the important teachings of The Church of Jesus Christ of Latter-day Saints. . . . We not only teach this doctrine, but we also participate in it. We do so as we help to gather the elect of the Lord on both sides of the veil. *The Book of Mormon is central to this work. It declares the doctrine of the gathering. It causes people to learn about Jesus Christ, to believe His gospel, and to join His Church.* In fact, *if there were no Book of Mormon, the promised gathering of Israel would not occur.*"[14]

A modern revelation declares, "Keep all the commandments and covenants by which ye are bound; and I will cause the heavens to shake for your good, and Satan shall tremble and Zion shall rejoice upon the hills and flourish; and *Israel shall be saved in mine own due time;* and by the keys which I have given shall they be led, and no more be confounded at all" (Doctrine and Covenants 35:24–25, emphasis added; compare 38:33; 101:12; Romans 11:26).

Moroni, son of Mormon, gave voice to a prayer and a plea that had been expressed by the prophet leaders since the days of father Lehi. In speaking of the Lamanites, he wrote, "These things which we have desired concerning our brethren, yea, even *their restoration to the knowledge of Christ,* are according to the prayers of all the saints who have dwelt in the land. And may the Lord Jesus Christ grant that their prayers may be answered according to their faith; and *may God the Father remember the covenant which he hath made with the house of Israel;* and may he bless them forever, through faith on the name of Jesus Christ" (Mormon 9:36–37; emphasis added).

The Book of Mormon bears a powerful testimony of the supernal gift of God's never-ending love for and infinite patience with the house of Israel. As we noted earlier, Jacob, the son of Lehi, quoted from the complex but profound allegory of Zenos. He then rejoiced in the mercy of God: "For he remembereth the house of Israel, both roots [ancestry] and branches [posterity]; and he stretches forth his hands unto them all the day long; and they are a stiffnecked and gainsaying people; but as many as will not harden their hearts shall be saved in the kingdom of God." Jacob then pleaded with his people, and with all people for that matter, to repent "and come with full purpose of heart, and cleave unto God as he cleaveth unto you" (Jacob 6:4–5).

The allegory of Zenos says it all—God simply will not let Israel go! To be involved in the gathering of Israel in these latter days is a sacred and sobering responsibility, but it is also a supernal and soul-satisfying opportunity and privilege. As we do our part in this the greatest work in all the world, we are being loyal to the royal within us and thereby helping to fulfill God's promises to Father Abraham.

ROBERT L. MILLET *is a professor emeritus of ancient scripture at Brigham Young University.*

Notes

1. Letter to the Elders of the Church, November 16, 1835; emphasis added.
2. See Russell M. Nelson, "Covenants," *Ensign*, November 2011; see also *Teachings of Russell M. Nelson* (Salt Lake City: Deseret Book, 2018), 7.
3. Letter to Noah C. Saxton, January 4, 1833. In the Wentworth Letter, Joseph explained that Moroni had been "sent to bring the joyful tidings that *the covenant which God made with ancient Israel was at hand to be fulfilled,* that the preparatory work for the second coming of the Messiah was speedily to commence; that the time was at hand for the Gospel in all its fullness, to be preached in power, unto all nations that a people might be prepared for the Millennial reign. I was informed that I was chosen to be an instrument in the hands of God to bring about some of His purposes in this glorious dispensation." *Times and Seasons*, March 1, 1842, 707.
4. Some have distinguished between those passages in the Book of Mormon that refer to Israel being *restored* from those that speak of Israel being *gathered*. They suggest that the people of Israel are *restored* to Christ, to the gospel, to the covenants, while they are physically *gathered* to the lands of their inheritance. While I understand the reasoning, in this paper I have chosen instead to refer to the whole process as the gathering of Israel and to speak of two stages of gathering: (1) to the Lord and his gospel; and (2) to the lands of their inheritance or the congregations of the Saints.
5. Bruce R. McConkie, *A New Witness for the Articles of Faith* (Salt Lake City: Deseret Book, 1985), 519–20.
6. *Teachings of Russell M. Nelson*, 100–101.
7. *Teachings of Presidents of the Church: Joseph Smith* (Salt Lake City: The Church of Jesus Christ of Latter-day Saints, 2007), 416–17, 419.
8. Clyde J. Williams, ed., *Mine Errand from the Lord: Selections from the Sermons and Writings of Boyd K. Packer*, (Salt Lake City: Bookcraft, 2008), 490.
9. "Children of the Covenant," *Ensign*, May 1995; emphasis added.
10. Russell M. Nelson, "Hope of Israel" (worldwide youth devotional, June 3, 2018, Conference Center in Salt Lake City); emphasis added.
11. "President Nelson Extends Three Invitations to Latter-day Saints in California," February 27, 2022, newsroom.churchofjesuschrist.org; in *Liahona*, August 2022.
12. Bengaluru, India, Member Meeting, April 19, 2018; see *Teachings of Russell M. Nelson*, 130; emphasis in original.
13. McConkie, *New Witness for the Articles of Faith*, 554–55; emphasis in original.
14. *Hope in Our Hearts* (Salt Lake City: Deseret Book, 2009), 69–70; emphasis added; see also Nelson, *Accomplishing the Impossible* (Salt Lake City: Deseret Book, 2015), 59–60.

3

Coming to Know Christ through the "I Am" Statements in the Book of Mormon

Joshua M. Matson

One of the covenants members of The Church of Jesus Christ of Latter-day Saints make each week when they participate in the ordinance of the sacrament is "to take upon them the *name* of [God's] Son" (Moroni 4:3; emphasis added). In the October 2022 general conference, Elder Jonathan S. Schmitt sought to deepen our commitment to this covenant by challenging individuals to ask, "Which of Jesus's names should I take upon myself?"[1] Elder Schmitt then observed, "One way we can come to better know Jesus is by learning His many names; . . . many of Jesus's names are titles that help us understand his mission, purpose, character, and attributes; . . . knowing his many names also inspires us to become more like Him—to develop Christlike attributes that bring joy and purpose to our lives."[2] Elder Schmitt's statement establishes a connection between an increase in our understanding of the many names and titles of Jesus Christ with our personal witness and knowledge of him; which ultimately helps us become like him. As this year's *Come, Follow Me* Symposium is focused on coming to know Christ in the Book of Mormon, I would like to explore numerous names and titles for the Savior found within this book of scripture that can lead us to know him better. While an exhaustive analysis of all the possible names and titles of Jesus Christ found in the Book of Mormon is beyond the constraints of this study, I would like to explore the names and titles Jesus Christ used to refer to himself. Specifically, I would like us to consider the titles and names employed by the Savior in "I am" statements.

For centuries Christian faith communities and individuals have carefully studied the "I am" statements of the Savior in the New Testament to shape their understanding of the teachings and person of Jesus Christ.[3] As Latter-day Saints, we are blessed by the addition of numerous "I am" statements pronounced by the Savior and recorded in Restoration scripture. The Savior employed fifty-three "I am" statements while conversing with the ancient authors of the Book of Mormon. While many of these statements are reiterated titles and names used by Christ as recorded in the Bible, twenty-one are unique to the Book of Mormon text. In the discussion that follows, we will identify each of the fifty-three "I am" statements and then employ a systematic analysis developed by New Testament scholars to derive meaning and understanding from those that are unique to this book of Restoration scripture. Studying the "I am" statements of the Book of Mormon in this manner provides the modern reader with a greater understanding of how the "I am" statements establish the Book of Mormon as "another testament of Jesus Christ" alongside the Old and New Testaments. Furthermore, this study intends to help each of us better understand how Jesus viewed himself and assist us to obtain a personal knowledge of the Savior, gain a greater appreciation for the Messiah's life and ministry, and increase our intentionality to keep our covenant to take upon us the Son's names.

New Testament Categories for Studying the "I Am" Statements

While it is tempting to delve into a detailed recitation of the history and importance of the "I am" statements in the world of both the Old and New Testaments, such an exploration is beyond the goals of our discussion and can be adequately found in the studies cited above. However, one component of such studies—namely, the methods employed by New Testament scholars to better understand the "I am" proclamations by the Savior—is helpful to establish a foundation for our study in the Book of Mormon.

In David Ball's study of the "I am" statements in the Gospel of John, he observes that these declarations can be divided into two distinct categories. The first category is identified as the metaphorical "I am" statements. These pronouncements use "I am" with an accompanying concrete image, such as "the bread of life" (John 6:35). The second category is identified as the absolute "I am" statements. These declarations lack an image, but frequently include an additional title or identifier, as shown in the statement, "I am he" (John 18:5).[4] Put simply, metaphorical utilizations of "I am" statements focus on "Jesus' role and mission"[5] and provide insight into how Jesus Christ is *acting* as the promised Messiah. The absolute "I am" statements are a revelation of who Jesus Christ is—his titles and names by which individuals would recognize him as the promised Messiah and God of Israel.

The "I Am" Statements in the Book of Mormon

Now that we have established the value for and criteria set forth by New Testament scholars in their studies of the "I am" statements, we can apply their methodology to the study of similar statements in the Book of Mormon and observe how these statements help the modern reader better understand who Jesus Christ is, what the Messiah does, and how we can follow his example in our daily lives. The fifty-three "I am" statements in the Book of Mormon were identified by employing three primary criteria. First, an "I am" statement must be spoken by or attributed directly to Jesus Christ. Second, the metaphorical "I am" statements must conform to the formula structure seen in the New Testament as outlined in the previous section. Third, the absolute "I am" statements must contain a title by which the Savior would be recognized to an ancient audience, specifically finding roots in the Old Testament. This final criterion does not mean that an absolute "I am" statement has to have a biblical parallel but instead requires that the title emphasized by the "I am" is recognizable to an ancient Jewish audience. Having outlined the definitions of the metaphorical and absolute "I am" statements above, we can divide the "I am" statements of the Book of Mormon into these two categories and analyze them respectively. A comprehensive table categorizing each statement is included in the appendix.

The analysis that follows will look at the metaphorical and absolute "I am" statements at two different periods within the Book of Mormon: those given by the premortal Jehovah and those given by the resurrected Jesus Christ, creating four sections for our study (metaphorical "I am" statements by the premortal Jehovah, absolute "I am" statements by the premortal Jehovah, metaphorical "I am" statements by the resurrected Jesus Christ, and absolute "I am" statements by the resurrected Jesus Christ). While dividing our discussion into these four categories helps contextualize the statements made by Jesus Christ at various times during his premortal and resurrected ministries and shows how the Book of Mormon fits within the ancient chronology of the Bible, it also reveals things about the Savior that are lacking in our current biblical text and that if simply attributed to a time after the New Testament would be obsolete. For example, concerning the premortal Jehovah, the Book of Mormon preserves examples that his role as the Messiah was explicitly revealed to ancient prophets (2 Nephi 10:7), that working miracles among the children of men is central to his mission and character (2 Nephi 27:23), and that he would be known by the name of Jesus (Ether 3:14). Furthermore, concerning the resurrected Jesus Christ, the Book of Mormon preserves examples that explicitly connect him with the premortal Jehovah (3 Nephi 11:14; 15:5; 20:23), that reveal that his ministry continues beyond the resurrection (3 Nephi 19:22), and that provide insight into the divine nature of the resurrected Messiah (3 Nephi 28:10). These insights are valuable additions to our knowledge of the premortal Jehovah and the resurrected Jesus Christ because they clearly show that they are one in the same individual. Each section will consist of four elements of analysis: an introduction to the "I am" statements, a table presenting the verses from the Book of Mormon that contain the "I am" statements, a comparison of Book of Mormon "I am" statements with similar statements from the Bible, and an articulation of new insights provided by the Book of Mormon "I am" statements that emphasizes who the Savior is, what he does, and how we can keep our covenant to take his unique names upon us.

Metaphorical "I am" statements by the premortal Jehovah in the Book of Mormon

Twenty-six of the "I am" statements from the Book of Mormon are proclaimed by the premortal Jehovah to various prophets spanning the book's history. Of these twenty-six statements, ten are metaphorical, though this includes two sets of statements that are the same pronouncement (table 1), and the remaining sixteen are absolute (table 2). As emphasized above, metaphorical "I am" statements follow a predictable formula in their presentation. Each of the ten metaphorical statements given by the premortal Jehovah in the Book of Mormon follows this prescribed pattern by first emphasizing the self-predication (I am) followed by a description of the salvific power or actions of the Messiah (italicized in the table below). Of these statements, three are unique to the Book of Mormon and are presented in bold.

Table 1: Premortal Jehovah "I am" statements in the Book of Mormon

METAPHORICAL "I AM" STATEMENTS	
I Am Statement	*Reference*
Hearken unto me, O Jacob, and Israel my called, for I am he; *I am the first, and I am also the last.*	1 Nephi 20:12; compare Isaiah 48:12
I am he; yea, *I am he that comforteth you.* Behold, who art thou, that thou shouldest be afraid of man, who shall die, and of the son of man, who shall be made like unto grass?	2 Nephi 8:12; compare Isaiah 51:12
For he saith: By the strength of my hand and by my wisdom I have done these things; for *I am prudent*; and I have moved the borders of the people, and have robbed their treasures, and I have put down the inhabitants like a valiant man;	2 Nephi 20:13; compare Isaiah 10:13
Then shall the Lord God say unto him: The learned shall not read them, for they have rejected them, and *I am able to do mine own work*; wherefore thou shalt read the words which I shall give unto thee.	2 Nephi 27:20; compare Isaiah 29:11–12

Touch not the things which are sealed, for I will bring them forth in mine own due time; for I will show unto the children of men that *I am able to do mine own work.*	2 Nephi 27:21
For behold, I am God; and *I am a God of miracles;* and I will show unto the world that *I am the same yesterday, today, and forever;* and I work not among the children of men save it be according to their faith.	2 Nephi 27:23
And I do this that I may prove unto many that *I am the same yesterday, today, and forever;* and that I speak forth my words according to mine own pleasure. And because I have spoken one word ye need not suppose that I cannot speak another; for my work is not yet finished; neither shall it be until the end of man, neither from that time henceforth and forever.	2 Nephi 29:9
And it shall come to pass that they shall know that I am the Lord their God, and *am a jealous God,* visiting the iniquities of my people.	Mosiah 11:22; compare Exodus 20:5
And then shall they know that I am the Lord their God, that *I am their Redeemer;* but they would not be redeemed.	Mosiah 26:26
Behold, *I am he who was prepared from the foundation of the world to redeem my people.* Behold, I am Jesus Christ. I am the Father and the Son. In me shall all mankind have life, and that eternally, even they who shall believe on my name; and they shall become my sons and my daughters.	Ether 3:14

The Book of Mormon shares five salvific statements of Jehovah with the Old Testament. These include "I am he that comforteth you" (2 Nephi 8:12// Isaiah 51:12), "I am prudent" (2 Nephi 20:13//Isaiah 10:13), "I . . . am a jealous God" (Mosiah 11:22//Exodus 20:5), "I am their redeemer" (Mosiah 26:26// Isaiah 41:14; 43:14), and "I am the first, and I am also the last" (1 Nephi 20:12//Isaiah 48:12). Some of these statements not only share verbiage with their counterparts in the Bible, but in the cases of 1 Nephi 20:12, 2 Nephi 8:12, and 2 Nephi 20:13 are direct quotations from Isaiah. While these shared statements are valuable for studying the mission of the coming Messiah, the focus of our discussion is on the proclamations that are unique to the Book of Mormon—namely, "I am able to do mine own work" (2 Nephi 27:21), "I am a God of miracles" (2 Nephi 27:23), and "I am the same yesterday, today, and forever" (2 Nephi 29:9).

Jehovah's proclamation "I am able to do mine own work" (2 Nephi 27:21) is one of the more intriguing "I am" statements in the Book of Mormon because of its connection with the Old Testament. Second Nephi 27 consists of Nephi's quotation and explanation of Isaiah 29. Although based on the Isaiah text, the statement "I am able to do mine own work" does not appear in the ancient or modern texts of Isaiah. While this "I am" statement does not have a direct textual parallel within Isaiah, it aligns with one of the primary purposes of invoking an "I am" statement in antiquity—namely, to show supremacy over other gods and earthly rulers.[6] The connection between this power and salvation is clearly articulated by Elder Neal A. Maxwell, who said, "Because the centerpiece of the Atonement is already in place, we know that everything else in God's plan will likewise finally succeed. God is surely to do his own work!"[7] One of the divine components of the Savior's earthly ministry emphasized by this "I am" statement is that because of his atoning sacrifice, we can be assured that salvation is available and will work for all God's children who will follow him. The fact that this "I am" statement is given before the Savior's earthly ministry emphasizes that Jesus Christ would fulfill his divine mission to atone for the sins of humankind. Elder D. Todd Christofferson aligned this truth to repentance stating, "Only through repentance do we gain access to the atoning grace of Jesus Christ and salvation."[8] Thus, by examining ourselves and repenting as we participate in the ordinance of the sacrament (see 1 Corinthians 11:31–32), we take upon ourselves the work of salvation completed by Jesus Christ.

Jehovah's proclamation "I am a God of miracles" (2 Nephi 27:23) is a wonderful addition to the study of the "I am" statements from antiquity and teaches us of a primary component of the Messiah's divine mission. The connection between miracles and the Messiah is a dominant theme throughout the Book of Mormon. In Mosiah 3, King Benjamin declares, "The Lord Omnipotent who reigneth . . . shall come down from heaven among the children of men, and shall dwell in a tabernacle of clay, and shall go forth amongst men, working mighty miracles, such as healing the sick, raising the dead, causing the lame to walk, the blind to receive their sight, and the deaf to hear, and curing all manner of diseases" (Mosiah 3:5). While one could easily point to numerous stories from the Savior's life in the New Testament as a fulfillment of this prophecy, we should keep in mind that King Benjamin is directing his remarks to an audience in the Americas, whose posterity would see them fulfilled. In 3 Nephi 17, this "I am" statement by the premortal Jehovah is made manifest as the resurrected Jesus Christ calls upon the people to bring him "any that are sick, . . . lame, or blind, or halt, or maimed, or leprous, or that are withered, or that are deaf, or that are afflicted in any manner. . . . Bring them hither and I will heal them" (3 Nephi 17:7). Connecting these miracles to the Messiah suggests that one of the important saving components of the Lord's divine ministry is to heal physical ailments of those who believe on his name. In the April 2021 general conference, Elder Ronald A. Rasband commented on the importance of connecting God to miracles when he stated, "The Lord performs miracles to remind us of His power, His love for us, His reach from the heavens to our mortal experience, and His desire to teach that which is of most worth."[9] The manifestation of miracles, either anciently or in modern times, is an indication to us that Jesus Christ is a God of miracles and that an important aspect of his divine mission is to work miracles among God's children. As we reflect upon this title as one of the names of the Savior that we take upon ourselves, we can approach the throne of God with confidence that he will do miracles among us (see Mormon 9:21).

The final metaphorical "I am" statement by the premortal Jehovah that is unique in the Book of Mormon highlights the unchanging nature of God—namely, "I am the same yesterday, today, and forever" (2 Nephi 27:23 and 29:9). While the Old Testament does not preserve an "I am" statement that parallels that of these Book of Mormon passages, the concept of the unchanging nature of Jehovah is emphasized by the prophet Malachi, who records the Lord as saying, "I am the Lord, I change not" (Malachi 3:6). This inability to change according to Andrew E. Hill suggests that part of the divine mission of Jehovah is to be of such a holy character that one can be assured that the covenants made by him are effectual in life and eternity.[10] This teaching is also articulated by the later author of Hebrews, who preserves an almost identical statement to those in the Book of Mormon characterizing "Jesus Christ the same yesterday, and to day, and forever" (Hebrews 13:8). In context of Hebrews 13 and Malachi 3, the focus is not necessarily on the person of Jesus never changing but on the word of Christ, promising that he will always keep his covenant and maintain his doctrines. The discussion in 2 Nephi 27 and 29 likewise surrounds the word of the Lord and its ability to be fulfilled, according to the timing of God. In light of our sacramental covenants, it is an assurance that we can trust in the promise from God that we may "always have his spirit to be with [us]" (Moroni 4:3).

Absolute "I am" statements by the premortal Jehovah in the Book of Mormon

The Book of Mormon preserves sixteen absolute "I am" statements uttered by the premortal Jehovah. These absolute statements contain six primary titles associated with Jehovah: *God, Lord, Christ, Jesus Christ, the Father and the Son,* and *he*. From these titles, we can easily show that all but two have a parallel in the Old Testament, suggesting that their primary purpose is to reiterate the divine identity of Jehovah to a Book of Mormon and modern audience. Jehovah's pronouncement to Jacob of "I am Christ" (2 Nephi 10:7) and again to the brother of Jared, "I am Jesus Christ. I am the father and the Son" (Ether 3:14) are vivid proclamations that Jehovah is the Messiah and stand as the only examples of absolute "I am" statements in the Book of Mormon that are not found in a parallel Old Testament text. These are presented in bold in the table below. While these are the only unique absolute "I am" statements in the Book of Mormon, it is helpful to discuss how the other titles reiterate Jehovah's divine titles, in both the Bible and modern scripture.

Table 2: Premortal Jehovah "I am" statements in the Book of Mormon

Absolute "I am" statements	
I Am Statement	*Reference*
And it came to pass that the Lord said unto me: Stretch forth thine hand again unto thy brethren, and they shall not wither before thee, but I will shock them, saith the Lord, and this will I do, that they may know that *I am the Lord their God*.	1 Nephi 17:53
Hearken unto me, O Jacob, and Israel my called, for *I am he*; I am the first, and I am also the last.	1 Nephi 20:12; compare Isaiah 48:12
And kings shall be thy nursing fathers, and their queens thy nursing mothers; they shall bow down to thee with their face towards the earth, and lick up the dust of thy feet; and thou shalt know that *I am the Lord*; for they shall not be ashamed that wait for me.	1 Nephi 21:23; compare Isaiah 49:23
And kings shall be thy nursing fathers, and their queens thy nursing mothers; they shall bow down to thee with their faces towards the earth, and lick up the dust of thy feet; and thou shalt know that *I am the Lord*; for they shall not be ashamed that wait for me.	2 Nephi 6:7; compare Isaiah 49:23
I am he; yeah, I am he that comforteth you. Behold, who art thou, that thou shouldest be afraid of man, who shall die, and of the son of man, who shall be made like unto grass?	2 Nephi 8:12; compare Isaiah 51:12
But *I am the Lord thy God*, whose waves roared; the Lord of Hosts is my name.	2 Nephi 8:15; compare Isaiah 51:15
But behold, thus saith the Lord God: When the day cometh that they shall believe in me, that *I am Christ*, then have I covenanted with their fathers that they shall be restored in the flesh, upon the earth, unto the lands of their inheritance.	2 Nephi 10:7
For behold, *I am God*; and I am a God of miracles; and I will show unto the world that I am the same yesterday, today, and forever; and I work not among the children of men save it be according to their faith.	2 Nephi 27:23
Wherefore murmur ye, because that ye shall receive more of my word? Know ye not that the testimony of two nations is a witness unto you that *I am God*, that I remember one nation like unto another? Wherefore, I speak the same words unto one nation like unto another. And when the two nations shall run together the testimony of the two nations shall run together also.	2 Nephi 29:8

And it shall come to pass that my people, which are of the house of Israel, shall be gathered home unto the lands of their possessions; and my word also shall be gathered in one. And I will show unto them that fight against my word and against my people, who are of the house of Israel, that *I am God*, and that I covenanted with Abraham that I would remember his seed forever.	2 Nephi 29:14
And it shall come to pass that they shall know that *I am the Lord their God*, and am a jealous God, visiting the iniquities of my people.	Mosiah 11:22; compare Exodus 20:5
And it shall come to pass that the life of king Noah shall be valued even as a garment in a hot finance; for he shall know that *I am the Lord*.	Mosiah 12:3
I am the Lord thy God, who hath brought thee out of the land of Egypt, out of the house of bondage.	Mosiah 12:34; compare Exodus 20:2
And then shall they know that *I am the Lord their God*, that I am their Redeemer; but they would not be redeemed.	Mosiah 26:26
Behold, thou art Nephi, and *I am God*. Behold, I declare it unto thee in the presence of mine angels, that ye shall have power over this people, and shall smite the earth with famine, and with pestilence, and destruction, according to the wickedness of this people.	Helaman 10:6
Behold, I am he who was prepared from the foundation of the world to redeem my people. Behold, *I am Jesus Christ*. I am the Father and the Son. In me shall all mankind have life, and that eternally, even they who shall believe on my name; and they shall become my sons and my daughters.	Ether 3:14

Each title that has parallels in the Old Testament can be best understood by the Hebrew roots from which they likely derive. The absolute "I am God" statement is an emphasis of the Hebrew word אלהים (*'elohim*). This exact "I am" statement is made nine times in the Old Testament as a title for the one true God (see Isaiah 44:8), emphasizing God's unique position among all other gods.

The absolute "I am the Lord" is connected to the title Lord (appearing in small capital letters throughout the King James text) which frequently appears in the Old Testament as a substitute for the divine name Jehovah, יהוה (*yhwh*), (see Exodus 29:46 and "Jehovah" in the Bible Dictionary). When this title appears in the Book of Mormon, as it does in 2 Nephi 6:7 and Mosiah 12:3, there is a high probability that the phrase could be translated as "I am Jehovah," as it appears in the Hebrew Bible nearly 162 times. This frequently invoked title emphasizes that the individual speaking to the ancient prophets was indeed the God of Israel, the premortal Jehovah.

The absolute "I am Christ" found in 2 Nephi 10:7 and "I am Jesus Christ" in Ether 3:14 at first glance may appear anachronistic to a modern reader. This title, revealed to Jacob by an angel and spoken to the brother of Jared, is an anglicized form of the Greek word χριστος (*christos*) used frequently in the Greek translation of the Old Testament as the equivalent to the Hebrew משיח (*mashiach*) and meaning "the anointed one." This title in an "I am" statement is found three times in the New Testament (Matthew 24:5; Mark 13:6; and Luke 21:8), rooted in the Old Testament's description of the act of anointing high priests and kings as part of their ascension to leadership within the community. The title takes on a higher meaning in the Dead Sea Scrolls as it is associated with a future anointed high priest and an "anointed one of the spirit" (see 11Q13 2:18), perhaps indicating an explicit prophecy of the coming Messiah as the anointed one circulating among Jewish communities in the late Second Temple period. Especially among the writings of Paul and early Christian communities in the first century AD, the term came to be synonymous with the ministry of Jesus Christ. This is visually portrayed by the anointing scenes preserved in the gospels (see Matthew 26:6–13; Mark 14:3–9; Luke 7:36–50; and John 12:1–8). As observed by Marinus de Jonge, "For Paul and the tradition before him, the designation 'Christ' was thus linked with Jesus' death and resurrection and their salvific effects."[11] This title underscores the blurriness that can sometimes exist when categorizing the "I am" statements, the title of who Christ *is* overlaps with the actions that he performed, thus "I am the Christ,"(2 Nephi 10:7) can be read either as "I am the Messiah" or "I am the one who is anointed to save."

The absolute "I am" statement found in Ether 3:14 includes further identities of Jehovah that do not have an Old Testament parallel—namely, "I am the Father and the Son." These titles, also alluded to in Mosiah 5:7–8, emphasize the nature of our relationship to Jesus Christ because of our covenants, rather than a reference to a literal fatherhood. As D. Kelly Ogden and Andrew C. Skinner have observed, "When we become the children of Christ, he becomes our covenant Father, and every week we remember the sacred covenant by taking upon us the name of Christ."[12] This insight, provided by the Book of Mormon, shows that the nature of the premortal Jehovah is that of a loving parent to his covenant children, an image that is absent in the "I am" statements of the Bible but is invoked again by the resurrected Jesus Christ when he appears to the Nephites.

Metaphorical "I am" statements by the resurrected Jesus Christ in the Book of Mormon

The final twenty-eight "I am" statements in the Book of Mormon are pronounced by the resurrected Jesus Christ. Unlike the statements uttered by the premortal Jehovah, these declarations reflect on the mortal ministry of the Savior rather than prophetically looking forward to it. Because of this, many statements organized here have parallels in the New Testament Gospels. Of these twenty-eight statements, fifteen are metaphorical (see table 3) and thirteen are absolute (see table 4).

The fifteen metaphorical statements pronounced by the resurrected Jesus Christ to the inhabitants of the New World have striking similarities to those given in the New Testament. The resurrected Jesus Christ's proclamation "I am the light of the world" (3 Nephi 9:18; 11:11; 15:5, 9; 18:16, 24; and Ether 4:12) has parallels with the Savior's pronouncement of being the light of the world in John 8:12 and 9:5. Additionally, the resurrected Savior's metaphorical statement "I am he that gave the law and I am he who covenanted with my people Israel" (see 3 Nephi 12:17; 15:5, 9) is directly connected with the statement he made in the Sermon on the Mount in Matthew 5:17 of coming to fulfill the law, not to destroy it. The metaphorical "I am Alpha and Omega, the beginning and the end" recorded in 3 Nephi 9:18 parallels the Savior's statement to John the Revelator in Revelation 1:8, 11; 21:16; and 22:13. A final parallel "I am" statement appears in Ether 4:8, where the Lord emphasizes "I am he who speaketh," a reiteration of Isaiah 52:6. Such parallels, like those pronounced above by the premortal Jehovah, will not be discussed here. The three remaining metaphorical "I am" statements, "I am with them" (3 Nephi 19:22), "I am he who doeth it" (3 Nephi 20:19), and "I am the same that leadeth men to all good" (Ether 4:12) provide unique insights to the mission and actions of Jesus Christ as our Savior and are bolded in the table below.

Table 3: Resurrected Jesus Christ "I am" statements in the Book of Mormon

Metaphorical "I am" statements	
I am statement	*Reference*
I am the light and the life of the world. I am Alpha and Omega, the beginning and the end.	3 Nephi 9:18; compare Revelation 22:13
And behold, *I am the light and the life of the world*; and I have drunk out of that bitter cup which the Father hath given me, and have glorified the Father in taking upon me the sins of the world, in the which, I have suffered the will of the Father in all things from the beginning.	3 Nephi 11:11
Think not that I am come to destroy the law or the prophets. *I am not come to destroy but to fulfil*;	3 Nephi 12:17; compare Matthew 5:17
Behold, *I am he that gave the law*, and *I am he who covenanted with my people Israel*; therefore, the law in me is fulfilled, for I have come to fulfill the law; therefore it hath an end.	3 Nephi 15:5
Behold, *I am the law, and the light*. Look unto me, and endure to the end, and ye shall live; for unto him that endureth to the end will I give eternal life.	3 Nephi 15:9
And I have prayed among you even so shall ye pray in my church, among my people who do repent and are baptized in my name. Behold *I am the light*; I have set an example for you.	3 Nephi 18:16
Therefore, hold up your light that it may shine unto the world. Behold *I am the light which ye shall hold up* that which ye have seen me do. Behold ye see that I have prayed unto the Father, and ye all have witnessed.	3 Nephi 18:24
Father, thou hast given them the Holy Ghost because they believe in me; and thou seest that they believe in me because thou hearest them, and they pray unto me; and they pray unto me because *I am with them*.	3 Nephi 19:22

For I will make my people with whom the Father hath covenanted, yea, I will make thy horn iron, and I will make thy hoofs brass. And thou shalt beat in pieces many people; and I will consecrate their gain unto the Lord, and their substance unto the Lord of the whole earth. And behold, *I am he who doeth it.*	3 Nephi 20:19; compare Micah 4:13
Verily, verily I say unto you, that my people shall know my name; yea, in that day they shall know that *I am he that doth speak.*	3 Nephi 20:39; compare Isaiah 52:6
And he that will content against the word of the Lord, let him be accursed; and he that shall deny these things, let him be accursed; for unto them will I show no greater things, saith Jesus Christ; for *I am he who speaketh.*	Ether 4:8
And whatsoever thing persuadeth men to do good is of me; for good cometh of none save it be of me. *I am the same that leadeth men to all good;* he that will not believe my words will not believe me—that I am; and he that will not believe me will not believe the Father who sent me. For behold, I am the Father, *I am the light, and the life, and the truth of the world.*	Ether 4:12

The "I am" statement by the resurrected Jesus Christ in 3 Nephi 19:22 that proclaims, "I am with them" is a beautiful reminder of the Savior's constant care for God's children. While we do not know the original language from which the words used here are drawn, there is an interesting parallel between this phrase and a Hebrew phrase utilized by Isaiah and quoted by Nephi. In 2 Nephi 17:14 the prophet proclaims, "Therefore, the Lord himself shall give you a sign—Behold, a virgin shall conceive, and shall bear a son, and shall call his name Immanuel." This prophecy is quoted by the author of Matthew, who then adds "which being interpreted is, God with us" (Matthew 1:23). The Savior's pronouncement to the inhabitants of the New World that he is with them is a fulfilment of Isaiah's prophecy. President Thomas S. Monson reiterated this promise and component of the Savior's salvific ministry in our day when he said, "Whether it is the best of times or the worst of times, He is with us. He has promised that this will never change."[13] This reassurance is particularly poignant when thinking of the names of the Savior during the sacrament because this title provides comfort that in addition to his spirit being with us, we can know he is with us as well.

The second unique metaphorical "I am" statement in the Book of Mormon is ambiguous if read outside its context. In this statement Jesus Christ proclaims, "I am he who doeth it" (3 Nephi 20:19). This statement, situated within a discussion of how he will gather his covenant people together (3 Nephi 20:18), articulates the importance of gathering scattered Israel. Thus, the gathering of Israel is a primary responsibility of the Savior and a way in which he brings about salvation to all God's children. President Russell M. Nelson has connected salvation with the gathering of Israel by stating, "When we speak of the gathering, we are simply saying this fundamental truth: everyone of Heavenly Father's children, on both sides of the veil, deserves to hear the message of the restored gospel of Jesus Christ. They decide for themselves if they want to know more."[14] He further declared, "The gathering is the most important thing taking place on earth today."[15] Because of the Book of Mormon, the importance of this part of the Savior's continuing mission in the salvific plan of our Heavenly Father is known to extend to every nation, kindred, tongue, and people.

The final metaphorical "I am" statement by the resurrected Jesus Christ comes in his addressing Moroni in Ether 4:12. Here the Messiah proclaims, "I am the same that leadeth men to all good." This role of the Savior is succinctly described by Ogden and Skinner, who state, "Whatever persuades people to do good originates from God; he is the source of all good. He is the Most High God, and he is the most high good."[16] This characteristic was equally imprinted upon Moroni by his father as he sought to encourage others to follow the Savior and do his will. Mormon wrote, "Every thing which inviteth to do good, and to persuade to believe in Christ, is sent forth by the power and gift of Christ; wherefore ye may know with a perfect knowledge it is of God" (Moroni 7:16). A key component of the Savior's salvific ministry is to not only teach good but to help all to do good. As we reflect on the sacramental covenant to take upon us the name of God's son, we should equally ponder on whether what we do on a regular basis reflects his good.

Absolute "I am" statements by the resurrected Jesus Christ in the Book of Mormon

While the thirteen absolute "I am" statements given by the resurrected Jesus Christ in the Book of Mormon share many titles pronounced by the premortal Jehovah, studying the statements alongside one another produces a unique observation. Noticeably, the Savior shifts his emphasis in titles: while his premortal statements focused more heavily on his divinity as a god, his post-resurrection statements are more focused on his mortal experience. The titles emphasized by the "I am" statements include a more pronounced emphasis on his earthly title of Jesus Christ (see 3 Nephi 9:15; 11:10; and 20:31), his covenantal role as the Father (3 Nephi 9:15; 11:27; 28:10; and Ether 4:12), two references to the absolute "I am" (3 Nephi 12:1–2), with only a single reference to his roles as the God of Israel (3 Nephi 11:14) and as the Lord (3 Nephi 24:6). While each of these titles was discussed previously, our attention turns to the title not analyzed above, "the Son of God," a title that has ample representation in the New Testament but is surprisingly not spoken directly by the Savior except here in the Book of Mormon.

Table 4: Resurrected Jesus Christ "I am" statements in the Book of Mormon

Absolute "I am" statements	
I am statement	*Reference*
Behold, *I am Jesus Christ the Son of God*. I created the heavens and the earth, and all things that in them are. I was with the Father from the beginning. *I am in the Father*, and the Father in me; and in me hath the Father glorified his name.	3 Nephi 9:15
Behold, *I am Jesus Christ*, whom the prophets testified shall come into the world.	3 Nephi 11:10
Arise and come forth unto me, that ye may thrust your hands into my side, and also that ye may feel the prints of the nails in my hands and in my feet, that ye may know that *I am the God of Israel*, and the God of the whole earth, and have been slain for the sins of the world.	3 Nephi 11:14

And after this manner shall ye baptize in my name; for behold, verily I say unto you, that the Father, and the Son, and the Holy Ghost are one; and *I am in the Father*, and the Father in me, and the Father and I are one.	3 Nephi 11:27
Blessed are ye if ye shall give heed unto the words of these twelve whom I have chosen among you to minister unto you, and to be your servants; and unto them I have given power that they may baptize you with water; and after that ye are baptized with water, behold, I will baptize you with fire and with the Holy Ghost; therefore blessed are ye if ye shall believe in me and be baptized, after that ye have seen me and know that *I am*.	3 Nephi 12:1
And again, more blessed are they who shall believe in your words because that ye shall testify that ye have seen me, and that ye know that *I am*. Yea, blessed are they who shall believe in your words, and come down into the depths of humility and be baptized, for they shall be visited with fire and with the Holy Ghost, and shall receive a remission of their sins.	3 Nephi 12:2
And they shall believe in me, that *I am Jesus Christ, the Son of God*, and shall pray unto the Father in my name.	3 Nephi 20:31
For *I am the Lord*, I change not; therefore my sons of Jacob are not consumed.	3 Nephi 24:6; compare Matthew 3:6
And for this cause ye shall have fulness of joy; and ye shall sit down in the kingdom of my Father; yea, your joy shall be full, even as the Father hath given me fulness of joy; and ye shall be even as *I am*, and *I am even as the Father*; and the Father and I are one.	3 Nephi 28:10
And whatsoever thing persuadeth men to do good is of me; for good cometh of none save it be of me. I am the same that leadeth men to all good; he that will not believe my words will not believe me—that *I am*; and he that will not believe me will not believe the Father who sent me. For behold, *I am the Father*, I am the light, and the life, and the truth of the world.	Ether 4:12

The Savior's statement of clarification, that "I am Jesus Christ, *the Son of God*" (3 Nephi 9:15 and 20:31; emphasis added), appears once in the Old Testament (see Daniel 3:25) and is frequently employed throughout the New Testament, especially by Matthew (see Matthew 2:15; 3:17; 4:3, 6; 8:29; 14:33; 16:16; 26:63), but is not directly stated by the Messiah anywhere in biblical texts. Aaron M. Gale emphasizes such references by stating, "Matthew presents Jesus also as the divine Son of God who will save his people."[17] The sonship of Jesus Christ is equally emphasized in the Gospel of John. "These are written, that ye might believe that Jesus is the Christ, the Son of God; and that believing ye might have life through his name" (John 20:31). Neither of these Gospel authors, however, records the Savior referring to himself as the Son of God. The closest parallel "I am" statement is given in the Gospel of Matthew, though admittedly by a secondhand account. According to Matthew 27:43, one of the guards positioned at the cross mocks the dying Messiah by stating, "He trusted in God; let him deliver him now, if he will have him: for he said, I am the Son of God." Perhaps this is a reference to John 10:36, where the Savior recounts opposition to his statement "I am the Son of God," but no further context is given. No explicit account exists where the Savior proclaims himself as the Son of God, except here in the Book of Mormon, providing another valuable addition as to how the Messiah himself spoke of his role, mission, and identity. For modern readers, this statement solidifies the position of Jesus Christ as the only begotten son of God and assures us that as we take upon ourselves the identity as children of God, this identity, as Elder Jeffrey R. Holland states, "teaches us as mortal men and women that we can be one with the Father in a crucial, fundamental, eternally significant way: We can obey him. We can subject the flesh to the spirit. We can yield our will as children to the will of our Heavenly Father."[18]

The Book of Mormon "I Am" Statements and Our Coming to Know Christ

This study of the "I am" statements, proclaimed by the Lord and recorded in the Book of Mormon, has provided us with important insights that aid us in coming to know Jesus Christ and by reflecting upon the various names we can take upon ourselves as we participate in the ordinance of the sacrament. First, as we have discussed the metaphorical "I am" statements of the Savior, we have obtained a clearer picture of the work of salvation that surrounds Jesus Christ. The salvific actions of the Savior as a worker of miracles, an independent and almighty deity, and the consistency of his character teaches us that the Savior desires to be an intricate part of each of our lives. As the Messiah, he desires to continue to perform miracles for us, to be mighty to save, and to be true and faithful to covenants so that we can obtain eternal life. Additionally, the metaphorical "I am" statements have reassured us that Christ is still involved in our lives by being with us, gathering scattered Israel, and aiding each of us to learn good and to do it. The metaphorical "I am" statements recorded in the Book of Mormon give us direction for our own lives and the assurance that as "we come unto Christ and help others to do the same, we are participating in God's work of salvation and exaltation."[19] Second, as we have discussed absolute "I am" statements pronounced by the Savior and recorded in the Book of Mormon, we have come to know more about who the Savior is and the titles that help us know how he relates to God's children. The titles *God, Lord, Christ, Jesus Christ*, as well as *the Father and the Son*, though commonly used in our day, take on greater meaning when we recognize that these are specifically chosen by the Savior to help us know him at various times in his premortal and resurrected ministries. As we come to know him better, we have an increase in our resolve to be intentional in keeping the covenant to take upon ourselves the names of Christ. Ultimately, the "I am" statements further contribute to one of the primary purposes of the Book of Mormon to "convinc[e] Jew and Gentile that Jesus is the Christ" (title page of the Book of Mormon).

JOSHUA M. MATSON *is a religious educator with Seminaries and Institutes of Religion and currently teaches at the Bingham High School Seminary.*

Appendix

"I am" statements by the Savior in the Book of Mormon (unique Book of Mormon "I am" statements are in bold)

I am statement	Category of "I am" statement	Book of Mormon reference	Biblical quotations	Biblical parallel
I am the Lord their God	Absolute	1 Nephi 17:53		Exodus 29:46; Leviticus 26:44
I am he, I am the first, and I am also the last	Absolute	1 Nephi 20:12	Isaiah 48:12	
I am the Lord	Absolute	1 Nephi 21:23	Isaiah 49:23	
I am the Lord	Absolute	2 Nephi 6:7		
I am he, yea, I am he that comforteth you	Metaphorical	2 Nephi 8:12	Isaiah 51:12	
I am the Lord thy God	Absolute	2 Nephi 8:15	Isaiah 51:15	
I am Christ	Absolute	2 Nephi 10:7		
I am prudent	Metaphorical	2 Nephi 20:13	Isaiah 10:13	
I am able to do mine own work	Metaphorical	2 Nephi 27:20		
I am able to do mine own work	Metaphorical	2 Nephi 27:21		
I am God	Absolute	2 Nephi 27:23		Genesis 46:3
I am a God of miracles	Metaphorical	2 Nephi 27:23		
I am the same yesterday, today, and forever	Metaphorical	2 Nephi 27:23		Malachi 3:6
I am God	Absolute	2 Nephi 29:8		Genesis 46:3

I am the same yesterday, today, and forever	Metaphorical	2 Nephi 29:9		Malachi 3:6
I am God	Absolute	2 Nephi 29:14		Isaiah 43:12; 46:9
I am the Lord their God and am a jealous God	Absolute/ Metaphorical	Mosiah 11:22		Exodus 20:5
I am the Lord	Absolute	Mosiah 12:3		162 occurences
I am the Lord thy God	Absolute	Mosiah 12:34		Isaiah 43:3; 48:17; Deuteronomy 5:6; Exodus 20:2
I am the Lord their God	Absolute	Mosiah 26:26		Exodus 29:46; Leviticus 26:44
I am their Redeemer	Metaphorical	Mosiah 26:26		Isaiah 41:14; 43:14
I am God	Absolute	Helaman 10:6		Isaiah 43:12; 46:9
I am Jesus Christ, the Son of God	Absolute	3 Nephi 9:15		
I am in the Father	Absolute	3 Nephi 9:15		John 14:10
I am the light and the life of the world	Metaphorical	3 Nephi 9:18		John 8:12; 9:5
I am Alpha and Omega, the beginning and the end	Metaphorical	3 Nephi 9:18		Revelation 1:8; 1:11; 21:16; 22:13
I am Jesus Christ	Absolute	3 Nephi 11:10		
I am the light and life of the world	Metaphorical	3 Nephi 11:11		John 8:12; 9:5
I am the God of Israel	Absolute	3 Nephi 11:14		Exodus 32:27

I am in the Father	Absolute	3 Nephi 11:27		John 14:10
Know that I am	Absolute	3 Nephi 12:1		Isaiah 43:10; 52:6
Ye know that I am	Absolute	3 Nephi 12:2		Isaiah 43:10; 52:6
I am not come to destroy, but to fulfill	Metaphorical	3 Nephi 12:17	Matthew 5:17	
I am he that gave the law	Metaphorical	3 Nephi 15:5		John 8:12; 9:5
I am he who covenanted with my people Israel	Metaphorical	3 Nephi 15:5		Genesis 15:18
I am the law and the light	Metaphorical	3 Nephi 15:9		John 8:12; 9:5
I am the light	Metaphorical	3 Nephi 18:16		John 8:12; 9:5
I am the light which ye shall hold up	Metaphorical	3 Nephi 18:24		John 8:12; 9:5
I am with them	Metaphorical	3 Nephi 19:22		
I am he who doeth it	Metaphorical	3 Nephi 20:19		
I am he of whom Moses spake	Absolute	3 Nephi 20:23		Deuteronomy 18:15–19
I am Jesus Christ, the Son of God	Absolute	3 Nephi 20:31		
I am he that doth speak	Absolute	3 Nephi 20:39		Hebrews 12:25
I am the Lord	Absolute	3 Nephi 24:6	Malachi 3:6	
I am even as the Father	Absolute	3 Nephi 28:10		John 5:19

I am he who was prepared from the foundation of the world to redeem my people	Metaphorical	Ether 3:14		1 Peter 1:20
I am Jesus Christ	Absolute	Ether 3:14		
I am the Father and the Son	Absolute	Ether 3:14		
I am he who speaketh	Metaphorical	Ether 4:8	Isaiah 52:6	
I am the same that leadeth men to all good	Metaphorical	Ether 4:12		
I am the Father	Absolute	Ether 4:12		
I am the light, and the life, and the truth of the world	Metaphorical	Ether 4:12		John 8:12; 9:5

Notes

1. Jonathan S. Schmitt, "That They Might Know Thee," *Liahona*, November 2022, 106.
2. Schmitt, "That They Might Know Thee," 107–8.
3. See Catrin H. Williams, *I Am He: The Interpretation of 'Ani Hû' in Jewish and Early Christian Literature* (Tübingen: Mohr Siebeck, 2000); David M. Ball, *I Am in John's Gospel: Literary Function, Background and Theological Implications* (Sheffield: Sheffield, 1996); Jonathan H. Stephenson, "'I Am He': Jesus' Publication Declarations of His Own Identity," in *The Lord of the Gospels: 1990 Sperry Symposium on the New Testament*, ed. Bruce A. Van Orden and Brent L. Top (Salt Lake City: Deseret Book, 1991), 162–72; and Raymond E. Brown, "The Ego Eimi ('I AM') Passages in the Fourth Gospel," *Companion to John: Readings in Johannine Theology (John's Gospel and Epistles)*, ed. Michael J. Taylor (New York: Alba House, 1977), 117–26.
4. Ball, *I Am in John's Gospel*, 14.
5. Williams, *I Am He*, 9.
6. Williams, *I Am He*, 150.
7. Neal A. Maxwell, "Put Off the Natural Man, and Come Off Conqueror," *Ensign*, November 1990, 15.
8. D. Todd Christofferson, "The Divine Gift of Repentance," *Ensign*, November 2011, 38.

9. Ronald A. Rasband, "Behold! I am a God of Miracles," *Liahona*, May 2021, 112.
10. Andrew E. Hill, *Malachi: A New Translation with Introduction and Commentary* (New York: Doubleday, 1998), 295.
11. Marinus de Jonge, "Christ" in *Anchor Bible Dictionary*, 914.
12. D. Kelly Ogden and Andrew C. Skinner, *Verse by Verse The Book of Mormon, Volume 1: 1 Nephi through Alma 29* (Salt Lake City: Deseret Book, 2011), 322–23.
13. Thomas S. Monson, "I Will Not Fail Thee, Nor Forsake Thee," *Ensign*, November 2013, 87.
14. Russell M. Nelson, "Hope of Israel" (worldwide youth devotional, June 3, 2018).
15. Nelson, "Hope of Israel."
16. D. Kelly Ogden and Andrew C. Skinner, *Verse by Verse Book of Mormon*, vol. 2: *Alma 30 through Moroni 10* (Salt Lake City: Deseret Book, 2011), 269.
17. Aaron M. Gale, "The Gospel of Matthew," *The Jewish Annotated New Testament*, ed. Amy-Jill Levine and Marc Zvi Brettler (Oxford: Oxford, 2017), 10.
18. Jeffrey R. Holland, *Christ and the New Covenant* (Salt Lake City: Deseret Book, 2006), 189.
19. *General Handbook: Serving in the Church of Jesus Christ of Latter-day Saints*, 1.2 (Salt Lake City: Intellectual Reserve, 2022).

4

Remember Him
The Christ-Centered Focus of Remembering in the Book of Mormon

Michael David Ricks

President Spencer W. Kimball asserted that a dictionary's most important word "could be 'remember,'" adding that "because all of [us] have made covenants.... 'Remember' is the word."[1] Forms of the word *remember* appear more than 550 times in the standard works—disproportionately in the Book of Mormon.[2] If remembering characterizes our covenantal relationship with Jesus Christ and is uniquely emphasized in the Book of Mormon, then a deeper understanding of Book of Mormon teachings about remembering can contribute to our covenantal conversion to Christ.

This essay explores remembering in the Book of Mormon and demonstrates a connection between remembering and our Savior Jesus Christ. Academic work studying the remembering in the Book of Mormon has documented linguistic parallels with other ancient texts;[3] has connected remembering theologically with action, repentance, and obedience;[4] and has demonstrated how remembering builds themes of covenant identity both linguistically and narratively.[5] This paper complements these specific research

Figure 1. Common words in Book of Mormon passages with *remember*.

topics by taking a fully categorical approach to what the Book of Mormon teaches about remembering.

In total, there are 221 references to *remember* and its derivatives[6] in the Book of Mormon; 150 of these are directly connected to Jesus Christ. Christ is repeatedly featured in passages containing the word *remember*: inviting remembrance, being remembered, and himself remembering. Furthermore, seven doctrinal themes about remembering emerge, providing practical insights into our covenantal connection with Christ—especially our promises to "always remember him" (Moroni 4:3).

In the Book of Mormon Remembering Is Connected to Jesus Christ

In the Book of Mormon, passages that mention remembering are filled with titles of Christ. Figure 1 is a word cloud that visualizes the 250 most common

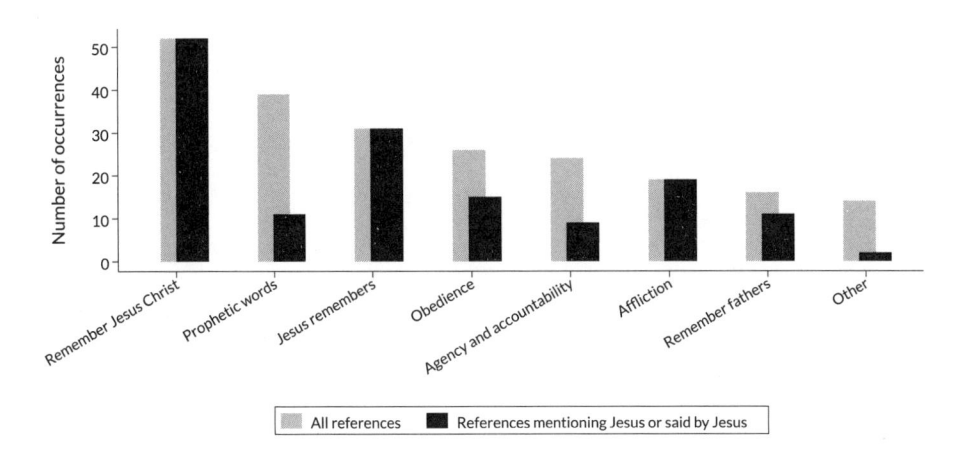

Figure 2. Seven *remember* themes and Christ-connected passages.

words in the verses where *remember* is used.[7] Larger and more central words occur with greater frequency.[8]

Words like "Lord God," "Son," "Christ," and "Jesus" occur with great regularity in these passages—more than words anecdotally associated with remembrance like "words," "commandments," "spoken," and "fathers." Furthermore, explicit mentions of "Jesus," "Christ," "Lord," and "Redeemer" occur about twice as often in these verses than in the Book of Mormon on average.[9] Clearly Christ is central.

Word clouds are intuitive and fully data-driven but cannot identify broader themes or less explicit connections with Christ. To explore these connections, I grouped the passages into one of seven themes using an emergent coding procedure.[10] These seven themes, ordered from most to least prevalent, are (1) remembering Jesus Christ; (2) remembering prophetic words; (3) that Jesus remembers; (4) remembering and obedience; (5) agency, accountability, and remembering; (6) afflictions and remembering; and (7) remembering our fathers.

These seven themes teach about Christ and connect him with remembering. Figure 2 visualizes the frequency of each theme as well as what share of the references are connected to Christ. Lighter bars show how many passages are in each theme, and darker bars show how many of these passages are connected to Christ, which I define as explicitly or contextually referencing Jesus or being spoken by him.[11]

Figure 2 identifies two important patterns about *remembering* and Jesus Christ in the Book of Mormon. First, when Book of Mormon scriptures mention *remembering*, they are most likely teaching us to remember Jesus Christ. Although this emphasis can be obscured by our focus on oft-repeated phrases like "remember the captivity of your fathers," or "remember the words of the prophet," the theme of remembering Christ is the most common—more than twice as prevalent as most other themes. Second, many of the *remembering* themes are intensely Christ-centered. For example, more than half of the passages in the themes about obedience, afflictions, and fathers are directly connected to Jesus Christ. This is in addition to the two full themes that are entirely about him. Jesus Christ is central to themes of remembering in the Book of Mormon.

Specific Themes Related to Remembering

The previous section cemented the connection between Jesus and the idea of remembrance in the Book of Mormon. With that connection in mind, this section explores each of the seven themes, the key truths they teach, and what they can mean in the life of a latter-day disciple. While I divide each theme into subtopics based on the truths they teach, many of the passages could reasonably fit in other subtopics, and other reasonable sets of groupings exist. For each theme I present a table with all the related verses divided by subtopic, but for concision I limit the discussion in the text to one or two key truths taught by the passages.

Remember him

At the heart of the themes of remembering in the Book of Mormon is remembering Jesus Christ. This theme is almost 50 percent larger than the next most common theme. Prophets and our Savior himself emphasize the importance of remembering Jesus, his perfection, his salvific role, and what he has said and done for us. Table 1 reports the related scriptural passages.

TABLE 1. REMEMBER JESUS

REMEMBER WHAT JESUS HAS SAID AND DONE

1 Nephi 14:8	Do you remember his covenants with the house of Israel?
1 Nephi 15:10–11	Remember, if you ask me in faith, you will know these things.
2 Nephi 9:52	Remember his words, pray, and rejoice.
Mosiah 2:41	Remember, those who keep the commandments will be happy and blessed.
Mosiah 25:16	Remember that he was who delivered them from bondage.
Alma 5:52	"Behold and remember, the Holy One hath spoken it."
Alma 13:1	Remember, he ordained priests to teach the people.
Alma 37:13	Remember, if we keep the commandments, we will prosper in the land.
Alma 60:23	Remember, clean the inward vessel first.
Alma 62:50	Remember, he delivered from death, bonds, prisons, afflictions, and out of the hands of enemies.
3 Nephi 13:25	Jesus asks twelve disciples to remember his words to teach them.
3 Nephi 15:1	Remembering his words to do them leads to salvation.
3 Nephi 27:12	Remember what he taught to build church on his gospel.
Ether 12:32–33	Remember, he loved us unto laying down his life and now prepares a place for us.
Moroni 7:5	Remember, by their works we shall know them.

REMEMBER THAT HE SAVES

2 Nephi 10:20	Remember him to lay aside our sins and use his mercy.
2 Nephi 10:24	Remember, we are only saved in and through his grace.
Mosiah 4:30	Remember to continue in faith in him to perish not.
Mosiah 16:13	Remember, we are only saved in and through Christ.

Mosiah 23:27	Alma exhorts people to remember the Lord and he will deliver them.
Alma 29:10	Alma remembers the Lord heard his prayer for mercy and forgiveness.
Alma 34:37	Remember to work out your salvation by his cleansing blood.
Alma 42:11	Remember that without his plan of redemption, all would be miserable and cut off.
Helaman 5:12	Remember to build on Christ so that we won't fall.

Remember the character of Christ

2 Nephi 9:40–41	Remember that he is great and that his paths are righteous.
Mosiah 4:11	Remember his greatness, goodness, longsuffering, and love.
Alma 29:10	Alma remembers his merciful arm was extended toward him.
Alma 32:22	Remember, he is merciful unto all who believe and wants us to believe.
Moroni 10:3	Remember how merciful he has been.
Moroni 10:18–19	Remember, every good gift comes from him, and he will never change.

Remember him with the sacrament

3 Nephi 18:7	Eat bread in remembrance of his body that he showed; if we will always remember, we'll have his Spirit.
3 Nephi 18:11	Wine in remembrance of blood which he shed; testify that we will always remember; if we remember, we'll have his Spirit.
Moroni 4:3	Eat bread in remembrance and witness willingness to always remember.
Moroni 5:2	Drink wine in remembrance, and witness that we do always remember.
Moroni 6:6	Met oft to take bread and wine in remembrance of Lord Jesus.

PROPHETS INVITE US TO REMEMBER HIM

1 Nephi 19:8	Purpose of scripture is to persuade us to remember our Redeemer.
Mosiah 5:11–12	Remember that Jesus's name comes by covenant; write it in our hearts.
Alma 37:14	Alma asks Helaman to remember God entrusted him with the plates for his purposes.
Moroni 10:27	Remember Christ's teachings to prepare for judgment.

There are many rich and repeatedly reinforced truths related to this theme, but two types of verses emerge. Some passages teach us about Christ and ask us to remember what he has done (e.g., delivering us), what he has said (e.g., he laid down his life because he loved us), and what his character is like (e.g., he is merciful, longsuffering, and full of love). These passages reflect the fact that a correct understanding of Christ's character, perfection, and attributes empowers our faith in him[12] and inspires us to become even as he is (3 Nephi 27:27).

Other passages emphasize remembering that Jesus is the only source of our salvation. We are saved only in his grace (2 Nephi 10:24), we can be clean through his blood (Alma 34:36–37), and we are safe when we build upon the rock of our Redeemer (Helaman 5:6–12). Remembering that he alone can save is the crux of faith, but that doctrine also empowers us to abandon the distractions, false gods, and illusions of control that are so easy to put our trust in.

Interestingly, sacramental ordinances provide double assistance to help us to remember him. In the first place, we partake of his body and blood as an act of remembrance, but in the same moment we additionally demonstrate our covenantal intent to continue that remembrance with renewed dedication in life. Together these experiential and forward-looking acts of remembrance connect us to him. We can remember him, and as we do, we also become more like him.

Remembering prophetic words

The second prominent invitation to remember in the Book of Mormon is to remember prophetic words. Whether from prophets' public discourses or from inspired parental counsel, the invitation to "remember my words" is repeated again and again. Table 2 lists all occurrences of this invitation.

Table 2. Remember my words

Remembering prophetic words points us to Christ

2 Nephi 9:44, 51	Remember Jacob's words and come unto the Holy One of Israel.
Jacob 5:1	Remember Zenos's words to understand how Israel can return to him.
Alma 33:3	Remember Zenos's words to know how to worship God and grow faith in him.
Alma 36:17	Remembering Alma's words led his son to call upon Christ for mercy.
Alma 46:24	Remember Jacob's words to stand fast in the faith and cause of Christians.
Helaman 5:9–14	Nephi and Lehi remember prophets' words about Christ and teach.
3 Nephi 11:12	Nephites remember prophecies about Christ and worship him.

Remembering prophetic words leads us to live Jesus's gospel

2 Nephi 3:25	Remember the words of thy dying father.
2 Nephi 31:4	Remembering Lehi's prophecy about Jesus's baptism teaches our need to be baptized.
2 Nephi 32:2	Remember, receiving the Holy Ghost enables speaking with the tongue of angels.
Alma 7:16	Remembering Alma's promise encourages baptism.
Alma 57:21	Remembering mothers' words leads Ammonites to exact obedience.
Ether 15:1–3	Remembering Ether's words leads Coriantumr to repent.

Making prophecies that will be remembered when fulfilled

1 Nephi 7:15		If Laman and others return to Jerusalem, they will remember that Nephi said they would perish.
1 Nephi 12:9		Does Nephi remember Lehi's prophecy about apostles of the Lamb?
Helaman 4:21		The wicked remember prophecies and realize their own depravity.
Helaman 11:7		The wicked remember the famine Nephi said would come.
Helaman 16:5		When fulfilled and remembered, prophecies inspire belief.

Prophet-to-prophet instructions on keeping sacred records

Mosiah 1:3,6		Remember the importance and truth of scriptural records.
Alma 37:32		Remember to maintain sacred plates, and not to publish secret combinations.
Mormon 1:5		Remember where the records are hidden.

Most scriptures from this theme reflect one key principle: if we remember prophecies and inspired teachings, they will point us to Christ and help us live his gospel. One-third of these passages explicitly connect remembering prophetic words to Jesus, and there is a lot we can learn from the Nephites about finding these connections. For example, remembering prophecies about Christ led the Nephites to worship him at the temple in Bountiful (3 Nephi 11:12). When the Lord fulfills his promises to us, the only way we can recognize it and worship him for it is if we remember the words by which he made those promises to us. Similarly, remembering the words of Zenos helped early Nephites understand Jacob's teaching that those who reject Christ will one day build a sure foundation on him—this is the rhetorical purpose of the olive tree allegory (see Jacob 4:15–18, 5:1). This account underscores the truth that the words of prophets (even those as infamously dense as Zenos's words in Jacob 5) will point us to Christ when aptly remembered and applied.

An interesting implication of this theme is that remembering prophetic promises builds our faith in Christ as we see the promises fulfilled. For example, remembering President Russell M. Nelson's promise that by "working to remodel your home into a center of gospel learning, over time . . . your children will be excited to learn and to live the Savior's teachings"[13] has pointed our family to Christ and has grown our faith as we see it fulfilled (we taped this promise on a bathroom mirror). Knowing that we remember prophets' words to point us to Christ can also change how we hear, study, and apply them.

Jesus Christ remembers

Contrasting with the other six themes, which highlight things that we should remember as we strive to come unto Christ, this third theme is about how Jesus Christ remembers. In a sense, this theme sets a perfect example of remembering that we can apply as we seek to become like him. Table 3 lists the associated passages.

TABLE 3. JESUS REMEMBERS

JESUS REMEMBERS ALL PEOPLE

1 Nephi 15:16	He will remember Lehi's seed to graft a remnant into the house of Israel.
1 Nephi 19:16	He promises to remember and gather those on the isles of the sea.
2 Nephi 10:22	He remembers all he has scattered, so he must remember us.
2 Nephi 10:24	He also remembers the heathen because all are alike to him.
2 Nephi 29:7–8	I remember all the nations of the earth.
Jacob 6:4	He remembers Israel and stretches forth his hands to them—always.
Mosiah 27:30	Jesus's birth is a sign that he remembers every creature of his creating.

JESUS WILL REMEMBER THE CHILDREN OF THE COVENANT

1 Nephi 17:40	He remembered his covenant with the fathers, so he delivered them.
1 Nephi 19:15	He will remember the covenant with their fathers when they turn to him.

2 Nephi 29:1–2	By the restoration he remembers his covenants to the children of men and his promises to remember the children of Lehi and Nephi.
2 Nephi 29:14	I covenanted with Abraham that I would remember his seed forever.
2 Nephi 3:21	By remembering his covenant with the fathers, he brings their words to their children.
Mormon 5:20	He will remember his covenant with Abraham after Abraham's seed are smitten.

Jesus Remembers His Covenants

2 Nephi 3:5	He will visit the Nephites because they are remembered in his covenant.
3 Nephi 20:29	I will remember the covenant which I made with my people that I would gather them.
3 Nephi 29:3, 8	He remembers his covenant and will do what he has promised.
Mormon 8:21	Don't say that he has forgotten; he will remember.

The Restoration Is a Sign of Remembering

3 Nephi 16:11–12	I will remember my covenant which I made to my people and will bring the gospel to them and they will come to the knowledge of its fullness.
3 Nephi 20:11	Remember, when Isaiah's words are fulfilled, the covenant will be too.
Ether 4:15–16	Seeing prophecies fulfilled helps us remember that he has remembered his covenants with our fathers.

The Prayers of the Righteous Are Connected with His Remembering

Mormon 5:21	He will remember the prayers of the righteous in favor of the scattered.
Mormon 8:23	Saints from before will cry, and he will remember.
Mormon 9:37	Saints prayed that he would remember them and bless their brethren.

Two fundamental truths stand out from the richness of these verses. First, Jesus Christ remembers all people everywhere, and second, Jesus remembers his covenants. The teaching that Jesus Christ remembers all people features prominently in the early parts of the Book of Mormon. After fleeing Jerusalem and learning by revelation that their home had been destroyed, the people are reassured by Jacob that "the Lord remembereth all them who have been broken off [from the house of Israel], wherefore he remembereth us also" (2 Nephi 10:22). No matter who we are or how broken off we feel, Jesus Christ remembers us.

Whereas remembering his people demonstrates Jesus's love for them, remembering his covenants demonstrates his faithfulness to them. Jesus himself repeatedly promises, "I will remember the covenant which I have made with my people" (3 Nephi 20:29; see also 29:3, 8). In fact, the evidence Jesus gives that he remembers is his desire to gather us (see 1 Nephi 19:15–16). This sign began through his atoning sacrifice which he performed so that he could "draw all men unto" him (3 Nephi 27:14)—and this ultimate gathering in him is made possible through his Restoration (see 3 Nephi 16:11–12). Because of his sacrifice, because of the Restoration, and because he remembers forever and will fulfill his promises (see 2 Nephi 29:14; 3 Nephi 29:3–8), Jesus Christ will "sustain us in our hour of need—and always will."[14]

These truths build our faith in Jesus Christ as our perfect Savior. For example, when we worry that "the Lord hath forsaken me, and my Lord hath forgotten me," these passages assure us of his promise "I will not forget thee.... Behold I have graven thee upon the palms of my hands" (1 Nephi 21:14–16; compare Isaiah 49:14–16). These passages also set an inspiring standard of covenantal remembering for which we can strive as we seek to use our moral agency to obey him and to become like him.

Obedience and remembering

A fourth theme of remembering relates remembering to obedience. As scholar Louis Midgley suggested, remembering implies action in the Book of Mormon, such as remembering to keep the commandments of God always (1 Nephi 15:25) or remembering the Sabbath day to keep it Holy (Mosiah 13:16).[15] Table 4 lists the passages relating these ideas.

Table 4: Remember to obey

Remember to keep specific commandments

2 Nephi 1:10–12	Remember to follow the prophets' words.
Mosiah 1:7	Remember to search the scriptures diligently.
Mosiah 4:28	Remember, if you borrow something, give it back.
Mosiah 13:12	Remember that thou shalt not make graven images.
Mosiah 13:16	Remember the sabbath day to keep it holy.
Alma 34:29	Remember to have charity, or you will be cast out like dross.
3 Nephi 25:4	Remember the law of Moses with its statutes and judgments.

Remember to keep Christ's commandments

1 Nephi 15:25	Remember to keep God's commandments always and in all things.
2 Nephi 1:16	Remember to observe the statutes and judgments of God.
Alma 37:35	Remember and learn in youth to keep the commandments of God.
Alma 46:23	Remember to keep the commandments so that we are not scattered like Joseph's coat.
Helaman 5:6	Remember to keep the commandments of God.

Remember Jehovah's covenant ("Inasmuch as thy seed shall keep my commandments, they shall prosper in the land")

1 Nephi 4:14	Remembering his promise gives Nephi strength to obey.
Alma 9:13–14	Remember this promise and that the Lamanites have been cut off from his presence inasmuch as they have not kept his commandments.
Alma 37:13	Remember that his commandments are strict because of this promise.
Alma 50:20	Remember that as much as Lehi's seed will not keep the commandments, they shall be cut off from the presence of the Lord.

The law and church help us remember

Mosiah 6:3	Priests stir the people up in remembrance of the oath they made.
Mosiah 13:29–30	The law of Moses was strict and daily to keep the people in remembrance of God and to stop them from being slow to remember him.
Alma 4:19	Alma preached to stir the people up in remembrance of their duty.

Remembering Jesus helps us obey him

1 Nephi 17:45	Ye are swift to do iniquity but slow to remember the Lord.
Alma 58:40	Ammonites remember the Lord their God from day to day and keep his statutes and his judgments and his commandments continually.
Ether 2:14–15	Brother of Jared is chastened for not remembering to call on the Lord and is warned to remember that if his people sin and don't repent, they will be cut off.

The scriptures from this theme reinforce two main truths. First, the Lord asks us to remember to obey. Prophets, teachers, and Jesus Christ explicitly ask their audiences to remember specific commandments. For example, Benjamin asks his sons to remember to search the scriptures (Mosiah 1:7), Abinadi tells Noah's priests to remember the Ten Commandments (Mosiah 13:12, 16), and Jesus quotes Malachi's invitation to remember the full law of Moses (3 Nephi 25:4). This type of remembering is critical to our enduring to the end. How long will we press forward if we start forgetting to "feast upon the word of Christ" (see 2 Nephi 31:19–20)? Perhaps this is why President Harold B. Lee taught, "The most important of all the commandments of God is that one that you are having the most difficulty keeping today."[16] We can either choose to repent or rebel, but when we don't remember, there is no decision left to us.

The complementary half of this theme is that while the Lord does ask us to remember to obey, remembering also enables us to obey. Because Jesus doesn't demand obedience without assistance, he provides resources like a church and teachers that help us to remember to obey (see Mosiah 6:3). More importantly, he also provides covenants and an unfailingly perfect example which (if remembered) can motivate faith, sustain diligence, and change hearts as we strive to obey him. For example, Alma tries to inspire Helaman's continued faithfulness by inviting him to remember Jehovah's covenant that "inasmuch as thy seed shall keep my commandments, they shall prosper in the land" (1 Nephi 4:14; referenced in Alma 37:13; he also tried this with the people in Ammonihah to lesser effect in Alma 9:13–14). Later Helaman himself explicitly connects his warriors' strict remembrance of Jesus to their observance of his commandments and their success and deliverance (see Alma 58:40).

For busy, distractable mortals, obedience can be hard, but as we try to remember to obey, we can also remember *in order* to obey. Jesus promises to prosper us in his presence as we do, and in time both remembering and obeying become more natural. When we forget or disobey, we trust that by remembering again we will grow in obedience and in Christ.

Accountability, agency, and remembering

As we are invited to remember to keep his commandments, one resource to do so is the next theme of remembering: remembering our agency and eventual accountability before Christ. Table 5 documents these patterns.

TABLE 5. REMEMBER ACCOUNTABILITY AND AGENCY

REMEMBER THE CONSEQUENCES OF SIN

2 Nephi 9:39	Remember the awfulness of sin, and carnal mindedness is death.
Jacob 3:10	Remember that sins hurt children and may bring them to destruction.
Mosiah 20:18	Remember, the wicked priests of Noah did this evil.
Mosiah 23:9	Remember, the wicked example of Noah brought many to sin.
Mosiah 29:18	Remember, wickedness brought bondage and destruction.

Helaman 13:33	If we had remembered the Lord, we would not have lost our riches.
Ether 10:2	Shez remembers fathers' destruction and builds a righteous kingdom.

Remember judgment day, for we will remember at judgment day

1 Nephi 10:19–20	Remember that for all our doings we will be brought to judgment.
2 Nephi 9:46	At the day of judgment, we will remember our guilt in perfectness.
Alma 5:18	Imagine remembering guilt, wickedness, and defiance against God at judgment.

Remember our own sins and nothingness

Jacob 3:9	Remember your own filthiness; at least the Lamanites did not choose theirs.
Mosiah 2:40	Awake to a remembrance of the awfulness of falling into transgression.
Mosiah 16:5	Remember, persisting in rebellion gives the devil power over us.

Remember we can always choose him (allusions to 2 Nephi 2:27)

2 Nephi 10:23	Remember that we are free to choose eternal life or death.
Helaman 14:30	Remember that if we do evil, we do evil to ourselves because we are free to choose.

Coming to Christ resolves remembered sins, guilt, or grudges

Alma 36:13, 19	Alma remembered the pains of sin until he called on Jesus for mercy.
3 Nephi 12:23	If I want to come unto Christ and remember that someone has anything against me, I need to be reconciled with them first.

Consider two complementary principles. First, remembering our accountability prepares us to be accountable to Jesus at our eventual judgment. This is true for recognizing sin's consequences, remembering we will be judged, and feeling our nothingness compared to God. Second, remembering our agency to choose Christ helps him free us from sin and its consequences now. Passages teaching this echo Lehi's proclamation that we "are free to choose liberty and eternal life, through the great Mediator of all men" (2 Nephi 2:27).

By remembering that I am free to choose and am accountable for my choices, I become a more intentional agent and a more Christlike disciple. This type of remembering lets him change recollections of sorrow, guilt, and pain into experiences of hope, life, and joy. As Mediator and Judge, he clears my account, remembers no more, and make me his.

Affliction and remembering

Situated between the themes of remembering our eventual judgment and remembering the captivity of our fathers in the past, this sixth theme shows remembering is also closely connected with how we experience afflictions in the present. Even when eventual judgment and accountability seem so distant that we forget Jesus as our Judge, our afflictions are often so unforgettably present in our lives that we can still remember Jesus our Deliverer. Table 6 presents the verses in this theme.

TABLE 6. REMEMBERING AND AFFLICTION

AFFLICTIONS CAN "STIR US UP" TO REMEMBERING JESUS

1 Nephi 2:24	The Lamanites will stir the Nephites up to remember if they rebel against him.
2 Nephi 5:25	The Lamanites scourge the Nephites to stir them up in remembrance of me.
Mosiah 1:17	Lehi's family's afflictions were to stir them up in remembrance of their duty.
Alma 4:3	Great afflictions stirred the Nephites up in remembrance of their duty.
Alma 25:6	Afflictions stir the Lamanites up to remember Aaron's words and to believe in the Lord.

Helaman 11:4	Nephi prays for a famine for the people to remember the Lord, repent, and turn to him.
Helaman 11:7	The Nephites remember the Lord when they were about to perish by famine.
Helaman 11:34	Robbers stir the people up again in remembrance of the Lord their God.

IF WE REMEMBER WE WILL EXPERIENCE ADDITIONAL DELIVERANCE, BUT IF WE ARE SLOW TO REMEMBER WE WILL EXPERIENCE ADDITIONAL AFFLICTIONS

2 Nephi 5:25	Inasmuch as the Nephites will not remember Jesus and hearken unto his words, the Lamanites will scourge them unto destruction.
Mosiah 9:3	People were smitten because they were slow to remember the Lord.
Alma 38:5	Remember, as much as we shall put our trust in God, we will be delivered.
Alma 55:31	Because the Nephites were not slow to remember the Lord, they could not be ensnared.
Alma 62:49	Notwithstanding their strength and prosperity, the Nephites were not slow to remember the Lord.

THE NATURAL MAN IS SLOW TO REMEMBER JESUS

Helaman 12:3–5	The Lord's people do not remember him unless he chastens them.
Helaman 12:5	Men are so slow to remember the Lord or heed his counsels.
Helaman 13:22	Nephites remember riches but not the Lord who gave them.

These passages teach two main principles. First, although we are naturally slow to remember Jesus, afflictions can help us remember him. Second, remembering Jesus can help us find deliverance in and from affliction. This second principle is also taught in its converse: not remembering Jesus may lead to additional afflictions (to help us remember).

Despite being about affliction, this principle surprisingly offers a lot of hope. Even in our worst situations, if we remember we will be delivered (even in afflictions that did not come from our slowness to remember him). And whether we are delivered sooner or later, that deliverance comes, which can then motivate our faithfulness and our remembering.

Remembering our fathers

Although it is the least common theme of remembrance in the Book of Mormon, the invitation to remember our fathers and their captivity is a memorable one. Critically, the Book of Mormon teaches us to remember that our predecessors were delivered from their captivity by Jesus Christ. Table 7 reports the related passages.

TABLE 7. REMEMBERING OUR FATHERS

REMEMBER CAPTIVITY OF FATHERS AND DELIVERANCE BY THE LORD

Mosiah 9:17	Remembering fathers' deliverance led Zeniff's people to receive the Lord's strength.
Mosiah 27:16	An angel commands Alma to remember the captivity of his fathers and their deliverance by Christ.
Alma 5:6	Alma asks if the Nephites have retained in remembrance the captivity of your fathers and God's mercy in delivering them from captivity and hell.
Alma 29:11–12	Alma remembers and learns from the captivity of his fathers and learns about deliverance.
Alma 36:2, 29	Alma encourages Helaman to remember their fathers' captivity as he has.

REMEMBER THE MIRACLES THE LORD WORKED FOR OUR FATHERS

Alma 9:9	Remember that Lehi was led through the wilderness.
Ether 6:30; Ether 7:27; Ether 10:2	Orihah, Shule, and Shez remember the great things the Lord had done for their fathers in bringing them across the great deep into the promised land. This inspiring humility, righteous judgment, and walking in the ways of the Lord.

REMEMBER THEIR FATHERS' NAMES AND WORKS

| Jacob 1:11 | People call kings after Nephi to remember his name. |
| Helaman 5:6 | Helaman named Nephi and Lehi after their first parents to remember them, their works, and their goodness. |

The main doctrine taught through this theme is that the Lord delivers his people from spiritual and temporal captivity through miraculous means. Whether the miracles are those surrounding Alma's escape from the land of Helam, the families of Lehi and Jared being led to the promised land, or the ultimate deliverance of humankind from death and hell, Jesus is the Deliverer who saved our fathers. Remembering this is of paramount import.

Because Jesus has delivered our fathers, we have evidence to inspire us to have faith in him as well. As we act in faith, trusting in his deliverance, methods, and timing, the captivity and miraculous deliverance of our fathers serve as points of departure for our own upward cycle of faith, conversion, and discipleship. By exercising even a particle of faith in Jesus Christ (Alma 32:27), we become more like the faithful saints who came before us, more able to endure our own afflictions, and in the end more like him.

A Thought on Always Remembering Him

The Book of Mormon is brimming with the word *remember*. By exploring *remember*, this paper documented its close connection to Christ and discussed how remembering relates to our journeys of discipleship. As a reluctantly forgetful disciple, I found studying remembering enriched my observance of sacramental covenants to "always remember him." I conclude with this last insight that has enriched my relationship with my Redeemer.

When I think of "always remembering him," invitations like "let all [our] thoughts be directed unto the Lord" come to mind (see Alma 37:36). President Russell M. Nelson taught, "Our focus must be riveted on the Savior and his gospel. It is mentally rigorous to strive to look unto him in *every* thought."[17] But if this constant focus is the "perfect even as I" ideal (see 3 Nephi 12:48), the reality is that no mortal disciple always remembers him in this way.

Defining *remember* expanded my understanding of the sacramental covenant. Webster's 1828 dictionary presents two sets of meanings of the word *remember*. The first set involves bringing back to mind something that has left (in the sense of *recall* or *recollect*). The other set involves retaining something in the forefront of one's attention (in the sense of *bear in mind*).[18]

These two types of remembering are reflected in the Book of Mormon. For example, to encourage repentance King Benjamin invites his people to "awake to a remembrance" of sin and "remember" that God's promises to the righteous are true (or bring it back to mind; see Mosiah 2:40–41). After his people experience the joy of a remission of sin, he points them back to God saying, "I would that ye should . . . always retain in remembrance the greatness of God . . . and [his] long-suffering towards you" (or bear in mind; see Mosiah 4:11). Whereas King Benjamin repeatedly ties *bringing* Christ back to mind to repentance and receiving a remission of sins, he connects *bearing* Christ in mind with daily devotion, steadfast faith, and retaining a remission of sins (see Mosiah 4:9–12).

This distinction between types of remembering suggests that our covenant to always remember Christ is not limited to always bearing him in mind. Always bringing him back to mind again is a necessary and complementary facet of our covenant efforts to always remember. When we (inevitably) forget our Master, our only course of action is to repent and return to him. To repent for having forgotten, our faith and repentance must bring Jesus Christ back to our mind. In other words, to repent we must remember him again.

Personally, this insight is enriching my weekly devotion at the altar of the Lord's supper. Each Sabbath I covenant anew to "always remember him." And despite my best intentions, each week I forget him again. These insights about remembering reveal that an indispensable part of my covenant to always remember Jesus is my promise that I will always remember him again each time I forget.

This type of remembering guarantees our eventual salvation, for we can only fall by permanently forgetting. Remembering is essential in enduring to the end. Bringing him back to mind makes us better at bearing him in mind, and in the process he perfects us. Our covenant to always remember him is a promise to keep trying until one day we never forget again. Indeed, we will "remember and perish not" (Mosiah 4:30).

MICHAEL DAVID RICKS *is an assistant professor of economics at the University of Nebraska–Lincoln.*

Notes

1. Spencer W. Kimball, *Circles of Exaltation* (address to religious educators, June 28, 1968), 8.
2. The word *remember* occurs once every 1,200 words in the Book of Mormon, more than twice as frequently as in the other standard works (once every 2,800 words).
3. Louis C. Midgley, "The Ways of Remembrance," in *Rediscovering the Book of Mormon. Insights You May Have Missed Before*, ed. John L. Sorenson and Melvin J. Thorne (Salt Lake City and Provo: Deseret Book and FARMS, 1991), 168. See also Louis C. Midgley, "'O Man, Remember and Perish Not' (Mosiah 4:30)," in *Reexploring the Book of Mormon*, ed. John W. Welch (Salt Lake City and Provo: Deseret Book and FARMS, 1992), 127–29.
4. Midgley, "Ways of Remembrance," 168.
5. Steven L. Olsen, "Memory and Identity in the Book of Mormon," *Journal of the Book of Mormon and Other Restoration Scripture* 22, no. 2 (2013): 40–51.
6. These derivatives include the verb forms *remember, remembered, rememberest, remembereth, remembering,* and the noun *remembrance.*
7. The data underlying figure 1 came from a corpus of all Book of Mormon verses containing any form of the verb *remember* and for the nouns *remembering* and *remembrance.* Because the focus was on the word *remember*, I did not include related words such as *memory, remind,* or *forget.* Furthermore, the corpus only includes words used within the scriptural text, not within chapter headings or footnotes. After identifying 221 uses of *remember*, I included any noun and verb phrases directly connected with the word in my corpus. As such if a verse contained multiple *remember* words, words from that verse may appear multiple times in the corpus to appropriately weight the words that *remember* is collocated with. The result of this search was a corpus of 7601 words with 221 uses of *remember.*
8. Figure 1 is built from the text from the verses that contain the 221 uses of *remember* in the Book of Mormon as detailed in note 6. The word cloud includes the 250 most common words in the corpus. The font size of each word is proportional to the square root of the number of occurrences in the corpus. For example, the word *remember* occurs 158 times and is presented roughly twice as large as the word *words* which occurs 44 times (since $\sqrt{158}=12.6$ and $\sqrt{44}=6.3$). The figure was generated with online using public software from https://www.jasondavies.com/wordcloud/.
9. There are 115 uses of these titles out of the 7,601 words from the remember-related passages (1.5%) compared to 2,175 uses of these titles or "Savior" out of the 267,170 words in

the Book of Mormon (0.8%). Overall Book of Mormon numbers are accessed from Jeffrey McNeal, "Word Counts in LDS Scriptures," https://public.tableau.com/app/profile/jeffrey.mcneal/viz/WordCountinBibleandBookofMormon/WordCounts.

10. Themes were identified using a series of three sequential emergent coding exercises. First, I identified the main noun and verb clauses associated with the *remember* word as discussed in footnote 6 and determined a theme for each verse. For example, I assigned these themes to the first four passages: 1 Nephi 2:24, "affliction leads to remembering"; 1 Nephi 4:14, "The Lehite covenant"; 1 Nephi 7:15, "Remember inspired/prophetic words"; 1 Nephi 10:19–20, "Remember judgement/consequences for actions." This exercise resulted in 88 themes. Next, I compared these themes and identified natural groupings between them. For example, I combined the themes "Remember judgment/consequences," "remember the consequences of sin," "remember agency," and "the Spirit will not always strive" into one group I called Agency, Accountability, and Remembering. Through this process of aggregation, seven larger patterns emerged as well as an eighth "other" category. The other category mainly included narrative uses of *remember* like "do ye not remember the priests of your father, whom this people sought to destroy?" or "for he doth remember all of my commands to execute them". Finally, I aggregated the 88 themes into three to five subgroups within each group for exposition in the paper. These are the groups and subgroups reported in tables 1–7.

11. I define a passage as being connected to Christ if one of three conditions is met. First, a passage is connected to Christ if it explicitly mentions him or one of his titles (e.g., "I remembered my father speak of one Jesus Christ, a Son of God"). Second, it is connected to Christ if it contains a contextual reference to him or his roles even if not explicit (e.g., "remember also that this is the name that I said I should give unto you"). Finally, a passage may be connected Christ if it is spoken directly by him such as the discourses in 3 Nephi or words reported as a direct quotation by a prophet (e.g., "Know ye not that I, the Lord your God, have created all men, and that I remember those who are upon the isles of the sea").

12. Joseph Smith, comp., *Lectures on Faith* (Salt Lake City: Deseret Book, 1985), 3.4.

13. Russell M. Nelson, "Becoming Exemplary Latter-day Saints," *Ensign*, November 2018, 113.

14. Jeffrey R. Holland, "'An High Priest of Good Things to Come,'" *Ensign*, November 1999, 38; original emphasis removed.

15. Midgley, "The Ways of Remembrance," 168.

16. Harold B. Lee, *The Teachings of Harold B. Lee* (Salt Lake City: Deseret Book, 2000), 82.

17. Russell M. Nelson, "Drawing the Power of Jesus Christ into Our Lives," *Ensign*, May 2017, 41; emphasis in original.

18. Definitions 1 and 2 are in the first category, whereas 3–4 and 7–14 are in the second (5–6 were archaic in 1828).

5

The Brazen Serpent as a Symbol of Jesus Christ
A Dichotomy of Benevolence and Admonition

Krystal V. L. Pierce

The narrative surrounding the brazen serpent in the Old Testament is mentioned six times in the Book of Mormon, where it is always likened to Jesus Christ. Nephi, Alma the Younger, and Nephi the son of Helaman all speak of the brazen serpent as a symbol of Christ, who was also lifted up like the serpent in order to heal and save those who would look to him. However, the serpent not only represents the Savior, mercy, salvation, and life in the Book of Mormon and Bible but also the adversary, justice, punishment, and death.

Although it seems difficult to reconcile the dual nature of the serpent in the Book of Mormon and Old Testament, this was a common theme in the ancient Near East. Serpents represented deities who would spit fire as protectors and healers but also as arbiters and rebukers. These aspects of serpents were viewed as cooperative, essential, and purposeful. Through an examination of the dichotomy of the serpent as a symbol of both admonition and benevolence, we can better understand how Jesus Christ represents justice and mercy, chastisement and forgiveness, judgment and grace, temporal death (crucifixion) and resurrection, and infinite power and infinite love.

The Dual Symbolism of the Serpent in the Bible

The full narrative surrounding the brazen serpent is given in Numbers 21:4–9 of the Old Testament. The Israelites were traveling on their forty-year journey to the promised land when they reached the land of Edom, a territory ranging south of the Dead Sea to the Gulf of Aqaba. The king of Edom would not allow safe passage across his land, so the Israelites began the long circumnavigation of Edom, where they became discouraged and complained about the lack of food and water in the wilderness (see verses 4–5). The Lord then sent "fiery serpents" (*nahashim seraphim*) among the people of Israel, many of whom were bitten and died (verse 6). The Hebrew word used to describe the serpents as "fiery" (*seraphim*) comes from the verb "to burn" (*saraph*), which was likely a reference to the inflammatory pain that results from a venomous snakebite, although it could also refer to their vividly reflective scales.[1]

The Lord's dispatch of the serpents, which lead to snakebites and death, seems like a severe consequence for complaints regarding hunger and thirst; however, the murmurings in the wilderness were not merely "muttered complaints" but could be viewed as "mocking God's plan," or even "open rebellion" against God and his prophet Moses.[2] The Israelites recognized their unfaithfulness, confessed their sin in speaking against the Lord, and requested that Moses pray for the serpents to be removed (see verse 7). The Lord instructed Moses to "make thee a fiery serpent [*saraph*], and set it upon a pole: and it shall come to pass, that every one that is bitten, when he looketh upon it, shall live" (verse 8). Moses created a "serpent of brass" (*nehash nehosheth*), placed it upon a pole, and those who had been bitten were healed after looking at the brazen serpent, whose "fiery" nature was likely due to the reflective shine of its bronze material (verse 9).

The conflicting dichotomy of the serpent in this narrative has been discussed by many scholars and theologians.[3] On the one hand, fiery serpents were sent by the Lord as a consequence of the unfaithfulness of the Israelites, which led to punishment and death. On the other hand, instructions for the creation of a fiery serpent were provided by the Lord as a reward for the repentance of the Israelites, which led to blessings and life. According to Andrew Skinner, the opposing dualities in the narrative of the brazen serpent can be perplexing, as "the agent of both harm and healing, death and life, is, in this instance, the serpent."[4] Later in their journey, the Israelites were reminded of both the dangerous "fiery serpents" (*nahash saraph*) in the wilderness, as well as the benevolent guidance the Lord provided to the Israelites (Deuteronomy 8:15).[5]

Some scholars believe that the brazen serpent was eventually placed in the temple as "a valid and important representation of God's ultimate power over life and death."[6] However, by the reign of Hezekiah, the brazen serpent had been turned into an object of worship by the Israelites, who were burning incense to it, probably to seek healing (2 Kings 18:4).[7] King Hezekiah referred to the brazen serpent as "Nehushtan" (*nehosheth*, "copper, bronze"), drawing attention to the inert material of an inanimate object that should not be worshipped. Hezekiah destroyed Nehushtan, along with other idols, as part of his iconoclastic reform.[8] The ambivalent symbolism of the serpent had shifted again, in this case, from an object representing the healing power of the Lord for the faithful, to an object of unfaithful idol worship that needed to be destroyed.

The brazen serpent also appears in the New Testament, where Jesus tells Nicodemus that "as Moses lifted up the serpent [*ophis*] in the wilderness, even so must the Son of man be lifted up: that whosoever believeth in him should not perish, but have eternal life" (John 3:14–15). Here, the brazen serpent is again linked with the life-saving power of the Lord. In order for the faithful to obtain eternal life, the Savior will be "lifted up" through the atonement, crucifixion, and resurrection. In the same way that the faithful Israelites looked up to the raised brazen serpent as a symbol of healing and life, the followers of Christ will need to look up to the resurrected Savior for salvation and eternal life (also see John 8:28). He will "be lifted up from the earth" and "will draw all men" to him (John 12:32). The messianic prophecy of the raising or lifting up of the Savior is mentioned in the Old Testament, New Testament, Book of Mormon, Doctrine and Covenants, and Pearl of Great Price, which "binds all the holy prophets and scriptural records" and "seals the testimony of the Old World to that of the New World."[9]

Fluctuations between the negative and positive symbolism of the brazen serpent throughout the Bible follow that of the serpent in general. The serpent was commonly associated with the adversary throughout the Old Testament and New Testament. In the Garden of Eden, Satan was able to beguile Eve through the "heart" and "mouth" of the serpent because it was the most "subtle" beast (Genesis 3:1, 13; Moses 4:5–7, 19). The Hebrew word for "subtle" (*arum*) used here can also be translated as "crafty" and can refer to the ability of easily concealing one's true identity in order to mislead others, which is also connected to the homophonic wordplay between "snake" (*nahash*) and "beguile" (*nasha*).[10] The adversary often attempts to deceive others through usurping symbols of power and authority that are then twisted for his own use, leading some to suggest that he purposefully used the serpent in the Garden of Eden, knowing that it would later represent the Messiah in the brazen serpent narrative.[11]

Because of the serpent's role in beguiling Eve, the Lord cursed the snake to go "upon thy belly" (Genesis 3:14), a characteristic that was later referenced in the Mosaic law as "an abomination" (Leviticus 11:42). The connection between Satan and the subtle serpent continued into the New Testament, where the adversary was referred to as "that old serpent, called the Devil, and Satan, which deceiveth the whole world" (Revelation 12:9; compare 20:2). After instructing the seventy about the fall of Satan from heaven, Jesus gave them the "power to tread on serpents," a power also referenced in verse 13 of the messianic Psalm 91 (Luke 10:18–19). The defeat of snakes was likewise connected to the Lord's subduing of the watery chaos prior to creation and at the end of time (see Job 26:12–13; Isaiah 27:1; Amos 9:3). The poisonous sting of the snakebite and serpents as symbols of Israel's enemies, oppressors, or the wicked were common themes throughout the Old Testament.[12]

However, there are also several examples across the Bible of the serpent associated with a more positive symbolism. When Jacob gave a final blessing to each of his sons, he blessed Dan to "judge his people" and to "be a serpent by the way, an adder in the path, that biteth the horse heels, so that his rider shall fall backward" (Genesis 49:16–17). Even though the tribe of Dan will be small compared to its oppressors, like a serpent, it will end up being more powerful and victorious than its larger prey or enemies, seen in the deliverance of the tribe from the Philistines by the Danite judge Samson (see Judges 12–16).

The winged serpent was also depicted as part of Judean royal iconography, which is why some scholars believe it was used by Isaiah as a symbol of a future Davidic king or Messiah that would save Israel.[13] The winged *seraphim* ("fiery ones") also played an important role in Isaiah's own theophany in the temple, where they stood above the throne of the Lord (see Isaiah 6:2). After Isaiah confessed his unworthiness to be in the presence of the Lord, one of the seraphim took a coal from the altar and put it to Isaiah's mouth, saying, "Lo, this hath touched thy lips; and thine iniquity is taken away, and thy sin purged" (see verses 5–7). Here, the burning characteristics of the seraphim symbolize the purification and refinement that resulted from Isaiah's repentance. In the New Testament, Jesus encouragingly instructed his disciples to be "wise as serpents, and harmless as doves" when sending them out to preach and minister (Matthew 10:16; see also Doctrine and Covenants 111:11). The serpent is also referenced as a symbol of the peace that will mark the Millennium, when children will be able to play over the hole of the asp, even placing their hands on its den (see Isaiah 11:8).

The Dual Symbolism of the Serpent in the Book of Mormon

The dual symbolism of the brazen serpent is also found throughout the Book of Mormon, where "witnesses repeatedly reference this symbol in teaching lessons about obedience, faith in Jesus Christ, mercy, and the easiness of the path to return to God."[14] The first mention of the brazen serpent occurred in 1 Nephi 17, where Nephi was speaking to his brothers at Bountiful about building a ship to cross the ocean to the promised land (see verse 17). Nephi's brothers thought he was foolish for attempting these tasks, and Nephi compared their reaction to that of the children of Israel in the wilderness, who "hardened their hearts, even as ye have; and the Lord straitened them because of their iniquity. He sent fiery flying serpents among them." Nephi continued by stating that even though the Lord had prepared a way for those who had been bitten to be healed through the brazen serpent, "the labor which they had to perform was to look; and because of the simpleness of the way, or the easiness of it, there were many who perished" (verse 41).

Here Nephi introduced two new aspects to the brazen serpent narrative that are not extant in Numbers.[15] First, there were many who would not look at the serpent because they thought it was too simple and easy, and second, there were many who perished because they refused to look. Elder Dale G. Renlund taught that those who perished might have "lacked the faith to look, . . . did not believe that such a simple action would trigger the promised healing, or . . . willfully hardened their hearts and rejected the counsel of God's prophet."[16] Whether the problem was faith, overcomplication, or not following the prophet, "most blessings that God desires to give us require action on our part—action based on our faith in Jesus Christ. Faith in the Savior is a principle of action and power. First we act in faith; then the power comes."[17] Nephi was attempting to teach his brothers that following the commandments of the Lord takes both personal faith *and* dynamic action, whether it is believing that you could be healed and then looking at the brazen serpent or believing that you could reach the promised land and then building a ship to get there. Nephi used the more unpleasant aspects of the serpent narrative to show that faith and action must be centered in Jesus Christ and his gospel.

However, in Nephi's second reference to the brazen serpent, he linked four positive aspects of the narrative directly to his prophecy of the Messiah in 2 Nephi 25:20. Nephi first focused on the healing power of the Lord, who "gave unto Moses power that he should heal the nations after they had been bitten by the poisonous serpents." He then referenced the brazen serpent, "if they would cast their eyes unto the serpent," again remarking on the faith and action required for healing. Third, Nephi described the serpent as "raise[d] up before them," not only linking the brazen serpent with the Lamb of God that Nephi saw "lifted up upon the cross" in his vision (1 Nephi 11:33) but also with Jesus's later teachings that "the Son of man be lifted up" (John 3:14) and "I had been lifted up upon the cross" (3 Nephi 27:14).[18]

Nephi then ended with an oath and testimony that "there is none other name given under heaven save it be this Jesus Christ, of which I have spoken, whereby man can be saved" (2 Nephi 25:20). Here the brazen serpent is again linked with the life-saving power of the Lord, who was lifted up through the atonement, crucifixion, and resurrection so that all can be "lifted up at the last day" (3 Nephi 27:22).[19] Nephi tied all four of these positive aspects together just before his remarks about the brazen serpent, stating that the Messiah "shall *rise* from the dead, with *healing* in his wings; and all those who shall *believe* on his name shall be *saved* in the kingdom of God" (2 Nephi 25:13; emphasis added). For Nephi, the brazen serpent can symbolize the resurrection, healing, faith, and salvation of the Lord.

The next prophet who mentioned the brazen serpent in the Book of Mormon was Alma the Younger, who combined and wove Nephi's earlier negative and later positive statements about the narrative into one cohesive interpretation while teaching the Zoramites.[20] Like Nephi, Alma connected Jesus Christ with the brazen serpent, which was "raised up in the wilderness, that whosoever would look upon it might live"; however, Alma also explicitly identified the serpent as "a type," or symbol of the Savior (Alma 33:19). Similar to Nephi, Alma commented specifically on the lack of faith and action of those who would not look at the serpent "because of the hardness of their hearts . . . [and] they did not believe that it would heal them" (verse 20). However, Alma was able to turn this negative aspect of the brazen serpent narrative into a positive teaching tool for the Zoramites, asking, "If ye could be healed by merely casting about your eyes that ye might be healed, would ye not behold quickly?" (verse 21). Alma clearly defined that it is a personal choice to believe and actively look to the Lord or not, with the two very different results of eternal life or spiritual death.

Alma used some of the same terminology as Nephi in connecting the brazen serpent with the Savior but augmented Nephi's discussion with further clarifications. Akin to Nephi, Alma mentioned looking to the Son of God to "be healed," but also added that he will "redeem his people" (Alma 33:21–22). The life-saving power of Jesus Christ will not only heal his people, like the brazen serpent, but also redeem them from sin and death. Similar to Nephi, Alma mentioned the prophecy of the Messiah being lifted or "raised up," but chose to add the aspect "that he shall rise again from the dead," focusing on the resurrection (verses 19, 22). Alma added one new component in his connection between the serpent narrative and the Savior, "that all men shall stand before him, to be judged at the last and judgment day, according to their works" (verse

22). The brazen serpent not only represented the healing, redeeming, and resurrecting power of Jesus Christ for those who choose to look to him but also the power to judge properly and arbitrate justice at the last day, whether the outcome is positive or negative.

Alma the Younger referenced the brazen serpent narrative again when giving a final blessing to his son Helaman. In the blessing, Alma explained that the Liahona was a "type," or symbol, for "the words of Christ," which, "if we follow their course, [shall] carry us beyond this vale of sorrow into a far better land of promise" (Alma 37:45). Alma then added that the Liahona and the words of Christ were "prepared for them, that if they would look they might live" (Alma 37:46), succinctly paraphrasing the Lord's instructions about the brazen serpent, "when he looketh upon it, shall live" (Numbers 21:8) as well as Alma's own earlier statement, "whosoever would look upon it might live" (Alma 33:19).[21] In this instance, Alma made a strong connection between the words of Jesus Christ, the Liahona, and the brazen serpent.[22] According to Elder Carlos E. Asay, these things are examples of a "sextant," so that if "we focus our minds and hearts on the word of Christ, and then look to God, by doing so we will not only find the right spiritual latitude but also set our course toward eternal life."[23]

Alma also paraphrased Nephi in his admonition that the words of Christ, as symbolized by the Liahona and brazen serpent, must be actively followed, warning "do not let us be slothful because of the easiness of the way" (Alma 37:46; see 1 Nephi 17:41). Like Nephi, Alma taught that following the commandments of the Lord takes personal belief and dynamic action, or "faith and diligence" (Alma 37:41), so that the Liahona, brazen serpent, or words of Christ can truly be used as a guide to the promised land, whether a temporary location or place of "eternal bliss" (verse 44). Alma again focused on the life-giving power of the Savior, like the Liahona and the brazen serpent: "The way is prepared, and if we will look we may live forever" (verse 46). Alma purposely used the brazen serpent and Liahona as paradoxical symbols not only to warn the Zoramites and his son about the dangers of not actively looking to the Lord but also to promise the blessings and eternal life that can result from following the words of Christ.

About fifty years later, Nephi the son of Helaman combined the words of Moses, Nephi, and Alma about the brazen serpent to teach "concerning the coming of the Messiah" (Helaman 8:13). Like those earlier prophets, Nephi recognized a life-saving connection between looking to the "lifted up" serpent in the wilderness and looking to the "lifted up" Savior, who would bring "life which is eternal" (verses 14–15).[24] Helaman also mentioned the requirement that one "should look upon the Son of God with faith," referencing the personal belief needed for following the Lord also mentioned by Nephi and Alma, but added an additional requirement of "having a contrite spirit" (verse 15). Nephi realized that the brazen serpent was not only an outward symbol of the future atonement, crucifixion, and resurrection of Jesus Christ but also an inward symbol of "the requisite acceptance of his sacrifice, . . . the outward action of looking had to be accompanied by a pair or inward qualifiers," faith and a contrite spirit.[25]

Jesus used some of the same terminology as the prophets of the Book of Mormon in connecting the brazen serpent to the Lord when addressing the multitude at the temple in Bountiful.[26] He instructed the multitude, "Look unto me, and endure to the end, and ye shall live; for unto him that endureth to the end will I give eternal life" (3 Nephi 15:9). Jesus was not only teaching his followers that they must look to him for eternal life, like the Israelites looked to the brazen serpent, but also purposefully declaring how "the prophets," like Moses, Nephi, Alma, and Nephi son of Helaman, are "fulfilled in me" (verse 6). Every revelation or prophecy spoken by the true prophets of God about the Messiah was fulfilled in Jesus Christ.

Like the prophets of the Old Testament, those in the Book of Mormon also understood that the Lord, or his power, could be represented by the serpent itself. In quoting Isaiah 6 and 14:29, Nephi shared the role of the seraphim in Isaiah's theophany and may have also been commenting on the serpent as a symbol of a future Davidic king or Messiah that would save Israel (see 2 Nephi 16; 24:29).[27] Nephi likewise quoted and paraphrased Isaiah 11:8, where the serpent was a symbol of the peace of the Millennium under the rulership of the Lord (see 2 Nephi 21:8; 30:14). However, the prophets of the Book of Mormon also understood that Satan could be represented by the serpent. Both Lehi and Abinadi refer to Satan as "that old serpent" when teaching about the

Fall of Adam and Eve (2 Nephi 2:18; Mosiah 16:3). These prophets focused on the deceptive nature of Satan as the serpent, "who is the father of all lies" (2 Nephi 2:18) and "did beguile our first parents" (Mosiah 16:3).

The dual symbolism of the serpent, as shown in the brazen serpent narrative, was also demonstrated at the end of the Book of Mormon. During the reign of the wicked King Heth, prophets came among the Jaredites crying repentance and prophesying of a curse on the land (see Ether 9:27–28). After the prophets were imprisoned or killed, a famine and poisonous serpents arrived in the land and many people perished (verses 29–32). The Lord stopped the serpents from pursuing the people, but then used them to block the path southwards to new hunting grounds (verse 33). The people "humbled themselves sufficiently before the Lord," and eventually, under the reign of the righteous King Lib, "the poisonous serpents were destroyed," allowing the people to seek food southward (Ether 9:35; 10:19). Like in the brazen serpent narrative, the serpents among the Jaredites represented the negative consequences of sin, but also the positive forgiving and nurturing power of the Lord, who provided a way for them to be saved and find new nourishment.

The Dual Symbolism of the Serpent in the Ancient Near East

The dual symbolism of the serpent in the Bible and Book of Mormon fits well into an ancient Near Eastern context. In ancient Egypt, Mesopotamia, Canaan, Phoenicia, and Arabia, the serpent could represent creation and destruction, friend and enemy, divinity and mortality, blessings and punishment, or healing and harming. These roles were not viewed as contrary, antagonistic, and meaningless but actually as cooperative, beneficial, and purposeful, because they were meant to help teach humanity how to understand and interact with divinity.

The serpent played an important role in many ancient Near Eastern creation myths, sometimes as a protagonist and sometimes as an antagonist. In Egypt, several creator deities were personified as serpents or serpent headed.[28] These primeval serpentine gods and goddesses swam in the primeval flood, where they were associated with the creation of land, other deities, and eventually humankind. Narratives from Mesopotamia also related the creation of deities from a primeval serpent.[29]

However, other primordial serpent deities, such as the Babylonian Tiamat or Egyptian Apophis, were "symbolic of unformed chaos" that needed to be subdued in order for creation to occur.[30] In the Enuma Elish, a Babylonian creation myth, the goddess Tiamat created a group of serpent deities, who planned to wage war against the supreme council of the "great gods" of heaven.[31] Tiamat lost the war, was cast out of heaven, and her body was used to form the earth and the sky. The serpent deity Apophis also existed in the waters of primeval chaos before creation and was an antagonist to the sun god Re, fighting against him for all eternity. Alternatively, sometimes Re would be encircled or swallowed by Apophis, who, as the "Serpent of Rebirth" would assist in the sun-god's rebirth in the morning.[32]

In the ancient Near East, the serpent could represent renewal and immortality due to the sloughing off of old skin, which continually exposed a "new body," leading to the circular snake-biting-its-tail as an emblem for eternity.[33] While some serpent deities assisted in the resurrection of humans in the afterlife, other serpents, like the deceptive snake from the Epic of Gilgamesh, stole the ability to become immortal from humankind.[34] According to the Egyptian Book of the Dead, the creator god Atum will eventually become the "uncreator," destroy everything he made, and return to the form of a primeval serpent at the end of the world.[35] In the ancient Near East, the serpent not only represented creation, rebirth, and immortality but also destruction, death, and mortality.

The serpent was commonly portrayed or positioned as sentinels at the doorways or gateposts of Mesopotamian temples and cities as well as Egyptian tombs. These guardians were also posted at the entrance to heaven or at the gateways of the Egyptian netherworld, like the cavern deity known as the "Flame-Eyed" serpent.[36] These guardians fulfilled the dual roles of welcoming worthy claimants and repelling the dishonorable ones. The serpent in Egypt not only protected physical and metaphysical locations but also deities and humans. As mentioned above, while the sun-god Re traveled through the underworld, the serpent god Apophis, as the personification of evil, continually attempted to thwart Re's journey. Several gods and goddesses in serpentine form, such as

Mehen and Neith, protected Re through spitting venomous fire at Apophis.[37] According to the Egyptian Law of Duality, everything evil had something equal and opposite that was good, and so it took a good serpent to fight an evil serpent.[38] Sometimes these roles were not always clearly demarcated because Re could also appear in the form of a serpent or the god Seth "could be identified with the chaos serpent Apophis, or also the sun god's defender against the same monster."[39]

Serpents were also used to protect and fight for the king during war, where they were portrayed on divine battle standards that were raised up to guide the Pharaoh to victory.[40] One of these protective warrior goddesses was the cobra Wadjet, who was attached to the front of the royal crown as a uraeus that would spit fire and frighten enemies. Wadjet was also part of the formalized titulary of the king, and the uraeus eventually became a symbol of royalty, unification, and sovereignty as well as an emblem of the Pharaoh's rulership, control, and power.[41]

The divinity of the serpent has already been shown for Egypt and Mesopotamia, and there is evidence of Canaanite and Arabian serpent worship; however, sometimes the serpent was partly divine and partly mortal and was therefore viewed as a mediator between deities and humankind.[42] Some epithets of these serpents show their intermediary status, such as the underworld guardian called "Great One on His Belly," who was great in power but still must crawl on the ground in humility.[43] Uraei and serpents in the Pyramid Texts, including one called the "Ka[Spirit]-Allocator," were considered intercessors between the living and the "akhs" (transfigured spirits) and assisted with interactions between mortals and the divine.[44]

The dual intermediary roles of the serpent in the ancient Near East also included aspects of blessings and punishment. On the one hand, several serpent gods and goddesses related to the harvest cycle, such as Renenutet of Egypt or Dumuzi of Mesopotamia, could bless humankind with fertile land and vegetation in the autumn but punish the earth with barren ground and aridity during the summer.[45] These characteristics were also related to the appearance of serpent deities as judges or dispensers of justice and mercy in the ancient Near East. There were two serpent gods among the Judgment Tribunal in the Egyptian Hall of Justice, where the deceased were sent to be judged and either found justified and blessed or dishonored and punished.[46] In much the same way, the uraeus was said to perceive the soul in the Pyramid Texts.[47] The inhabitants of the Egyptian village of Deir el-Medina continually implored the cobra goddess Meretseger for forgiveness and mercy in penitential letters.[48]

As a dispenser of mercy or justice, the serpent was also commonly associated with healing and purification, so it became "the quintessential symbol of healing, health, and rejuvenation in the ancient Near East."[49] The Phoenician deity Eshmun, who was the god of medicine and healing, was always shown standing between two serpents or holding a serpent-encircled staff.[50] The burning sting of the snake was also symbolic of purification. Several Egyptian narratives recorded how serpents used flames in what seemed like a painful punishment for the wicked but then later revealed the burning to be a refining and purifying experience for the righteous.[51]

Discussion and Conclusion: The Dual Roles of Jesus Christ

The serpent clearly had a dual positive and negative symbolism in the Bible, Book of Mormon, and ancient Near East, where its many roles were not always viewed as contrary and antagonistic but as cooperative and beneficial. The brazen serpent was referenced many times in both the Bible and Book of Mormon as a symbol of the Savior, mercy, salvation, and life; however, the serpent was also connected with the adversary, justice, consequences, and death. An examination of the many roles of Jesus Christ show that the dual symbolism of the serpent was purposefully used to help us understand all aspects of his life, atonement, death, and resurrection so that we can better understand his gospel and know how to truly follow him.

Much of the brazen serpent narrative illustrated how the Lord has given us commandments, instructions, prophets, and warnings through his role as a law-giver and teacher. The children of Israel had been given commandments, and when they broke them, he taught them how to be healed. His instructions were to look to him, the brazen serpent, for repentance. The narrative was also meant to show how the Lord clarifies his teachings through his prophets, who share his original message (Moses), add that personal faith and dynamic action are required for healing (Nephi and Alma), and that a contrite spirit is needed for repentance (Nephi son of Helaman). Through his role as a teacher, the Lord also warns us of challenges we might encounter when we try to look to him. We are taught by Nephi that some might think it is too easy or simple, while Hezekiah's reform taught us that some will focus on the symbol itself (Nehushtan) and miss the intended message, both of which might constitute "looking beyond the mark" (Jacob 4:14).

The brazen serpent narrative further illustrates that even though Jesus Christ is a law-giver and teacher, he also has given us our independence and agency, allowing us to freely choose to follow him. The Lord prepared a way and gave instructions for the Israelites to be healed, but it was their choice to look. The serpent in the Garden of Eden and ancient Near Eastern mythology teach us that there must be "an opposition in all things" (2 Nephi 2:11) so that we have options to choose from. These serpents were also meant to show us that this opposition can sometimes be deceptive, beguiling, and purposely confusing. Alma sums up the dual roles of Jesus Christ as both law-giver and agency-giver in his declaration that once you have been taught what will happen when you look and know that it is your choice to look, you should look quickly!

Along with Jesus's role as a law-giver, the brazen serpent narrative shows us that Jesus Christ is a judge and arbiter of both justice and mercy. The Lord not only gave the children of Israel laws but also warned them of the consequences (fiery serpents) when those laws were broken. We are taught that according to the law of justice, sin always leads to pain (snakebites), and can lead to (spiritual) death. However, the Lord has also provided a way (a lifted-up brazen serpent) for us to overcome our pain through repentance (look and be healed), which is possible only through the atonement of Jesus Christ. In tandem with the law of justice, the law of mercy shows that obedience and repentance can lead to blessings and eternal life.

Nephi and Alma both used the narrative to show the dual nature of justice and mercy. Nephi mentioned that his brothers were being unfaithful like the Israelites, but that they also could be healed through personal faith and dynamic action. Alma taught that the Lord will judge us according to our works and that we will receive blessings for choosing righteousness. The dual roles of

Jesus Christ as judge of justice and mercy are also recognized in the narrative of the Jaredites and the poisonous serpents, which were sent by the Lord as a just consequence for sin, but then also removed by the Lord as a merciful reward for repentance. In the Old Testament and ancient Near East, several serpents were tribunal judges, while others represented wicked enemies and oppressors that were sent as consequences (justice) but also righteous benefactors who blessed the land and provided forgiveness (mercy). When examined together, serpents in the Bible, Book of Mormon, and ancient Near East help us better understand the dual roles of Jesus Christ as both a just and merciful judge.

In much the same way, these serpentine symbols teach us that the Lord is a physician who both heals us and purifies us. Many poisonous serpents were symbols of doctors, medicines, and treatments in the ancient Near East. While the Lord will always provide a way for us to be healed and give us a path to eternal life, sometimes the process can be painful. On the one hand, the burning sting of the fiery serpents in the brazen serpent narrative illustrates that the consequences of sin can hurt; on the other hand, the fiery serpent, made from molten metal and raised up on a pole, shows us that the refining process of repentance can also sometimes feel like painful burning. Isaiah described his repentance experience with the Lord as a purification through the burning coal of the seraphim. Many times, the chastisement of the Lord, or other painful events, can feel like a "furnace of affliction," but as Elder Dallin H. Oaks taught, "through the justice and mercy of a loving Father in Heaven, the refinement and sanctification possible through such experiences can help us achieve what God desires us to become."[52]

The symbolism of serpents in the Bible, Book of Mormon, and ancient Near East also help us understand the dual nature of Jesus Christ as both the Son of God and the son of Mary. On the one hand, serpents could be representations of creators, kings, and gods, but on the other hand, representations of mediators, followers, and mortals. We know Jesus Christ played a role in creation, will rule as king during the Millennium, and has the divine powers of his Father in Heaven, but we also know that he chose to come to earth in a mortal body, be our advocate, suffer the atonement, and allow himself to be taken and crucified.

Likewise, Jesus Christ fulfills the dual roles of Prince of Peace but also protector and warrior. In the Old Testament and ancient Near East, unformed chaos, symbolized as serpents, had to be subdued and organized before creation, while a war was fought in heaven between good and evil. These symbols were meant to teach us about Jesus Christ's roles in creation, premortality, and the plan of salvation. He fought for our agency then and continues to fight for our spiritual welfare now, like the serpent guardians of the ancient Near East, who protected and assisted during times of physical or spiritual warfare. Nevertheless, serpents also represent the peace and reconciliation that will commemorate the Millennium, when the adversary has been bound and Jesus reigns as the Prince of Peace.

Above all, the most important role that the brazen serpent narrative teaches us about is that of Jesus Christ as our Savior. In almost every reference to the narrative, whether Moses, Nephi, Alma, or Nephi the son of Helaman, there is an emphasis on looking to gain life. The lifting or raising up of the brazen serpent represents the lifting or raising up of the Savior for the atonement, crucifixion, and resurrection so that we too can be lifted or raised up to eternal life. Nephi testified that through all this symbolism, including believing with faith, healing with salvation, and rising with resurrection, Jesus Christ is the only way to be saved. Alma and Nephi son of Helaman added that we must have faith, action, and a contrite spirit to truly look to the Lord and follow him on the path to eternal life. Therefore, the brazen serpent not only teaches us about the many important dual roles of Jesus Christ but could also "constitute a symbol of the whole doctrine of Christ: faith; repentance; baptism by immersion for the remission of sins; receiving (and retaining) the Holy Ghost; enduring to the end in faith, hope, and charity; and salvation in the kingdom of God, or eternal life."[53]

Krystal V. L. Pierce *is an assistant professor of ancient scripture at Brigham Young University.*

Notes

1. The translators of the Septuagint (the Greek translation of the Old Testament) interpreted the "fiery serpents" as "serpents, the ones causing death." James Strong, *New Strong's Exhaustive Concordance* (Nashville: Thomas Nelson, 2003), 2289, 3789, 8313, and 8314; John D. Currid, *Ancient Egypt and the Old Testament* (Grand Rapids, MI: Baker Books, 1997), 146–47.
2. Neal A. Maxwell, "Murmur Not," *Ensign*, November 1989, 82, 84; George W. Coats, *Rebellion in the Wilderness* (Nashville: Abingdon Press, 1968), 249.
3. For a comprehensive bibliography, see James H. Charlesworth, *The Good and Evil Serpent: How a Universal Symbol Became Christianized* (Des Moines: Anchor Bible, 2010), 614–78.
4. Andrew C. Skinner, "Serpent Symbols and Salvation in the Ancient Near East and the Book of Mormon," *Journal of Book of Mormon Studies* 10, no. 2 (2001): 49.
5. The dual symbolism surrounding a staff and serpent also occurred earlier in Exodus. While in Egypt, Aaron was told by the Lord to cast down a rod and it would be turned into a serpent to "shew a miracle" to Pharaoh (Exodus 7:9; see also 4:1–5). In turn, the Egyptian magicians were able to also turn their rods into serpents; however, the serpent of Aaron swallowed the serpents of the Egyptians (verses 10–12). The serpent was used by both sides to show power, but in the end the power of the Lord was, and always will be, stronger.
6. Skinner, "Serpent Symbols," 49. See Alex Douglas, "The Garden of Eden, the Ancient Temple, and Receiving a New Name," in *Ascending the Mountain of the Lord*, ed. David Rolph Seely, Jeffrey R. Chadwick, and Matthew J. Grey (Salt Lake City: Deseret Book, 2013), 40.
7. Victor Avigdor Hurowitz, "Healing and Hissing Snakes," *Scriptura* 87 (2004): 278–87.
8. A later Jewish tradition claimed that Hezekiah did not destroy Nehushtan, but instead "hid it away" so the Israelites would not continue to "follow it in error." Jacob Neusner, trans., *The Tosefta: Translated from the Hebrew with a New Introduction* (Peabody, MA: Hendrickson, 2002), 1274.
9. RoseAnn Benson and Joseph Fielding McConkie, "A Prophet . . . like unto Thee," *Religious Educator* 12, no. 3: 109–10.
10. Strong, *Concordance*, 5377 and 6175. The word *arum* can also have positive connotations related to "prudence and wisdom." See A. Luc, "Arum," in *A Compendium of Contemporary Biblical Scholarship*, ed. T. D. Alexander and D. W. Baker (Leicester: InterVarsity Press, 2003) 539.
11. Skinner, "Serpent Symbols," 44.
12. See Deuteronomy 32:24; Job 20:16; Psalm 58:4; 140:3; Proverbs 23:32; Ecclesiastes 10:8, 11; Isaiah 30:6; 59:5; 65:25; Jeremiah 8:17; 46:22; Amos 5:19; Micah 7:17.
13. See Isaiah 14:29; 11:1; Doctrine and Covenants 113:1–2. J. J. M. Roberts, *First Isaiah*, ed. Peter Machinist (Minneapolis: Fortress Press, 2015), 179, 226. Charlesworth, *Serpent*, 248.
14. Benson and McConkie, "Prophet," 124.

15. Nephi also described the serpents as "flying," which is not mentioned in Numbers but is in accordance with the flying seraphim and serpent described in Isaiah 6:6 and Isaiah 14:29.
16. Dale G. Renlund, "Abound with Blessings," *Ensign*, May 2019, 71.
17. Renlund, "Blessings," 70.
18. See also 1 Nephi 19:10, where Nephi quoted Zenock that the Messiah would be "lifted up."
19. Although the phrase "lifted up" generally refers to the crucifixion, when it is connected with concepts surrounding salvation, eternal life, and the lifting up of his followers, the term can also encompass the atonement and resurrection.
20. For a thorough analysis of the shifting trajectory of the brazen serpent narrative in the Book of Mormon, see Neal Rappleye, "Serpents of Fire and Brass," *Interpreter* 50 (2022): 217–98.
21. A potential etymology of Liahona ("look to the Lord") might have also facilitated a connection with the brazen serpent, see Matthew L. Bowen, "Look to the Lord," in *Give Ear to My Words*, ed. Kerry Hull, Nicholas J. Frederick, and Hank R. Smith (Salt Lake City: Deseret Book, 2019), 275.
22. The Book of Mormon itself might have also been seen as another brazen serpent, see Scott Stenson, "'Wherefore, for This Cause,'" *Interpreter* 43 (2021): 291–318.
23. Carlos E. Asay, "Stay on the True Course," *Ensign*, May 1996, 61.
24. John Hilton III, *Considering the Cross* (Salt Lake City: Deseret Book, 2021), 80.
25. Jared M. Halverson, "Swine's Blood and Broken Serpents," in Seely, Chadwick, and Grey, *Ascending the Mountain of the Lord*, 187.
26. Kristian S. Heal, "Look to God and Live," *Insights* 26, no. 2 (2006): 2–3, 6.
27. Moroni also used serpents to demonstrate the protective power of the Lord when testifying that past prophets were able to use their faith "in his name" to withstand poisonous serpents, who were not able to harm them "because of the power of his word" (Mormon 8:24).
28. These deities included Atum and Tefnut of the Heliopolitan Cosmogony and Amun Kematef, Naunet, Hauhet, Kauket, and Amunet of the Hermopolitan Cosmogony. Richard H. Wilkinson, *The Complete Gods and Goddesses of Ancient Egypt* (London: Thames & Hudson, 2003), 78, 92–93, 99, 183.
29. These texts include both Akkadian and Sumerian examples. Charlesworth, *Serpent*, 232.
30. Wilkinson, *Gods and Goddesses*, 22.
31. Karel van der Toorn et al., eds., *Dictionary of Deities and Demons in the Bible* (Leiden: Brill, 1999), 205, 853.
32. Wilkinson, *Gods and Goddesses*, 221.
33. This emblem is also known as *Ouroboros*. Skinner, "Serpent Symbols," 44.
34. For example, the Egyptian goddess Kebehwet helped open the "windows of the sky" for the resurrection of the deceased. Wilkinson, *Gods and Goddesses*, 223; Van der Toorn, et al., *Deities and Demons*, 744.
35. Wilkinson, *Gods and Goddesses*, 99.

36. For example, the Mesopotamian deity Ningizzida was posted at the entrance to heaven. Van der Toorn, et al., *Deities and Demons*, 830; Wilkinson, *Gods and Goddesses*, 80–82.
37. Wilkinson, *Gods and Goddesses*, 158, 221-224.
38. For an introduction to the Law of Duality in Egypt, see Ian Shaw and Paul Nicholson, *The British Museum Dictionary of Ancient Egypt* (Cairo: American University in Cairo Press, 1997) 88.
39. Wilkinson, *Gods and Goddesses*, 198, 208.
40. Currid, *Ancient Egypt*, 90.
41. Currid, *Ancient Egypt*, 88–92.
42. Charlesworth, *Serpent*, 60–83, 116–24.
43. Wilkinson, *Gods and Goddesses*, 80.
44. Pyramid Texts 221 and 609, James P. Allen, *The Ancient Egyptian Pyramid Texts* (Atlanta: SBL Press, 2015), 42, 228.
45. Wilkinson, *Gods and Goddesses*, 225–26; Van der Toorn, et al., *Deities and Demons*, 831.
46. Wilkinson, *Gods and Goddesses*, 84.
47. Pyramid Text 273, Allen, *Pyramid Texts*, 54.
48. Wilkinson, *Gods and Goddesses*, 224.
49. Charlesworth, *Serpent*, 336.
50. Eshmun would late become the Greek Asclepius, whose serpent-wrapped rod became the predominant emblem for modern medicine and healthcare. Van der Toorn, et al., *Deities and Demons*, 307–8.
51. Currid, *Ancient Egypt*, 88; Wilkinson, *Gods and Goddesses*, 147. The goddess Qebehut ("Celestial Serpent") also purified the heart of the deceased (Pyramid Text 515, Allen, *Pyramid Texts*, 163).
52. Dallin H. Oaks, "The Challenge to Become," *Ensign*, October 2000, 33–34.
53. Bowen, "Look to the Lord," 276.

6

"That They May Bear Testimony of Him"

Jesus Christ's Communication to and about Prophets in the Book of Mormon

STEPHANIE DIBB SORENSEN

The Book of Mormon begins with the account of a prophetic vision in which Lehi sees the coming Messiah, and a thousand years later it ends with Moroni's testimony of the Christ (see 1 Nephi 1:6–15; Moroni 10:18–32). Although Jesus Christ is physically present for less than one percent of the timespan of the Book of Mormon, he is the central figure throughout the book. President Russell M. Nelson taught, "Few things build faith more than does regular immersion in the Book of Mormon. No other book testifies of Jesus Christ with such power and clarity. Its prophets, as inspired by the Lord, saw our day, and selected the doctrine and truths that would help us most."[1] How can a book written by mortals living in times and places so far removed from the geographic homeland and the mortal ministry of Jesus Christ give so much insight about the Son of God? The Book of Mormon was written by prophets, individuals called by God and tutored spiritually by the Savior himself to communicate his teachings and his guidance.

These prophets revealed his will for the people in the Book of Mormon lands and time, but also for the future audience that would receive their record after a period of Restoration. Moroni proclaimed, "Behold, I speak unto you as if ye were present, and yet ye are not. But behold, Jesus Christ hath shown you unto me, and I know your doing" (Mormon 8:35).

In the Doctrine and Covenants, Jesus testified of prophets' authority to teach his words: "What I the Lord have spoken, I have spoken, and I excuse not myself; . . . whether by mine own voice or by the voice of my servants, it is the same" (Doctrine and Covenants 1:38). This Restoration-era declaration continues a revelatory pattern found in ancient scripture. The Savior's divine communication with his prophets and servants in the Book of Mormon can educate modern Book of Mormon readers about the role and importance of living prophets.[2]

The Book of Mormon stands as a testament of Jesus Christ as the Son of God and the Savior of the world. It also stands as a testament of his revelation to prophets. A careful study of the Book of Mormon establishes the extent to which Jesus Christ values and uses prophets, identifying the ongoing pattern by which he communicates with them to direct his church and teach his gospel.[3] I will first discuss instances in which Jesus Christ personally appeared to Book of Mormon prophets, followed by additional occasions where he spoke directly to his prophets but did not appear. Finally, I examine what Jesus Christ taught *about* prophets as he revealed himself to peoples and individuals in the Book of Mormon.

In His Own Person

Although relatively uncommon in the Book of Mormon, Jesus Christ communicated at times with prophets in person. The culminating event in the chronicle of the Nephite civilization is his appearance in the Americas following his death and resurrection in Jerusalem. The glorious account found in 3 Nephi proclaims, "Behold, they saw a Man descending out of heaven; and he was clothed in a white robe; and he came down and stood in the midst of them; and the eyes of the whole multitude were turned upon him. . . . And it came to pass that he stretched forth his hand and spake unto the people, saying: Behold, I am Jesus Christ, whom the prophets testified shall come into the world" (3 Nephi 11:8–10).

The Savior referenced the prophets, discussed more fully in a later section, and identified himself as Jesus Christ, of whom they prophesied. Shortly thereafter, Jesus ministered to the people "one by one" (3 Nephi 11:15) and specifically invited the prophet Nephi to come to him (see 3 Nephi 11:18). Jesus said to Nephi, "I give unto you power that ye shall baptize this people when I am again ascended into heaven" (3 Nephi 11:21). Thus, one of Christ's very first acts after his appearance was to clearly confer his authority upon Nephi.

Nephi was not the only individual to receive this authority. Jesus "called others, and said unto them likewise; and he gave unto them power to baptize" (3 Nephi 11:22). By giving primacy and special designation to Nephi and others, Jesus Christ showed the significance of those whom he had called to lead. Over many days, he taught, blessed, and ministered to individuals and multitudes. He also specifically called and focused on twelve disciples. Commenting on this event, Moroni wrote that Christ called each disciple by name and said, "Ye shall call on the Father in my name, in mighty prayer; and after ye have done this ye shall have power that to him upon whom ye shall lay your hands, ye shall give the Holy Ghost; and in my name shall ye give it, for thus do mine apostles" (Moroni 2:2). Jesus Christ's communication with his chosen servants included instruction in doctrine and a bestowal of authority to act in his name and perform saving ordinances for his people.

For example, he asked the disciples to bring bread and wine, and then indicated, "There shall be one ordained among you, and to him will I give power that he shall break bread and bless it and give it unto the people of my church" (3 Nephi 18:5). He then taught them about the symbolism of the sacrament and the commandment to partake of it. He instructed them about its relationship to the covenant of baptism and outlined the promised blessings of protection (3 Nephi 18:6–13). Before addressing the multitude, Jesus specifically counseled his disciples to watch and pray always to avoid temptation and to pray throughout the church as he had shown them (3 Nephi 18:15–16).

He then directed the disciples in matters of administration, to authoritatively preside over participation in the ordinance of the sacrament and to exercise judgment concerning the worthiness of individuals who partake of it (3 Nephi 18:26–29). Regarding those who may be unworthy, he encouraged his disciples to not cast them out but to pray for them, warn them, and invite them to repent and to participate in the ordinances of baptism and sacrament (3 Nephi 18:30–33). The next day Jesus renewed his exhortation to pray, and he prayed with the disciples and for them (3 Nephi 19:15–21). He also miraculously provided the sacrament again, commanded the disciples to administer it to the multitude, and testified of its power to fill their souls (3 Nephi 20:1–8). The Savior's assignment to direct the work of ordinances is a prophetic pattern that has been restored in our day as well. Elder Robert E. Wells taught, "To prepare the way for the Second Coming, the Restoration took place—through Joseph Smith—of every necessary doctrine and sacred ordinance given by God to the prophets of past dispensations."[4]

Later, while the disciples journeyed and preached as Jesus had taught them, he appeared among them and addressed several topics. He told them the church should be in his name and be built upon him and his gospel. He reminded them to always follow his example in all things in the church and to help others repent and be baptized and endure to the end. He testified of his own atoning mission and their responsibility to teach and write about it and declared that they would be judges among the people (3 Nephi 27:3–27). When he asked them about the desires of their hearts, they dared not confess their hopes to either tarry with him in his work or quickly return to him in heaven. "And he said unto them: Behold, I know your thoughts" (3 Nephi 28:6), and he reported each of their desires with a promise that they would be granted. The account relates, "When Jesus had spoken these words, he touched every one of them with his finger save it were the three who were to tarry, and then he departed. And behold, the heavens were opened, and they were caught up into heaven, and saw and heard unspeakable things" (3 Nephi 28:12–13).

Jesus Christ's interactions with his chosen disciples demonstrates the principle of revelation in a council setting. After his ascension into heaven, the disciples ministered to the people and prepared them for his return the next day, teaching the words they had been specifically instructed by Jesus (3 Nephi 19:8). They gathered by the water's edge and continued to pray, and angels came and ministered to them until "Jesus came and stood in the midst and ministered unto them" (3 Nephi 19:15). Because of the great faith they exercised together, Jesus taught them miraculous things and said, "There are none [among the Jews] that have seen so great things as ye have seen; neither have they heard so great things as ye have heard" (3 Nephi 19:36). On the previously mentioned occasion where they were journeying together and united in prayer, "Jesus came and stood in the midst of them" (3 Nephi 27:2).

In both instances, as they counseled and prayed together, he answered their questions and instructed them in the ways of church governance, organization, ordinances, and his doctrine. For example, regarding the importance of consensus and unity of doctrine, he said, "I give you these commandments because of the disputations which have been among you. And blessed are ye if ye have no disputations among you" (3 Nephi 18:34). These accounts document a revelatory pattern still seen in communication to prophets and apostles today. According to Elder John H. Smith, "We not only believe that the Lord did in ancient days reveal Himself to man, but we accept the doctrine of revelation as necessary for the guidance of the Church today; that the same Lord who so signally blessed and sustained His people anciently can bestow similar blessings in our day."[5]

While the primary accounts of Jesus Christ's in-person visitations take place in 3 Nephi, there are other occasions of his appearance in the Book of Mormon. For example, Nephi recorded, "And now I, Nephi, write more of the words of Isaiah, for my soul delighteth in his words . . . , for he verily saw my Redeemer, even as I have seen him. And my brother, Jacob, also has seen him as I have seen him" (2 Nephi 11:2–3). Their combined witness serves to establish early in the Book of Mormon the reality and divinity of Jesus Christ as the promised Redeemer.

The book of Ether recounts how a group of individuals left the Tower of Babel and journeyed to the promised land. In preparation for such a journey, the brother of Jared sought guidance for completing their barges. The Lord answered his request to light the provided stones, and the brother of Jared remarkably saw the Lord's finger touch the stones. He expressed his astonishment to know the Lord had a body, and in response Jesus said, "Because of thy faith thou hast seen that I shall take upon me flesh and blood; and never has man come before me with such exceeding faith as thou hast; for were it not so ye could not have seen my finger. Sawest thou more than this?" The brother of Jared asked the Lord to reveal himself. "And when he had said these words, behold, the Lord showed himself unto him, and said: Because thou knowest these things ye are redeemed from the fall; therefore ye are brought back into my presence; therefore I show myself unto you. . . . Behold, I am Jesus Christ" (see Ether 3:9–14). In Moroni's summary, he reaffirmed the brother of Jared's experience: "Wherefore, having this perfect knowledge of God, he could not be kept from within the veil; therefore he saw Jesus; and he did minister unto him" (Ether 3:20).

In later commentary, as Moroni finished his record of the Jaredite people, he shared that he too had been visited by the Lord. "And now I, Moroni, bid farewell unto the Gentiles, yea, and also unto my brethren whom I love, until we shall meet before the judgment-seat of Christ. . . . And then shall ye know that I have seen Jesus, and that he hath talked with me face to face, and that he told me in plain humility, even as a man telleth another in mine own language, concerning these things" (Ether 12:38–39). Moroni's father, Mormon, had also been taught personally by the Lord. Mormon stated, "And I, being fifteen years of age and being somewhat of a sober mind, therefore I was visited of the Lord, and tasted and knew of the goodness of Jesus" (Mormon 1:15).

These foregoing accounts describe occasions where individuals witnessed the personal appearance of Jesus Christ. In addition, other prophets and servants in the Book of Mormon saw and were taught by the personage of Christ in visions. For example, Lehi, Nephi, and Jacob saw scenes of the future Messiah's life and ministry as shown to them in vision (see 1 Nephi 1:8; 10:17; and 2 Nephi 2:2–4). Alma the Younger alluded to having seen the Lord in the vision he experienced upon the angel's visit: "For because of the word which he has imparted unto me, behold, many . . . have seen eye to eye as I have seen" (Alma 36:26). After being taught by Ammon, King Lamoni also experienced such a vision and declared his joy, saying, "For as sure as thou livest, behold, I have seen my Redeemer" (Alma 19:13).

In both ancient and modern times, those servants with a special knowledge of the Lord are called to boldly share their witness of Jesus Christ. Book of Mormon readers can come to know of the reality and divinity of Jesus Christ through the testimony of these witnesses. Elder Adney Y. Komatsu taught,

"Throughout the thousand years of Book of Mormon history, many prophets bore solemn witness of the divinity of Jesus Christ as the Son of God. . . . These prophets spoke from pure knowledge, knowledge that came by personal visitations of the Savior to them, by the testimony of angels who spoke with them, by visions, and by the power of the Holy Ghost. They knew whereof they spoke and could not be shaken from their testimonies."[6]

By His Own Voice

All the previous examples of Jesus Christ's communication to his servants were both seen and heard, but not all revelation came visually. In fact, there are far more examples of communication that came through the voice of the Lord. Book of Mormon examples abound where prophets heard the voice of the Lord as instruction, warning, counsel, command, or reassurance. The Lord told Lehi to remove his family from Jerusalem and travel to the wilderness (1 Nephi 2:2) and then return for the brass plates (1 Nephi 3:2–3) and Ishmael's family (1 Nephi 7:1–2). The voice of the Lord commanded Nephi to keep records (1 Nephi 9:3), to build a ship (1 Nephi 17:8), to shock his brothers (1 Nephi 17:53), and to take his followers and flee from their brethren (2 Nephi 5:5). It also comforted him when his brothers threatened and hurt him (1 Nephi 2:19). Jacob taught his people in the temple and on other occasions words he had been commanded by the Lord (Jacob 1:17; 2:9). When contending with Sherem, he mentioned multiple times that he had been taught by the voice of the Lord (Jacob 7:5).

Enos wrestled in mighty prayer to receive remission of his sins, and he heard the voice of the Lord granting him forgiveness and then promising to visit his brethren the Nephites.[7] Abinadi experienced this divine confirmation as he fulfilled the commandment to speak the words of the Lord to the wicked King Noah and his priests: "Thus hath he commanded me, saying, Go forth, and say unto this people, thus saith the Lord—Wo be unto this people, for I have seen their abominations, and their wickedness" (Mosiah 11:20). Because he would not deny the words the Lord had commanded him to teach, Abinadi died as a martyr, but the priest Alma believed his words, repented, and became a servant of the Lord. Later, when Alma was discouraged by wickedness in the church, he too heard the Lord's voice: "Blessed art thou, Alma, and blessed are they who were baptized in the waters of Mormon. Thou art blessed because of thy exceeding faith in the words alone of my servant Abinadi" (Mosiah 26:15). This declaration reaffirms the Lord's consideration that the words taught by his prophets represent his own voice and will.

Shortly thereafter Alma the Younger and the sons of Mosiah experienced their miraculous change of heart because of an angelic visit and a vision of the Redeemer. When King Mosiah asked the Lord if he should send his newly converted sons to teach the Lamanites, the Lord spoke and said, "Let them go up, for many shall believe on their words" (Mosiah 28:7). On that mission Ammon heard the voice of the Lord on many occasions, directing him where to travel or avoid, and warning him that his brethren were in prison (Alma 20:2). He became a leader among the Anti-Nephi-Lehies, and the Lord's voice revealed the evil designs of the Amalekites and commanded them to relocate to a safer land (Alma 27:12).

Alma the Younger later traveled to Ammonihah, where the Lord's voice came to him, giving him the exact words to invite Amulek to join his ministry of preaching repentance. These two men then taught together for at least the next eight years. When the Lamanites came against the Nephites in war, Captain Moroni led the Nephite army but sought Alma's guidance. The voice of the Lord told Alma his desired strategy, and when the armies obeyed, "they were prepared against the time of the coming of the Lamanites" (Alma 43:26).

Despite being cast out, Samuel the Lamanite went back to teach the wicked Nephites because "the voice of the Lord came unto him, that he should return again, and prophesy unto the people whatsoever things should come into his heart" (Helaman 13:3). He stood atop a wall and cried out, calling them to repentance and testifying that his words were "the words of the Lord which he doth put into my heart" (Helaman 13:5), and he "did prophesy a great many more things" (Helaman 14:1).

A remarkable occurrence of the Lord speaking to prophets is when he announced his own birth. Nephi, the son of Helaman, was distraught because the believers were all facing execution for refusing to abandon their faith in Christ. "And it came to pass that he cried mightily unto the Lord all that day;

and behold, the voice of the Lord came unto him, saying: Lift up your head and be of good cheer; for behold, the time is at hand, and on this night shall the sign be given, and on the morrow come I into the world" (3 Nephi 1:12–13). The Son of God announced to Nephi that his long-awaited mortal ministry would begin.[8] Thirty-three years later, in the days leading up to Jesus's appearance among the Nephites, his voice from heaven chastised the unrepentant and prepared the people to meet the resurrected Lord (3 Nephi 9:1; 10:3).

The book of Ether reports many accounts of prophets hearing the voice of the Lord. Before the brother of Jared saw him in his spirit body, he first heard the voice of the Lord as he stood in a cloud and talked with him for three hours (Ether 2:4–5, 14). There are also multiple unnamed prophets throughout the book of Ether who brought messages of repentance and warning from the Lord (see Ether 7:23; 9:28; 11:1, 12, 20). The prophet Ether heard the voice of the Lord on two recorded occasions as well. First, "the word of the Lord came to Ether, that he should go and prophesy unto Coriantumr" (Ether 13:20), and after Coriantumr's final battle the Lord's voice said, "Go forth," that Ether might see what had been done (Ether 15:33).

Moroni recorded in the book of Ether that the Lord's voice told him what to write, what to include and exclude, and what to seal up for his purposes (Ether 4:5–8). He complained to the Lord that people might mock his writing, and by his account, "when I had said this, the Lord spake unto me, saying: Fools mock, but they shall mourn" (Ether 12:26), and the Savior taught him how he would use weaknesses to accomplish his work and bring men unto him. Furthermore, the Lord spoke reassuring words to dissuade Moroni from worrying about judgment from the Gentiles (Ether 12:37).

Finally, when Mormon began to witness the downfall of his people, the Lord's voice came to him, first telling him to cry repentance that they might be spared, and later to declare, "Vengeance is mine, and I will repay . . . because this people repented not" (Mormon 3:15). In all these circumstances throughout the Book of Mormon, the Lord spoke to his servants, either to comfort or strengthen them in their calling or to deliver a message that his people needed to hear.[9] Book of Mormon readers can learn through these examples that prophets become authorized intermediaries for the voice of the Lord. Elder Francisco J. Viñas taught, "The voice of the Lord may be received by listening to the

Lord's servants."[10] President Russell M. Nelson affirmed, "We hear Him as we heed the words of prophets, seers, and revelators. Ordained Apostles of Jesus Christ always testify of Him. They point the way as we make our way through the heart-wrenching maze of our mortal experiences."[11]

Jesus Christ Taught about Prophets

The many different accounts shared here demonstrate the consistent pattern of Jesus Christ's communication to his chosen servants throughout the Book of Mormon. In addition to these interactions *with* them, he also spoke on several occasions *about* his prophets, directing his people toward those whom he had called. In Nephi's vision of the tree of life, he was shown that prophets would be called to prepare the way for the Messiah (1 Nephi 11:27). The Lord's voice to Alma praised him for accepting his prophet, saying, "Thou art blessed because of thy exceeding faith in the words alone of my servant Abinadi" (Mosiah 26:15). When Samuel the Lamanite spoke the words the Lord had put into his heart, he included this rebuke:

> Wo unto this people, because of this time which has arrived, that ye do cast out the prophets, and do mock them, and cast stones at them, and do slay them, and do all manner of iniquity unto them, even as they did of old time. . . .
>
> Behold ye are worse than they; for as the Lord liveth, if a prophet come among you and declareth unto you the word of the Lord, which testifieth of your sins and iniquities, ye are angry with him, and cast him out and seek all manner of ways to destroy him; . . .
>
> Your destruction is made sure; and then shall ye weep and howl in that day, saith the Lord of Hosts. And then shall ye lament, and say:
>
> O that I had repented, and had not killed the prophets, and stoned them, and cast them out. (Helaman 13:24, 26, 32–33)

This prophecy was powerfully fulfilled a few decades later when Jesus Christ made his appearance among the Nephites.[12] In the days preceding his arrival, the lands of the Nephites were in disastrous upheaval, being buried in earthquakes or swallowed up into the sea. During this dark time, a voice from heaven mourned their wickedness, and the most often repeated accusation against them was their collective rejection of prophets.

And behold, that great city Moronihah have I covered with earth, and the inhabitants thereof, to hide their iniquities and their abominations from before my face, *that the blood of the prophets and the saints shall not come any more unto me against them*....

Yea, and the city of Onihah and the inhabitants thereof, and the city of Mocum and the inhabitants thereof, and the city of Jerusalem and the inhabitants thereof; and waters have I caused to come up in the stead thereof, to hide their wickedness and abominations from before my face, *that the blood of the prophets and the saints shall not come up any more unto me against them*. (3 Nephi 9:5, 7; emphasis added)

The Lord continued to name city after city whose destruction happened "because of their wickedness in casting out the prophets, and stoning those whom I did send to declare unto them concerning their wickedness and their abominations" (3 Nephi 9:10). These words from Jesus Christ identify the great importance of prophets to him and his great displeasure when they are rejected.

The darkness and upheaval came to an end; God the Father's voice introduced his Son; and then the resurrected Jesus Christ descended from heaven to appear among the Nephite people. "And it came to pass that he stretched forth his hand and spake unto the people, saying: Behold, I am Jesus Christ, whom the prophets testified shall come into the world" (3 Nephi 11:9–10). In the very same sentence where he named and presented himself for the first time, he identified himself as the one foretold by prophets. The Savior's first words to the Nephites vindicated the words of the prophets. He acknowledged their teachings and their prophecies as the means of letting people know who he really was.

On this momentous occasion, Jesus Christ proclaimed the invaluable role that prophets played in preparing the world for his coming. We read, "And it came to pass that the multitude went forth, and thrust their hands into his side, and did feel the prints of the nails in his hands and in his feet; and this they did do, going forth one by one until they had all gone forth, and did see with their eyes and did feel with their hands, *and did know of a surety and did bear record, that it was he, of whom it was written by the prophets, that should come*" (3 Nephi 11:15; emphasis added). Their testimony of Jesus Christ was ratified by what they had been taught by prophets.

Shortly after introducing himself, the Savior gave an extended sermon in 3 Nephi 12–16. He prefaced these words by specifically pointing to the twelve disciples he had just called and said, "Blessed are ye if ye shall give heed unto the words of these twelve whom I have chosen from among you to minister unto you, and to be your servants; and unto them I have given power that they may baptize you with water; and after that ye are baptized with water, behold, I will baptize you with fire and with the Holy Ghost" (3 Nephi 12:1).

Later, as he prayed with and for his disciples, he said, "Father, I thank thee that thou hast given the Holy Ghost unto these whom I have chosen; and it is because of their belief in me that I have chosen them out of the world. Father, I pray thee that thou wilt give the Holy Ghost unto all them that shall believe in their words" (3 Nephi 19:20). His prayer requested that those who believed his disciples' words would have the Holy Ghost. He also linked faith in his servants to faith in him. He said, "Father, I pray unto thee for them, and also for all those who shall believe on their words, that they may believe in me, that I may be in them as thou, Father, art in me, that we may be one" (3 Nephi 19:23). Then, when he commanded the disciples to write the words he had taught them and keep a record of the people, he declared, "Out of the books which have been written, and which shall be written, shall this people be judged . . . ; therefore out of the books which shall be written shall the world be judged. And know ye that ye shall be judges of this people, according to the judgment which I shall give unto you" (3 Nephi 27:25–27). The Lord used these occasions to affirm the power and authority of those whom he had called, and he promised blessings to those who would hearken to their words.

During his sojourn among the Nephites, the Savior reiterated his continued endorsement of prophets: "Think not that I am come to destroy the law or the prophets. I am not come to destroy but to fulfil" (3 Nephi 12:17). He often answered their questions and taught them by reminding them, "Search the prophets, for many there be that testify of these things" (3 Nephi 23:5).[13] When he discovered that some of Samuel the Lamanite's teachings had not yet been recorded, he commanded them to write his words (3 Nephi 23:9–13). The way that Jesus Christ spoke about his prophets testified *of them*, demonstrating the importance of their missions and their special connection to his mission. His declarations and directions among the Nephites echoed the principle, "Surely the Lord God will do nothing, but he revealeth his secret unto his servants the prophets" (Amos 3:7).

Conclusion

In the Book of Mormon, Jesus Christ revealed to his prophets that he would *continue* to call prophets to prepare the way for him. Nephi saw John the Baptist in vision, laying the foundation for the coming of the Messiah. He and his father also understood that a future prophet would be prepared to bring the gospel to their descendants. RoseAnn Benson explained, "In the patriarchal blessing that Lehi gave his son Joseph, we learn that God foreordained Joseph Smith to be a seer long before Joseph was born. . . . He promised that in the latter days, [Joseph of Egypt's posterity] would learn of covenants with God by a 'choice seer' whom the Lord would 'raise up' (see 2 Nephi 3:5–7). Joseph of Egypt knew that this latter-day seer and the seer's father would have his same name, 'Joseph' (see 2 Nephi 3:15)."[14]

Perhaps the most notable mention of future prophets was Jesus Christ's own account of Joseph Smith's coming role, given in his visit among the Nephites:

> For in that day, for my sake shall the Father work a work, which shall be a great and a marvelous work among them; and there shall be among them those who will not believe it, although a man shall declare it unto them. . . .
>
> Therefore it shall come to pass that whosoever will not believe in my words, who am Jesus Christ, which the Father shall cause him to bring forth unto the Gentiles, and shall give unto him power that he shall bring them forth unto the Gentiles, (it shall be done even as Moses said) they shall be cut off from among my people who are of the covenant. (3 Nephi 21:9, 11)

Of this account, Scott Esplin summarized, "Christ, speaking to the Nephites during his visit, further prophesied of Joseph Smith and his mission of restoration and clarification."[15] Many other gospel scholars have concluded that Joseph Smith and the coming forth of the Book of Mormon are the subject of and fulfillment of the Savior's prophecy here.[16]

Throughout the Book of Mormon, Jesus Christ highlighted the importance of prophets: those who had prophesied of his coming, those whom he called and organized during his time among the Nephites, and those who would subsequently testify of him and restore his truths. Regarding restored prophetic authority, President Spencer W. Kimball testified, "I say, in the deepest of humility, but also by the power and force of a burning testimony in my soul, that from the prophet of the Restoration to the prophet of our own year, the communication line is unbroken, the authority is continuous, a light, brilliant and penetrating, continues to shine. The sound of the voice of the Lord is a continuous melody and a thunderous appeal."[17]

The Church of Jesus Christ of Latter-day Saints is led today by prophets and apostles who are called by God to act with authority and teach in his name. They, like ancient prophets, teach that which is revealed to them by Jesus Christ, who leads his church. President Henry B. Eyring testified, "First, Jesus Christ is the head of the Church in all the earth. Second, He leads His Church today by speaking to men called as prophets, and He does it through revelation. Third, He gave revelation to His prophets long ago, still does, and will continue to do so. Fourth, He gives confirming revelation to those who serve under the leadership of His prophets. From those fundamentals, we recognize that the Lord's leadership of His Church requires great and steady faith from all who serve Him on earth."[18] Speaking of divine revelation today, President Russell M. Nelson stated emphatically, "The living Lord leads His living Church! The Lord reveals His will for the Church to His prophet."[19]

The Book of Mormon repeatedly bears witness that Jesus Christ spoke to prophets to direct his work, and the Restoration bears witness that he still does. The Nephite and Lamanite civilizations rejected the prophets and faced total destruction. Perhaps one of the most important principles the Book of Mormon teaches us about Jesus Christ is his power to save us, even by sending prophets to protect us. Just as he did in Book of Mormon times, the Lord communicates with living prophets today, and through their ministry he continues to carry out his eternal work and the salvation of mankind.

STEPHANIE DIBB SORENSEN *is an adjunct instructor in the Department of Church*

History and Doctrine at Brigham Young University.

Notes

1. Russell M. Nelson, "Embrace the Future with Faith," *Ensign*, November 2020, 75.
2. For the purposes of this paper, I will use the terms *prophets*, *apostles*, *disciples*, and *servants* to represent those in scripture who are generally understood to have appointed roles as witnesses of Christ. Speaking of the Book of Mormon, Elder Parley P. Pratt stated, "[We] profess that it is inspired, and was written by Prophets, and men that enjoyed the ministering of angels, more or less of them, and had communion with the heavens, and the spirit of prophecy." "Mormonism," in *Journal of Discourses* (London: Latter-day Saints' Book Depot, 1854–86), 1:43 (July 10, 1853). In addition to its authors, this paper also considers what Shon Hopkin identified as "those figures who could be called 'minor prophets' in the Book of Mormon, whose important teachings only span pages instead of full books but whose recorded sermons have a powerful impact on the rest of the book and on its modern-day readership." "Introduction," in *Abinadi: He Came Among Them in Disguise*, ed. Shon D. Hopkin (Provo, UT: Religious Studies Center; Salt Lake City: Deseret Book, 2018), v–xiv. I acknowledge that the modern church structure is not completely analogous to the Nephite structure of spiritual leadership or its designated titles. Regardless of these semantic distinctions, I believe that there are applicable principles that we can learn from the Savior's interactions with and words about Book of Mormon prophets.
3. Jesus Christ uses a variety of means to communicate with prophets. Elder D. Todd Christofferson taught, "In the Church today, just as anciently, establishing the doctrine of Christ or correcting doctrinal deviations is a matter of divine revelation to those the Lord endows with apostolic authority." He then outlined the established methods by which that revelation is received: "How does the Savior reveal His will and doctrine to prophets, seers, and revelators? He may act by messenger or in His own person. He may speak by His own voice or by the voice of the Holy Spirit—a communication of Spirit to spirit that may be expressed in words or in feelings that convey understanding beyond words. He may direct Himself to His servants individually or acting in council." This chapter will focus on the specific communications of Jesus Christ in the Book of Mormon, either given in person or spoken, where the speaker is identified as Jesus Christ or "the Lord." Accounts of the additional revelatory methods suggested by Elder Christofferson are also found in the Book of Mormon, but they are beyond the scope of this paper. See D. Todd Christofferson, "The Doctrine of Christ," *Ensign*, May 2012, 86.
4. Robert E. Wells, "Our Message to the World," *Ensign*, November 1995, 65.
5. John H. Smith, "Value of Liberty, etc.," in *Journal of Discourses*, 26:29 (July 27, 1885).
6. Adney Y. Komatsu, "Looking to the Savior," *Ensign*, May 1987, 78.
7. Of this account, Elder James E. Faust explained, "So how can we recognize inspiration when it comes? Enos stated, 'While I was thus struggling in the spirit, behold, the voice of the Lord came into my mind' (Enos 1:10). The voice of the spirit of revelation is not

necessarily audible, but it gives us divine confirmation through our thoughts and feelings." "Did You Get the Right Message?," *Ensign*, May 2004, 61.
8. See also 3 Nephi 7:15–17 for a summary of Nephi's communications with the Lord.
9. This chapter has attempted to list and briefly summarize all the occasions where Jesus Christ spoke directly to his servants in the Book of Mormon. Future research could analyze dialogic revelation, comparing the Savior's style of communication to prophets across different books of scripture, similar to Terryl L. Givens' work in *By the Hand of Mormon: The American Scripture that Launched a New World Religion* (Oxford: Oxford University Press, 2003). See also Terryl L. Givens, "The Book of Mormon and Dialogic Revelation," *Journal of Book of Mormon Studies* 10: No. 2 (2001): 16–27, 69–70.
10. Francisco J. Viñas, "Listening to the Voice of the Lord," *Ensign*, November 1996, 78.
11. Russell M. Nelson, "Hear Him," *Ensign*, May 2020, 88.
12. Like Samuel the Lamanite, Nephi had also prophesied of the destruction that would come to those who rejected the prophets. Fulfillment of that prophecy can be found in 3 Nephi 9, in the details of the calamitous events preceding the Savior's appearance to the Nephites. See Nephi's prophecy and doctrinal discourse on following prophets in 2 Nephi 26:1–10.
13. In this case, "prophets" refers to their recorded words in scripture.
14. RoseAnn Benson, "Joseph Smith and the Messiah: Prophetically Linked," *Religious Educator* 3, no. 3 (2002): 65–81.
15. Scott C. Esplin, "'Millions Shall Know Brother Joseph Again': Joseph Smith's Place among the Prophets," in *Joseph Smith and the Doctrinal Restoration* (Provo, UT: Brigham Young University, Religious Studies Center, 2005), 172–86.
16. See also RoseAnn Benson and Shon D. Hopkin, "Finding Doctrine and Meaning in Book of Mormon Isaiah," *Religious Educator* 15, no. 1 (2014): 95–122; Robert L. Millet, "Joseph Smith and the Rise of a World Religion," in *Global Mormonism in the 21st Century*, ed. Reid L. Neilson (Provo, UT: Religious Studies Center, Brigham Young University, 2008), 3–29; and RoseAnn Benson and Joseph Fielding McConkie, "A Prophet . . . like unto Thee," *Religious Educator* 12, no. 3 (2011): 109–27.
17. Spencer W. Kimball, "Revelation: The Word of the Lord to His Prophets," *Ensign*, May 1977, 78; see also *Teachings of Presidents of the Church: Spencer W. Kimball* (Salt Lake City: The Church of Jesus Christ of Latter-day Saints, 2006), 241.
18. Henry B. Eyring, "The Lord Leads His Church," *Ensign*, November 2017, 81.
19. Russell M. Nelson, "Sustaining the Prophets," *Ensign*, November 2014, 74.

7

According to Their Faith
Alma and Amulek Typify Jesus in Overcoming Evil

Stephan D. Taeger

On Sunday morning, November 17, 1957, Martin Luther King Jr. was told by a doctor that he should not preach. Regardless, Dr. King stood at a pulpit in Montgomery, Alabama, to deliver a sermon called "Loving Your Enemies."[1] The doctor allowed him to preach only if Dr. King would "immediately go back home and get in the bed."[2] King based his sermon on Matthew 5:43–45, where Jesus taught his disciples, "Love your enemies, bless them that curse you, do good to them that hate you, and pray for them which despitefully use you, and persecute you" (Matthew 5:44). In explaining why one should love their enemies, Dr. King said, "Hate for hate only intensifies the existence of hate and evil in the universe. If I hit you and you hit me and I hit you back and you hit me back and go on, you see, that goes on ad infinitum. It just never ends. . . . Somebody must have religion enough and morality enough to cut it off and inject within the very structure of the universe that strong and powerful element of love."[3] Dr. King's message teaches that we cannot use hatred to end wickedness in our families and communities—that would simply add more suffering to the world. The *way* that we seek to eliminate evil matters immensely. Ultimately, the only way to defeat wickedness is through Christlike love.

In a world that is increasingly more divisive, contentious, and fractured, Latter-day Saints need to identify principles that allow us to overcome evil in the Savior's way. Elder Robert D. Hales taught, "When we do not retaliate—when we turn the other cheek and resist feelings of anger—we too stand with the Savior. We show forth His love, which is the only power that can subdue the adversary and answer our accusers without accusing them in return. That is not weakness. That is Christian courage."[4] The Book of Mormon contains numerous examples of prophets and disciples confronting wickedness in Christlike ways.

In this essay I will show that Alma and Amulek act as types of Christ in the way they triumph over evil while imprisoned at Ammonihah. To do so, I will demonstrate that Alma and Amulek typify the Savior in overcoming evil in three ways. First, Alma and Amulek respond peacefully to the attacks inflicted by the people of Ammonihah. Second, Alma and Amulek indirectly expose the moral corruption of the Ammonihah leadership. Finally, Alma and Amulek ultimately defeat evil at Ammonihah by allowing wickedness to collapse on itself.

Establishing Types

In seeking to establish intentional types of Christ in a text, we have to be careful not to succumb to "parallelomania" (suggesting unfounded or excessive parallels). Obviously, there are differing opinions on how a text may or may not relate to the Savior.[5] In addition, we have all been subject to teachers or writers who force us to squint to see how a text, event, or scriptural character points to Jesus Christ. However, seeing correspondences between scripture and Jesus is at the very heart of what it means to read scripture as a believer. For example, as New Testament scholar Richard Hays points out, "All four of the four canonical Evangelists, in interestingly distinct ways, embody and enact [a] figural christological reading."[6] In a similar manner, in this essay I will seek to show how the language used in Alma 14 suggests parallels between the events surrounding the Alma and Amulek imprisonment at Ammonihah and the life and mission of Jesus.[7] In so doing, I will not seek to definitively demonstrate that Mormon or Alma are responsible for the language that depicts Alma and Amulek as types. It's impossible to know how much Mormon or Alma knew about the Savior's ministry to highlight parallels between the Ammonihah prison narrative and Jesus. In addition, I am not claiming to prove if all the following similarities I identify between the Savior and Alma and Amulek are intentional. Considering the number and specificity of some of the parallels, it seems at least plausible that some of the following types may be intentional. Regardless, the Book of Mormon is an ancient prophetic Christian text that teaches, "All things which have been given of God from the beginning of the world, unto man, are the typifying of him" (2 Nephi 11:4). Ultimately, whether intentional or not, the way that Alma and Amulek overcome evil in Ammonihah can certainly embody the principles and manner in which Jesus defeated evil through his suffering, death, and resurrection.

Although the debate has a long and nuanced history around the definition of typology and allegory,[8] in this essay I will use the following definition of a type: "A person, thing, or event that prophetically foreshadows another person, thing, or event of greater magnitude."[9] In this sense we are simply looking for ways that the story of Alma and Amulek in Ammonihah might point to and teach us something about the mission of Jesus Christ. For modern readers, it may be surprising to think that certain highlighted typological details may have been included intentionally. However, the ancients reported stories in extremely thoughtful and deliberate ways to add layers of meaning to their narratives. The Book of Mormon is no exception.[10]

Responding Peacefully to Persecution

During his mortal ministry, Jesus never hurt any other person. Even when false accusations, hatred, and physical suffering were inflicted upon him, the Savior responded with peace. As C. Terry Warner said, "He absorbed the terrible poison of vengeance into Himself and metabolized it by His love."[11]

Before seeing how Alma and Amulek respond in like manner, it's important to note that Alma and Amulek are persecuted and mocked in similar ways to the Savior during his final sufferings. For example, Mormon reports that the leadership at Ammonihah "did withhold food from [Alma and Amulek] that they might hunger, and water that they might thirst" (Alma 14:22). John indicates that one of the statements Jesus said from the cross was "I thirst" (John 19:28). Instead of satisfying that thirst, Jesus was offered "vinegar . . . mingled with gall" (Matthew 27:34). When the judge in Ammonihah confronted Alma and Amulek, he said, "Know ye not that I have power to deliver you up unto the flames?" (Alma 14:19). With similar language Pilate asked Jesus, "Knowest thou not that I have power to crucify thee, and have power to release thee?" (John 19:10).

Mormon also explains that the Ammonihah leadership "did take from [Alma and Amulek] their clothes that they were naked" (Alma 14:22). After Jesus was crucified, the Roman soldiers "parted his garments" (Matthew 27:35). A modern translation reads, "They divided his clothes among themselves by casting lots" (Matthew 27:35 New Revised International Version). Latter-day Saint scholar John Hilton III explained, "While complete nudity was not part of all crucifixions, the general lack of clothing was a physically and emotionally painful aspect of this method of execution."[12]

In addition, Alma and Amulek "were bound with strong cords, and confined in prison" (Alma 14:22). After Jesus suffered in Gethsemane, "a great multitude with swords and staves . . . laid their hands on [Jesus], and took him" (Mark 14:43, 46). Mormon reports that the leadership spat upon Alma and Amulek while they were in prison (Alma 14:21). Likewise, when Jesus was brought before "the chief priests and all the council" (Mark 14:55) "some began to spit on him" (Mark 14:65). Finally, Alma and Amulek were mocked "for many days" (Alma 14:22) while in prison. Jesus was mocked by "the men that held" him (Luke 22:63), by "Herod with his men of war," who "arrayed him in a gorgeous robe" (Luke 23:11), and by the soldiers at the cross (Luke 23:36–37). In light of all these similarities, it seems possible that Alma and Amulek are intentionally depicted as types of Christ in the way they experience suffering and persecution.

Responding with silence

However, Alma and Amulek typify the Savior not only in the way they suffered but also in the way that they peacefully respond to the persecution heaped upon them by the Ammonihah leadership. After witnessing the horrific murder of many women and children by fire, Alma and Amulek were asked by the Ammonihah chief judge if they were going to continue to preach the doctrine of hell (Alma 14:14). The judge smote Alma and Amulek on "their cheeks and asked: What say ye for yourselves?" (Alma 14:15). In response, Alma and Amulek "answered him nothing" (Alma 14:17). Following three days of imprisonment, Alma and Amulek were questioned again by "many lawyers, and judges, and priests, and teachers, who were of the profession of Nehor," and again "they answered them nothing" (Alma 14:18). This led the judge to arise and say, "Why do ye not answer the words of this people? . . . And he commanded them to speak; but [Alma and Amulek] answered nothing" (Alma 14:19). This may be a surprising response to evil, but as Elder Neil L. Andersen has taught, "There are times when being a peacemaker means that we resist the impulse to respond and instead, with dignity, remain quiet."[13]

Similarity, when Jesus was accused of claiming that he was "able to destroy the temple of God, and to build it in three days" (Matthew 26:61), the high priest asked, "Answerest thou nothing? what is it which these witness against thee?" (Matthew 26:62). In response, Matthew simply says that "Jesus held his peace" (Matthew 26:63). Later, when Jesus was accused in front of Pilate by "the chief priests and elders, he [again] answered nothing" (Matthew 27:12). In the Book of Mormon and New Testament accounts, the authors highlight that both Alma and Amulek and the Savior respond to multiple accusations by remaining silent.

The suffering servant and Alma and Amulek

Many scholars today recognize that the New Testament authors may have intentionally highlighted this detail about Jesus remaining silent to point to certain passages in Isaiah commonly referred to as "the servant songs."[14] At the end of the nineteenth century, a German theologian named Bernhard Duhm identified four passages (or songs) in Isaiah that speak of a servant (see Isaiah 42:1–4; 49:1–6; 50:4–7; 52:13–53:12) who suffers vicariously on behalf of Israel. In the last of these passages, the suffering servant (who is identified as Jesus by both traditional Christians and Latter-day Saint interpreters) is depicted as both "oppressed" and "afflicted" (Isaiah 53:7). However, in response to this persecution, Isaiah writes that the suffering servant "opened not his mouth: he is brought as a lamb to the slaughter, and as a sheep before her shearers is dumb,[15] so he openeth not his mouth" (Isaiah 53:7). Earlier in this same suffering servant passage, the servant is depicted as standing before "kings" (Isaiah 52:15). Consequently, early Christians would have been reminded of the suffering servant when Jesus repeatedly answered nothing during his persecution and when he was brought before Pilate (Matthew 27:11–14).

It seems that Alma and Amulek typify Jesus as suffering servants. One can identify at least five reasons to support this claim. First, like Jesus, Alma and Amulek do not respond to accusations. Of all the aspects of the imprisonment story Mormon could have emphasized, it's surprising that Mormon highlights this detail multiple times. Second, as mentioned above, Alma and Amulek experience persecution in similar ways to the suffering servant. Both the suffering servant and Alma and Amulek are struck (Isaiah 50:6; Alma 14:14), spit upon (Isaiah 50:6; Alma 14:21), and shamed (Isaiah 50:6; Alma 14:22). In addition, Mormon uses the word "suffer" when he points out that Alma and Amulek "*suffered* for many days" (Alma 14:23; emphasis added) and when Alma cries out, "How long shall we *suffer* these great afflictions, O Lord?" (Alma 14:26; emphasis added). Third, like the suffering servant who stands before kings (Isaiah 52:15), Alma and Amulek are depicted as standing before those who hold power (Alma 14:15). Fourth, both the suffering servant and Alma and Amulek are both eventually vindicated (Isaiah 50:8; Alma 14:28). Fifth, since Alma and Mormon had access to Abinadi's teachings, we know that there is a possibility they would have been aware of the similarities between the Ammonihah prison narrative, Isaiah's servant songs, and the life of Jesus. Additionally, the servant songs play an important role in Book of Mormon history. For example, Nephi (1 Nephi 21), Jacob (2 Nephi 7), Abinadi (Mosiah 14), and Jesus (3 Nephi 20) all quote from the servant songs.

Responding with prayer

Besides remaining silent in the face of persecution, the only other behavior that Alma and Amulek are described doing in the Ammonihah prison is offering prayer. After being imprisoned for many days, Alma said: "O Lord, give us strength according to our faith which is in Christ, even unto deliverance" (Alma 14:26). Ultimately, Alma and Amulek do not rely on their own potential strength or show of force to escape prison, but instead they rely on the power of God to deliver them. In other words, they respond to persecution and accusation with the peaceful practice of prayer. Interestingly, when Alma the Elder's people were threatened with an attack from the Lamanites in the land of Helam, Alma taught his people "that they should remember the Lord their God and he would deliver them" (Mosiah 23:27). In response, the people "began to cry unto the Lord that he would soften the hearts of the Lamanites" (Mosiah 23:28). Rather than respond to an attack from the Lamanites with force (as did King Limhi's people), Alma instructed his people to pray. Eventually, Alma's people were delivered through nonviolent means when "the Lord caused a deep sleep to come upon the Lamanites" (Mosiah 24:19), allowing Alma's people to escape. Perhaps Alma the Younger learned from his father that prayer can be an effective response to violence.

Like Alma the Elder and Alma and Amulek, Jesus demonstrated prayerful trust in God during his hours of greatest distress. In Gethsemane, Jesus offered this prayer: "Take away this cup from me: nevertheless not what I will, but what thou wilt" (Mark 14:36). On the cross, Jesus was mocked for his reliance on God: "He trusted in God; let him deliver him now, if he will have him" (Matthew 27:43). Finally, according to Luke, the last thing that Jesus said on the cross was "Father, into thy hands I commend my spirit" (Luke 23:46). In moments of profound distress and persecution, both Alma and Amulek and the Son of God respond with trusting prayer instead of returning hatred for hatred.

The fruits of peace

There are at least two ways that Alma and Amulek's peaceful response[16] to persecution ultimately helped to overcome evil in Ammonihah in a manner that typified Jesus. First, if Alma and Amulek had responded by an inappropriate show of force, there was a high likelihood they would have been killed. In the same chapter (Alma 14) we see that those who held power in Ammonihah could be brutally violent to those they opposed. Although their lives were not guaranteed (many presumably nonviolent individuals were killed in Alma 14), Alma and Amulek left open the possibility of deliverance by responding nonviolently. Jesus himself warned of escalating violence when he was arrested the night before his crucifixion. After Peter cut off the ear of Malchus, Jesus said, "Put up again thy sword into his place: for all they that take the sword shall perish with the sword" (Matthew 26:52). Second, by offering prayer instead of using force, Alma and Amulek permitted God to provide a miraculous liberation. Instead of taking justice into their own hands, they allowed God to act on their behalf to accomplish his righteous purposes. Likewise, when Jesus submitted to suffering and death, he was providing means for the defeat of sin and triumphant resurrection. In these ways, we can see how peaceful response to persecution is ultimately an act of trust in God. By responding with nonviolence, Alma and Amulek and Jesus were showing faith that their Father in Heaven would provide a way for redemption.

Indirectly Exposing Lack of Moral Authority

Another way that Alma and Amulek overcome evil in Ammonihah is to indirectly expose the Ammonihah leadership's lack of moral authority and character. There seems to be at least two ways that the narrative highlights this in a manner that can typify Jesus. First, just as those who put Jesus to death were shown to be corrupt by convicting an innocent person, so the Ammonihah leadership is seen as evil by condemning the guiltless Alma and Amulek. Second, during both the crucifixion and Ammonihah prison narrative, the accused are mockingly invited to demonstrate the power of God to deliver themselves. In both cases, the power of God is manifested so the innocent parties are rescued—thus showing the corruption of the persecutors.

The innocent wrongly accused

Alma and Amulek are clearly innocent of any crime (legal or theological) that would justify casting them into prison. Obviously, the fact that Alma and Amulek were inspired by God (Alma 8:32), preached to an apostate group (Alma 8:9), did not respond with violence (Alma 14:15–29), and were ultimately vindicated (Alma 14:28–29) demonstrates that they were undeserving of the punishment they received. Likewise, in Luke's Gospel the innocence of Jesus is repeatedly emphasized. Pilate stated three times that he could find no fault in Jesus (Luke 23:4, 14, 22), one of the malefactors crucified with Jesus said, "This man hath done nothing amiss" (Luke 23:41), and the centurion at the cross said, "Certainly this was a righteous man" (Luke 23:47), which a modern translation renders, "Certainly this man was innocent" (Luke 23:47 NSRV). In speaking of this final comment, N. T. Wright said, "Just in case anyone in Luke's audience, perhaps an educated Roman, might comment that if Roman justice executed Jesus then there must have been some reason, Luke presents his Roman witness to make it clear . . . that Jesus was not guilty, that he had done nothing worthy of death."[17]

Whenever one reads a narrative where the innocent are wrongly convicted, we consequently see the accusers as corrupt. The false charges against Alma and Amulek illustrate that the people of Ammonihah were wicked. Likewise, as one scholar pointed out regarding Jesus's trial, "Given the self-interest of the alliance of Rome and the leaders, and the bias of 'justice' toward the elite and against low-status provincials, Jesus cannot receive a fair trial. *The chapter exposes the self-serving agenda of Roman 'justice.'*"[18] When Alma and Amulek and Jesus are falsely accused, we can't help but see the corrupt nature of those who hold power in Ammonihah and Judea.

If

A second way that the Alma and Amulek narrative seems to typify Jesus in indirectly exposing evil is in the use of the word *if*. While in prison, Alma and Amulek were asked, "*If* ye have such great power why do ye not deliver yourselves?" (Alma 14:20; emphasis added). Later, the chief judge asked Alma and Amulek, "*If* ye have the power of God deliver yourselves from these bands, and then we will believe that the Lord will destroy this people according to your words" (Alma 14:24; emphasis added). In like manner, Satan asked Jesus in the Judean wilderness, "*If* thou be the Son of God, command that these stones be made bread" (Matthew 4:3; emphasis added) and "*If* thou be the Son of God, cast thyself down" (Matthew 4:6; emphasis added). While Jesus was hanging from the cross some of the people passing by said, "*If* thou be the Son of God, come down from the cross" (Matthew 27:40; emphasis added). The chief priests, scribes, and elders also said, "*If* he be the King of Israel, let him now come down from the cross, and we will believe him" (Matthew 27:42; emphasis added). The use of the word *if* in both the temptation and crucifixion narrative is something that appears to be deliberately highlighted by Matthew.[19] The leadership in both narratives claim that they would come to belief if Alma and Amulek or Jesus demonstrated their power by delivering themselves. The repetitive and central use of the word *if* might indicate that there is a deliberate connection between the Alma and Amulek prison experience and the story of Jesus.

These direct challenges to Alma and Amulek and Jesus which employ the word *if* all set up to expose the corruption of the elite in both narratives. When those who hold power in Ammonihah say, "Why do ye not deliver yourselves?" (Alma 14:20), they are eventually shown to be in the wrong when, in fact, Alma and Amulek are delivered (Alma 14:28). In addition, the chief judge exposes his own evil when he says if Alma and Amulek demonstrate the power of God by delivering themselves, "then [the elite in Ammonihah] will believe that the Lord will destroy this people according to your words" (Alma 14:24). Two chapters later the Lamanites "began to slay the people and destroy the city" (Alma 16:2).

Mormon also could be emphasizing the inability of the elite in Ammonihah to discern righteousness when he reports the chief judge as saying, "*If* ye have the power of God deliver yourselves from these bands" (Alma 14:24; emphasis added). Mormon then adds this intriguing detail: "And it came to pass that they all went forth and smote them, saying the same words, even until the last; and when the last had spoken unto them the power of God was upon Alma and Amulek, and they rose and stood upon their feet" (Alma 14:25). One rightly asks, why did Mormon point out that *every one* of the elite in the prison mocked

Alma and Amulek? Brant Gardner suggests "that the physical abuse appears to be ritualized at least to the point that each person not only participates, but repeats the same words."[20] Whether this is true or not, Mormon later *twice* identifies that those who persecuted Alma and Amulek were the very ones who were destroyed during the collapse of the prison (Alma 14:27–28). Perhaps the reason Mormon highlighted that the Ammonihah elite "all went forth and smote" Alma and Amulek was to show that everyone in the prison was deserving of the justice they received. In this sense, the fact that *all* the leadership in prison wrongly mocked Alma and Amulek illustrates they were deeply morally flawed.

Exposing the powers

The elite in Jerusalem who mocked Jesus during the crucifixion (Matthew 27:40) were also eventually shown to be exposed in their corruption and misjudgment when God raised Jesus from the dead. Like the Alma and Amulek story, this indirect exposing of evil had sweeping consequences. The doctrine that Jesus triumphed over and exposed evil during his atonement is something that is repeatedly taught in scripture but is not often emphasized in common discourse in the church. For example, Paul taught the Colossians saints that when the Savior completed his work on the cross, he "spoiled principalities and powers, he made a shew of them openly, triumphing over them" (Colossians 2:15). Two modern commentators describe this verse as saying, "The spirit powers with their hold over human lives have been disarmed, stripped of their authority, and paraded publicly as defeated enemies."[21]

The Savior himself taught a related principle in John 16. The night before his crucifixion, Jesus, speaking of the Comforter, said, "And when he is come, he will reprove the world of sin, and of righteousness, and of judgment: of sin, because they believe not on me; of righteousness, because I go to my Father, and ye see me no more; of judgment, because the prince of this world is judged" (John 16:8–11). The "reprove" in these verses can also be translated as "prove" (NRSV). Jesus was teaching that the world is wrong in three crucial areas. First, the Comforter proves the world is wrong about the nature of sin because it has rejected Christ. In other words, how could the world claim to know what evil is if they reject the most holy of all? Second, when Jesus said the Comforter proves the world is wrong about "righteousness, because I go to my Father, and ye see me no more" (John 16:10) he means the world is also mistaken about their conception of righteousness because it did not accept him. Because he has gone to the Father, we know Jesus is vindicated[22] and is thus shown to be righteous. Third, the world is also wrong about judgment as manifested by its incorrect judgment of Jesus. The prince of this world (Satan) "is judged (see also 12:30; 14:30) because evil is shown to be powerless before God."[23] All this is to demonstrate that Jesus was vindicated through his death and resurrection and that Satan (or the world) is exposed to be in the wrong.

Interestingly, in the Ammonihah prison narrative, the chief judge struck Alma and Amulek and then asked, "Will ye stand again and judge this people, and condemn our law?" (Alma 14:20). At this point in the narrative, Alma and Amulek had prophesied that Ammonihah would be destroyed if they did not repent (Alma 8:10; 9:12). Alma had also testified that those who die in their sins will experience torments "as a lake of fire and brimstone, whose flame ascendeth up forever and ever" (Alma 12:17). At stake in this story was who was right about God and judgment (Alma 14:5). When the chief judge falsely accused Alma and Amulek of judging the people and condemning their law, he set himself up for the possibility of being proved wrong. Like the suffering servant and Jesus, Alma and Amulek were vindicated when they responded peacefully and let God indirectly testify (Alma 14:26–28) through their deliverance that they were righteous. Ammonihah, on the other hand, was exposed in its wickedness.

Allowing Evil to Destroy Itself

Not only did the nonviolent response of Alma and Amulek indirectly help convict Ammonihah, but it also provided a space for the corrupt leadership of Ammonihah to cause their own destruction. This principle seems to be a key point of the Ammonihah narrative. While witnessing the appalling burning of women and children at the hands of the people of Ammonihah, Amulek suggested to Alma that they should "stretch forth [their] hands, and exercise the power of God which is in [them], and save them from the flames"

(Alma 14:10). In response, Alma explained that the people of Ammonihah "may do this thing unto them, according to the hardness of [the people of Ammonihah's] hearts, that the judgments which [God] shall exercise upon them in his wrath may be just; and the blood of the innocent shall stand as a witness against them" (Alma 14:11). In other words, by not using the power of God to force the agency of the people of Ammonihah, Alma and Amulek were allowing for the judgments of God to "exercise upon them . . . at the last day" (Alma 14:11). In this moment, Alma and Amulek were allowing evil to lead eventually to its own destruction.

Destroyed by their own prison

We also see this principle play out quite dramatically within the prison narrative. After Alma and Amulek cried out with faith in Christ for deliverance and "broke the cords with which they were bound," the people "began to flee, for the fear of destruction had come upon them" (Alma 14:26). Then "the earth shook mightily, and the walls of the prison were rent in twain, so that they fell to the earth; and the chief judge, and the lawyers, and priests, and teachers, who smote upon Alma and Amulek, were slain by the fall thereof" (Alma 14:27). Quite strikingly, the prison that was used to unjustly hold Alma and Amulek ended up being the very means that destroyed the chief judge, lawyers, and priests of Ammonihah. Mormon could have stated more generally, as he does later, that "every soul within the walls thereof, save it were Alma and Amulek" (Alma 14:28) was killed, but instead he takes time to emphasize that the Ammonihah elite were the ones who slain by the fall of the prison walls.

The death and resurrection of Jesus Christ uses similar means (at least in part) to overcome evil. Satan inspired wicked people (John 13:27; Acts 2:23) to crucify Jesus, not knowing that this would be the way that God would overcome sin and death. In Corinthians, Paul speaks of the "hidden wisdom, which God ordained before the world unto our glory: which none of the princes of this world knew: for had they known it, they would not have crucified the Lord of glory" (1 Corinthians 2:7–8). Additionally, the author of Hebrews states, "Forasmuch then as the children are partakers of flesh and blood, he also himself likewise took part of the same; that through death he might destroy him that had the power of death, that is, the devil" (Hebrews 2:14). As one modern theologian explained, "By withdrawing his protection and delivering over his Son to these wicked powers, allowing them to carry out the violence that was in their hearts, the Father caused their evil intentions to recoil back on their own heads (cf. Ps 7:16), thereby using evil to punish evil."[24]

Pointing to the resurrection

To see another potential link between this principle and the Ammonihah prison narrative, it is important to first note how the resurrection plays a central role in defeating evil. Obviously, it would not have been enough simply for Jesus to suffer for sin and die; God raising him from the dead was integral in overcoming sin and death. As Jacob taught in 2 Nephi 9:8, "For behold, if the flesh should rise no more our spirits must become subject to that angel who fell from before the presence of the Eternal God, and became the devil, to rise no more." Without the Savior's resurrection, humankind would never have been set free from the captivity of the devil.

In what might be an allusion to the resurrection, Mormon highlighted that Alma and Amulek were in prison "three days" when "lawyers, and judges, and priests, and teachers . . . of the profession of Nehor" (Alma 14:18) began to question them. Obviously, claiming that the use of "three days" is an allusion to Jesus in the tomb for three days can be written off as simple coincidence. However, when we note how much both Book of Mormon and New Testament writers highlight the use of "three days" in their writing, one can consider the possibility that this detail was intentionally emphasized in this narrative. Although sometimes the use of "three days" or "third day" seems to simply be a detail of the story (1 Nephi 2:6; Alma 8:6; 56:42; 3 Nephi 26:13; Ether 13:28), other times "three days" is used in stories that are arguably typological in nature (1 Nephi 18:13; Mosiah 17:6; Alma 14:18; 17:26; 36:16; 38:8). We know for certain that Book of Mormon writers were aware that Jesus would be in the tomb for three days (1 Nephi 19:10; 2 Nephi 25:13; Mosiah 3:10), so we can at least be open to the possibility that this detail is highlighted typologically. In the New Testament "three days" or "third day" might be highlighted typologically in the story of the feeding of the five thousand (Mark 8:2),[25] turning water to wine (John 2:1),[26] and Paul receiving sight (Acts 9:9). Furthermore, it's important to remember that the ancients were very intentional with the numbers they highlighted in narrative. It seems at least plausible that "three days" was intentionally mentioned to draw a connection to the resurrection.

There may be at least two other ways that the narrative indirectly points to the resurrection. The first possibility regards the use of language related to the phrase "bands of death." When speaking to Alma and Amulek, the chief judge said, "If ye have the power of God deliver yourselves from these bands" (Alma 14:24). After Alma prayed for deliverance, Alma and Amulek "broke the cords with which they were bound" (Alma 14:26). This kind of language may allude to phrases like "broken the bands of death" (Mosiah 15:9, 23) and "the bands of death shall be broken" (Mosiah 15:20). Abinadi, who helped convert Alma the Elder, used the phrase "bands of death" at least four times (Mosiah 15:9, 20, 23; 16:7), and Alma the Younger himself used the phrase at least four times (Alma 5:9–10; 7:12; 11:41), including when speaking to the people of Ammonihah. Perhaps this language was meant to intentionally echo the resurrection and therefore point to the ultimate example of evil destroying itself.

Another way this narrative may allude to the resurrection is when Mormon highlighted that "the earth shook mightily" shortly before "the walls of the prison were rent in twain" (Alma 14:27). In Matthew's account of the resurrection, he described how on "the first day of the week" Mary and "the other Mary" (Matthew 28:1) came to the tomb of Jesus. "And . . . there was a great earthquake: for the angel of the Lord descended from heaven" (Matthew 28:2). Again, this may be a small way that this story points to the ultimate triumph over evil by highlighting details that remind the reader of the resurrection.

Theological precedence

Finally, the idea that evil eventually works to destroy itself is taught throughout Book of Mormon history. It seems reasonable that Mormon or Alma the Younger would have noticed this idea when they realized the prison walls destroyed those who falsely accused Alma and Amulek. The Book of Mormon contains multiple instances of evil eventually hurting itself. For example, when speaking of the great and abominable church, Nephi said, "That great pit which hath been digged for the destruction of men shall be filled by those who digged it, unto their utter destruction" (1 Nephi 14:3). Speaking again of the great and abominable church, Nephi said, "The blood of that great and abominable church ... shall turn upon their own heads" (1 Nephi 22:13). In a related way, Abinadi warned King Noah that "what you do with me ... shall be as a type and a shadow of things which are to come" (Mosiah 13:10). Later, as Abinadi was being put to death by fire, he warned King Noah by declaring, "Ye shall be taken by the hand of your enemies, and then ye shall suffer, as I suffer, the pains of death by fire" (Mosiah 17:18). Mormon himself wrote this principle and applied it to his own people: "And it is by the wicked that the wicked are punished" (Mormon 4:5). We see this idea manifested with the city of Ammonihah itself when the Lamanites "began to slay the people and destroy the city" (Alma 16:2). The principle that evil will eventually cause its own destruction is taught from the beginning of the Book of Mormon until the end. This concept is powerfully illustrated when the prison that is used to hold Alma and Amulek became the very instrument that destroyed the wicked leadership in Ammonihah.

Conclusion

During a recent Brigham Young University devotional, Elder Jeffrey R. Holland clarified that God never harms or hurts his children. He then added, "Now *allowing* something is a different matter! God can and will do *that* if it is ultimately for our good."[27] In other words, punishment from God comes when he simply allows us to deal with the effects of our own decisions. In many ways, Alma and Amulek embody this principle when they responded peacefully to suffering, exposed the moral corruption of the people of Ammonihah, and allowed evil to collapse on itself.

Modern Latter-day Saints would do well to find ways to follow the example of Jesus and Alma and Amulek in seeking peaceful ways to overcome evil. For example, when people attack our beliefs, sometimes we should clarify misunderstandings and other times we should stay silent. But regardless of what is needed in each situation we should respond peacefully. Also, we would do well to remember that when others offend or hurt us, we indirectly expose their wickedness by responding in authentic, Christlike ways. Finally, we do not need to take ultimate justice into our own hands because evil will eventually destroy itself. Of course, this does not mean we do not work proactively to improve our families, communities, and societies. Rather, we must let Christian love guide whatever methods we use in seeking to eliminate evil and establishing righteousness.

In a classic example of a Christlike response to persecution, Bishop Edward Partridge recorded this incident during the Missouri persecutions:

> I was taken from my house by the mob . . . who escorted me about half a mile, to the courthouse, on the public square in Independence; and then and there . . . I was stripped of my hat, coat and vest and daubed with tar from head to foot, and then had a quantity of feathers put upon me; and all this because I would not agree to leave the county, <and> my home where I had lived two years. . . . I bore my abuse with so much resignation and meekness, that it appeared to astound the multitude, who permitted me to retire in silence, many looking very solemn, their sympathies having been touched. . . . And as to myself, I was so filled with the Spirit and love of God, that I had no hatred towards my persecutors, or anyone else.[28]

It is striking that Bishop Partridge's meekness convicted the multitude who then left in silence. In that moment, Christian love overcame evil and wickedness itself withdrew. In the words of Dr. King, someone had "inject[ed] within the very structure of the universe that strong and powerful element of love."[29] Whenever anyone works to overcome evil through self-sacrificial love without allowing themselves to be filled with hate, they too typify Jesus as "The Prince of Peace" (Isaiah 9:6). As Elder Robert D. Hales said, "That is not weakness. That is Christian courage."[30]

STEPHAN D. TAEGER *is an assistant professor of ancient scripture at Brigham Young University.*

Notes

1. Martin Luther King Jr., "Loving Your Enemies" (sermon delivered at Dexter Avenue Baptist Church, Montgomery, AL, December 17, 1957), https://kinginstitute.stanford.edu/king-papers/documents/loving-your-enemies-sermon-delivered-dexter-avenue-baptist-church.

2. King, "Loving Your Enemies."
3. King, "Loving Your Enemies."
4. Robert D. Hales, "Christian Courage: The Price of Discipleship," *Ensign*, November 2008, 72–75.
5. Amy-Jill Levine and Mark Zvi Brettler, *The Bible With and Without Jesus: How Jews and Christians Read the Same Stories Differently* (New York: HarperCollins, 2020), ix–xii.
6. Richard B. Hays, *Echoes of Scripture in the Gospels* (Waco, TX: Baylor University Press, 2018), 2.
7. Brian D. Garner, *Search These Things Diligently: A Personal Study Guide to the Book of Mormon* (Salt Lake City, UT: Deseret Book, 2003) 188–90. Garner also sees Alma and Amulek as typological, but there are differences in the types we identify in the narrative.
8. Peter W. Martens, "Revisiting the Allegory/Typology Distinction: The Case of Origen," *Journal of Early Christian Studies* 16, no. 3 (2008): 283–317.
9. Robert James Norman, "Types," in *The Book of Mormon Reference Companion*, ed. Dennis Largey (Salt Lake City: Deseret Book, 2003), 768.
10. Grant Hardy, *Understanding the Book of Mormon: A Reader's Guide* (Oxford: Oxford University Press, 2010), xvii.
11. C. Terry Warner, "Honest, Simple, Solid, True" (speech delivered at Brigham Young University, Provo, UT, January 16, 1996).
12. John Hilton, *Considering the Cross: How Calvary Connects Us with Christ* (Salt Lake City: Deseret Book, 2021), 126.
13. Neil L. Anderson, "Following Jesus: Being a Peacemaker," April 2022 general conference, https://www.churchofjesuschrist.org/study/general-conference/2022/04/15andersen.
14. Aaron M. Gale, *The Jewish Annotated New Testament*, ed. Amy-Jill Levine and Marc Zvi Brettler (New York: Oxford University Press, 2011), 50; Warren Carter, *The New Interpreter's Study Bible: New Revised Standard Version With the Apocrypha*, ed. Walter Harrelson (Nashville: Abingdon Press, 2003), 1795–96.
15. Or "silent" in the NRSV.
16. It may be important to point out that the Book of Mormon does not have a simplistic view of nonviolent resistance. Other narratives in the Book of Mormon suggest that the use of force is justified when defending oneself or protecting others (Alma 43:45–46). In suggesting that Alma and Amulek respond nonviolently is not to suggest that there is one single method for overcoming evil. What seems to be essential is that disciples of Christ maintain a heart like Moroni that sincerely does "not delight in bloodshed" (Alma 48:11) and seeks to find peaceful means to resolve conflict whenever possible. For more on how the Book of Mormon presents war, see Kent P. Jackson, "War and Peace—Lessons from the Upper Room," in *To Save the Lost*, ed. Richard Neitzel Holzapfel and Kent P. Jackson (Provo, UT: Religious Studies Center, Brigham Young University, 2009), 35–59.
17. N. T. Wright, *Luke for Everyone* (Louisville, KY: Westminster John Knox Press, 2004), 268.
18. Carter, *New Interpreter's Study Bible*, 1796.

19. N. T. Wright, *Matthew for Everyone, Part 2* (Louisville, KY: Westminster John Knox Press, 2004), 186.
20. Brant A. Gardener, *Second Witness: Analytical and Contextual Commentary on the Book of Mormon, Volume 4, Alma* (Sandy, UT: Greg Kofford Books, 2001), 240.
21. M. Eugene Boring and Fred B. Craddock, *The People's New Testament Commentary* (Louisville, KY: Westminster John Knox Press, 2010), 630.
22. N. T. Wright, *John for Everyone, Part 2* (Louisville, KY: Westminster John Knox Press, 2004), 82.
23. Gail R. O'Day, *The New Interpreter's Study Bible: New Revised Standard Version With the Apocrypha*, ed. Walter Harrelson (Nashville: Abingdon Press, 2003), 1941.
24. Gregory A. Boyd, *The Crucifixion of the Warrior God*, volumes 1–2 (Fortress Press, 2017), 803.
25. Boring and Craddock, *People's New Testament Commentary*, 142.
26. Boring and Craddock, *People's New Testament Commentary*, 294.
27. Jeffrey R. Holland, "A Saint Through the Atonement of Christ the Lord" (speech delivered at Brigham Young University, Provo, UT, January 18, 2022).
28. "History, 1838–1856, volume A-1 [23 December 1805–30 August 1834]," p. 327, The Joseph Smith Papers.
29. King, "Loving Your Enemies."
30. Robert D. Hales, "Christian Courage: The Price of Discipleship," *Ensign*, November 2008, 72–75.

8

"I Am the Law"

Jesus Christ and the Law of Moses in the Book of Mormon

THORA FLORENCE SHANNON
AND AVRAM R. SHANNON

One way the Book of Mormon bears witness of Jesus Christ is by testifying of the eternal nature of his saving work. In the Book of Mormon, Christ identifies himself as the giver of the law of Moses and the Sinai covenant (3 Nephi 15:5). The connection between Jesus and the law of Moses starts from the beginning of the Book of Mormon. When Lehi₁ and his family came to the promised land from Jerusalem they bring with them the brass plates, which contained the law of Moses (1 Nephi 4:15–16).[1] Early in the Book of Mormon, the Lord begins to reveal to Lehi₁ and his family about his bodily coming to earth to save the world through his sacrificial blood atonement. Edward J. Brandt has shown that there are three separate revelational periods where Jesus Christ is specifically introduced by name to the Nephites before his post-resurrection appearances.[2] These occasions are composed first of the grouped revelations of Lehi₁, Nephi₁, and Jacob. Then, when the specific knowledge of Jesus Christ and his atoning sacrifice appears to have been lost among the general Nephites, there are separate but roughly contemporaneous revelations, first in the book of Mosiah by King Benjamin, and then by Abinadi.[3] These revelations each explicitly connect with the law of Moses, because Jesus Christ and the atoning blood of his sacrifice are inextricably connected with the law of Moses.

Thus, the revelation about Jesus Christ from the beginning of the Book of Mormon down to his coming did not supersede either the ethical and moral belief system or the ritual practices of the law of Moses. Rather, the introduction of Christ and the understanding of his blood atonement complemented and completed the law of Moses. The Nephites looked forward to the coming of Jesus Christ not so he would save them *from* the law of Moses but rather that he would fulfill the law of Moses as the ultimate and final blood atoning sacrifice to complete all the other animal blood sacrifices called for from the time of Adam and Eve up through Jesus Christ's mortal life (see Alma 34:9–13).[4]

The Law of Moses

The book of Exodus records that after Jehovah had rescued the Israelites from Egypt, he brought them to Mount Sinai and there offered to them his covenant. In Exodus 19:5–6 Jehovah states the purpose of the law; "Now therefore, if ye will obey my voice indeed, and keep my covenant, then ye shall be a peculiar treasure unto me above all people . . . and ye shall be unto me a kingdom of priests, and an holy nation." The people agreed to the offered covenant, and this became the basis for the relationship between Israel and Jehovah.[5] The various commandments of the law of Moses were designed to help Israel become holy, in the way that Jehovah himself was holy (Leviticus 11:44).[6]

As a covenant path designed to give the ancient Israelites the means to be a holy people, the law of Moses provided a complete religious system for them. This included both ritual (including sacrificial) and ethical/moral systems. Although Jesus Christ would end many of the ritual and sacrificial aspects of the law, many of the ethical and moral ideas are eternal.[7] This is why commandments such as the Ten Commandments are still binding on Christians today, although the law has been fulfilled through Jesus Christ. While the sacrificial system was a complex system that included the sacrifices of various animals such as birds, bulls, and male and female goats, it also served as a valuable teaching tool, much as ordinances do for Latter-day Saints today.[8] These sacrifices taught the Israelites to give up material possessions and to learn how to consecrate themselves to Jehovah.[9] They also effected atonement for the ancient Israelites (see, for example, Leviticus 4:20).[10] In fact, in the King James Version of the Bible, of the eighty-one times that the word atone and its variants appear in the Old Testament, seventy-seven of those are in the law of Moses (Genesis–Deuteronomy).[11]

The Sinai covenant was the standard way in which the children of Israel interacted with and worshipped Jehovah throughout the Old Testament and into the New Testament. In his mortal ministry, Jesus himself continued to live the law of Moses.[12] Among the earliest members of Jesus Christ's church in the Old World, there were some who continued to live the law of Moses, while non-Jewish converts did not need to (see Acts 15:22–29). Because the question of living the law of Moses generated a lot of discussion in the partially Jewish and partially non-Jewish early church, the New Testament sometimes makes strong statements against the law of Moses (such as Galatians 3). These strong statements made by inspired individuals such as Paul need to be read alongside the indicators that even after Jesus, early Christians continued to live the law of Moses. For example, Paul goes to the temple to offer sacrifices and pay his vows, specifically to show people opposed to Christianity that he still lived the law (Acts 21:20–26).[13] The law of Moses was part of the religious experiences of God's covenant people up to and even after the coming of Jesus, which helps to explain the ways in which the Nephites both believed in Jesus and lived the law of Moses.[14] The close connection between Christ and the law of Moses in Nephite religious thought begins at the very beginning of the Book of Mormon, and it is to Lehi$_1$ and his children that we turn to next.

Jesus and the Law in the Small Plates

The Lehites begin their relationship with Jehovah through the Sinai covenant from the very outset, but Nephi$_1$ preserves a record of the process of revelation where Lehi$_1$ and his family gradually learned about the coming of Jesus

Christ. The first few chapters of 1 Nephi contain references both to a coming Messiah[15] (1 Nephi 1:19) and the need to live the law of Moses (1 Nephi 4:15). As the Book of Mormon progresses and the Nephites begin to receive more knowledge about the coming of Jesus Christ, they work to incorporate their knowledge into their existing religious systems. The small plates do not indicate that the increased knowledge about Jesus possessed by Nephi₁, Jacob, and Jacob's descendants led them to stop living the law. In fact, the evidence in some places suggests the opposite. Not only does the Book of Mormon show that Nephites worshipped Jesus through the law of Moses, but the specific name *Jesus Christ* is used precisely when the authors in the small plates are talking about the law of Moses.

Because of the abbreviated nature of Nephi₁'s abridgment of his father's record, we do not have much of Lehi₁'s early teachings in the Book of Mormon, but Nephi₁ does preserve a record of their growing understanding of Jesus Christ. In the current Book of Mormon, the terms *Jesus* and *Christ* do not appear in the text of 1 Nephi at all. Jacob is the first to use the distinctive title of *Christ* in 2 Nephi 10:3, while Nephi₁ is the first to use the complete name *Jesus Christ* as a set phrase, in 2 Nephi 25:19.[16] Before 2 Nephi 10 (and often after it), Lehi₁, Nephi₁, and Jacob would use other titles, such as *Redeemer* (1 Nephi 10:515) and *Holy One of Israel* (1 Nephi 19:14–15).[17] After the names *Christ* and *Jesus Christ* are revealed to the Nephites through angelic ministration, these specific names become the framework through which the Nephites build their relationship with Jesus.

Although Lehi₁ never uses either distinctive name, the process of learning about Jesus Christ's mission begins with him. From the very outset, Lehi₁ "testified that the things which he saw and heard . . . manifested plainly of the coming of a Messiah" (1 Nephi 1:19). Usually when *Messiah* is used in the Old Testament, it means the king. In Lehi₁'s day, the primary meaning of *Messiah* would have been King Zedekiah, and this seems to be the understanding that Lehi starts out with.[18]

After his vision of the tree of life, Lehi₁ prophecies that the Lord God would raise up a prophet (1 Nephi 10:4). Lehi₁'s language is highly reminiscent of prophecy now found in Deuteronomy 18:18–19, where Jehovah promises Moses, "I will raise them up a Prophet from among their brethren, like unto thee, and will put my words in his mouth; and he shall speak unto them all that I shall command him."[19] The biblical tradition looks forward only to a new Mosaic prophet.[20] Lehi₁ makes an intriguing expansion to the understanding of the Mosaic prophet, however, by continuing in 1 Nephi 10:4, "Even a Messiah, or, in other words, a Savior of the world." This shows that, for Lehi₁, the prophet like Moses will be a Messiah, which in his ancient Judahite context meant a king. This king and prophet will be a savior of the world, which in 1 Nephi 10:6 Lehi₁ indicates will be a salvation from a "lost and ... fallen state." The connection between the coming kingly Messiah and prophet like Moses is the thread that will underscore the teachings in the small plates.

Following his father's lead, in 1 Nephi 22:20, Nephi₁ paraphrases Deuteronomy 18:18–19, changing the pronouns around so that it is Moses speaking of a prophet, rather than the Lord to Moses. Nephi₁ makes his own intriguing connection to the prophet like Moses in the immediately following verse, "And now I, Nephi, declare unto you, that this prophet of whom Moses spake was the Holy One of Israel; wherefore, he shall execute judgment in righteousness" (1 Nephi 22:21). Nephi₁ explicitly connects the prophet like Moses with the Holy One of Israel. Within the confines of the Old Testament, the Holy One of Israel was Jehovah, the covenant God of Israel (Isaiah 48:17 // 1 Nephi 20:17 is one example). In his version of his father's dream, Nephi₁ learned about the "condescension of God" (1 Nephi 11:16), including and especially the coming of Jehovah in the flesh. Nephi₁'s connecting his father's coming Messiah and prophet to the coming of Jehovah is a natural progression of the Nephites' learning about Jehovah's coming in the flesh to save his people.

In his final address to his children, Father Lehi continues this line of thinking, calling the coming salvific figure "the Holy Messiah." This phrase is unique in the scriptures to Lehi₁ and is an example of Lehi₁ connecting the Messiah as king and savior of the world with the sacrificial system under the law of Moses. In many ways this title is a combination of the kingly Messiah and the prophet like Moses. According to Lehi₁, this Messiah "offereth himself a sacrifice for sin, to answer the ends of the law, unto all those who have a broken heart and a contrite spirit, and unto none else can the ends of the law be answered" (2 Nephi 2:7). This explicitly connects the kingly idea of the Messiah to the atoning and sacrificial ideas from the law of Moses.

The Nephites' growing belief that Jehovah would come as a Holy Messiah who would save them from their sins did not change their commitment to living the commandments under the law of Moses. This is made clear by Nephi₁ building a temple after the manner of the temple of Solomon (2 Nephi 5:16). Solomon's temple was a place of animal sacrifice under the law.[21] From an ancient Israelite perspective, the primary reason to build a temple was to keep the law of Moses, just as in this dispensation our temples are built to perform ritual ordinances.

As part of this, Nephi₁ ordains Jacob a priest, whose primary responsibility would have been to administer the ordinances described in the law of Moses at the temple built by Nephi₁ (2 Nephi 5:26).[22] In his role as a priest, Jacob teaches the people in a sermon (2 Nephi 6–10) that is heavily rooted in concepts from the law of Moses such as "holiness" and "atonement." As part of his sermon, Jacob first introduces the idea of "infinite atonement" (2 Nephi 9:7). In the sacrificial system of the law of Moses, atonement was effected by animal sacrifice.[23] By introducing the Lord's saving sacrifice as an infinite atonement, Jacob is explicitly connecting it to animal sacrifice and implicitly contrasting the temporary nature of the law with the eternal nature of salvation. Jacob divides his sermon into two different days, and in between the first and the second day, he receives revelation through an angel that the coming saving figure would be named Christ (2 Nephi 10:3).

Christ derives from the Greek word for "anointed," so in one sense, the title of Christ is not different from the title *Messiah*. The Book of Mormon clearly differentiates between Christ and Messiah, however, often using them side by side in the same chapter. This means that it is likely the name revealed to Nephi₁ and Jacob was not Hebrew, which would have been something like *Yehoshua ha Mashiah*, or *Mashiah*, but something specific that was related to or perhaps sounded like Greek *Christ*. The Nephites then seem to prefer this term, perhaps because it does not have the associations with Judahite kingship of Messiah, which would have been largely negative to Lehi and his family.[24] Not only have Lehi₁ and Nephi₁ been teaching about the coming Messiah in terms of Moses and the law but the first explicit revelation of the name *Christ* to the people in the Book of Mormon as we now have it is part of a sermon heavily rooted in the law of Moses.

Nephi₁ continues to expand this thread of understanding the coming of Christ through the law of Moses. In commenting on Jacob's sermon, he states, "Behold, my soul delighteth in proving unto my people the truth of the coming of Christ; for, for this end hath the law of Moses been given; and all things which have been given of God from the beginning of the world, unto man, are the typifying of him" (2 Nephi 11:4). For Nephi₁, the law points toward, not away from, Jesus Christ. Nephi₁ further explores this when he also notes that he "delight[s] in the covenants of the Lord" (2 Nephi 11:5), which in Nephi₁'s day referred to the Sinai covenant. Nephi₁'s statement that the purpose of the law was to prove the coming of Christ is a clear development from his revelation of the condescension of God.

In 2 Nephi 25, Nephi₁ continues his close association between Christ's coming and the law of Moses. In his commentary on the teaching of Isaiah that he just quoted, Nephi₁ prophecies about the Lord's bodily coming to earth using the names or titles *Christ* (first seen in Jacob's sermon) and *Messiah* (the preferred term of his father). In 2 Nephi 25:19, Nephi₁ uses the full name and title *Jesus Christ* for the first time in the Book of Mormon as we currently have it, telling us that, like Jacob, he learned the name from an angelic revelation. Like Jacob's teachings, Nephi₁'s teachings here are also explicitly connected to the law. In 2 Nephi 25:24, Nephi₁ says, "And, notwithstanding we believe in Christ, we keep the law of Moses, and look forward with steadfastness unto Christ, until the law shall be fulfilled."[25] Nephi₁ and Jacob both receive divine manifestations through angels of specific names for Jesus Christ, and they reveal them to their people in contexts that are associated with the law of Moses. This is because for the Nephites, the coming of Jesus, and especially his sacrificial blood atonement, is part and parcel of their living of God's law as revealed to Moses on Mount Sinai.

The explicit connection between the law and Christ does not appear to have been universally accepted among the people of Nephi₁, however. Jacob's encounter at the end of his life with Sherem illustrates that Nephi₁ and Jacob's teachings on the law and its relationship to Christ are not the only teachings current among the Nephites. On the contrary, Sherem teaches "among the people" that "there should be no Christ" (Jacob 7:2).[26] Much ink has been spilled about the identity of Sherem and his relationship to the Nephites.[27] For the purposes of the present discussion, it is sufficient to observe that whoever Sherem was and wherever he came from, he was a fervent believer in the efficacy of the law of Moses, but not in a Christ/Messiah who would atone for the sins of the world.[28] Indeed, he accuses Jacob (and, by extension, Nephi₁), saying, "Ye have led away much of this people that they pervert the right way of God, and keep not the law of Moses which is the right way; and convert the law of Moses into the worship of a being which ye say shall come many hundred years hence" (Jacob 7:7). There are two intriguing elements to Sherem's denunciation. The first is that Jacob has led away "much" of the people, suggesting that there were Nephites who kept the law of Moses, but did not necessarily accept Nephi₁ and Jacob's Christ-centered approach to the law. This is closely related to his second claim that Jacob had changed the law of Moses into the worship of Christ. There is some legitimacy to Sherem's accusation against Jacob, but this is the point of the distinctive revelations that Jacob and his brother have received. Simply put, for Nephi and Jacob, they are not transforming the law of Moses into the worship of another being—they are properly using it to worship Jehovah in his role as Jesus Christ and his promise to come bodily to the earth and atone for the world.

Despite the evidence of Sherem illustrating that there were some Nephites who did not use the law of Moses to look forward to Jesus, the record of Jacob's descendants through the remaining small plates shows that they preserve at least some knowledge of Jesus Christ. Enos is told by God that salvation from sin comes from his faith in Christ (Enos 1:8), and he closes out his record with a memorial to his commission to preach "the truth which is in Christ" (Enos 1:26). Jarom reverts to the usage "Messiah," stating that "the prophets, and the priests, and the teachers" teach the law of Moses, connecting it with the coming of the Messiah (Jarom 1:11), although he himself does not appear to be a priest teaching it. Jarom's son, Omni, describes himself as "a wicked man" (Omni 1:2), but there still seems to be preservation of the knowledge of Jesus Christ through this Jacobite record. The last keeper of the small plates, Amaleki, testifies of Jesus using language reminiscent of Lehi₁ and Nephi₁, stating, "And now, my beloved brethren, I would that ye should come unto Christ, who is the Holy One of Israel, and partake of his salvation, and the power of his redemption. Yea, come unto him, and offer your whole souls as an offering unto him, and continue in fasting and praying, and endure to the end; and as the Lord liveth ye will be saved" (Omni 1:26). From all this we can see that even though the keepers of the small plates were not all direct preachers of Christ or the law of Moses, they did preserve a memory of it through their generations.

King Benjamin

At the beginning of what we currently have of Mormon's summary of the large plates, King Benjamin reigns over the Nephites and the people of Zarahemla almost five hundred years after Lehi$_1$ and his family left Jerusalem. Amaleki, contemporaneous with Benjamin, closes out the small plates by stating his intent to give the plates to Benjamin (Omni 1:25).[29] All we know for sure about what happens to the plates is what Mormon tells us:

> After I had made an abridgment from the plates of Nephi, down to the reign of this king Benjamin, of whom Amaleki spake, I searched among the records which had been delivered into my hands, and I found these plates, which contained this small account of the prophets, from Jacob down to the reign of this king Benjamin, and also many of the words of Nephi.
>
> *And the things which are upon these plates pleasing me, because of the prophecies of the coming of Christ....*
>
> Wherefore, I chose these things, to finish my record....
>
> Wherefore, it came to pass that after Amaleki had delivered up these plates into the hands of *king Benjamin, he took them and put them with the other plates*, which contained records which had been handed down by the kings, from generation to generation until the days of king Benjamin. (Words of Mormon 1:3–5, 10; emphasis added)

This quote by Mormon indicates that the small plates contain more explicit prophecies of the coming of Christ than those found in the large plates to this point. It also indicates that Benjamin placed the plates with other records, but not whether he made a close study of them.

When Benjamin delivers his speech, he first gives what he calls "my words which I shall speak unto you" (Mosiah 2:9), but when he begins what is now Mosiah 3 Benjamin states that the things he is now saying come directly from an angel (Mosiah 3:2). Then the rest of his sermon, including the name and atoning mission of Jesus Christ, comprises the words of that angel. That

Benjamin receives the name of Jesus Christ and his blood sacrifice by angelic revelation suggests that this was not general knowledge among the Nephites living in Zarahemla. This further indicates that the small plates were not in general circulation among the people of Zarahemla.

Benjamin calls his people to come to the temple to hear his message (Mosiah 1:18), and there "they also took of the firstlings of their flocks, that they might offer sacrifice and burnt offerings according to the law of Moses" (Mosiah 2:3). This shows that the populace was still living the law of Moses, including the sacrificial laws, even if the people had not retained the full understanding of the law of Moses and its connection to Jesus Christ. It also shows that Benjamin will reveal the angel's message of Jesus's name in a temple and therefore a law of Moses context.

Like with the vision where Nephi first sees the condescension of God, the angel speaking to Benjamin also goes through the Lord's birth to Mary and his ministry, healings, and death.[30] Unlike with Nephi's vision, the angel visiting Benjamin continues beyond this to explain to Benjamin, "And he shall be called Jesus Christ, the Son of God, the Father of heaven and earth, the Creator of all things from the beginning" (Mosiah 3:8). The angel details out what Christ shall do, by noting that "salvation might come unto the children of men even through faith on his name" (Mosiah 3:9) and that he shall be crucified: "And he shall rise the third day from the dead" (Mosiah 3:10). Then the angel makes the connection between Jesus Christ and the law of Moses: "For behold, and also his blood atoneth for the sins of those who have fallen by the transgression of Adam. . . . For salvation cometh to none such except it be through repentance and faith on the Lord Jesus Christ" (Mosiah 3:11–12). This explicitly connects Jesus Christ's death with the law of Moses that the people of Zarahemla are already keeping. Blood atonement is a common principle in the law of Moses, and the people of Zarahemla, who had just barely brought sacrifices to the temple to be killed, would have immediately understood and connected Jesus Christ's blood atoning for their sins to how priests sacrificed animals to atone for their sins under the law of Moses.

The angel continues in Mosiah 3:14 to say, "Yet the Lord God saw that his people were a stiffnecked people, and he appointed unto them a law, even the law of Moses." This could be used to show that the law of Moses is a law only given because of sin, and that perhaps if the Israelites had been righteous when Moses went up Mount Sinai that they would not have received the law of Moses. Yet, taken in context, the next verse gives an insight into how the law of Moses itself is not what is inferior, but when the Lord's people "hardened their hearts, and understood not that the law of Moses availeth nothing except it were through the atonement of his blood" (Mosiah 3:15), that is the problem.

The angel brings together the name of Jesus Christ and the law of Moses notion of atonement through blood with his climactic statement: "There shall be no other name given nor any other way nor means whereby salvation can come unto the children of men, only in and through the name of Christ, the Lord Omnipotent.... Salvation was, and is, and is to come, in and through the atoning blood of Christ, the Lord Omnipotent" (Mosiah 3:17–18). Benjamin's speech as delivered to him by an angel is foundational for revealing to King Benjamin's people not only the name of Jesus Christ but also Christ's atoning blood sacrifice through his own death. This sacrifice is inextricably connected with the law of Moses, illustrating that Christ's atonement is the ultimate fulfillment of that very law. Benjamin's teaching his people of Jesus Christ and his atoning blood is an epochal moment that, along with Abinadi's preaching of Christ to Alma$_1$, who then founds the church of Christ, will provide the basis of understanding for Nephite belief in Jesus Christ for the rest of the Nephite civilization until Jesus himself comes.[31]

Abinadi

Later in the book of Mosiah, but earlier in chronology than the speech of King Benjamin,[32] Mormon directly quotes the record of Zeniff, which tells about the group of Nephites that Zeniff took back to the land of Nephi. These people separated from the main group in either Mosiah 1 or King Benjamin's reign.[33] Zeniff's people, like the general Nephites of their time, do not seem to be aware of Nephi$_1$ or Jacob's revelations on the name and mission of Christ, as the words *Jesus, Christ,* and *Messiah* never appear in Zeniff's record in the Book of Mormon. The people still live the law of Moses—in fact, the temple and priesthood are central to the reign of even the wicked king Noah. They do not understand the coming of Christ, and so, like with Nephi$_1$, Jacob, and Benjamin, the Lord sends a messenger to reveal Christ's name and salvation through his atoning blood. In those cases, it was an angel, while Abinadi in Mosiah 15:21 does so as a prophet. As we will show in this section, Abinadi does not assume his audience knows Christ's name.

The Lord sends Abinadi to preach warning and repentance to the people of Zeniff, now under the rule of Zeniff's son Noah and his decadent priests. In his first preaching, there is no mention of Christ or his mission—what we see instead is a mission preaching repentance like many Old Testament prophets. It is possible, and perhaps likely, that Abinadi was himself a priest through Zeniff and then later was put down by Noah.[34] The people of Noah have a temple and priests, and those priests speak of keeping the law of Moses.[35] Yet they do not seem to be aware of a specific figure named Jesus Christ who would come and save them through his sacrifice and fulfill the law of Moses.[36] This could theoretically be a forgetting because of wickedness, but it is as likely that it simply was not preserved among the people of Zeniff.[37]

Even though Abinadi's speech in his second mission comes in response to a question about the writings of Isaiah from the priests of Noah, he spends most of his sermon discussing first the law of Moses and then introducing Christ and his salvific sacrificial role in connection with that law. Grant Hardy even observes ways in which Mormon presents Abinadi as a new Moses.[38] Abinadi's emphasis on the law can be seen in elements of his speech, such as his quoting the entire Ten Commandments. Abinadi castigates Noah's priests for not keeping or teaching the law of Moses, but he does not condemn them for not understanding that salvation does not come by the law of Moses. He even says if you keep the commandments in the law of Moses you will be saved (Mosiah 12:25–33). In fact, he ends his entire argument with a specific statement about still teaching the law of Moses, showing that even though he has testified of Christ, the expectation is still of keeping the law along with the new understanding that redemption comes through Christ.

In response to their question, Abinadi begins to lay out for the priests the doctrine of salvation, Christ[39], and the law of Moses.

> And now ye have said that salvation cometh by the law of Moses. I say unto you that it is expedient that ye should keep the law of Moses as yet; but I say unto you, that the time shall come when it shall no more be expedient to keep the law of Moses.
>
> And moreover, I say unto you, that salvation doth not come by the law alone; and were it not for the atonement, which God himself shall make for the sins and iniquities of his people, that they must unavoidably perish, notwithstanding the law of Moses. (Mosiah 13:27–28)

Like Benjamin in his speech, Abinadi then discusses how the law of Moses was a strict law for a stiff-necked people but notes that they "understood not that there could not any man be saved except it were through the redemption of God" (Mosiah 13:32). Abinadi speaks of how prophets have prophesied of God and his redemption and then quotes what we have as Isaiah 53 in the current Old Testament, focusing before and after this chapter on how God will be oppressed when he will "come down among the children of men, and shall redeem his people" (Mosiah 15:1).

Having laid the groundwork for understanding that God should atone for the sins of his people through his blood (with a direct connection to the law of Moses) and that God is the suffering servant that Isaiah talks about in Isaiah 53, Abinadi tells how the prophets are the ones who will declare his generation (see Mosiah 14:8 // Isaiah 53:8) and that the prophets and those who hear them are those who will publish peace, which the priests first asked Abinadi about (see Mosiah 12:20–24 // Isaiah 52:7–10). It is in this discussion that Abinadi reveals the name of God who will come down, die as an atoning sacrifice for the sins of his people, and be resurrected again, "And there cometh a resurrection, even a first resurrection; yea, even a resurrection of those that have been, and who are, and who shall be, even until the resurrection of Christ—*for so he shall be called*" (Mosiah 15:21; emphasis added). This verse makes clear that Abinadi assumes that the priests of Noah do not already know the name of Christ, illustrating that this knowledge had been generally lost at some point after Nephi₁ and Jacob.

Abinadi finishes the end of his sermon by reiterating what he has taught the priests: "Therefore, if ye teach the law of Moses, also teach that it is a shadow of those things which are to come—teach them that redemption cometh through

Christ the Lord, who is the very Eternal Father. Amen" (Mosiah 16:14–15). Thus, for the second time chronologically and the third time in the canonical order of the Book of Mormon, the Lord reveals to his people in the Americas Jesus Christ's name and mission as the Redeemer through his atoning sacrifice. All three times that Jesus Christ is revealed as their savior to the Nephites, it is done in connection with the law of Moses because with his own sacrificial death he makes the blood atonement that will be the end of the law.

After Abinadi finishes his sermon, King Noah and his priests, who outwardly follow the law of Moses's legal precepts, despite their lack of practicing that law, look for a reason to put Abinadi to death under a rule of law.[40] The reason they come up with for their justification shows again that the knowledge of Jesus Christ had been lost among the Nephites while the law of Moses from the brass plates had remained. They tell Abinadi he is being killed for preaching "that God himself should come down among the children of men; and now, for this cause thou shalt be put to death" (Mosiah 17:8), showing that they believe that is a justifiable case of blasphemy that would stand up among the people of Zeniff, who therefore can also be seen as generally not knowing about Christ or his prophesied coming.

Yet Abinadi's message of Christ and his redeeming blood atonement as the fulfillment of the law of Moses is not lost with his death. One of the priests of Noah, Alma$_1$, repents when he hears Abinadi's sermon and founds the church of Christ based on Abinadi's teachings. When Alma$_1$ and his people later unite with the rest of the Nephites and the people of Zarahemla, the church of Christ is founded among the entire populace (Mosiah 24). Thus, the teachings about Jesus Christ are not lost again like they were at some point after Jacob's time, and knowledge of Christ and his redeeming blood atonement continues down to the coming of Jesus Christ himself to the Americas.

From Alma$_1$ to Jesus Christ

We have shown that there are three separate examples where the Nephites receive specific revelation about the name and mission of Jesus Christ before his coming to the Nephites. These revelations to the Nephites not only revealed to them important truths about Jesus Christ but did so through the law of Moses. Although this can be unusual to us looking backward from two thousand years of Christian history, this should not be surprising because the Sinai covenant was how Israelites understood their relationship with Jehovah. After Benjamin and Abinadi, however, we see a continuation up to the coming of Jesus Christ. The church founded by Alma$_1$ preserves the teachings about the coming of Jesus Christ in ways that do not seem to be the case previously, but they do not stop keeping the law of Moses as part of their covenant relationship with God.[41]

Two examples in the Book of Mormon show the staying religious power of the Sinai covenant among the Nephites, even with a church focused on the teachings of Benjamin and Abinadi about Christ.[42] The first is the conversion of the former Lamanites who become the Anti-Nephi-Lehies. They are converted by a preaching mission led by the sons of Mosiah$_2$, and this mission is explicit in its basis in preaching salvation through the coming sacrifice of Jesus Christ. Ammon explains to Lamoni about Christ in Alma 18:39 and Aaron similarly teaches Lamoni's father in Alma 22:13–14.[43] When Lamoni's wife comes out of her spiritual coma, she cries out, "O blessed Jesus, who has saved me from an awful hell!" (Alma 19:29). Because the sons of Mosiah$_2$ left the land of Zarahemla after the return of Alma$_1$ and his church, their understanding of the coming of Jesus Christ comes through both the revelations given to Benjamin and Abinadi, as discussed previously.[44]

The explicit conversion of the Anti-Nephi-Lehies to Jesus makes Mormon's historical note in Alma 25:15–16 intriguing. There Mormon describes the converted Lamanites as beginning to keep the law of Moses *after* their conversion. This presumably included the sacrificial and purity components. Although Mormon tells us that the Anti-Nephi-Lehies did not "suppose that salvation came by the law of Moses" (with echoes of Abinadi's teachings here), he also claims, "The law of Moses did serve to strengthen their faith in Christ" (Alma 25:16). Rather than taking away from their belief in the coming Jesus Christ, the Anti-Nephi-Lehies saw living the law as an enhancement to their faith.

The other example between Alma$_1$ and Jesus Christ is the negative example of the Zoramites. The creation of the church among the people in the land of Zarahemla had created space for other religious organizations, such as the order of Nehor.[45] The Nehorites were different from the Zoramites, because the followers of Nehor appear to have continued to keep the law. Mormon tells us about the Zoramites: "But [the Zoramites] had fallen into great errors, for they would not observe to keep the commandments of God, and his statutes, according to the law of Moses. Neither would they observe the performances of the church, to continue in prayer and supplication to God daily, that they might not enter into temptation" (Alma 31:9–10). The Zoramites rejected both the church and the law of Moses, which astonished Alma$_2$ and his companions and fed their desire to return the Zoramites to both church *and* law. This helps to explain Amulek's discussion to the Zoramites of Jesus Christ's mission in connection with the atoning sacrifices of the law of Moses (Alma 34:9–14). The Nephite church continues to teach the specific teaching about Jesus Christ's coming and to live the law of Moses as part of their worship of Jesus.

Jesus Christ's Post-Resurrection Ministry to the Nephites

Jesus's interactions with the law of Moses during his visit to the Nephites are in continuity with what we have seen from the earliest stages of Lehi$_1$ and his family up to the special revelations given through Benjamin and Abinadi. When Jesus does come, he teaches about himself and his mission in connection to the law of Moses. Jesus's statements about fulfilling the law should not be seen as denigration against the law, because Jesus actively connects his life and ministry to the law of Moses.

When he announces the end of animal sacrifice, he does so with a quotation from Psalm 51.[46] This psalm is fundamentally about contrition and the sorrow of repentance. Towards the end of the psalm, the psalmist makes this remarkable statement: "For thou desirest not sacrifice; else I would give it: thou delightest not in burnt offering. The sacrifices of God are a broken spirit: a broken and a contrite heart, O God, thou wilt not despise" (Psalm 51:16–17). Jesus references this passage with his statement to the Nephites, "And ye shall offer for a sacrifice unto me a broken heart and a contrite spirit" (3 Nephi

9:20). Christian readers of these verses in the psalm have sometimes seen this as a statement that God never actually wanted animal sacrifice, even under the law of Moses, but this cannot be maintained from the psalm. Indeed, the psalm ends by noting after the sinner's forgiveness, "Then shalt thou [God] be pleased with the sacrifices of righteousness, with burnt offering and whole burnt offering: then shall they offer bullocks upon thine altar" (Psalm 51:19). Psalm 51 makes it clear that it is the psalmist's wicked state that prevents him from being able to offer sacrifices. Animal sacrifice without the proper penitence is empty and worthless, which accords especially well with the teachings of Abinadi that the law of Moses points to salvation through Christ (Mosiah 16:14–15).

When Jesus comes, he delivers a sermon very similar to the New Testament Sermon on the Mount (Matthew 5–7).[47] After finishing this sermon, Jesus revisits his role as the giver of the law of Moses. Specifically, there were some Nephites who were wondering about Jesus's statement in 3 Nephi 12:47, "Old things are done away, and all things have become new." The Nephite confusion about what to do with the law of Moses suggests that it was not simply a cut-and-dry circumstance where the Nephites were simply happy to get rid of the "lower" law. There was place for some confusion.

In answer to their question, Jesus reiterates his statement that "the law is fulfilled that was given unto Moses" (3 Nephi 15:4). He then explains his relationship to the law, and with that his authority to fulfill the law, "Behold, I am he that gave the law, and I am he who covenanted with my people Israel; therefore, the law in me is fulfilled, for I have come to fulfil the law; therefore it hath an end" (3 Nephi 15:5). Jesus here explicitly connects himself with the giving of the law on Mount Sinai, reminding the Nephites that as the giver of the law, it is his law, and not really the law of Moses at all but rather the law of Jehovah. Even at this point in Nephite history, the destruction of the law of Moses is not what was on Jesus's mind here, because he himself gave that law. He is the God of Israel, revealing himself and his covenant to his people.

Conclusion

It is no accident that all three times the Lord introduces the knowledge of the coming of Jesus Christ to the Nephites, he does so explicitly in conjunction with the law of Moses and Jesus's atoning sacrifice. Jesus Christ and his atonement is not simply something better instead of the law of Moses. In the book of Moses, the Lord sent an angel to tell Adam and Eve to keep a sacrificial law of animal sacrifice as a sign of his coming (Moses 5:6–8). Jesus Christ as Jehovah gave the law and covenant on Mount Sinai, something he reminds the people of in the New World (3 Nephi 15:5). Although scripture indicates that the ancient Israelites received a lesser law because of their own actions (see Doctrine and Covenants 84:23–26), the "lesser" part of this law is not the system of animal sacrifice nor the ethical and moral commandments that are also integral to the law of Moses such as the Ten Commandments, which were never rescinded and that we still keep and believe today. What is lesser in the law of Moses seems to be the Israelites' ignorance of the fullest significance of the law pointing to a great and last sacrifice by Jesus Christ. Jehovah revealed that knowledge to the subsection of Israelites he led away to the promised land. Lehi$_1$, Nephi$_1$ and Jacob, King Benjamin, and Abinadi all received revelation about Jesus Christ. These revelations were not separate from or instead of the law of Moses and Sinai covenant. Instead, Jesus Christ and the knowledge of his coming was explicitly bound up in the law of Moses the Nephites were already keeping. Within the Book of Mormon, Jesus Christ and his mortal life, atonement, sacrificial death, and resurrection are inextricably connected with the law of Moses and Jehovah's covenant purposes for his children.

This can help explain what Jesus means both by the law being fulfilled as well as what it means that it has an end. Jesus is the lord of the everlasting covenant, and our relationship to him is a covenant relationship, as it has always been. There are aspects of the law of Moses and the Sinai covenant that are still operative and binding on Latter-day Saints to this day. We still live and try to keep the commandments, like the two great commandments to love God (Deuteronomy 6:5) and to love our neighbor (Leviticus 19:18). Latter-day Saints are a covenant part of the house of Israel, which is why it matters to us that it was Jesus Christ as Jehovah who covenanted with Israel. The Book of

Mormon revelations of Jesus Christ's name in connection with his blood sacrifice is something that we encounter every week as we take the sacrament and take upon us the name of Jesus Christ and drink in remembrance of his blood (Moroni 5:2). We ourselves are in continuity with the Nephites and the law of Moses as we also experience the name and blood of Jesus together during the sacrament. All of this reminds us that salvation only comes through Jesus Christ, not through specific ordinances or commandments in *any* dispensation. It is Jesus Christ himself who teaches us, "Behold, I am the law, and the light. Look unto me, and endure to the end, and ye shall live; for unto him that endureth to the end will I give eternal life" (3 Nephi 15:9).

AVRAM R. SHANNON *is an assistant professor of ancient scripture at Brigham Young University.*

THORA SHANNON *is an independent scholar from Provo, Utah.*

Notes

1. The form of the content on the brass plates is subject to scholarly discussion. John L. Sorenson argued that it derived from traditions from the northern kingdom of Israel. See John L. Sorenson, "The 'Brass Plates' and Biblical Scholarship," *Dialogue: A Journal of Mormon Thought* 10, no. 4 (1977): 31–39; Robert L. Millet, "The Influence of the Brass Plates on the Teachings of Nephi," in *Second Nephi, The Doctrinal Structure*, ed. Monte S. Nyman and Charles D. Tate Jr. (Provo, UT: Religious Studies Center, Brigham Young University, 1989), 207–25. See further Avram R. Shannon, "The Book of Mormon and the Documentary Hypothesis," in *They Shall Grow Together: The Bible in the Book of Mormon*, eds. Charles Swift and Nicholas J. Frederick (Provo, UT: Religious Studies Center, Brigham Young University, 2022), 249–75.
2. See Edward J. Brandt, "The Name *Jesus Christ* Revealed to the Nephites," in *The Book of Mormon: Second Nephi, The Doctrinal Structure*, ed. Monte S. Nyman and Charles D. Tate Jr. (Provo, UT: Religious Studies Center, Brigham Young University, 1989), 201–6. Brandt identifies the three different revelations to Nephi$_1$ and Jacob, Abinadi, and Benjamin, but does not indicate why there needed to be these revelations of the name of Jesus. As we discuss later in the paper, Jesus Christ identifies as the fulfillment of these prophecies. According to Ether 3:14, he also identified himself as Jesus Christ to the brother of Jared, but the Jaredite records were not generally known among the Nephites. See Alma 37:21–29.

3. John W. Welch discusses ten individuals who bear testimony of Jesus in the Book of Mormon. Welch's focus is on how these various testimonies both teach the same basic doctrine and reflect their own experiences. John W. Welch, "Ten Testimonies of Jesus Christ from the Book of Mormon," in *A Book of Mormon Treasury: Gospel Insights from General Authorities and Religious Educators* (Provo, UT: Religious Studies Center, Young University, 2003), 316–42. Welch discusses Nephi$_1$ on 324–5, Jacob on 325–7, Benjamin on 329–31, and Abinadi on 327–29.
4. We do not see the Abinadi as "untethering" the law of Moses from salvation but argue in this paper that instead of disconnecting salvation from the law, Abinadi is simply clarifying how the law and salvation are connected. For an alternative perspective, see Daniel L. Belnap, "The Abinadi Narrative: Redemption and the Struggle of Nephite Identity," in *Abinadi: He Came Among Them in Disguise*, ed. Shon D. Hopkin (Provo, UT: Religious Studies Center; Salt Lake City: Deseret Book, 2018), 27–66, discussion on 41–44.
5. There is a very nice overview for Latter-day Saints in Daniel L. Belnap, "The Law of Moses: An Overview," in *New Testament History, Culture, and Society: A Background to the Texts of the New Testament*, ed. Lincoln H. Blumell (Religious Studies Center, Brigham Young University; Salt Lake City: Deseret Book, 2019), 19-34.
6. This continues in the Restoration, where the Saints who receive celestial glory are promised that they will be "priests and kings" (Doctrine and Covenants 76:56). For a discussion of notions of consecration and holiness in the Old Testament law see Avram R. Shannon, "'Be Ye Therefore Holy': Consecration in the Sinai Covenant," in *Old Testament Insights: The Sacrifice of a Broken Heart and Contrite Spirit*, eds. Kenneth L. Alford, Gaye Strathearn, and Mary Jane Woodger (American Fork, UT: Covenant Communications, 2021), 79–87.
7. See Kerry Muhlestein, Joshua M. Sears, and Avram R. Shannon, "New and Everlasting: The Relationship between Gospel Covenants in History," *Religious Educator* 21, no. 2 (2020): 20–40.
8. For a description of the sacrificial system as described in the book of Leviticus, see Jacob Milgrom, *Leviticus 1–16* (New Haven, CT: Yale University Press, 2001), 133–378. There is an accessible discussion focused on Latter-day Saints in Richard Neitzel Holzapfel, Dana M. Pike, and David Rolph Seely, *Jehovah and the World of the Old Testament* (Salt Lake City: Deseret Book, 2009), 219–25.
9. Shannon, "Consecration in the Sinai Covenant," 83–6.
10. Milgrom, *Leviticus 1–16*, 1079–84; T. Benjamin Spackman, "The Israelite Roots of Atonement Terminology," *BYU Studies Quarterly* 55, no. 1 (2016): 39–64.
11. The Hebrew verb that "atone" translates (Q/P/R) appears 101 times in the Hebrew Bible, but it is not always translated using "atone" or variants in the KJV. For example, it is translated as "purge" in Psalm 79:9 and Proverbs 16:6. It is translated as "forgave" in Psalm 78:38.
12. On Jesus's Jewish background see Trevan G. Hatch, *A Stranger in Jerusalem* (Eugene, OR: Wipf and Stock, 2019); Geza Vermes, *Jesus the Jew: A Historian's Readings of the Gospel* (Minneapolis: Fortress Press, 1981); Daniel Boyarin, *The Jewish Gospels*; David Daube, *The New Testament and Rabbinic Judaism* (Peabody, MA: Hendrickson, 1956). On the

background of Jesus and his specific teachings about how to teach the law of Moses, see Philip Sigal, *The Halakhah of Jesus of Nazareth According to the Gospel of Matthew* (Atlanta: Society of Biblical Literature, 2007).

13. Paul's relationship to the law and to Judaism is a fairly fraught question. As with Jesus, scholarly opinion on Paul's position vis-à-vis Judaism and the law of Moses runs the gamut from being a Torah-faithful Jew to rejecting Judaism entirely in favor of the new religious system. The New Testament presents a fairly nuanced version of Paul's relationship to the systems of the law of Moses. For a perspective that focuses on Paul's essential Jewishness, see Kimberly Ambrose, *Jew Among Jews: Rehabilitating Paul* (Eugene, OR: Wipf and Stock, 2015). See also David Nirenberg, *Anti-Judaism: the Western Tradition* (New York: W. W. Norton, 2013), 53–66.

14. Jeffrey R. Chadwick, "What Jesus Taught the Jews About the Law of Moses" in *The Life and Teachings of Jesus Christ*, volume 2: *From the Transfiguration through the Triumphal Entry*, ed. Richard Neitzel Holzapfel and Thomas A. Wayment (Salt Lake City: Deseret, 2006), 176–207.

15. Hebrew "anointed one," referring to the specific ceremony involved in the creation of the ancient Israelite king. See 1 Samuel 10:1 and the poetic parallelism in 1 Samuel 2:10.

16. This statement needs to be nuanced a little bit. In the initial translation of the Book of Mormon, an angel reveals to Nephi the name of Jesus Christ in what is now 1 Nephi 12:18. In preparation for the publication of the 1837 edition, Joseph Smith edited "Jesus Christ" to say "Messiah." Royal Skousen suggests that "Jesus Christ" should be maintained, since he sees 2 Nephi 25:18 as referring back to 1 Nephi 12:18. This observation is legitimate, but it does not explain why Jacob then needs to be told by an angel in 2 Nephi 10:3. This observation also does not diminish the relative prominence of titles such as Redeemer or Messiah in the small plates relative to the rest of the Book of Mormon. If Skousen is right, this simply shows that even the revelation of the name Jesus Christ through Nephi$_1$ does not make the name universal among the Nephites. See Royal Skousen, *Analysis of Textual Variants of the Book of Mormon: Part One, 1 Nephi 1–2 Nephi 10*, The Book of Mormon Critical Text Project, vol. 4 (Provo, UT: FARMS, 2004), 259.

17. As an example of this, the title *Messiah* appears thirty times in the small plates, but only twice in Mormon's abridgement (and both of those examples are quoting Moses). These are Mosiah 13:33 and Helaman 8:13.

18. See the discussion in Roland de Vaux, *Ancient Israel: Its Life and Institutions*, trans. John McHugh (New York: McGraw-Hill, 1961), 103–6; Marinus de Jonge, "Christ," *Dictionary of Deities and Demons* (Leiden: Brill, 1999),192–200, discussion of the Old Testament notion of Messiah at 193–4; David Rolph Seely and Jo Ann H. Seely, "Jesus the Messiah: Prophet, Priest and King," in *Jesus Christ: Son of God, Savior*, ed. Paul H. Peterson, Gary L. Hatch, and Laura D. Card (Provo, UT: Religious Studies Center, Brigham Young University, 2002), 248–69, discussion of anointing kings on pages 252–53. This kingly definition means, among other things, that Lehi could be construed as preaching treason against Zedekiah in 1 Nephi 1 by promising the coming of another king.

19. For discussions of this prophecy, see RoseAnn Benson and Joseph Fielding McConkie, "A Prophet . . . like unto Thee," *Religious Educator* 12, no. 3 (2011): 109–27; "'A Prophet like Moses' (Deuteronomy 18:15–18) in the Bible, Book of Mormon, and the Dead Sea Scrolls," *Interpreter: A Journal of Latter-day Saint Faith and Scholarship* 41 (2020): 266–80, originally published as David R. Seely, "'A Prophet like Moses' (Deuteronomy 18:15–18) in the Book of Mormon, the Bible, and the Dead Sea Scrolls," in *"To Seek the Law of the Lord": Essays in Honor of John W. Welch*, ed. Paul Y. Hoskisson and Daniel C. Peterson (Orem, UT: The Interpreter Foundation, 2017), 359–74.
20. See Jeffrey Stackert, *A Prophet Like Moses: Prophecy, Law, and Israelite Religion* (Oxford: Oxford University Press, 2014), 36–69, 136–40; Benson and McConkie, "Prophet . . . like unto Thee," 110–11.
21. See Richard Neitzel Holzapfel, Dana M. Pike, and David Rolph Seely, *Jehovah and the World of the Old Testament* (Salt Lake City: Deseret Book, 2009), 219–25.
22. Jacob's teachings and writings are pervaded with ideas and doctrine coming out of the law of Moses. Avram R. Shannon, "'After Whose Order?': Kingship and Priesthood in the Book of Mormon," *BYU Studies Quarterly* 60, no. 4 (2021): 75–91, discussion on pages 80–82.
23. See, for example, Leviticus 1:1-4.
24. See Brandt, "The Name *Jesus Christ*," 201–2.
25. In 2 Nephi 25:25, Nephi$_1$ makes the statement that the law had become dead to the Nephites, but this seems to be less a statement against the law, and more an acknowledgement of their living it in connection with their expectation of Jesus. Although it is not recorded in the Book of Mormon, Nephi$_1$'s use of fulfilled in 25:24 shows that the Nephites have been given the understanding that some of the ritual portions of the law will be ended.
26. For a discussion of Sherem and the legal issues in his interaction with Jacob, see John W. Welch, *The Legal Cases in the Book of Mormon* (Provo, UT: Brigham Young University Press and Neal A. Maxwell Institute for Religious Scholarship, 2008), 107–38.
27. There is a discussion and overview of previous scholarship in A. Keith Thompson, "Who was Sherem?" *Interpreter: A Journal of Mormon Scripture* 14 (2015): 1–15. Thompson argues that Sherem was a member of the original Lehite party whose identity Jacob has suppressed.
28. John W. Welch, *Legal Cases in the Book of Mormon*, 109–11.
29. There is some evidence that Benjamin read from at least Jacob's work, although we do not know what that looked like or whether Benjamin shared that with others. John Hilton III, "Jacob's Textual Legacy," *Journal of Book of Mormon and Restoration Scripture* 22, no. 2 (2013): 52–65. Hilton does an excellent job showing places where language that first appears in Jacob again appears in Benjamin's speech, but without the plates it remains difficult to say much about Benjamin's source for Jacob. It is possible, for example, that the allusions to Jacob found in Benjamin's speech could come from the large plates. It is clear from the angelic revelation that the knowledge of Jesus Christ was not general among the Nephites in Benjamin's day.

30. See also 1 Nephi 11:13–33. According to the earliest versions of the Book of Mormon, Nephi learns Jesus Christ's name through angelic revelation in 1 Nephi 12:18. See the discussion in note 16. Either way, Nephi's vision is also based on law of Moses ideas, which is made clear from his constant reference to the "Lamb of God."
31. See Helaman 5:9, recalling Helaman teaching his sons to remember the words of King Benjamin teaching how salvation comes "only through the atoning blood of Jesus Christ." This is especially of note because Helaman names his sons Nephi$_2$ and Lehi$_2$, showing his knowledge and reverence for his ancestors, while still basing his knowledge of Christ dating from Benjamin's speech. (Note that not just Jesus Christ was retained, but also Christ's connection with the law of Moses.)
32. Alma$_1$ is nineteen years older than Mosiah and is a "young man" when he hears the words of Abinadi (Mosiah 17:2). See Hilton, "Abinadi's Legacy," 107–8.
33. Omni 1:27–30.
34. See John A. Tvedtnes, *The Most Correct Book: Insights from a Book of Mormon Scholar* (Salt Lake City: Cornerstone Publishing, 1999), 323–4; Brant Gardner, *Second Witness: Enos through Mosiah* (Salt Lake City: Greg Kofford Books), 260. Abinadi is able to quote from memory the beginning of the Ten Commandments, showing a deep familiarity with scripture that in the ancient world only priests would have.
35. After the death of Noah, the temple retains its importance, and Limhi summons his people to the temple in Mosiah 7:17.
36. Hugh Nibley described the people as having "well-nigh forgotten" the doctrine of the coming of Christ. Hugh Nibley, *An Approach to the Book of Mormon* (Provo, UT: Foundation for Ancient Research and Mormon Studies, 1988), 121.
37. When Limhi tells Ammon$_1$ about everything that has transpired among the people of Zeniff, he notes that Abinadi prophesied about the coming of Christ and was killed for saying that Christ is God (Mosiah 7:26–27). Since this is precisely what Nephi$_1$ taught, this shows that the people of Zeniff did not accept this. The fact that Abinadi actually reveals the name of Christ in 15:21 suggests that they were unaware of it.
38. Grant Hardy, *Understanding the Book of Mormon: A Reader's Guide* (Oxford: Oxford University Press), 157–60.
39. Like Benjamin, Abinadi uses other words before coming to the revelation of the specific name of Christ. Abinadi prefers "God himself."
40. Welch, *Legal Cases in the Book of Mormon*, 200.
41. Kerry Hull discusses the founding of the Nephite church and compares it with the experience in the New Testament. See Kerry M. Hull, "Two Case Studies on the Development of the Concept of Religion: The New Testament and the Book of Mormon," *Religious Educator* 17, no. 1 (2016): 40–63.
42. Mosiah 18:1 makes it clear that the teachings of the church founded by Alma$_1$ were based on what he had heard from Abinadi. Alma$_2$ bases his teachings on what he learned from his father, making the teachings of the church of Christ from Alma$_1$ to Jesus firmly rooted in the teachings of Abinadi before Noah and his priests.

43. Aaron is one of the few individuals in the Book of Mormon who use the priestly word "atonement" to describe Jesus Christ's saving work in his preaching in Alma 21:9. The others are Lehi$_1$, Nephi$_1$, Jacob, Benjamin, Abinadi, Alma$_2$, Anti-Nephi-Lehi, Amulek, Helaman$_2$ (quoting Benjamin), and Mormon.
44. Aaron seems to quote Abinadi in Alma 22:12–13. See Hilton, "Abinadi's Legacy," 101–2.
45. Shannon, "Kingship and Priesthood," 84–5.
46. For a discussion of the Psalms in the Book of Mormon broadly, see John Hilton III, "Old Testament Psalms in the Book of Mormon," in *Ascending the Mountain of the Lord: Temple, Praise, and Worship in the Old Testament* (2013 Sperry Symposium), ed. Jeffrey R. Chadwick, Matthew J. Grey, and David Rolph Seely (Provo, UT: Religious Studies Center, Brigham Young University; Salt Lake City: Deseret Book, 2013), 291–311.
47. Hardy, *Understanding the Book of Mormon*, 193–4.

9

The Redeemer
Taking upon Him the Sins of the World

Jennifer C. Lane

The biblical identification of the Lord Jehovah as the Redeemer of Israel and the redemption of Israel in the event of the Exodus are foundational for Book of Mormon prophets.[1] They knew that the covenant between Jehovah and the patriarchs created a family relationship in which he became the *gō 'ēl*, or kinsman-redeemer, of Israel (see Exodus 6:3–6).[2] They knew that because the Lord remembered his covenant, he redeemed the Israelites from slavery to the Egyptians (see 1 Nephi 17:40; Deuteronomy 7:8). Their covenant identity gave them confidence that the Lord would remember them when they were in trouble or were separated from God.[3] They knew that covenants bound them to the Lord and his redeeming power.

In the Exodus, the redemption of Israel came after the destruction of the firstborn, the last of the plagues of Egypt and the one that finally persuaded Pharaoh to let the children of Israel leave their bondage (see Exodus 13:14–16). This redemption was connected to the blood of the lambs that were slain, providing protection for those Israelites who applied that blood to their doorposts and lintels (see Exodus 12:3–7, 12–13). While the Exodus pattern and covenant redemption have been explored, I believe that the connection between redemption and the blood of the Lamb in Book of Mormon teaching needs additional attention. Given the consistent language relating to applying the blood of the Lamb, or Christ, in the Book of Mormon, I believe that the Exodus Passover and then the temple sacrifices as a way for Israel to be redeemed, cleansed, and restored to God's presence was a formative metaphor by which Lehi's descendants understood redemption and the role of the Redeemer, primarily in terms of spiritual redemption.

The Book of Mormon brings together the identity of Christ both as Jehovah, the kinsman-redeemer of Israel, and as the prophesied suffering servant who would act to bring about a new exodus to allow for a redemption of the world from the bondage of sin. The writings of Isaiah, particularly Isaiah 40–55, look ahead to a new, larger scale exodus. These prophecies were critical for the early Christian understanding of Christ, and I believe we see the same understanding in the Book of Mormon prophets.[4]

In the Book of Mormon, the Passover image of applying the blood of the Lamb is understood to have cleansing power. The cleansing made possible by the blood of the Lamb is part of the prophets' understanding of how this spiritual redemption would take place. We will see that they bring in the language of Isaiah 53 to see Christ's redemption coming in his "taking upon himself" the sins of the world, allowing those who applied that sacrifice, his atoning blood, to become clean through him. In this paper I will explore the shift in understanding to a spiritual redemption and survey different phases of this teaching, including early Book of Mormon teachings, Abinadi's witness, Alma and Amulek's witness, and Christ's own witness, and then consider implications for what this redemption imagery can tell us about how to think about Christ's atonement.

Spiritual Reframing of Redemption

In the Book of Mormon, the past redemption of the children of Israel from Egypt was important in shaping their confidence in God's power and disposition to help and is referred to on many occasions (see 1 Nephi 17:23–44; Mosiah 7:19–20; Helaman 8:11–12). But while there are times that people call upon their memory of the Redeemer's acts of deliverance in the past to seek for deliverance from physical bondage, it is striking that the Book of Mormon prophets' teaching about redemption is primarily forward-looking and universal in its effects. Most often the bondage from which people seek redemption is spiritual, characterized as the chains or bonds of hell, of death, of iniquity, or of Satan (see 2 Nephi 1:13; 9:45; 28:19; Mosiah 23:13; 27:29; Alma 5:7; 12:6; 13:30; 26:14; 36:18; 41:11; Mormon 8:31; Moroni 8:14). Sin is bondage, a way of being that we need redemption from to be able to leave.

The Book of Mormon model for redemption draws on the prophecy of Isaiah in which we learn that, as God himself coming to redeem his people, Christ willingly *takes upon himself* the sins and transgressions of the world: "The Lord hath laid on him the iniquity of us all" (Isaiah 53:6). Their understanding of the cleansing power of his blood seems to be tied to his willing intervention to absorb the bitterness of sin that sickens us all. Alma testified, "The Son of God suffereth according to the flesh that he might *take upon him the sins of his people, that he might blot out their transgressions* according to the power of his deliverance" (Alma 7:13; emphasis added). This seems to quote Psalm 51:1–2: "Have mercy upon me, O God, according to thy lovingkindness [*ḥesed*]: according unto the multitude of thy tender mercies *blot out my transgressions*. Wash me throughly from mine iniquity, and cleanse me from my sin" (emphasis added). It is the Lord's *ḥesed*, his covenant love and covenant faithfulness, that the Psalmist relies on to be restored, to be redeemed.[5]

The expression "blotting out" appears many times in the Old Testament and its root has to do with wiping.[6] The verb for "atone" (*kpr*) likewise has at its root the action of wiping off and cleansing.[7] Wiping a liquid with a cloth can erase the liquid, but it is erased only as it is absorbed. The idea that the consequences of what we have done, our sins and transgressions, can be wiped away and erased is a powerful concept, but the verb "blot out" reminds us how that erasing is made possible. Through his vicarious sacrifice, Christ has power to absorb, to "take upon him the sins of his people, that he might blot out their transgressions according to the power of his deliverance" (Alma 7:13). On the Day of Atonement, the blood sprinkled by the high priest on the mercy seat had a cleansing power, redeeming Israel from their uncleanness and separation from God (see Leviticus 16:14–19). In the teachings of Book of Mormon prophets, the blood of the Lamb is shown to have redemptive power for those who choose to apply it through making and keeping covenants.

In the Book of Mormon, the redemption from sin through the blood of the Lamb is tied to the remission of sins. Sinfulness as a state of being is a bondage that we are freed from. This suggests more than just a forgiving nature on God's part, but rather remission of our sins being tied to our leaving the state of sin. "Remission" in the New Testament is *aphesin*, which can be translated as forgiveness but means release from bondage or imprisonment—redemption. As the Messiah, Christ came to fulfill the messianic prophesy, "to proclaim liberty to the captives, and the opening of the prison to them that are bound" (Isaiah 61:1) as he "set at liberty [*aphesin*] them that are bruised" (Luke 4:18).

We see the power of Christ's redeeming blood in the remission of sin in Moroni's closing statement of the Book of Mormon: "If ye by the grace of God are perfect in Christ, and deny not his power, then are ye sanctified in Christ by the grace of God, *through the shedding of the blood of Christ*, which is in the covenant of the Father *unto the remission of your sins*, that ye become holy, without spot" (Moroni 10:33; emphasis added). As part of his covenant relationship with us, we can experience this redemption from sin as, with faith and repentance, we choose to apply the blood of the Lamb and leave the bondage of sin.

Early Book of Mormon Teachings on Christ as the Redeemer of the World

The message that there would come a Redeemer of the world is one of the earliest teachings in the Book of Mormon. In 1 Nephi 1 we learn that Lehi "manifested plainly of the coming of a Messiah, and also the redemption of the world" (1 Nephi 1:19). The term *Messiah* is, of course, the Hebrew equivalent of *Christ*, both meaning "Anointed One." Lehi preaches that this Messiah would be the Redeemer of the world (see 1 Nephi 10:5–6, 14).

Lehi testified of the global need for the Redeemer Messiah, that "all mankind were in a lost and in a fallen state, and ever would be save they should rely on this Redeemer" (1 Nephi 10:6). This frames our condition without a Redeemer as a state of being that is lost and fallen, but we can *choose* to rely on him to experience a change of state. The Messiah is also described as "the Lamb of God, who should take away the sins of the world" (1 Nephi 10:10). As the Lamb of God, he offers redemption from the bondage of sin. Just as the children of Israel applied the blood of the lamb and could leave their bondage, as we rely on our Redeemer and choose to leave a sinful state we are redeemed from sin. We also learn that this Redeemer-Messiah would be slain and rise from the dead (see 1 Nephi 10:11).

At this point Lehi described the Messiah as "the Lord," whose way would be prepared by a prophet who "should baptize the Messiah with water" (1 Nephi 10:9). We do not yet, however, have as full a sense of the Anointed One's relationship to Deity. Later in the chapter, written decades after these events, Nephi explains that his father "spake by the power of the Holy Ghost, which power he received by faith on the Son of God—and the Son of God was the Messiah who should come" (1 Nephi 10:17). Nephi had come to understand that the Redeemer-Messiah of whom his father testified was the Son of God. We can see this revelation coming to Nephi in his own vision recorded in the next chapter.

As Nephi sought to understand his father's teachings, he received further revelation and clarification of who this Redeemer-Messiah would be. While the title *Redeemer* is not used in the vision recorded in 1 Nephi 11–14, Lehi's language of the Redeemer-Messiah who would be slain informs Nephi's vision of the Lamb of God and the meaning of his death. The Spirit who spoke to him asked him if he believed, and then told Nephi that he is blessed "because thou believest in the Son of the most high God" (1 Nephi 11:6). Nephi is told after he beholds the tree that bore the fruit his father tasted that he shall "behold a man descending out of heaven, and him shall ye witness; and after ye have witnessed him ye shall bear record that it is the Son of God" (1 Nephi 11:7). Nephi is given a vision of Christ as an infant and told, "Behold the Lamb of God, yea, even the Son of the Eternal Father!" (1 Nephi 11:21).

Significantly, in the original manuscript and the 1830 edition, the connection between the Lamb of God and Jehovah (the Eternal Father) is even clearer: "Behold the Lamb of God, yea, even the Eternal Father!" This builds on Lehi's teaching that the Messiah would be "the Lamb of God, who should take away the sins of the world" (1 Nephi 10:10). We start to see a vision of Jehovah himself coming down as the Son of God and as the Lamb of God–Redeemer of the world to take away the sins of the world.

After seeing the components of Lehi's dream that Nephi came to understand as representations of the love of God, the angel says, "Look and behold the condescension of God!" (1 Nephi 11:26). The language of "the condescension of God" reinforces the message of the coming down of Jehovah, the Eternal God, to be with his people. At this point Nephi sees Christ going to be baptized, and Nephi beholds him as "the Redeemer of the world, of whom my father had spoken" and repeats the title of "Lamb of God" (1 Nephi 11:27). Given Nephi's personal experience with Jerusalem temple sacrifices and the Passover festival, the cultic resonance of the title *Lamb of God* for the Redeemer is striking.

Nephi articulates a relationship between the "condescension of God" and the redemption of the world that resonates with the redemption model contained in the story of Passover and the temple sacrifices. Throughout this vision, Nephi consistently refers to Christ as "the Lamb of God." It is "the Lamb of God [who goes] forth among the children of men," and the people "were healed by the power of the Lamb of God" (1 Nephi 11:31). Then, finally, Nephi beholds "the Lamb of God, that he was taken by the people; yea, the Son of the everlasting God was judged of the world; and I saw and bear record. And I, Nephi, saw that he was lifted up upon the cross and slain for the sins of the world" (1 Nephi 11:32–33).

Nephi sees in vision what his father had taught. Lehi had testified that the Messiah was "the Lamb of God, who should take away the sins of the world" (1 Nephi 10:10) and that he would be slain and rise from the dead (see 1 Nephi 10:11). Lehi gave the critical doctrinal background to see the need for spiritual redemption: that "all mankind were in a lost and in a fallen state, and ever would be save they should rely on this Redeemer" (1 Nephi 10:6).

Lehi's language of the Redeemer-Messiah who would be slain explains the redemption made possible by the Lamb of God being "lifted up upon the cross and slain for the sins of the world" (1 Nephi 11:33). Nephi also learns from the angel that application of the blood of the Lamb makes one's garments white, representing a righteous state: "Because of their faith in the Lamb of God their garments are made white in his blood" (1 Nephi 12:10; see also verse 11). In

Nephi's vision we see a Redeemer-Messiah who is both the Eternal Father and the Son of God. As the Lamb of God, he is "slain for the sins of the world," and we learn that the blood of the Lamb has a cleansing effect. This model of the blood of the Lamb as the means for redemption from sin will be part of the ongoing revelations in the Book of Mormon.

Understanding these critical truths, Nephi works to persuade his brothers to "remember the Lord their Redeemer" (1 Nephi 19:18). Seeking to "more fully persuade them to believe in the Lord their Redeemer [Nephi] did read unto them that which was written by the prophet Isaiah" (1 Nephi 19:23). In these chapters from Isaiah, the Lord is repeatedly referred to as the Redeemer, the Holy One of Israel (see 1 Nephi 20:17; 21:7, 26). While neither Nephi nor Jacob quote Isaiah 53, that chapter's vision of how the Redeemer offers redemption from sin will be particularly important for later prophets. Nephi explains that as the Lord God fulfills his covenants, the house of Israel "shall be brought out of obscurity and out of darkness; and they shall *know that the Lord is their Savior and their Redeemer*, the Mighty One of Israel" (1 Nephi 22:12; emphasis added). Knowing that the Lord is the Redeemer is key to understanding the importance of the witness that "Jesus is the Christ, the Eternal God" (Book of Mormon title page).

Both Lehi and Nephi testify of the Redeemer of the world who would come. Lehi says he knows that Jacob is "redeemed, because of the righteousness of thy Redeemer; for thou hast beheld that in the fulness of time he cometh to bring salvation unto men" (2 Nephi 2:3). The Redeemer comes to bring salvation and that salvation includes redemption from sin to those who trust and repent, even before his coming. Lehi teaches Jacob, "Redemption cometh in and through the Holy Messiah; for he is full of grace and truth. Behold, he offereth himself a sacrifice for sin, to answer the ends of the law, unto all those who have a broken heart and a contrite spirit; and unto none else can the ends of the law be answered" (2 Nephi 2:6–7).[8] The Redeemer's sacrifice is the means for redemption from sin, if received and applied.

By framing the redemption offered by the Holy Messiah as him *offering himself as a sacrifice for sin*, Lehi reinforces the sacrificial identification of the Redeemer-Messiah as the Lamb of God. Lehi emphasizes redemption's global reach: "The Messiah cometh in the fulness of time, that he may redeem the children of men from the fall. And because that they are redeemed from the fall they have become free forever, knowing good from evil; to act for themselves and not to be acted upon, save it be by the punishment of the law at the great and last day, according to the commandments which God hath given" (2 Nephi 2:26). As the Redeemer of the world, Christ reverses the effects of the Fall and puts all in a position to choose for themselves.

The redemption from the Fall is universal, but redemption from sin is to be sought out personally. Nephi seeks for redemption from his own sins: "O Lord, wilt thou redeem my soul? Wilt thou deliver me out of the hands of mine enemies? Wilt thou make me that I may shake at the appearance of sin?" (2 Nephi 4:31). Redemption here is equated with deliverance, with a particular focus on a change of nature. "May the gates of hell be shut continually before me, because that my heart is broken and my spirit is contrite!" (2 Nephi 4:32). By the end of his writings, Nephi can say, "I glory in my Jesus, for he hath redeemed my soul from hell" (2 Nephi 33:6).

Abinadi's Witness

Some of the Book of Mormon's most striking statements about the Redeemer as the condescending God coming to redeem his covenant people by providing an offering for sin are found in the teachings of Abinadi.[9] His teachings are spurred by the question of the priests of King Noah about the meaning of the passage in Isaiah 52 referring to the Lord comforting his people and redeeming Jerusalem (see Mosiah 12:20–24).

Abinadi first emphasizes the need for keeping covenants to receive the blessings of redemption from sin, something that the priests and King Noah were not doing. After repeating the covenant expectations laid out in the Decalogue, Abinadi stresses that the law alone could not save. He testifies of the condescension of God to come as the Redeemer: "Were it not for the atonement, which God himself shall make for the sins and iniquities of his people, ... they must unavoidably perish, notwithstanding the law of Moses" (Mosiah 13:28). God shall make atonement with an offering as the priests do, but *he himself* shall be the offering. He himself shall bear the sins and iniquities of his people.

Abinadi argues that Moses and the prophets have said, "God himself should come down among the children of men, and *take upon him* the form of man, and go forth in mighty power upon the face of the earth" (Mosiah 13:34; emphasis added). At this point, Abinadi quotes Isaiah 53 to explain how redemption from sin comes: "He has *borne* our griefs, and *carried* our sorrows; yet we did esteem him stricken, smitten of God, and afflicted. But he was wounded for our transgressions, he was bruised for our iniquities; the chastisement of our peace was *upon him*; and with his stripes we are healed" (Mosiah 14:4–5; emphasis added); the Lord shall "make his soul *an offering for sin*" (Mosiah 14:10; emphasis added), "he shall *bear* their iniquities," and he "*bore* the sins of many" (Mosiah 14:11–12; emphasis added).

After quoting Isaiah 53, Abinadi interprets this passage, declaring, "I would that ye should understand that God himself shall come down among the children of men, and *shall redeem his people*" (Mosiah 15:1; emphasis added). Using the language of Isaiah 53, Abinadi looks ahead to see the redemption of the covenant people, that the Lord had "*taken upon himself* their iniquity and their transgressions, *having redeemed them*" (Mosiah 15:9; emphasis added). Abinadi's connection between the Lord taking upon himself transgressions and the redemption that this makes possible are reiterated later by both Alma and Amulek (see Alma 7:11–13; Alma 11:40; Alma 34:8).

Redemption as release from bondage can be seen in Abinadi's teaching that Christ took upon him human sin to allow people to leave the bondage of sin: "these are they whose sins he has *borne*; these are they for whom he has died, *to redeem them from their transgressions*" (Mosiah 15:12). Abinadi emphasizes that redemption only happens for those who choose to leave the bondage of sin through making and keeping covenants, for "he that persists in his own carnal nature, and goes on in the ways of sin and rebellion against God, remaineth in his fallen state . . . [and] is as though there was no redemption made" (Mosiah 16:5).

Alma Teaching the People of Shiblon

Like Abinadi, Alma draws from the language of Isaiah 53 to explain the scope of the redemption that Christ offers. Alma explains, "He will *take upon him* the pains and the sicknesses of his people. And he will *take upon him* death, that he may loose the bands of death which bind his people; and he will *take upon him* their infirmities, that his bowels may be filled with mercy, according to the flesh, that he may know according to the flesh how to succor his people according to their infirmities" (Alma 7:11–12; emphasis added). Christ's suffering was not just for sin.

In giving this witness, Alma testifies that Christ "shall go forth, suffering pains and afflictions and temptations of every kind, . . . *that the word might be fulfilled* which saith he will take upon him the pains and the sicknesses of his people" (Alma 7:11; emphasis added). The prophetic "word" that Christ fulfills seems to be Isaiah 53. A closer translation from the Hebrew gives us the exact language of Alma's expression: "It was our sicknesses that He Himself bore, and our pains that He carried" (Isaiah 53:4 NASB).[10] Just as we saw in Abinadi's teaching, this language from Isaiah about the messianic suffering servant *bearing* and *carrying* our sicknesses and pains provides a scriptural root for Alma's language of Christ taking upon him our pains and sicknesses.

This language of taking upon him not only emphasizes the beautiful truth that Christ understands our pain and sickness but can also help us see how God provides a *way* for the redemption of humans from the bondage of sin. Alma states some results as certain: "He will take upon him death," and "he will take upon him their infirmities" (Alma 7:12). In addition to the things that he *will* take upon him, Alma *also* testifies that "the Son of God suffereth according to the flesh that he *might* take upon him the sins of his people, that he *might* blot out their transgressions according to the power of his deliverance" (Alma 7:13; emphasis added). The conditional nature of redemption from sin is a consistent aspect of the Book of Mormon redemption model. One must choose to apply the blood of the Lamb to leave the captivity of one's fallen state to become righteous, prepared to enter God's presence.

Amulek Teaching the People of Ammonihah and the Zoramites

Amulek uses the same language connected to Isaiah 53. He teaches Zeezrom that the Son of God "is the very Eternal Father of heaven and of earth, and all things which in them are; he is the beginning and the end, the first and the last; and he *shall come into the world to redeem his people*; and he shall *take upon him the transgressions* of those who believe on his name" (Alma 11:39–40; emphasis added). Like Abinadi and Alma, Amulek stresses that redemption from sin is conditional. It is tied to both Christ taking transgressions upon himself and individuals believing on his name, choosing to exercise faith and repent. "Therefore the wicked remain as though there had been no redemption made, except it be the loosing of the bands of death" (Alma 11:41).

Amulek later uses the same Isaiah-influenced language while teaching the Zoramites. He refers to Alma's quoting of Zenos, "that *redemption* cometh through the Son of God" (Alma 34:7; emphasis added), and confirms this, saying, "I do know that Christ shall come among the children of men, to *take upon him the transgressions* of his people, and that he shall atone for the sins of the world; for the Lord God hath spoken it" (Alma 34:8; emphasis added). Just as Isaiah taught that Christ would be "an offering for sin" (or *asham*, guilt offering), Amulek witnesses that Christ will come to "atone for the sins of the world" and that this infinite atonement is possible because "that great and last sacrifice will be the Son of God, yea, infinite and eternal" (Alma 34:14). The condition of humans is that "all are fallen and are lost, and must perish except it be through the atonement which it is expedient should be made" (Alma 34:9).

Amulek stresses that the gift of Christ's atoning blood is offered to all: "it must be an infinite and eternal sacrifice" (Alma 34:10), but he explains that while Christ atones for the sins of the world, he takes "upon him the transgressions of *his people*," those who choose to become his through covenant. The purpose of this sacrifice of Jehovah's own self will be to "bring salvation to all those who *shall believe on his name*; this being the intent of this last sacrifice, to bring about the bowels of mercy, which overpowereth justice, and bringeth about means unto men that they may have faith unto repentance" (Alma 34:15; emphasis added). Christ's vicarious atonement provides the *means* for all humans to have faith unto repentance and unto redemption, leaving the bondage of sin. Whether people use these means and apply his atoning blood is left to each to decide.

Alma's Teaching to the Zoramites

Alma also speaks to a people who did not believe in Christ and the need for redemption through him. Alma responds to their question about "in what manner they should begin to exercise their faith" (Alma 33:1) by quoting scriptures that emphasized the role of the Son in God's mercy: "It is because of thy Son that thou hast been thus merciful unto me, therefore I will cry unto thee in all mine afflictions, for in thee is my joy; for thou hast turned thy judgments away from me, because of thy Son" (Alma 33:11).

Alma then clearly lays out the Redeemer as the Son of God as the seed or word that they should plant in their hearts: "Begin to believe in the Son of God, that he will *come to redeem his people, and that he shall suffer and die to atone for their sins*; and that he shall rise again from the dead, which shall bring to pass the resurrection, that all men shall stand before him, to be judged at the last and judgment day, according to their works" (Alma 33:22; emphasis added).[11] Alma emphasizes that the Son of God "will come to redeem his people" and "shall suffer and die to atone for their sins." The redemption of his covenant people is made possible by his atoning suffering and death.

Christ's Witness of His Redeeming Sacrifice

When Christ appeared at the temple in Bountiful, he echoes the language from Isaiah that we have seen throughout the Book of Mormon. He declares that he "glorified the Father in *taking upon me* the sins of the world" (3 Nephi 11:11; emphasis added). This exact phrase appears elsewhere in the Book of Mormon, and again it comes directly from the voice of Jehovah. To Alma he taught, "It is I that *taketh upon me* the sins of the world" (Mosiah 26:23).

I believe that this first-person witness of his taking upon himself the sins of the world is a crucial lens through which we can understand the apostolic witness that "He gave His life to atone for the sins of all mankind. His was a great vicarious gift in behalf of all who would ever live upon the earth."[12] Christ took our sins upon himself. On our behalf, he was a victor over sin and death. He gave his life to atone for the sins of all people so we can repent and be redeemed as we receive that gift.

As Lehi taught, "All mankind were in a lost and in a fallen state, and ever would be save they should rely on this Redeemer" (1 Nephi 10:6). Christ is the Redeemer of Israel. He is *"the God of Israel, and the God of the whole earth,"* who was "slain for the sins of the world" (3 Nephi 11:14). As a faithful Son, accomplishing the Father's plan of redemption, Christ drank out of the bitter cup. Rather than leaving us to suffer the bitterness of our choices, in his atoning sacrifice Christ absorbed the consequences that belonged to us as well as the injustices that never should have been ours. All that we have done that we regret creates a very bitter cup. He says to us, in the words of Isaiah: "Thus saith thy Lord the Lord, and thy God that pleadeth the cause of his people, Behold, I have taken out of thine hand the cup of trembling, even the dregs of the cup of my fury; thou shalt no more drink it again" (Isaiah 51:22). He was willing to absorb that immensity of sin and iniquity by taking it upon himself, drinking our bitter cup to give us a fresh start, to wipe our slate clean.

Redemption through Applying Christ's Atoning Blood

With this perspective on *how* Christ redeems us by taking upon himself our sins, we can better understand the other statements about his atoning sacrifice throughout the Book of Mormon. The additional prophetic witnesses in the Book of Mormon that he atones for the sins of the world, takes away the sins of the world, and is slain for the sins of the world can best be understood in light of the redemption he offers as the Lamb of God.

Because redemption is deliverance from captivity through the payment of a ransom price, only those who choose to receive this ransom price and leave sin behind are freed. His was a great vicarious gift on behalf of all who would ever live upon the earth, but we must choose to receive that gift through our faith, repentance, and making and keeping covenants.

Understanding Christ's death as a sacrificial offering that can free us by his *taking upon himself* our sins helps us see the purpose and meaning of him being "lifted up upon the cross and *slain for the sins of the world*" (1 Nephi 11:32–33; emphasis added). The importance of this doctrine that his death was for the sins of the world can be seen in its denial by Korihor: "Ye say also that he shall be *slain for the sins of the world*" (Alma 30:26; emphasis added). Christ himself emphasizes that his death was for our redemption: "I am the God of Israel, and the God of the whole earth, and have been *slain for the sins of the world*" (3 Nephi 11:14; emphasis added). By applying his atoning blood, we can become clean and experience redemption from the bondage of a state of sin.

Conclusion: Our Need to Be Willing to Be Redeemed

With its powerful witness of Christ as our Redeemer, the Book of Mormon gives a vision of sin as bondage and stresses that Christ took our sins upon him so that we *could* be cleansed and sanctified, leaving the captivity of sin. His atoning sacrifice is universal, but our individual redemption is conditional on our willingness to accept and apply his redeeming blood. While providing for those who do not fully have personal accountability, the Book of Mormon redemption model consistently emphasizes personal agency in applying the atoning blood of Christ (see 2 Nephi 9:25–26; Mosiah 3:11, 16; Moroni 8:8–12).

Many Book of Mormon prophets stress the need to have our garments be made white through the application of the blood of the Lamb. This imagery may point to how the high priest dressed in white, carrying the blood of the sacrificial offering, could enter the presence of the Lord in the Holy of Holies on the Day of Atonement (see Leviticus 16:4–19; Hebrews 9:7). Likewise, through the blood of the Lamb, one's state can be changed from fallen to righteous so that one can enter God's presence (see Alma 13:11–12; 34:36; Mormon 9:6; Ether 13:10–11). The consistent message is that as an offering for sin, Christ took upon him the sins of the world so that we can have faith, repent, and make and keep covenants, to be redeemed and enter the Lord's presence.

Without the change and cleansing made possible by applying Christ's atoning blood, we are in the condition described by Lehi: "All mankind were in a lost and in a fallen state, and ever would be save they should rely on this Redeemer" (1 Nephi 10:6). Sin is a state of being that prophets compare to captivity and bondage. Lehi warns his sons to leave this state of captivity: "Awake from a deep sleep, yea, even from the sleep of hell, and shake off the awful chains by which ye are bound, which are the chains which bind the children of men, that they are carried away captive down to the eternal gulf of misery and woe" (2 Nephi 1:13).

Alma describes his own repentance as redemption from a state of bondage: "My soul hath been redeemed from the gall of bitterness and bonds of iniquity" (Mosiah 27:29). He shares that the Lord told him that redemption refers to a change of state: "Marvel not that all mankind, yea, men and women, all nations, kindreds, tongues and people, must be born again; yea, born of God, *changed from their carnal and fallen state*, to a state of righteousness, *being redeemed of God*, becoming his sons and daughters" (Mosiah 27:25; emphasis added). Our need for redemption from a state of bondage is stressed, as Alma explains to Corianton that "all men that are in a state of nature, or I would say, in a carnal state, are in the gall of bitterness and in the bonds of iniquity; they are without God in the world, and they have gone contrary to the nature of God; therefore, they are in a state contrary to the nature of happiness" (Alma 41:11).

Christ took our sins upon him so that we could be free to choose to leave the captivity of that way of being. Being sinful intrinsically separates us from God's presence and by its nature is a state of suffering. As Elder Dale G. Renlund has taught, "In the scriptures, getting off the path is referred to as sin, and the resultant decrease in happiness and forfeited blessings is called punishment. In this sense, God is not punishing us; punishment is a consequence of our own choices, not His."[13] What Elder Renlund describes is exactly what we see in the Book of Mormon. Sin is a state of bondage and separation from God. Christ's suffering offers a redemption from that state of sin. Christ takes our sins upon him so that we can leave them behind, being redeemed from sin.

Many contemporary atonement theories argue that there is no need for Christ to suffer for God to forgive us.[14] The Book of Mormon helps to show how God's forgiving us alone would not be enough to solve our problem because that would not change our state. We need redemption through the blood of the Lamb, to become "saint[s] through the atonement of Christ the

Lord" (Mosiah 3:19). King Benjamin's witness is summarized in Helaman's teachings to his sons: "There is no other way nor means whereby man can be saved, only through the atoning blood of Jesus Christ, who shall come; yea, remember that he cometh to redeem the world" (Helaman 5:9).

We experience redemption as we choose to apply the atoning blood of Christ. Our garments are made clean, and our souls become pure as we leave behind the bondage of a sinful state. Helaman taught this as he reiterated Amulek's teaching, "The Lord surely should come to redeem his people, but that he should not come to redeem them in their sins, but to redeem them from their sins" (Helaman 5:10). Redemption requires the atoning blood of Christ, but it also requires our agency. We choose redemption when we choose to exercise faith and repent. Christ "hath power given unto him from the Father to redeem them from their sins because of repentance" (Helaman 5:11). Knowing that Christ has taken upon him our sins and iniquities can give us the faith and the desire to leave sin behind. This faith will lead to our making and keeping covenants, through which we leave the bondage of sin and become prepared to enter the presence of the Lord.

Starting with Lehi's teaching of a Redeemer of the world who could deliver humans from their lost and fallen state (see 1 Nephi 10:5–6), the Book of Mormon has a consistent redemption model that focuses on being redeemed from sin. From Nephi's vision to Moroni's closing remarks, the means of that redemption is shown to be the application of the blood of the Lamb. People must choose to apply it to themselves to have "their garments ... made white in his blood" (1 Nephi 12:10) and to be "sanctified in Christ ... through the shedding of the blood of Christ" (Moroni 10:33).

In the words of President Gordon B. Hinckley, "He has done for each of us and for all mankind that which none other could have done. God be thanked for the gift of His Beloved Son, our Savior, the Redeemer of the world, the Lamb without blemish who was offered as a sacrifice for all mankind."[15] The Redeemer has power to redeem, having taken upon him "the sins of the world" (3 Nephi 11:11), but we must individually choose to receive that redemption by applying his atoning blood.

Jennifer C. Lane *is a Neal A. Maxwell Research Associate at the Maxwell Institute for Religious Scholarship and a professor emerita at Brigham Young University–Hawaii.*

Notes

1. Important studies of Exodus imagery in the Book of Mormon include George S. Tate, "The Typology of the Exodus Pattern in the Book of Mormon," in *Literature of Belief: Sacred Scripture and Religious Experience*, ed. Neal E. Lambert (Provo, UT: Religious Studies Center, Brigham Young University, 1981), 245–62, and S. Kent Brown, "The Exodus Pattern in the Book of Mormon," in *From Jerusalem to Zarahemla: Literary and Historical Studies of the Book of Mormon* (Provo, UT: Religious Studies Center, Brigham Young University, 1998), 75–98.
2. I discuss this background in more depth in "The Lord Will Redeem His People: Adoptive Covenant and Redemption in the Old Testament," in *Sperry Symposium Classics: The Old Testament*, ed. Paul Y. Hoskisson (Provo, UT: Religious Studies Center, Brigham Young University; Salt Lake City: Deseret Book, 2005), 298–310. Benjamin Spackman also gives a helpful development of the kinship dimension of covenant and redemption with references to more recent scholarship in "The Israelite Roots of Atonement Terminology," *BYU Studies Quarterly* 55, no. 1 (2016): 51–57.
3. It may be argued that this is a key thesis of the Book of Mormon: "Which is to show unto the remnant of the house of Israel what great things the Lord hath done for their fathers; and that they may know the covenants of the Lord, that they are not cast off forever" (title page; see also 1 Nephi 15:14, 19:15). As Nephi says, "But behold, I, Nephi, will show unto you that the tender mercies of the Lord are over all those whom he hath chosen, because of their faith, to make them mighty even unto the power of deliverance" (1 Nephi 1:20).
4. See Richard Bauckham, *Jesus and the God of Israel: God Crucified and Other Studies on the New Testament's Christology of Divine Identity* (Grand Rapids, MI: Eerdmans, 2008), 52, and N. T. Wright, *The Day the Revolution Began: Reconsidering the Meaning of Jesus's Crucifixion* (New York: HarperOne, 2016), 326–27.
5. We see the covenant love and loyalty that Jehovah, as the kinsman-redeemer, has towards his people in his actions of redemption. Redemption is an act of *ḥesed*, "which [*ḥesed* acts] may be described as a beneficent action performed, in the context of a deep and enduring commitment between two persons or parties, by one who is able to render assistance to the needy party who in the circumstances is unable to help him- or herself." Gordon R. Clark, *The Word Hesed in the Hebrew Bible*, Journal for the Study of the Old Testament Supplement Series 157. (Sheffield, England: JSOT Press, 1993), 267.
6. Francis Brown, S. R. Driver, and Charles Briggs, "*machah* wipe or wipe out," in *A Hebrew and English Lexicon of the Old Testament* (Oxford: Clarendon Press, 1996), 562.
7. "The lid of the Ark was called *kapporet*, a noun that derives from the verb *k-p-r*, 'to wipe clean, purify,' hence 'to expiate,' because it was God's seat of mercy whence atonement was

granted." Baruch A. Levine, *The JPS Torah Commentary: Leviticus* (Philadelphia: Jewish Publication Society, 1989), 100.

8. Lehi frames this atoning sacrifice for our redemption as stemming from the very essence of who God is, full of "grace and truth," very likely a translation of *ḥesed v emmet*, covenant love and faithfulness, the way in which Jehovah described himself to Moses when he appeared to him in Exodus 34:6. See Anthony Hanson, "John i.14–18 and Exodus xxxiv," *New Testament Studies* 23 (1976): 90–101.

9. An excellent contextualization of Abinadi's teachings and his use of Isaiah 52 and 53 is offered in Daniel L. Belnap, "The Abinadi Narrative, Redemption, and the Struggle of Nephite Identity," in *Abinadi: He Came Among Them in Disguise*, ed. Shon D. Hopkin (Provo, UT: Religious Studies Center; Salt Lake City: Deseret Book, 2018), 27–66. He notes, "Having placed the context of Isaiah 52 in line with all other prophets, including Moses, Abinadi now establishes what redemption really is—the granting of eternal life" (44).

10. I am grateful to Matthew Bowen for this insight.

11. A helpful examination of this expression as the summary of the Nephite profession of faith in Alma's day is found in John W. Welch, "Ten Testimonies of Jesus Christ from the Book of Mormon" in *A Book of Mormon Treasury: Gospel Insights from General Authorities and Religious Educators* (Provo, UT: Religious Studies Center, Brigham Young University, 2003), 316–42.

12. "The Living Christ: The Testimony of the Apostles," *Ensign*, April 2000, 2.

13. Dale G. Renlund, "Choose You This Day," *Ensign*, November 2018, 105–6.

14. See, for example, Brad Jersak and Michael Hardin, eds., *Stricken by God? Nonviolent Identification and the Victory of Christ* (Grand Rapids, MI: Eerdmans, 2008).

15. Gordon B. Hinckley, "A Season for Gratitude," *Ensign*, December 1997, 4.

10

Book of Mormon "Trinitarianism" and the Nature of Jesus Christ
Old and New World Contexts

STEPHEN O. SMOOT AND KERRY HULL

Readers of the Book of Mormon are sure to encounter what they may be tempted to call "trinitarian" depictions of the relationship between God the Father, Jesus Christ, and the Holy Ghost.[1] It is understandable why the text might leave this impression. Several passages in the Book of Mormon, after all, do in fact speak of the Father, Son, and Holy Spirit as being "one God." At the end of his record, Nephi bore testimony how "there is none other way nor name given under heaven whereby man can be saved in the kingdom of God" except through the name of Jesus Christ. He affirmed, "And now, behold, this is the doctrine of Christ, and the only and true doctrine of the Father, and of the Son, and of the Holy Ghost, which is one God, without end" (2 Nephi 31:21). Centuries later, the prophet Abinadi taught that "because he dwelleth in flesh," Jesus would be called the Son of God but that he would also be given the title of "Father, because he was conceived by the power of God," thus making him both "the Father and Son"[2] and "one God, yea, the very Eternal Father of heaven and of earth" (Mosiah 15:2–4).[3]

When he appeared to the assembled Lamanites and Nephites at the temple in the land of Bountiful, Jesus declared his gospel with precision and plainness, including the way the people would perform baptism (3 Nephi 11:21–41). As part of his instruction, Jesus affirmed, "The Father, and the Son, and the Holy Ghost are one," and, "I am in the Father, and the Father in me, and the Father and I are one" (3 Nephi 11:27). This Jesus would repeat later in a subsequent private discourse to his Nephite disciples, testifying, "All the ends of the earth shall see the salvation of the Father; and the Father and I are one" (3 Nephi 20:35). Finally, in closing his record Mormon assured that those who had been saved and who "dwell in the presence of God in his kingdom" would "sing ceaseless praises with the choirs above, unto the Father, and unto the Son, and unto the Holy Ghost, which are one God" (Mormon 7:7).

Although an instinctive reaction to these verses would be to deem them "trinitarian," one author writing in 1989 observed how "the important question becomes in what sense the Book of Mormon speaks of the oneness of the Godhead." This is an important and often overlooked point. "That the Book of Mormon includes passages about the oneness of God does not necessarily establish it as trinitarian,"[4] this author continues, meaning the text does not necessarily promote the classical orthodox Christian doctrine of the Trinity as codified by the Nicene Creed of AD 325 and clarified by subsequent orthodox writers and theologians.[5] Indeed, there has been considerable debate over the precise nature of the Godhead of Father, Son, and Holy Spirit as revealed in the pages of the Book of Mormon, and calling the passages seen above and others like them "trinitarian" merely because they speak of three persons in the Godhead is inadequate for properly situating the text in its ancient context, to say nothing of its theological context.

The clear distinction between God the Father and Jehovah as made and understood by contemporary Latter-day Saints may not have been fully grasped by Book of Mormon peoples; the same holds true for the ancient Israelites.[6] The Nephites at the time of Benjamin clearly understood God to be Yahweh or Jehovah (e.g., Mosiah 3:8), and on at least five occasions in the Book of Mormon prophets declared that he who would perform the atonement was "God himself" (Mosiah 13:28, 34; 15:1; 17:8; Alma 42:15). And yet there are fifty-one cases where the title "Son of God" was also applied to Jesus Christ, showing they understood at some level that Jesus as Jehovah was their God but also that God the Father existed in a supraordinate position to Jesus. This was certainly apparent when Jesus prayed to God the Father (3 Nephi 19:27, 31, 33), a pattern they immediately replicated when the Twelve "prayed to the Father in the name of Jesus" (3 Nephi 18:24; 19:8) and later noted in Moroni 3:2. This was not a new paradigm, for Nephi had taught that they should "pray unto the Father in the name of Christ" for his approval and blessing (2 Nephi 32:9).

While Jesus is referred to as "God" in the Book of Mormon and in some instances is identified with Jehovah, the God of Israel (compare 3 Nephi 11:14),[7] the Nephites nevertheless expressly worshipped the Father. Jacob noted how "all the holy prophets" who came before them had "believed in Christ and worshiped the Father in his name," which he stated they also continued to do (Jacob 4:4–5). In fact, God the Father is mentioned individually at many points throughout the text. While still in the Old World, Nephi saw that "the work of the Father shall commence, in preparing the way for the fulfilling of his covenants" in the last days (1 Nephi 14:17). Nephi later wrote that the day would come when "the Only Begotten of the Father, yea, even the Father of heaven and of earth, shall manifest himself unto them in the flesh" (2 Nephi 25:12). That all three members of the Godhead were viewed as individual beings is also particularly clear from 2 Nephi 31:12, which reads: "And also, the voice of the Son came unto me, saying: He that is baptized in my name, to him will the Father give the Holy Ghost." However, it is likely that the specific nature of the Godhead may not have been fully understood throughout Nephite history. It is possible that God the Father and Jehovah existed in a complex fashion as recipients of Nephite worship—thereby making this particular deity dyad less distinct at times. In our view, this blurring of lines between God the Father and Jesus Christ (Jehovah) in Nephite understanding was one contributing factor to the "trinitarian" language seen throughout the text of the Book of Mormon, and, concomitantly, made triadic deity complexes in both New and Old World contexts more mutually intelligible.

In this paper we seek to contribute to the ongoing discussion surrounding the trinitarian depiction of the Godhead in the Book of Mormon by situating its teaching about the nature of Jesus Christ and the relationship he shares with his Father in an ancient context. Specifically, this paper will explore how divine triads were understood and depicted in both the ancient Old and New Worlds. In terms of scope, this study will focus on two parts of the ancient world in making its comparisons with the Book of Mormon: Egypt and Mesoamerica. In our judgment, these two areas in particular offer interesting comparative data that afford useful ancient Near Eastern and ancient American cultural contexts for what readers encounter in the Book of Mormon. We are convinced that the divine triad of Father, Son, and Holy Spirit as depicted in the Book of Mormon can be greatly illuminated by this comparative cultural approach. We shall therefore draw on ancient Egyptian and Mesoamerican textual material that describes divine triads in making our comparisons with the Book of Mormon and will assess how this cross-cultural context may help inform a modern Latter-day Saint reading of the text.[8] We hope to show how situating the teachings of Book of Mormon prophets in their ancient Old and New World contexts heightens our understanding of the Godhead and the nature of Jesus Christ.

Ancient Egyptian Triads

The ancient Egyptians acknowledged and worshipped a diversity of divine triads. This fact can be abundantly demonstrated through a variety of textual and nontextual sources.[9] Here we offer just a sampling of the evidence, drawn partly from the thorough analysis offered by Egyptologist J. Gwyn Griffiths in his important 1996 study.[10] "The triadic grouping of gods was an early and persistent tradition in the religion of Ancient Egypt," Griffiths writes. "The best-known example is perhaps that of Osiris, Isis, and Horus, and the relationship within the triad is often on a family basis of father, mother, and child, although there are triads with three gods or three goddesses, the leading deities of one locality being sometimes this combined." As he elaborates, the "prominence of this structural element in Egyptian religion" is such that it raises the serious question of whether Egypt "may well have influenced, in this matter, the formulation of the Christian doctrine of the Trinity." In any case, "the triadic groupings are so conspicuous at all times in dynastic Egypt that they must be faced," and what Griffiths asks for the Trinity of later Christian orthodoxy might with the same seriousness be asked of the Book of Mormon's depiction of the Godhead.[11]

As Griffiths and others have observed, groupings of three divinities, or, alternatively, groupings of the king and two or three other patron deities, or general triadic groupings of a variety of figures, can be seen in the earliest epochs of Egyptian history in a number of different contexts.[12] In the mythological or heavenly realm, the Pyramid Texts from the Old Kingdom (circa 2700–2200 BC) display a "triadic schema" involving the deities Horus and Seth with the king and also Re addressing the king alongside Horus and Seth. In the pyramid of Unis these three gods are invoked in a recitation for the king's ascent into heaven (PT 305): "Stand, O Unis, (says) Horus; sit, O Unis, (says) Seth; receive his arm, (says) Re."[13] In another text from his pyramid (PT 268), Unis is said to be nursed by the divine triad of Isis, Nephthys, and Horus: "Isis shall nurture him; Nephthys shall give him suck; Horus shall receive him by his two fingers."[14] The fluidity of these triads can be seen in the next recitation (PT 269) from Unis's pyramid, where Isis and Nephthys are depicted together but Horus is substituted for Atum: "Unis shall go forth upon the thighs of Isis; this Unis shall climb upon the thighs of Nephthys; the father of Unis, Atum, shall take the arm of Unis for him."[15]

In the Middle Kingdom (circa 2100–1650 BC) Coffin Texts, triadic groupings of a variety of divine "souls" (*b3w*) of gods are associated with their respective cities, including Heliopolis (Re, Shu, and Tefnut), Hermopolis (Thoth, Sia, and Atum), Buto (Horus, Imsety, and Hapy), and Hieraconpolis (Horus, Duamutef, and Qebehsenuef).[16] "The connection [of these triads] with specified places implies a reference to local gods,"[17] and indeed ancient Egypt saw a nationwide manifestation of triadic groupings attached to multiple cities.[18] The language used in Egyptian texts to revere and describe these triads is sometimes strikingly trinitarian. Take, for instance, the depiction of the divine triad of Amun-Re-Ptah as preserved in a New Kingdom papyrus (pLeiden I 350) dating to the end of the reign of Rameses II (circa 1228 BC).[19] This Hymn to Amun, as it is commonly designated, is divided into 26 "chapters" or "sections" (*ḥwt*—"enclosure") and focuses on the "ultimate cause" of creation, namely, "the creator himself, conceptualized in the god Amun." Each chapter explores "a different aspect of the god" in what can otherwise be described as a fairly sophisticated theological exploration of the nature of the unity of Amun and his manifestations or appearances in other gods (and nature itself).[20] One passage from the text in particular stands out: "All the gods are three: Amun, Re, and Ptah, without their equal. His name is hidden as Amun; he is Re as the face; his body is Ptah. Their cities are upon the earth, established forever—Thebes, Heliopolis, and Memphis, for eternity."[21]

In what Wilson called "a statement of trinity"[22] and Gardiner "a trinity in unity,"[23] here Amun, Re, and Ptah appear to be in some manner assumed into one divine being or substance identifiable as various manifestations, including their terrestrial localities. Particularly noteworthy is the numerical and grammatical ambivalence witnessed in the use of both the singular and plural prenominal suffixes. So, while Amun, Re, and Ptah are without *their* (=*sn*) equal and establish *their* (=*sn*) cities, *his* (=*f*) name is Amun, *he* (*ntf*) is Re, and *his* (=*f*) body is Ptah. "Three is the first number to signify a plural," notes Otto. "But the number three contains at the same time the three components that express the essential qualities of a god—name, appearance, and essence. Amon, Ptah, and Ra embody in this sense all the gods, and at the same time they are only aspects of *one* god."[24]

As is true with any theological discussion of the Christian Trinity of Father, Son, and Holy Spirit, understanding what exactly the author of this text had in mind with this confusing formula is somewhat unclear. Gardiner understood this text as asserting Amun's omnipotence, "the other gods [existing] only at his good pleasure."[25] More recently Jan Assmann has explained that this trinitarian formula expresses the "three constituent elements of the divine person ... put into the context of the earthly personified presence of the gods."[26] In any case, this is not the only instance of a triadic conception of God in ancient Egypt.[27]

Given that the Book of Mormon depicts a Father-Son relationship between two of the persons in its triadic schema, it is interesting to further note how "the [Egyptian] deities are summarized in a pluralistic triad: the family. This theological solution of the problem of divine unity and plurality corresponds to the Egyptian conception of man not as a lone individual, but as a member of society."[28] It is therefore plausible in some sense to maybe speak of ancient Egyptian triads as something like a "social trinity" which preserved the ontological distinctiveness of the individual gods while affirming their unity in the triad, as some Christian writers have posited for the Christian Trinity.[29] "By aid of the triad," in other words, "divine plurality is explained as a unity."[30]

What is said of Amun-Re-Ptah in pLeiden I 350 is similar to what was said of Atum, the primordial deity of the Heliopolitan Ennead, centuries earlier in Spell 80 of the Coffin Texts (II, 39): "Atum achieved eldership through his power when he begets Shu and Tefnut in Heliopolis; when he is One, so he becomes as Three."[31] The determinative attached to "three" (*ḫmt*) in this passage is a seated god (with plural strokes), and, when coupled with the verbs in this text (*wn*, "to be"; followed by *ḫpr*, "to become"), would appear to indicate that "the doctrine emphasizes that Atum remained One after he became Three," a theological conception which Griffiths compares to the position arrived at by the Council of Chalcedon in AD 451.[32] The so-called Demotic Chronicle, dating to the early Ptolemaic period several centuries after the Amun hymn,[33] is also noteworthy given its description of the Apis Bull: "Apis, Apis, Apis, that means, Ptah, Pre, Harsiesis, who are the lords of the office of sovereign. . . . The three gods denote Apis. Apis is Ptah, Apis is Pre, Apis is Harsiesis."[34] "What is implied" in this passage, Griffiths remarks, "is that these three gods are incorporated in Apis; they are, in effect, three forms of him. This recalls the doctrine of some early Christians that God in the trinity is revealed in three aspects or modes, as Father, Son and Holy Spirit, the primacy being assigned to the concept of God per se."[35] It also recalls the depiction of Amun-Re-Ptah in pLeiden I 350 above, where the one god

(Apis) is manifested as three separate deities (Ptah, Pre, and Harsiesis) who are assumed into a composite unity while retaining their individual ontology.

For a book "which consists of the learning of the Jews and the language of the Egyptians" (1 Nephi 1:2), it is thus highly suggestive that we encounter comparable trinitarian concepts in the Book of Mormon. We are even tempted to apply Griffiths's musing on "the possibility that Egyptian influence may later have affected the Christian formulation of the trinity" to the Book of Mormon. At the very least, "it must be agreed that Egyptian religion provides clear cases of triune conceptions of deity"[36] and that this provides a useful lens by which to analyze Nephite conceptions of the triunity of the Godhead.

Mesoamerican Triads

As interesting and illustrative as the Egyptian evidence might be for the Book of Mormon, the New World data on this topic are of particular consequence given the centuries-long historical and cultural context of the Nephites and Lamanites in ancient America.[37] There remain, however, significant gaps in our understanding of Nephite and especially Lamanite religion. We are given precious little information on the nature of the pantheons of Lamanites and other non-Nephite groups in the Book of Mormon. There is a singular, clear reference to polytheism at the end of the text in Mormon 4:14 where the Lamanites are said to have taken "many prisoners both women and children," whom they offered "as sacrifices unto their idol gods." Our only specific discussion of a Lamanite deity comes around 90 BC, where Ammon's seemingly super-human abilities caused some Lamanites to ask if he were not in fact "the Great Spirit" come to punish them because of the murders they had committed (Alma 18:2; 19:25). This mention of "the Great Spirit" provides a singular emic description of the name of a Lamanite god. We also know from the text that the Great Spirit was viewed as a vengeful god because the Lamanites state that he "had destroyed so many of their brethren, the Lamanites" in the past (Alma 19:27). Lamoni initially believed that Ammon was this Great Spirit incarnate, a god spoken of by their fathers (Alma 18:4), indicating they believed the Great Spirit could assume bodily form. At this point in the narrative, Mormon interjects and clarifies that "this was the tradition of Lamoni, which he had received from his father, that there was a Great Spirit" (Alma 18:5). In other words, the belief of a Great Spirit was something held by Lamoni's ancestors; importantly, however, we are not told whether this was true for all Lamanite groups (of which there were many, each of which could have their own king [compare Mosiah 24:2]), or whether this was a local patron deity of his particular city. Lamoni's father attempted to reconcile his belief system with that of the Nephites' when he asked if the Great Spirit was the deity "that brought our fathers out of the land of Jerusalem," to which Aaron, Ammon's brother, responds in proper missionary bridge-building fashion, "Yea, he is that Great Spirit" (Alma 22:9–10).

While we make no direct effort to compare Lamanite gods to those of the ancient Maya or other Mesoamerican groups (because we have almost no data from the text for comparative purposes), there is one striking feature of the ancient Maya pantheon for which comparisons may be instructive: the presence of triadic deity complexes. The ancient Maya pantheon consisted of dozens of "gods" (*k'uh*), although the English term seems somewhat inadequate to describe the true nature of Maya supernatural beings. Gods in the Maya pantheon were not always discrete entities; rather they could conflate and overlap with other gods at times.[38] Martin suggests the term *theosynthesis*[39] to account for the fusion that takes place among Mesoamerican gods at times, and which he defines broadly as "the pictorial convergence of a deity with some other deity, creature, object, or material."[40]

Apart from the pan-regional gods that were shared among many ancient Maya groups, local patron deities often rose to particular prominence. While these tutelary deities sometimes appear as pairs[41]—likely a reflection of the symmetric dualism common to Mesoamerica—in many cases individual gods are manifest as a trinity. All indications are that the notion of a deity triad stretches back millennia in Mesoamerica, certainly into at least late Book of Mormon times.[42] One of the first such triads to be recognized was at the Maya city of Palenque by Heinrich Berlin.[43] Berlin, unable to read hieroglyphs for each of the god names, simply labeled them GI, GII, and GIII. These three gods are repeatedly mentioned as a group in numerous texts at the site of Palenque. In this case, there was a hierarchy among the three since GI was "clearly the dominant and senior member."[44] At Palenque and other Maya sites, the presence of deity triads often correlates with the construction of specific buildings dedicated to each of the three gods. Mesoamerican temples were commonly held to be dwelling places of particular gods. Epigraphic evidence shows the inner shrines of certain Maya buildings were conceived as being "god houses,"[45] either being owned by the gods themselves or by humans.[46] For example, at Palenque, the triad had at least one shrine dedicated to each member: GI the Temple of the Cross, GII the Temple of the Foliated Cross, and GIII the Temple of the Sun, thereby forming a triadic architectural complex. Beginning about 300 BC, we see triadic deities being mirrored by these triadic architectural groupings throughout the southern Maya lowlands.[47] Indeed, Hansen has argued that deity triads may have provided the "mythological basis" for these triadic architectural layouts.[48]

Several major Maya cities have clearly defined triadic deity complexes. For example, groupings of three gods in hieroglyphic texts appear on four separate monuments at Caracol (Stela 16), at Tikal on Stela 26, La Mar Stela 1, and at Naranjo on HS1 Step II (C2b-D2). At each of these four sites, however, the triad members do not fully correlate, clearly indicating the choice of which three deities was strictly a local phenomenon. The earliest appearance of a deity triad appears at Tikal on Stela 26, a reused basal fragment found in the shrine of Structure 5D-34-1st of the North Acropolis. In its original form, Stela 26 was likely a monument dating to the mid-fourth century AD during the reign of Chak Tok Ich'aak. A possible explanation for the reuse of this destroyed monument could lie in the content of the text itself, which contains a mention of the Tikal triad. Charcoal deposits around the stela show that burning ceremonies were being performed at the monument into the eighth and ninth centuries AD.[49] At Tikal the triad consists of "Baby Jaguar" (*Unehn K'awiil*), "The Principal Bird Deity" (*Muut Itzamnaaj*), and *Ehb K'inich* (possibly *Yax Ehb Xook*) on Stela 26. Here, however, the triad appears before the mention on a Tikal patron goddess, Ix Mut.[50] It is also noteworthy that triad gods are sometimes described as being "owned" by the rulers of a particular site. At Palenque, for example, on the tablet of the Temple of the Inscriptions and the Cross Group texts each of the three gods is said to be the *ujuntahn*, "sole/precious cared for one" or "receiver of the diligent care of" the king. The third person possessive pronoun *u-* marks the gods as being the "possession" or "thing owned" by each king.

As Houston and Stuart have noted, the Palenque triad are not universal throughout the Maya area; rather they are distinctly local patron gods linked to the Palenque dynasty—a pattern found at other major Maya sites.[51] As Stuart stated, "I prefer to see the Palenque Triad as a local expression of wider mode of categorizing gods into a triadic format having its own deep cosmological meaning."[52] The fact that all three Palenque Triad gods appear at others sites (not necessarily in triadic form) show that they "were members of the primary pantheon of Maya deities,"[53] but whose makeup of individual triads at different sites was not universal. Wright similarly emphasizes the site-specific nature of triadic deity complexes where "each triad created a diacritical marker of local identity and provided a unique mythological template for each city."[54] Furthermore, the presence of a deity triad did not preclude the worship of other deities at a particular site. Various supernatural beings were often simultaneously worshipped, and the specific prominence afforded one god at any given period likely changed over time.[55] In some cases, deity triads are introduced by a glyphic compound that seems to deictically mark a trinity. This phrase, which reads *ux-?-ti-k'uh* (three [?] gods), with one syllable of unsure reading,[56] appears before mentions of patron deity triads at various sites such as Palenque, Caracol, Tikal, and on polychrome ceramic vessels,[57] as well as in the Dresden Codex (P. 69, block C2-B2).[58]

In terms of function, triadic patron gods sometimes oversaw important events in the lives of rulers. Certain ceremonies were epigraphically stated to be performed *y-ichnal*, or "in the presence of" the Palenque Triad of patron deities. Stuart also notes that similar language appears on La Mar Stela 1 where a ruler is crowned *y-ichnal u k'uhuul*, "before his gods."[59] At the site of Piedras Negras, the elegantly carved Panel II depicts a banquet attended by

Itzam K'an Ahkul II where the ruler danced (*ak'taj*) and drank fermented cacao (*uch'un tikal kakaw*). The narrative then discusses an earlier event that took place in AD 518, at which Ruler 2 "took the [war] helmet" (*uch'amaw kohaw*) while "in the company of" (*y-ichnal*) three Piedras Negras patron gods (*uk'uhuul*).

There is also considerable ethnographic data to suggest different Maya groups worshipped a trinity of gods. For instance, the Northern Zapotecs of western Mexico had a deity triad.[60] Among the K'iche' Maya of Guatemala, early evangelization efforts confronted triadic deity complexes such as Jun Junajpu and his two sons, Junajpu and Xb'alanque. Quiroa has noted that sixteenth-century missionaries found this to be "an opportunity to teach the Judeo-Christian concept of the Trinity, associating Jun Junajpu with God the Father, and Junajpu as a personification of Christ, born from divine conception."[61] The K'iche' lineage rulers who had responsibility for community temples also recognized three main local deities, Tohil, Auilix, and Hacavitz.[62] Furthermore, the Yucatec Maya likewise had the concept of three principal gods,[63] and in larger, conceptual terms, they classified deities into three distinct groups: *balams* (village guardians), *chaacs* (rain deities), and *kuilob kaaxob* (forest gods).[64]

In short, deity triads are clearly present in ancient, colonial, and modern Mesoamerican groups. While we have here focused principally on the deity triads of Palenque, Naranjo, and Tikal, there are in fact twenty-six different triads in the Maya hieroglyphic corpus.[65] Other notable sites such as Calakmul (e.g., Stela 58), Cancuen (e.g., Cancuen Panel), Yaxchilan, La Corona, Naranjo, and Copan have triadic lists of gods at times, showing the conception of a triadic deity unity has deep roots in the ancient Maya systems of worship.

The Godhead in the Book of Mormon Reconsidered

Besides being interesting, what might all of this teach us about the Book of Mormon's depiction of the triunity of the Godhead? Several considerations come to mind. The first and most obvious is that these examples show just how widespread divine triads or trinities were throughout the ancient world.[66] The Book of Mormon's depiction of a specific triad of God the Father, Jesus Christ, and the Holy Ghost worshipped by the ancient Nephites was just one of a multiplicity of divine triads scattered throughout the religious landscape of antiquity.[67] Furthermore, as seen from the evidence reviewed above, divine triads in both the Old and New Worlds tended to be localized to specific cities or cultic sites. Recognizing this might provide a useful way to understand the Nephite Godhead in the broader cultural landscape of ancient Mesoamerica. As Mark Alan Wright explained, "The Mesoamerican landscape was home to countless cultures throughout its pre-Columbian history.... Some of these cultures are well known, such as the Olmec, Maya, and Aztecs, but the majority of these ancient societies remain obscure."[68] In what Wright describes as "localized diversity," it is apparent from "the diversity of material culture" and from other strands of evidence that Mesoamerican kings "ruled over a multiethnic population, a melting pot of cultures from the Maya heartland in the west to Central American cultures in the east."[69] We can perhaps situate the Nephites and their divine triad of Father, Son, and Holy Ghost into this diverse cultural landscape and understand their religious devotion as described in Mormon's record not as a pan-national or pan-ethnic phenomenon but as a localized religious custom observed only in those lands that at some point hosted Nephite occupation. This would be consistent with what we have seen when it comes to the worship of divine triads in the ancient world and would explain why some Book of Mormon peoples, like the Lamanite king Lamoni and his subjects, were evidently ignorant of the Nephite Godhead. It might also satisfy those who wonder why there does not appear to be unambiguous attestation of the worship of the specific deity Jehovah in ancient America in the available epigraphic and iconographic record.[70]

Understanding divine triads, especially Mesoamerican triads, also possibly adds additional context to the relationship shared by God the Father and Jesus Christ. First, the notion of a triadic deity complex would have been highly meaningful and would have situated well within either of these cultural contexts. The limited Mesoamerican data suggests that the trinitarian language in the Book of Mormon that speaks of three divinities being "one god" (e.g., 2 Nephi 31:21; Mosiah 15:4) could have been viewed through the lens of "theosynthesis," wherein individual deities could merge in some sense either physically or in terms of purpose and divine mission,[71] the latter being the clear intention of the Nephite authors. Also, Benjamin's teaching that the Lord "dwelleth not in unholy temples" (Mosiah 2:37), specific language not found in the Bible (although alluded to by Paul in 1 Corinthians 3:17), fully resonates with both an ancient Egyptian and a Mesoamerican understanding that gods dwelled in temples, often in triadic architectural complexes. While such terminology of temples as "god houses" is found throughout the Old and New Worlds,[72] both its prominence among Mesoamerican groups as well as the antiquity of attestations of this specific language lends special significance to Benjamin's phraseology and theology.

To be sure, Nephite prophets learned by revelation about God's nature and the character of his divine Son. Lehi, at the inauguration of his prophetic ministry, for example, was given a revelation where he learned "plainly of the coming of a Messiah, and also the redemption of the world" (1 Nephi 1:19). So likewise, Nephi and Benjamin learned the name of Jesus Christ by divine manifestation (2 Nephi 25:19; Mosiah 3:2, 8). But all revelation is bound to the culture and language of those receiving it (compare 2 Nephi 31:3; Doctrine and Covenants 1:24), just as manifestations of apostasy are constrained by the culture and language of those who fall away from divinely revealed truth.[73] Knowing something about divine triads as anciently conceptualized therefore helps us better appreciate the cultural context in which Nephite prophets taught about the nature of God and resisted opposing theological forces. As Wright and Gardner explain, "Syncretizing Nephite and Mesoamerican religions had to deal with concepts of deity. On this most fundamental point, where modern monotheists would see tremendous differences with the Mesoamerican polytheists, there were sufficient perceived similarities that the Nephite explanation of deity could accommodate, or be accommodated to, Mesoamerican ideas about the nature of the divine."[74] By putting its teachings about the Godhead against this ancient cultural backdrop, the Book of Mormon's message becomes all the more focused and clearer to modern readers who may otherwise not enjoy the benefit of this context.

From this study we therefore see emerge a plausible ancient context for the Book of Mormon's trinitarianism, and one that can increase our appreciation for and understanding of the book's theology. There is nothing really to suggest the Book of Mormon depicts the classical orthodox trinity of Nicaea. Never does the text suggest Jesus and God the Father are of one substance (*homoousios*), for example, which was precisely the metaphysical lynchpin of the Nicene council's theological determination.[75] Nor, for that matter, is there reason to suppose the text promotes trinitarian modalism, despite the insistence of some authors. The *social* Nephite triad of Father, Son, and Holy Ghost who act in concert as "one God" (or Godhead) but who also clearly retain their individual personhood is a trinitarian concept basically unique to the Book of Mormon, but one that does find intriguing parallel with the evidence reviewed above. The Book of Mormon's divine trinity, we contend, is best understood as a deity complex that reflects especially well an ancient Mesoamerican perspective on the nature of God but one that also finds significant parallel with Old World sources.[76]

Of course, the overtly Christological nature of the Nephite Godhead cannot be accounted for on historical grounds, because the book claims that its inspired authors derived that understanding from revelation, the ultimate reality of which historical inquiry can neither absolutely confirm nor deny. Yet it is striking that two cultural regions, Egypt and Mesoamerica, both of which arguably are linked to the Book of Mormon, have such highly developed but fluid notions of deity triads. Book of Mormon events did not take place in a vacuum, and so the theology expressed by authors in the text must be contextualized in the cultures that both informed them and with which they interacted. As we have shown here, the expression of trinitarian language in the Book of Mormon is certainly reflective of triadic deity complexes from ancient Egypt and Mesoamerica. Any attempt at grounded theological exposition on the nature of Jesus Christ and the relationship he shares with the other two members of this triad would do well to take this into account.

STEPHEN O. SMOOT *is a PhD student in Semitic and Egyptian languages and literature at the Catholic University of America and an adjunct instructor in Religious Education at Brigham Young University.*

KERRY HULL *is a professor of ancient scripture at Brigham Young University.*

Notes

1. An earlier and rough version of this paper originally appeared as Stephen O. Smoot, "A Note on Book of Mormon 'Trinitarianism,'" *Ploni Almoni*, March 5, 2018, https://www.plonialmonimormon.com/2018/03/a-note-on-book-of-mormon-trinitarianism.html. This current version of the paper at times slightly revises the language of the earlier blog version while also significantly expanding on it.
2. This reasoning is nearly the same Jesus himself uses to describe how he is both Father and Son. In Doctrine and Covenants 93, Jesus states how "I am in the Father, and the Father in me, and the Father and I are one" (verse 3), and then explicates, "The Father because he gave me of his fulness, and the Son because I was in the world and made flesh my tabernacle, and dwelt among the sons of men" (verse 4).
3. Abinadi's discourse to the priests of King Noah recorded in Mosiah 12–16 has received sustained attention by exegetes, including specifically his remarks on the relationship between the Father and the Son preserved in Mosiah 15:1–9. For representative samples of useful hermeneutical exploration of this text, see generally Richard L. Bushman, "Abinadi on the Nature of Christ," *Millennial Star*, April 1958, 104–6, 111–12; Robert L. Millet, "The Ministry of the Father and the Son," in *The Book of Mormon: The Keystone Scripture*, ed. Paul R. Cheesman (Provo, UT: Religious Studies Center, Brigham Young University, 1988), 44–72; Jeffrey R. Holland, *Christ and the New Covenant* (Salt Lake City: Deseret Book, 1997), 103–5; Paul Y. Hoskisson, "The Fatherhood of Christ and the Atonement," *Religious Educator* 1, no. 1 (2000): 71–80; Brian K. Ray, "Adoption and Atonement: Becoming Sons and Daughters of Christ," in *Religious Educator* 6, no. 3 (2005): 129–36; Jared T. Parker, "Abinadi on the Father and the Son: Interpretation and Application," in *Living the Book of Mormon: Abiding by Its Precepts*, ed. Gaye Strathearn and Charles Swift (Provo, UT: Religious Studies Center, Brigham Young University; Salt Lake City: Deseret Book, 2007), 136–50; Brant Gardner, *Second Witness: Analytical and Contextual Commentary on the Book of Mormon* (Salt Lake City: Greg Kofford Books, 2007), 3:299–308.
4. Dan Vogel, "The Earliest Mormon Concept of God," in *Line Upon Line: Essays on Mormon Doctrine*, ed. Gary James Bergera (Salt Lake City, UT: Signature Books, 1989), 21. Vogel, "The Earliest Mormon Concept of God," 22, goes on to argue that the Book of Mormon reflects a modalistic rather than classical trinitarian view of the Godhead because of its "failure to clearly distinguish between the person of the Father and the person of the Son," and, furthermore, because "modalistic elements such as the literal oneness of the Godhead,

the Father becoming the Son, and patripassianism are clearly expressed in the Book of Mormon." Vogel's arguments, and others like his that see the Book of Mormon as teaching a form of modalism, have been convincingly challenged by Ari D. Bruening and David L. Paulsen, "The Development of the Mormon Understanding of God: Early Mormon Modalism and Other Myths," *FARMS Review of Books* 13, no. 2 (2001): 109–69; Barry R. Bickmore, "Does the Book of Mormon Teach Mainstream Trinitarianism or Modalism?" (2001), online at https://www.fairlatterdaysaints.org/; Blake T. Ostler, "Re-vision-ing the Mormon Concept of Deity," *Element: The Journal of the Society for Mormon Philosophy and Theology* 1, no. 1 (Spring 2005): 31–58; David L. Paulsen and Ari D. Bruening, "The Social Model of the Trinity in 3 Nephi," in *Third Nephi: An Incomparable Scripture*, ed. Andrew C. Skinner and Gaye Strathearn (Salt Lake City: Deseret Book; Provo, UT: Neal A. Maxwell for Religious Scholarship, 2012), 191–233.

5. A highly useful and accessible overview of the council and its theological outcome specifically aimed for a Latter-day Saint audience can be found in Lincoln H. Blumell, "Rereading the Council of Nicaea and Its Creed," in *Standing Apart: Mormon Historical Consciousness and the Concept of Apostasy*, ed. Miranda Wilcox and John D. Young (New York: Oxford University Press, 2014), 196–217.

6. In 1916 the First Presidency and the Quorum of the Twelve published a "doctrinal exposition" clarifying the use of the titles "Father" and "Son" as they pertain to God the Eternal Father and His Son Jesus Christ, the first and second members of the Godhead. This treatise standardized and codified as a matter of official doctrine in The Church of Jesus Christ of Latter-day Saints the usage of the name Elohim to refer to God the Father and Jehovah to refer to Jesus Christ. It further delineated the ways in which Jesus Christ could rightly assume the title and role of "father," such as his role as Creator, his being the "father" of those who accept his Gospel, and his "fatherhood" being related to the investiture of authority given to him by his own Father. See "The Father and the Son. A Doctrinal Exposition by the First Presidency and the Twelve," *Deseret Evening News*, July 1, 1916, 4; "The Father and the Son," *Improvement Era*, August 1916, 934–42. This exposition was republished as "Gospel Classics: The Father and the Son," *Ensign*, April 2002, 13–18. However, as Latter-day Saint scholars have observed, while this usage of the names Elohim and Jehovah are normative for modern Latter-day Saints, these divine names and other titles, including "Lord," were not uniformly applied throughout the Hebrew Bible/Old Testament and among early Latter-day Saints. See the insightful comments in Ryan Conrad Davis and Paul Y. Hoskisson, "Usage of the Title *Elohim* in the Hebrew Bible and Early Latter-day Saint Literature," in *Bountiful Harvest: Essays in Honor of S. Kent Brown*, ed. Andrew C. Skinner, D. Morgan Davis, and Carl Griffin (Provo, UT: Neal A. Maxwell Institute for Religious Scholarship, Brigham Young University, 2011), 113–35; "Usage of the Title *Elohim*," *Religious Educator* 14, no. 1 (2013): 109–27. For a Latter-day Saint argument that the New Testament authors understood Jesus to be Jehovah, see Roger R. Keller, "Jesus is Jehovah (YHWH): A Study in the Gospels," in *Jesus Christ: Son of God, Savior*, ed. Paul H. Peterson, Gary L. Hatch, and Laura D. Card (Provo, UT: Religious Studies Center, Brigham Young University, 2002), 120–51. Throughout this paper we accept and employ

the conventional Latter-day Saint standard of using the divine name Jehovah (or Yahweh) to refer to Jesus Christ.

7. In addition to the examples cited above, consider also that the Book of Mormon frequently employs the divine title "Holy One of Israel," used in the Hebrew Bible for Jehovah (e.g., Psalm 89:18; Isaiah 1:4; 5:24; 10:20; 30:15; 31:1; 41:14, 16, 20; 43:3, 14; 45:11; 47:4; 48:17; 49:7; 55:5; 60:9, 14; Jeremiah 50:29) to refer unambiguously and explicitly to Jesus Christ (e.g., 2 Nephi 1:10; 3:2; 6:9–10, 15; 9:11–12, 19, 23–26, 40–41; 25:29; 30:2; Omni 1:25–26; 3 Nephi 22:5). This fact does not on its own prove the Nephites exclusively understood or applied the name Jehovah to Jesus Christ, but it is consistent with our claim that they in some manner did recognize him as such.

8. We are of course aware that The Church of Jesus Christ of Latter-day Saints takes no official position on the geographical setting of the events narrated in the Book of Mormon. As an official statement from the Church has made clear, "Since the publication of the Book of Mormon in 1830, members and leaders of The Church of Jesus Christ of Latter-day Saints have expressed numerous opinions about the specific locations of the events discussed in the book. Some believe that the history depicted in the Book of Mormon—with the exception of the events in the Near East—occurred in North America, while others believe that it occurred in Central America or South America. Although Church members continue to discuss such theories today, the Church's only position is that the events the Book of Mormon describes took place in the ancient Americas." See "Book of Mormon Geography," Gospel Topics, online at www.churchofjesuschrist.org. We respect and affirm the Church's neutrality on Book of Mormon geography as a matter of revealed doctrine. In this paper we assume a Mesoamerican cultural and geographical setting for the Book of Mormon not as such, but rather out of our own individual scholarly judgments that a Mesoamerican setting matches best the world of the Book of Mormon as described in the text and provides an especially illustrative cultural backdrop by which to read the text. We of course recognize that some readers of this paper may in good faith hold to different geography theories for the New World setting of the Book of Mormon but nevertheless hope that what we have to offer herein will be of interest.

9. See variously Herman Te Velde, "Some Remarks on the Structure of Egyptian Divine Triads," *Journal of Egyptian Archaeology* 57 (1971): 80–86; J. Gwyn Griffiths, "Triune Conceptions of Deity in Ancient Egypt," *Zeitschrift für ägyptische Sprache* 100 (1973): 28–32; Wendy Wood, "A Reconstruction of the Triads of King Mycerinus," *Journal of Egyptian Archaeology* 60 (1974): 82–93; L. Kákosy, "A Memphite Triad," *Journal of Egyptian Archaeology* 66 (1980): 48–53; Manana Khvedelidse, "Babylonian and Egyptian Triads," in *Gesellschaft und Kultur im alten Vorderasien*, ed. Horst Klengel, Schriften zur Geschichte und Kultur des Alten Orients (Berlin: Akademie Verlag, 1982), 137–41; L. Kákosy, "The Ptah-Shu-Tefnut Triad and the Gods of the Winds on a Ptolemaic Sarcophagus," in *Essays on Ancient Egypt in Honour of Herman Te Velde*, ed. Jacobus van Dijk, Egyptological Memoirs 1 (Leiden: Brill, 1997), 219–29; J. Gwyn Griffiths, *Triads and Trinity* (Cardiff: University of Wales Press, 1996), 11–113; Edward Brovarski, "A Traid for Pehenptah," in *Essays in Honour of Prof. Dr. Jadwiga Lipińska*, Warsaw Egyptological

Studies 1 (Warsaw: National Museum in Warsaw, 1997), 261–74; Florence Dunn Friedman, "Reading the Menkaure Triads, Part I," in *Palace and Temple: 5th Symposium on Egyptian Royal Ideology*, ed. Rolf Gundlach and Kate Spence, Königtum, Staat und Gesellschaft Früher Hochkulturen 4,2 (Wiesbaden: Harrassowitz Verlag, 2011), 23–56; "Reading the Menkaure Triads: Part II (Multi-directionality)," in *Old Kingdom, New Perspectives: Egyptian Art and Archaeology 2750–2150 BC*, ed. Nigel Strudwick and Helen Strudwick (Oxford and Oakville: Oxbow Books, 2011), 93–114; José das Candeias Sales, "Divine Triads of Ancient Egypt," *Hathor: Studies of Egyptology* 1 (2012): 115–35.

10. J. Gwyn Griffiths, *Triads and Trinity* (University of Wales Press, 1996): 11–113.
11. Griffiths, *Triads and Trinity*, 11.
12. See Griffiths, *Triads and Trinity*, 11–43, and the authorities cited in note 7 above.
13. Egyptian: *ḥꜥ Wnis in Ḥr ḥms Wnis in St ššp ꜥ=f in Rꜥ*. James P. Allen, *A New Concordance of the Pyramid Texts, Vol. III: PT 247–421* (Providence, RI: Brown University, 2013), §PT 305 473b–473c; Allen, *The Ancient Egyptian Pyramid Texts*, Writings from the Ancient World 23, ed. Peter Der Manuelian (Atlanta, GA: Society of Biblical Literature, 2005), 57; Griffiths, *Triads and Trinity*, 31. Unless otherwise indicated, translations from the Egyptian are ours.
14. Egyptian: *ꜣty sw 'Ist snk sw Nbt-ḥwt ššp sw Ḥr r ḏbꜥwy=f*. Allen, *A New Concordance of the Pyramid Texts, Vol. III*, §PT 268 371c–372a; *The Ancient Egyptian Pyramid Texts*, 49; Griffiths, *Triads and Trinity*, 32.
15. Egyptian: *pr Wnis ḥr mntwy 'Ist ḥfd Wnis pn ḥr mntwy Nbt-ḥwt nḏry n=f it Wnis 'Itm ꜥ n Wnis*. Allen, *A New Concordance of the Pyramid Texts, Vol. III*, §PT 269 379c–380a; *The Ancient Egyptian Pyramid Texts*, 49; Griffiths, *Triads and Trinity*, 32.
16. Griffiths, *Triads and Trinity*, 45, citing CT II, 286b–c, 323c–325e, 348b–c.
17. Griffiths, *Triads and Trinity*, 45.
18. Griffiths, *Triads and Trinity*, 80–113.
19. James P. Allen, *Genesis in Egypt: The Philosophy of Ancient Egyptian Creation Accounts*, Yale Egyptological Seminar (New Haven, CT: Yale University Press, 1988), 49.
20. James P. Allen, "From Papyrus Leiden I 350," in *The Context of Scripture*, Volume I: *Canonical Compositions from the Biblical World*, ed. William W. Hallo (Leiden: Brill, 1997), 23.
21. Egyptian: *ḥmt pw nṯrw nbw 'Imn Rꜥ Ptḥ nn nw=sn imn(.w) rn=f m 'Imn ntf Rꜥ m ḥr ḏt=f Ptḥ niwt=sn ḥr tꜣ smn(.w) r nḥḥ wꜣst ḥwt-kꜣ-Ptḥ r ḏt*. Alan H. Gardiner, "Hymns to Amon from a Leiden Papyrus," *Zeitschrift für ägyptische Sprache* 42 (1905): 35.
22. John A. Wilson, "Amon as the Sole God," in *Ancient Near Eastern Texts Relating to the Old Testament*, ed. James B. Pritchard, 3rd ed. (Princeton, NJ: Princeton University Press, 1969), 369n11.
23. Gardiner, "Hymns to Amon from a Leiden Papyrus," 36.
24. Eberhard Otto, *Egyptian Art and the Cults of Osiris and Amon*, trans. Kate Bosse Griffiths (London: Thames and Hudson, 1968), 52, emphasis in original. As Otto elaborates, "The two triads Osiris-Isis-Horus and Amon-Ptah-Ra are joined by the king himself [Sety I], the original owner of the mortuary temple [at Abydos]. In this way is reached the

otherwise uncommon number seven. Probably the Egyptians would have gone still one step further and explained the seven as a triad, that is, the gods around Osiris, the gods of the country, and the king."

25. Gardiner, "Hymns to Amon from a Leiden Papyrus," 36.
26. Jan Assmann, *Egyptian Solar Religion in the New Kingdom: Re, Amun and the Crisis of Polytheism*, trans. Anthony Alcock, 3rd ed. (London: Routledge, 2009), 141–42.
27. Herman Te Velde begins his 1971 study on this subject by observing, "Although the Egyptian word for triad rarely appears in Egyptian texts, the triad is undoubtedly a structural element of Egyptian religion." Te Velde, "Some Remarks on the Structure of Egyptian Divine Triads," 80. Such triads include Amun-Re-Ptah, Khepri-Re-Atum, Ptah-Sokar-Osiris, Qadesh-Astarte-Anat, Atum-Shu-Tefnut, Osiris-Isis-Horus, Amun-Re-Horakhty, Amun-Re-Montu, Re-Horaskhty-Osiris, Ptah-Sakhmet-Nefertem, and the Ennead of Heliopolis, "structured in three phases: Atum became Shu and Tefnut; Shu and Tefnut became Geb and Nut, Geb and Nut became Osiris, Isis, Seth, and Nephthys. Thus the triadic structure . . . is not 3 x 3 but 1+2+2+4. To the one god, gods were added three times." Te Velde, "Some Remarks on the Structure of Egyptian Divine Triads," 81–83, quote at 83; Griffiths, "Triune Conceptions of Deity in Ancient Egypt," 29.
28. Te Velde, "Some Remarks on the Structure of Egyptian Divine Triads," 83.
29. Compare Michael C. Rea, "Polytheism and Christian Belief," *Journal of Theological Studies* 57, no. 1 (2006): 133–48, who seems to recognize this but despairs of the theological consequences of admitting such.
30. Te Velde, "Some Remarks on the Structure of Egyptian Divine Triads," 82; Griffiths, "Triune Conceptions of Deity in Ancient Egypt," 29, points out that grammatically the Ennead is likewise ambivalently treated as both a singular and a plural.
31. Egyptian: *iri.n ʾItm smsw m ꜣḫw=f m mst=f Šw Tfnt m iwnw m wn=f wꜥy m ḫpr=f m ḥmt.* Adriaan de Buck, ed., *The Egyptian Coffin Texts, II: Texts of Spells 76–163* (Chicago: University of Chicago Press, 1938), 39.
32. Griffiths, "Triune Conceptions of Deity in Ancient Egypt," 29.
33. H. Felber, "Die Demotische Chronik," in *Apokalyptik und Ägypten: Eine Kritische Analyse der Relevanten Texte aus dem Griechisch-Römischen Ägypten*, ed. A. Blasius and B. U. Schipper (Leuven: Peeters, 2002), 68.
34. Egyptian: *Ḥꜥp Ḥꜥp Ḥꜥp ḏd Ptḥ pꜣ-Rꜥ Ḥr-sꜣ-ꜣst nt ꜥw nꜣ nbw n tꜣ ꜥꜣwt . . . Ḥꜥp pꜣ ḥmt nṯrw ḏd=f Ḥri nꜣi Ḥꜥp Ptḥ pꜣi Ḥꜥp pꜣ-Rꜥ pꜣi Ḥꜥp Ḥr-sꜣ-ꜣst pꜣi.* As translated in Griffiths, "Triune Conceptions of Deity in Ancient Egypt," 29. For the Demotic transliteration, see Wilhelm Spiegelberg, *Die sogenannte Demotische Chronik des Pap. 215 der Bibliothèque Nationale zu Paris* (Leipzig: Hinrichsche Buchhandlung, 1914), 12, lines 12–13; cf. Felber, "Die Demotische Chronik," 86, who renders this passage: "Apis, Apis, Apis! Ptah, Re, Harsiese, welche die Herren des Herscheramtes sind. . . . Apis ist die drei Götter, die er oben genannt hat. Apis ist Ptah; Apis ist Re; Apis ist Harsiese."
35. Griffiths, "Triune Conceptions of Deity in Ancient Egypt," 30; compare Griffiths, *Triads and Trinity*, 91.
36. Griffiths, "Triune Conceptions of Deity in Ancient Egypt," 32.

37. On which, see generally John L. Sorenson, *An Ancient American Setting for the Book of Mormon* (Salt Lake City: Deseret Book; Provo, UT: FARMS, 1985); *Mormon's Codex: An Ancient American Book* (Provo, UT: Neal A. Maxwell Institute for Religious Scholarship, 2013).
38. Jan Szymański, "Between Death and Divinity: Rethinking the Significance of Triadic Groups in Ancient Maya Culture," *Estudios de Cultura Maya* 44 (2014): 149, 158.
39. Simon Martin, *The Old Man of the Maya Universe: A Unitary Dimension to Ancient Maya Religion*, in *Maya Archaeology 3*, ed. Charles Golden, Stephen Houston, and Joel Skidmore (San Francisco: Precolumbia Mesoweb Press, 2015), 186–227.
40. Martin, *The Old Man of the Maya Universe*, 210.
41. Mark Alan Wright, "A Study of Classic Maya Rulership" (PhD diss., University of California, Riverside, 2001), 231.
42. David Stuart, "The Gods of Heaven and Earth," *Del saber ha hecho su razón de ser. Homenaje a Alfredo López Austin* 2 (2017): 257.
43. Heinrich Berlin, "The Palenque Triad," *Journal de la Societe des Americanistes* 59 (1963): 107–35.
44. David Stuart, "The Palenque Mythology," in *Sourcebook for the 2005 Maya Meetings, Austin*. The Mesoamerica Center, Department of Art and Art History, University of Texas (Austin, TX: The University of Texas at Austin, 2005), 88.
45. Stephen Houston, and David Stuart, "Of Gods, Glyphs and Kings: Divinity and Rulership among the Classic Maya," *Antiquity* 70, no. 268 (1996): 293.
46. William Saturno, Franco D. Rossi, David Stuart, and Heather Hurst, "A Maya *Curia Regis*: Evidence for a Hierarchical Specialist Order at Xultun, Guatemala," *Ancient Mesoamerica* 28, no. 2 (2017): 432.
47. Arlen F. Chase, and Diane Z. Chase, "Complex Societies in the Southern Maya Lowlands: Their Development and Florescence in the Archaeological Record," in *The Oxford Handbook of Mesoamerican Archaeology*, ed. Deborah L. Nichols and Christopher A. Pool (New York: Oxford University Press, 2012), 258.
48. Richard D. Hansen, "The Archaeology of Ideology: A Study of Maya Preclassic Architectural Sculpture at Nakbe, Peten, Guatemala" (PhD diss., Department of Archaeology, University of California, Los Angeles, 1992), 167–68.
49. William Coe, *Excavations in the Great Plaza, North Terrace, and North Acropolis of Tikal, Tikal Report #14*, University Monograph 61 (Philadelphia: University Museum, University of Pennsylvania, 1990), 476, 498–99. See also Megan E. O'Neil, "Ancient Maya Sculptures of Tikal, Seen and Unseen," *Res* 55/56 (Spring/Autumn 2009): 123–24.
50. Simon Martin, "Early Classic Co-Rulers on Tikal Temple VI," *Maya Decipherment: A Weblog on the Ancient Maya Script*, November 22, 2014, https://mayadecipherment.com/tag/tikal/.
51. Houston and Stuart, "Of Gods, Glyphs, and Kings," 301.
52. Stuart, "The Palenque Mythology," 90.
53. Karen Bassie-Sweet, "The Chahk Thunderbolt Deities and Flint Weapons," in *Maya Gods of War*, ed. Karen Bassie-Sweet (Boulder: University Press of Colorado, 2021), 41.

54. Wright, "A Study of Classic Maya Rulership," 230.
55. Christian M. Prager, "A Study of the Classic Maya *k'uh* Concept," in *Tiempo detenido, tiempo suficiente*, ed. Verónica Amellali Vázquez López et al. (Wayeb, 2018), 603.
56. The second sign resembles the *lu* syllable, which would yield a *lut* reading. Nicholas Hopkins first proposed a Ch'ol cognate *lot* meaning "together", suggesting a possible "three-together-gods" interpretation for this compound. Similar terminology appears in Tzotzil Maya (*ox lot*, lit. 'three together') as a name for three stars found in the belt of Orion. Evan Vogt, "Zinacanteco Astronomy," *Mexicon* 19, no. 6 (1997): 112. However, the *lu* syllable is not safely identifiable in this case, so the reading of this grouping remains unsecure.
57. Stuart, "The Palenque Mythology," 160.
58. Carl Callaway, *A Catalogue of Maya Era Day Inscriptions* (PhD thesis, La Trobe University, Australia, 2012), 255.
59. David Stuart, "Making a Mountain: The Reconstruction of Text Fragments from Palenque's Palace Tablet," *PARI Journal* 21, no. 3 (2021): 7.
60. David Tavárez, *Rethinking Zapotec Time: Cosmology, Ritual, and Resistance in Colonial Mexico* (Austin: University of Texas Press, 2022).
61. Nestor Quiroa, "Missionary Exegesis of the Popol Vuh: Maya-K'iche' Cultural and Religious Continuity in Colonial and Contemporary Highland Guatemala," *History of Religions* 53, no. 1 (2013): 78.
62. Hubert Howe Bancroft, *The Works of Hubert Howe Bancroft*, vol. 3: *The Native Races*, vol. 3, *Myths and Languages* (San Francisco: A. L. Bancroft, 1883), 554, 648. See also Allen Christenson, *Popol Vuh: The Sacred Book of the Maya* (Norman: University of Oklahoma Press, 2012), 212.
63. Luis Rosado Vega, *Amerindmaya* (Mexico: Botas, 1938), 82–83.
64. Robert Redfield and Alfonso Villa Rojas, *Chan Kom, A Maya Village* (Washington, DC: Carnegie Institution of Washington, 1934), 112–13, 134.
65. Joanne Baron, "Metapragmatics in Archaeological Analysis: Interpreting Classic Maya Patron Deity Veneration," *Signs and Society* 2, no. 2 (2014): 180.
66. Griffiths, *Triads and Trinity*, passim, reviews divine triads from a variety of ancient cultures and parts of the world, ranging from Iran to India to Mesopotamia to the Greco-Roman world.
67. In this regard, it is noteworthy that a contemporary critic of Joseph Smith thought the Book of Mormon anachronistic for its portrayal of the Trinity. See Alexander Campbell, "Delusions," *Millennial Harbinger*, February 1831, 92. Time, it would appear, continues to vindicate the prophets.
68. Mark Alan Wright, "The Cultural Tapestry of Mesoamerica," *Journal of the Book of Mormon and Other Restoration Scripture* 22, no. 2 (2013): 4.
69. Wright, "The Cultural Tapestry of Mesoamerica," 11.
70. Notwithstanding the well-intended efforts of writers such as L. Taylor Hansen, *He Walked the Americas* (Amherst, WI: Amherst Press, 1963), Bruce W. Warren and Thomas Stuart Ferguson, *The Messiah in Ancient America* (Provo, UT: Book of Mormon

Research Foundation, 1987), Diane E. Wirth, "Quetzalcoatl, the Maya Maize God, and Jesus Christ," *Journal of Book of Mormon Studies* 11, no. 1 (2002): 4–15, 107, and David G. Calderwood, *Voices from the Dust: New Insights into Ancient America a Comparative Evaluation of Early Spanish and Portuguese Chronicles, Archaeology and Art History, the Book of Mormon* (Austin, TX: Historical Publications, 2005), efforts to demonstrate the presence of the worship of Jesus Christ among the peoples of ancient America are fraught with both methodological and evidentiary problems. See, for example, the considered critique of this line of argumentation by Brant A. Gardner, "The Christianization of Quetzalcoatl," *Sunstone*, August 1986, 7–10; *Second Witness*, 5:353–95.

71. The unity of Jesus and God the Father in the Book of Mormon is certainly not one of substance but one aptly described by Abinadi (Mosiah 15:7) as a unity of *purpose*, "the will of the Son being swallowed up in the will of the Father."

72. For example, at the site of Copan, certain miniature stone temples were epigraphically labeled as *uwayib k'uh*, "the sleeping places of the god." Similarly, in Nahuatl, the language of the Aztecs, the term for "temple" was *teocalli*, literally "god-house." In the colonial period, the Yukatek Mayan referred likewise referred to a temple as *k'uh nah*, literally "god-house." For an informative discussion on the temple/house complex in Mesoamerica see Karl Taube, "The Classic Maya Temple: Centrality, Cosmology, and Sacred Geography in Ancient Mesoamerica," in *Heaven on Earth: Temples, Ritual, and Cosmic Symbolism in the Ancient World*, ed. Deena Ragavan (Chicago, IL: Oriental Institute of the University of Chicago, 2013), 90–91. In ancient Egypt the terminology is similar, with both *pr-nṯr* ("house of the god") and *ḥwt-nṯr* ("enclosure of the god") as the most common designations.

73. Mark Alan Wright, "'According to Their Language, unto Their Understanding': The Cultural Context of Hierophanies and Theophanies in Latter-day Saint Canon," *Studies in the Bible and Antiquity* 3 (2011): 51–65; Mark Alan Wright and Brant A. Gardner, "The Cultural Context of Nephite Apostasy," *Interpreter: A Journal of Latter-day Saint Faith and Scholarship* 1 (2012): 25–55.

74. Wright and Gardner, "The Cultural Context of Nephite Apostasy," 34, and passim, where they provide multiple examples of how the Nephite conception of deity could have easily translated into a Mesoamerican religious backdrop.

75. Blumell, "Rereading the Council of Nicaea and Its Creed," 206–8, explains how the Christology of both the Book of Mormon and the Doctrine and Covenants appears to significantly contradict the Nicene Creed.

76. See further Wright and Gardner, "The Cultural Context of Nephite Apostasy," 34–38.

11

"That Ye Might Feel and See"
Touch in the First Day of Christ's Ministry

Daniel L. Belnap

The culminating event of the Book of Mormon, the fulfillment of six hundred years of Nephite prophecy, was Christ's post-resurrection physical ministry. Comprising chapters 11–18 of 3 Nephi, the first day of that ministry is described in great detail, incorporating a number of teachings and events reflecting the supernal nature of the day. Much has been written concerning the discourses and experiences of that first day, yet perhaps the most intriguing are those events associated with touch with Christ's ministry beginning with and initial touching event described in 3 Nephi 11:14–15 and the day's ministry ending with an allusion to the earlier event in 3 Nephi 18:25: "And ye see that I have commanded that none of you should go away, but rather have commanded that ye should come unto me, that ye might feel and see."

This continuity suggests that touch was not just peripheral to his ministry but central to it. In fact, touch appears to have been used by Christ as a form of teaching, with Christ himself declaring that touching him would result in knowing that he was "the God of Israel and the God of the whole earth, and have been slain for the sins of the world" (3 Nephi 11:14). Yet touching Christ may have done more than what Christ explicitly said it would do, for the act of touching itself can be understood as a form of communication with physiological effects such as engendering social cohesiveness that communicate meaning even if the ones touching are not aware of it. This paper will explore the role of touch in Christ's first day ministry, beginning with the manner by which touching Christ taught what he said it would, thus possibly confirming uncertainty in Nephite prophecy, and then addressing the ways touch may have affected other aspects of his first day ministry, concluding with new insight into Christ's invitation to "come unto me" (3 Nephi 18:25) at the conclusion of that ministry.

"That You May Know"

According to Mormon, following Christ's condescension from heaven, the multitude "fell to the earth," thus associating their behavior with their recognition of the fulfillment of prophecy: "The whole multitude fell to the earth; for they remembered that it had been prophesied among them that Christ should show himself unto them after his ascension into heaven" (3 Nephi 11:12). At this point, Christ exhorted those assembled, "Arise and come forth unto me, that ye may thrust your hands into my side, and also that ye may feel the prints of the nails in my hands and in my feet, that ye may know that I am the God of Israel, and the God of the whole earth, and have been slain for the sins of the world" (3 Nephi 11:14). Mormon then recounts that everyone did so, "going forth one by one until they had all gone forth, and did see with their eyes and did feel with their hands, and did know of a surety and did bear record, that it was he, of whom it was written by the prophets, that should come" (3 Nephi 11:15).

As these verses suggest, a primary purpose to this initial touching event was to acquire knowledge, specifically the knowledge that Christ was the God of Israel and the God of the whole earth, and that he had been slain for the sins of the world. Though verse 12 implies that the gathered recognized Christ upon his arrival, a closer reading may indicate that they do not do so immediately. Only after Christ introduced himself using the language he had spoken during the three days of darkness (see 3 Nephi 9:14–18) did Mormon place their remembrance of earlier prophecy; a prophecy, interestingly, not mentioned anywhere else in the Book of Mormon. Their initial uncertainty and Christ's emphasis that touching him would give them knowledge that he was "the God of Israel, and the God the whole earth, and have been slain for the sins of the world" may indicate ignorance of (1) Christ's death by crucifixion, (2) that he would visit those in the New World, and (3) that Christ was, in fact, God, thus necessitating the acquisition of this knowledge by those gathered in Bountiful via touching the Savior.

Uncertainty Concerning Death by Crucifixion

Understanding that Christ died by crucifixion would appear at first glance to be obvious, the physical puncture marks associated with crucifixion clearly and tangibly present on Christ's body and attesting to the act of crucifixion. Yet it is possible that Christ's crucifixion, and crucifixion in general, was not widely understood by the survivors of the cataclysmic events described in 3 Nephi 8–10. The understanding that Christ was going to die to redeem the world can be found as late as the prophecies of Samuel the Lamanite, who noted that Christ "surely must die that salvation may come . . . , that thereby men may be brought into the presence of the Lord" (Helaman 14:15). Yet explicit references to crucifixion are found primarily in the prophecies associated with the small plates. The first explicit reference to the crucifixion is in Nephi$_1$'s paraphrase of certain prophecies found on the brass plates: "The God of our fathers, . . . yea, the God of Abraham, and of Isaac, and the God of Jacob, yieldeth himself . . . as a man, into the hands of wicked men, to be lifted up, according to the words of Zenock, and to be crucified, according to the words of Neum" (1 Nephi 19:10).[1] A few verses later, Nephi$_1$ again referenced crucifixion, this time suggesting that the prophet Zenos also prophesied of Christ's crucifixion.[2]

Jacob referenced the crucifixion in his discourse recorded in 2 Nephi 6–10. In 2 Nephi 6:9, Jacob proclaimed, "The Lord has shown unto me . . . that the Lord God, the Holy One of Israel, should manifest himself unto them in the flesh; and after he should manifest himself they should scourge him and crucify

214   Daniel L. Belnap

him, according to the words of the angel who spake it unto me." Jacob repeated the prophecy in 2 Nephi 10:3, again highlighting the prophecy's angelic origin: "And they shall crucify him—for thus it behooveth our God, and there is none other nation on earth that would crucify their God." Nephi$_1$ gave one last prophecy concerning Christ's crucifixion following his Isaiah citations, declaring that the Jews would "crucify him; and after he is laid in a sepulchre for the space of three days he shall rise from the dead" (2 Nephi 25:13). After these references, there is no explicit mention of crucifixion until the Nephite migration to Zarahemla.

The next set of prophecies are found in King Benjamin's discourse, also delivered angelically: "The things which I shall tell you are made known unto me by an angel from God. And he said ... they shall consider him a man, and say that he hath a devil, and they shall scourge him, and shall crucify him" (Mosiah 3:2, 9). The final explicit reference is in the words of Abinadi, who noted that Christ would be "crucified, and slain, the flesh becoming subject even unto death, the will of the Son being swallowed up in the will of the Father" (Mosiah 15:7).[3] This is the last explicit reference to the crucifixion until Christ's appearance, and it may suggest that the few generations preceding Christ's arrival were unaware of the act and it being a means by which one could identify Christ. In fact, the nature of the act itself may have been unknown outside of vision or direct angelic speech as there is no indication that Roman-style crucifixion was practiced in the New World; the only individual who appears to have seen the crucifixion was Nephi$_1$, who stated that he saw Christ lifted up (1 Nephi 11:33). Others were told that he would be lifted up, but there is no corresponding vision provided; therefore, it is unclear if the people understood what crucifixion was at the time of Christ's arrival.[4]

Uncertainty Concerning Christ's Coming

It is also unclear how well-known were prophecies concerning Christ's actual appearance in the New World. Prophecies concerning the coming of Christ as a mortal are found throughout the Book of Mormon; in fact, it is possible that this is one of the most common prophecies in the Nephite record. First noted in 1 Nephi 11:7, these prophecies continue until 3 Nephi 2:7 and range from simple observations that Christ would come to detailed prophecies concerning his birth and ministry. The designations associated with Christ's mortality include his identification as the Messiah, the Son of God, Lamb of God, Redeemer, Christ, and, importantly for this paper, Lord and God. The latter are significant as they indicate the prophecy that "God" would take on a mortal form was understood among at least some of the righteous.

Yet as common as these prophecies are, they emphasized Christ's birth and ministry in the Old World. Prophecies declaring Christ's ministry in the New World are rare in the text as we have it. The most explicit prophecies are again found in the writings of Nephi$_1$. As part of the vision concerning his descendants and after the destruction associated with Christ's death, he "saw the heavens open, and the Lamb of God descending out of heaven; and he came down and showed himself" to those who survived (1 Nephi 12:6).[5] Nephi$_1$ revisits the prophecy in 2 Nephi 26:1, noting, "After Christ shall have risen from the dead he shall show himself unto you, my children, and my beloved brethren." Reiterating the destruction that would take place at Christ's death, Nephi$_1$ then promises, "The Son of Righteousness shall appear unto them [the righteous who survive]; and he shall heal them, and they shall have peace with him" (2 Nephi 26:9). In both instances, Nephi$_1$ appears to be addressing later generations of Lehi's descendants who would experience Christ's visit, but their placement on the small plates may suggest they were not well known by later generations.[6]

Alma$_2$ also spoke of Christ's coming. For instance, Alma$_2$ would tell his son Corianton that their ministry was "to declare these glad tidings [the coming of Christ] unto this people, to prepare their minds; or rather that salvation might come unto them, that they may prepare the minds of their children to hear the word at the time of his coming" (Alma 39:16). A generation or two later, Helaman$_2$ would remind his sons, Nephi$_2$ and Lehi$_2$, of King Benjamin's prophecy, paraphrasing: "Jesus Christ, who shall come; yea, remember that he cometh to redeem the world" (Helaman 5:9). Nephi$_2$ would later declare that the Nephite "fathers . . . even down to this time, yea, they have testified of the coming of Christ" (Helaman 8:22). Significantly though, these prophecies only indicate an awareness that Christ was coming to earth to redeem it, not explicit prophecies concerning a visitation by him to those in the New World.

An explicit reference to Christ's coming to the New World following Nephi$_1$ is found in Alma 16:20. The verse is part of Mormon's summary of events for the latter half of the twelfth year of the reign of judges. In response to the ministering of the church's priests, "many of the people did inquire concerning the place where the Son of God should come." The interest appears to be based on the church's teachings, described a few verses earlier: "The Lord did pour out his Spirit on all the face of the land to prepare the minds of the children of men, or to prepare their hearts to receive the word which should be taught among them at the time of his coming" (Alma 16:16). As noted, the coming of Christ as a mortal was a common Book of Mormon prophecy; this continued as a part of the church's teachings in the reign of the judges, possibly reflecting the emphasis on Abinadi's teachings in the early church.[7] Mormon continues in Alma 16:20, noting that the people "were taught that [Christ] would appear unto them after his resurrection; and this the people did hear with great joy and gladness," thus suggesting that Christ's future appearance was a known element of the church's teachings.

Yet three years earlier in the ninth year of the reign of the judges, Alma$_2$, speaking to the people of Gideon, admitted, "The time is not far distant that the Redeemer liveth and cometh among his people. Behold, I do not say that he will come among us at the time of his dwelling in his mortal tabernacle; for behold, the Spirit hath not said unto me that this should be the case. Now as to this thing I do not know; but this much I do know, that the Lord God hath power to do all things which are according to his word" (Alma 7:7–8). According to the admission, Alma$_2$ acknowledges two things. The first is that he knows Christ will visit "his people" and the second is that Christ would not be in the New World during his "time of dwelling." The assumption as to whom "his people" are appears to be the church in the Book of Mormon, but if this is the case, then Alma$_2$ is acknowledging that he is unsure how exactly the prophecy would be fulfilled, his own uncertainty reflected in the admission.[8]

Perhaps most notable is the absence of this prophecy in the prophecies attributed to Samuel the Lamanite. As detailed as they were about the events that would take place in the New World at the birth and death of Christ,

Samuel's prophecies contain no explicit reference, or even allusion, to Christ's arrival in the New World.[9] In light of the above, it is possible that those gathered, as described in 3 Nephi 11, were not fully aware that Christ was to come.[10]

Uncertainty Concerning Christ as God

The final uncertainty mentioned above was the way Christ could also be identified as God. At issue was what the Nephites meant when they spoke of Christ as both "Son of God" and "God."[11] The identification for Christ as the Son of God is found fifty-one times in the Book of Mormon. The first mention is in 1 Nephi 10:17, where Lehi described Christ as the "Son of God." The designation is found four times in Nephi$_1$'s vision (1 Nephi 11:6, 7, 18, 24), with the angel also identifying Christ as the Lamb of God, who he later acknowledges as "the Son of the everlasting God" (1 Nephi 11:32) and "Son of the Eternal Father" (1 Nephi 11:21; 13:40). Later, in 2 Nephi 25, Nephi$_1$ uses the designation twice (2 Nephi 25:16, 19) in conjunction with "the Only Begotten of the Father" (2 Nephi 25:12; see also Alma 5:48; 9:26; 13:9). The text of King Benjamin's sermon contains the title three times (Mosiah 3:8; 4:2; 15:2), the first usage, as in 1 Nephi 11, used by an angel.

Alma$_2$ also uses the designation; in fact he uses the designation eighteen times, more than any other with its appearance in every major sermon he delivered.[12] The designation is used once by Helaman$_2$ when speaking to his sons, Nephi$_2$ and Lehi$_2$ (Helaman 5:12), with Nephi$_2$ using it three times in his sermon on the tower (Helaman 8:14, 15, 20). Samuel the Lamanite references Christ as "the Son of God" three times in Helaman 14 (verses 2, 8, 12). Of interest is the usage of the title by those who are critical of the church's teachings in Helaman 16:18: "It is not reasonable that such a being as a Christ should come; if so, and he be the Son of God, the Father of heaven and of earth." Though antagonistic, its usage here suggests a general understanding among the population as to Christ as the Son of God. One final note before moving on is that this designation is often associated with Christ's future mortal state. In fact, in at least two instances, Mosiah 15:3 and 3 Nephi 1:14, Christ's designation as "Son" is explicitly tied to his future, physical form.

Further prophetic utterances demonstrate that they distinguished between Christ and a figure identified as "God" even when not using the explicit designation of "Son of God." In 2 Nephi 25:23, Nephi₁ exhorts his people to believe in Christ and be reconciled unto God. In Nephi₁'s discourse concerning the eventual restoration of Israel, he notes, "The Lord covenanteth with none save it be with them that repent and believe in his Son, who is the Holy One of Israel" (2 Nephi 30:2). Nephi₁'s brother, Jacob, also suggests that there are two distinct and different divine beings. In Jacob 4:5, Jacob records that he and his people "believed in Christ and worshiped the Father in his name." Just a few verses later, Jacob would exhort his people to "be reconciled unto him [God] through the atonement of Christ, his Only Begotten Son" (Jacob 4:11). As with the designation of Christ as "Son of God," these references indicate a common understanding of Christ as a being separate from "God."

Yet even as these descriptions suggest that Christ and God were understood as two distinct beings, other references imply a more complex, ambiguous understanding to the designation of the term *God* and its application to Christ.[13] In 1 Nephi 19, Nephi₁ indicates that the "God of our fathers,... the God of Abraham, and of Isaac, and the God of Jacob" would be crucified, indicating that Christ was also "God" (1 Nephi 19:10). In 2 Nephi 10:3–4, Jacob explicitly designates Christ as God, who would be crucified and work miracles. A few chapters later, Nephi₁ would entitle Christ as "the Eternal God" (2 Nephi 26:12). A few hundred years later, Abinadi emphasized that "God would come down," this emphasis on divine condescension being one of the primary factors behind his martyrdom: "For thou hast said that God himself should come down among the children of men" (Mosiah 17:8; also Mosiah 13:34; 15:1). In at least one instance, the divine voice, identifying himself as Christ, refers to himself as "God." In Mosiah 26, which records the revelation setting out the church's regulations concerning membership, the divine voice declares, "This is my church;... whomsoever ye receive shall believe in my name; and him will I freely forgive. For it is I that taketh upon me the sins of the world;... then shall they know that I am the Lord their God, that I am their Redeemer" (Mosiah 26:22–23, 26).

A duality between the usage of the term *God* as a general term for divinity and as a designation for a specific entity is expressed in Alma 11. Part of the debate between Zeezrom and Amulek centers on this subject. In verse 25 Amulek referenced "the true and living God." After confirming this title, Zeezrom then asked if there was more than one God, implying that he understood Amulek to be discussing the title as the designation for a type of divine being. Amulek's answer is no, suggesting that his usage differed from what Zeezrom supposed. A few verses later, Zeezrom asks concerning the prophecy of Christ, "Who is he that should come? Is it the son of God?" (Alma 11:32). Amulek answers in the affirmative, to which Zeezrom then rejoins with, "He said there is but one God; yet he saith that the Son of God shall come" (Alma 11:35), which suggests that at some level "Son of God" was equated with the concept of "god" since Zeezrom is attempting to catch Amulek in a verbal error.

The subject is redressed again later in the confrontation, with Zeezrom asking if the Son of God was "the very Eternal Father" (Alma 11:38). Amulek responded again in the affirmative, noting that this individual would "come into the world to redeem his people" (Alma 11:40), an act that would allow for a judgment and resurrection by which all would "be brought and be arraigned before the bar of Christ the Son, and God the Father, and the Holy Spirit, which is one Eternal God" (Alma 11:44). In this verse, three usages of *God* are being used; God as entity is referenced in conjunction with the identification of the Father, while the entities of Christ, the Father, and the Holy Spirit are "one eternal God." Thus, there appears to be three concurrent usages of *God*: (1) individual entity, often but not always associated with a supreme deity equated either with God the Father, especially when used to designate Christ as Son or with Christ, (2) ontological descriptor, in which no specific identity is necessarily referenced, but purposes and behaviors of deity may include recognizing the deity's possible physical form, and (3) designation for organization of divine entities, or what we today would refer to as the Godhead.

Adding to the confusion, it appears that at some point the Nephite word *God* was not understood by the Lamanites. In Alma 18 the martial acts of Ammon$_2$ are ascribed to supernatural power, which leads Lamoni, a Lamanite king, to assume that Ammon is "the Great Spirit" (Alma 18:11). Later, when Ammon$_2$ demonstrates that he knows what Lamoni is thinking, Lamoni again equates him with the Great Spirit: "Who art thou? Art thou that Great Spirit, who knows all things" (verse 18). Still later, when Ammon asks if Lamoni believes in "God," Lamoni's answer is intriguing: "I do not know what that meaneth" (verse 25), suggesting that the terminology Ammon$_2$ uses, translated in the Book of Mormon as *God*, is not in the Lamanite lexicon or has a completely different meaning.[14] Ammon$_2$ then asks if Lamoni believes there is "a Great Spirit." When Lamoni responds in the affirmative, Ammon$_2$ declares, "This is God" (verse 28).

The same confusion appears later in Aaron's interaction with Lamoni's father. The exchange begins with Lamoni's father wondering why it is that Ammon$_2$ is not present. Aaron's response is that Ammon$_2$ had been called away to the land of Ishmael by "the Spirit of the Lord" (Alma 22:4). Lamoni's father then asks, "What is this that ye have said concerning the Spirit of the Lord? Behold, this is the thing which doth trouble me" (verse 5). What exactly it is that troubles him is not clear, though based on the confusion between the Nephite term *God* and the Lamanite term *Great Spirit*, it is possible that Lamoni's father is confused as to who is exactly interacting with Ammon$_2$. Aaron's response to this begins in the same manner as Ammon$_2$ with Lamoni: "Believest thou that there is a God?" (verse 7). Unlike Lamoni, who responded that he didn't know what that meant, Lamoni's father answers that he is aware of God but only through Nephite dissenters to whom he had granted religious rights of assembly and building of edifices. This awareness leads Lamoni's father to ask whether the Nephite God is equivalent to his Great Spirit, and, like his brother, Aaron responds in the affirmative (verses 9–10). What these narratives suggest is that Nephite terminology for deity is not the same as Lamanite terminology and that therefore the nature of God was not equally known among Lehi's descendants.

As to how they envisioned what a God was as a physical entity is never defined in the Book of Mormon. Christ is accorded a physical body, but only when he became mortal. For the Lamanites, deity, or at least a chief deity, was understood to be a Great Spirit, and though the terminology differed, all Nephite interactions with Christ in the Book of Mormon would have been with him in his premortal, precorporeal state, and thus a spirit as well, his designation as "Son" reflecting his future, corporeal state. The ontological nature of other individuals identified as God are either as spirit or not provided. Thus, not surprisingly, the Holy Ghost, or Spirit of God, is designated as a spirit. In the case of God the Father and his ontological state, the text is silent. Again, as noted above, it seems clear that the Nephites know of the existence of the Father as an independent entity and recognize generally his work regarding salvation, but there is no explicit interaction with God the Father outside of 2 Nephi 31, which records speech from both God the Father and Christ to Nephi$_1$. Thus, it is unclear if anyone in the Book of Mormon fully understood the ontological nature of God outside of spirit states, with the Lamanites possibly not even understanding the very terminology.[15]

"They ... Did Feel with Their Hands, and Did Know of a Surety"

These uncertainties—uncertainty as to the fulfillment of earlier Nephite prophecy, specifically prophecies concerning crucifixion and his actual appearance in the New World, as well as uncertainty concerning how Christ was God and if Gods had bodies—may have been answered in the touching experience. Unfortunately, Christ does not explain (nor Mormon for that matter), how exactly touching Christ was necessary for the acquisition of this knowledge. With that said, tactile manipulation is one of the primary avenues for early learning. Though rarely thought of in terms of the learning process—specifically abstract learning—tactile, or haptic, learning is formational at the beginning of the learning process. While haptic learning is crucial to spatial awareness, which includes such elements as temperature, air movement, object recognition, even balance, it also serves to make abstract thought concrete.

In little children and infants, some have suggested that approximately 60 percent of the early lexical development is simple nouns. This development begins with the child grasping and feeling the object. The act of touching creates rudimentary patterns of mental characteristics, which are the foundation of more complex mental representations. The "haptic schemas" (the patterns or characteristics associated with the object) then lead to "image schemas" in which the visual experience with the object harmonizes with the haptic memory; these then allow for the object to be associated with the more abstract identifying word.[16] For example, a child may first learn the concept of "apple" through the touch of one, which is reinforced by a picture of one, which is then assigned the abstract word *apple*. In the end, the child knows what an apple is and will associate the correct concept when presented with the word *apple*, but the process itself began with the tactile manipulation of one. In this manner Helen Keller was able to figure out how to communicate. It took her hands being placed under running water and then having her fingers manipulated into the signs for "water" that she grasped the concept of "water," which was the communicative breakthrough she needed. It was the tactile experience, the sense of touch, the water running over her skin, that led to the mental recognition.[17]

Based on the role of touch in learning, it is possible that the experience of touching Christ reinforced schema that already existed, such as the Nephite prophecies, while at the same time making concrete other schema, like the physical reality of a God. The experience itself would have entailed sensations such as pressure, temperature distribution, spatiality, and so forth—all of which would have revealed something of the nature of the object being touched. If, as Christ says, the object was his divinized body, then touch was being used to make aspects of a divine body concrete. This may seem elementary, but it has profound implications concerning the uncertainties mentioned above.

First, it would have confirmed the nature of crucifixion. As noted earlier, there is no evidence that Nephites earlier and the righteous present at Christ's arrival understood exactly what crucifixion entailed. Running fingers over the ridges and indentations of Christ's marks in his hands and in his feet would have initiated haptic learning, allowing for everyone present to grasp what crucifixion was which would have led to a greater understanding and appreciation of those prophecies; they would have truly understood what had been promised. Second, it would have confirmed the prophecies of Christ's coming and of his presence. This may seem obvious, but by handling and feeling Christ's body, those gathered would have no longer simply believed but known in a powerful, lasting way that Christ was real. That this is in fact what happened is realized in their response to the touching, recorded by Mormon: "And this they did do, going forth one by one until they had all gone forth . . . and did feel with their hands, and did know of a surety . . . that it was he, of whom it was written by the prophets, that should come" (3 Nephi 11:15).

Finally, the experience of touching Christ would have taught those gathered the physical reality of a divine body. Again, as obvious as it may sound, it would have revealed the spatial immediacy of Christ. A divine body took up space; it was present within a space not filled by anything else. It would have confirmed that deity had its own physical form independent of others. In this it would have contrasted with deity as spirit. The ontological implications of a spirit being were that they could be housed or embodied in anything, perhaps suggesting a fluidity to the concept of God. Feeling Christ's own body would have established that at least at some level, *God* includes an independent form. This experience would have affected that understanding from that moment forward. It also would have confirmed that the body was living. While it is not clear exactly what a resurrected body is like (does it have a pulse, does it have a circulatory system, does one breathe, and so forth), it is certainly not a corpse. Thus, his body would have been enlivened, possibly reacting to the stimuli of being touched by twitching, shivering, and so on. All of this would have confirmed his living nature, that deity was alive and therefore relatable at some level. Those gathered would know via this haptic learning the nature and very existence of deity. As Christ himself would recognize: "Ye have seen me and [now] know that I am" (3 Nephi 12:1).

"My Bowels Are Filled with Compassion towards You"

Though the tactile experience described in 3 Nephi 11 had an explicit purpose to teach those gathered about Christ, both in terms of prophecies uttered about him and his very ontological nature as God, the experience would have had other unspoken effects as well by virtue of the physiological aspect of the event. Perhaps the most significant would have been the hormonal changes enacted by this active form of touching, specifically the release of oxytocin. This physiological effect of touch has long been recognized and has been noted to be an essential feature of social interaction.[18] First noted as an effect of childbirth and labor, breastfeeding, and physical intimacy, oxytocin has since been found to be released in even casual touch such as handshakes, pats on the back, and so forth. While there is much that is still not known, one of the primary effects of oxytocin appears to reduce amygdala activity, an area of the brain that regulates fear and aggression and the release of hormones such as cortisol associated with stress and anxiety. At the same time, it helps facilitate the release of other hormones such as dopamine and serotonin, which have calming influences and are associated with prosocial behavior, such as creation and maintenance of long-term bonds, parental care, and other social affiliations.[19]

One of the intriguing outcomes of touch is that it appears the release of oxytocin associated with touch increases compliancy in those being touched. In one study, it was demonstrated that a waiter or waitress who touched a restaurant patron even in the most casual manner was more likely to receive a bigger tip.[20] Other studies have demonstrated that oxytocin makes one more socially aware, with one study noting that the presence of oxytocin led to greater visual concentration of another's eyes and facial expressions.[21] In light of the prosocial behavior that results from oxytocin, some have begun noting that oxytocin may play a role in one's spirituality and religiosity.[22]

Perhaps because touch has such a powerful physiological impact, touch experiences are highly regulated socially. No matter the culture, bodily contact is often limited to only certain situations and the type of touch is associated with one's spatiality.[23] One's understanding of self includes the physical separateness one has from objects and others, with the senses delineating the type of contact one has with another. Unlike the other senses though, touch possesses an immediacy in terms of response.[24] Unlike the other senses, touch includes an immediate awareness of being touched. One cannot be unaware of touch the same way one can be unaware of others looking at us or speaking to us.[25] It collapses personal space and is not an event that one is unaware of. As such, touch is one of the primary means of communication.

The space that separates us from others, and thus regulates the type of touching that can take place, demarcates the closeness of the individual with us. The more distant, the less attached we are to the individual. The closer they are to our body, the more likely we have attachment feelings to the individual. Moreover, the closer they are, the more they are allowed to touch and have access to more places to touch. Thus, not surprisingly, touch plays a role in determining social status. In a number of studies, initiation of touch seems to indicate one is of a higher social status, with the act elevating the individual in the lower status, since the act suggests access to higher social levels, as if some of the status rubbed off and is retained by the individual of lower status.[26] Other studies have demonstrated that because touch indicates status, the type of touch differs in those of higher and lower social status. Those in lower status positions are more likely to initiate touching and engage in more formal, polite touches such as handshakes that recognize and maintain spatial distance. Those of higher status are more likely to engage in more informal, friendly acts of touch such as hand-to-shoulder and hand-to-arm touch.[27]

Because the type of touch is significant as much as the act of touching itself, it is worth noting the terminology used to describe the touch type. In 3 Nephi 11 we are told that the individual was to "thrust" their hands (plural) into the side of Christ and "feel" the prints of the nails in his hands and feet. These suggest a tactile experience, which would have included feeling the ridges, the puckering of skin, pressure in or on the body, perhaps feeling the depressions or absence of flesh in the wounds themselves, sensing the warmth of the flesh. In the case of the spear mark, one would have also felt flesh surrounding the fingers inserted into the wound. If the above description of the tactile experience is somewhat uncomfortable, part of the reaction reflects the intimacy of the act itself. This was not simply a reaching out of a fingertip, but fully active form of touching of areas of the body normally off limits, particularly the lower torso. The social boundaries are not in effect and therefore result in our potentially reflexive discomfort.

In this sense, then, we can think of Christ's invitation as provocative. It certainly would have had social ramifications. In terms of status, Christ's invitation indicates his position of higher status, yet the type of touch is not one of social distance but of intimacy and closeness in which those gathered entered Christ's personal space and engaged in more than incidental, polite contact. They were invited not only to actively feel the contours and depressions of the marks but actually to place their hands inside the body of Christ in an area, either the torso or lower torso, that is restricted territory. Moreover, there is no record that Christ actively touched back. Instead, Christ stood there as twenty-five hundred people ran their hands over portions of his body, inserting them into his side. The invitation to enter his personal, intimate space suggests a reversal of status. Christ voluntarily placed himself into the lower status position regarding this touching event, elevating all those who actively touched him, in effect erasing the status as a marker. The closeness and the type and placement of the touching indicated that Christ did not view those touching as strangers but close, intimate friends or colleagues.

The effects, both in terms of the physiological effects and the resulting prosocial behavior, may provide insight into Christ's emphasis concerning social cohesion. Christ's instructions to the disciples concerning the proper manner of baptism immediately following the touching event include instruction that there be no "disputations" among the congregation (3 Nephi 11:22, 28). In verses 29–30, Christ teaches that there should be no contention and anger against one another in any situation, with Christ suggesting such antisocial behavior is the antithesis of his doctrine: "This is not my doctrine, to stir up the hearts of men with anger, one against another; but this is my doctrine, that such things should be done away." This is immediately followed by Christ's emphasis on the oneness that exists between him and other members of the Godhead (verses 32–36, see also verse 27).

Similar instruction is given to the multitude. While many have recognized themes in Christ's sermon at the temple, noting its similarities with Christ's Old World teachings, social cohesion plays a role in these as well.[28] Third Nephi 12:11–12 speaks to the importance of not responding in kind to negative social behaviors, as do verses 38–44, emphasizing the role of loving even your enemy, praying for those that despise and persecute you. Earlier, in verses 21–25, Christ again emphasized the role of reconciliation in proper worship, exhorting those gathered, "Go thy way unto thy brother, and first be reconciled" (verse 24) if they desired to come unto Christ. Christ's instruction concerning marriage in verses 27–32 may also be seen as an emphasis to greater cohesion, this time within the bonds of the marriage relationship.

Later in the day, oneness is again a theme. Beginning in chapter 15, Christ relates that there are "other sheep . . . which are not of this fold"; these too would receive Christ's ministrations so that there would be "one fold, and one shepherd" (verse 17). This is emphasized in verse 21, where Christ indicates that the righteous in the New World were those of whom he was speaking, again emphasizing the importance of one fold and one shepherd. Chapter 16 continues the theme, this time noting that there were still others that Christ would minister to, again because there was to be one fold and one shepherd (verse 3). Within this context of greater social cohesion established by the touching event, we place Christ's teachings on the gathering. Immediately following his emphasis on one fold and one shepherd, itself following on the heels of his teachings that had implied oneness among the gathered in Bountiful, Christ speaks concerning the manner by which he and the Father would gather all, both Israelite and Gentile (verses 4–5), placing the pivotal Isaianic prophecy concerning redemption and comfort within the context of the touching event and social cohesion of his earlier words (verses 17–20).[29]

"Even So Shall Ye Do"

The event described in 3 Nephi 11 was not the only tactile event of that day. Following his spoken discourses, Christ brought to him all who were "afflicted in any manner" (3 Nephi 17:7), who were then healed. We don't know precisely how the healing took place, but Christ suggested that he would do so in the same manner as he did in the Old World: "I perceive that ye desire that I should show unto you what I have done unto your brethren at Jerusalem" (verse 8). If he did heal in the same manner, this would have included touching the afflicted as this is the overwhelmingly predominant way he healed in the New Testament. A few verses later, we find that Christ invited all the little children in the gathering to come to him, where, following a prayer concerning all who had gathered, Christ "took their little children, one by one, and blessed them" (verse 21). Again, though it doesn't say explicitly that he touched them, the implication of his taking them one by one suggests that he would have held them, perhaps encircling them with his arms while blessing them, while at the same time reflecting the earlier experience. Just as they had come one by one to touch him, so he too touched them one by one. These later events would have had the same physiological results, and thus would have emphasized and reinforced the effects of the earlier event resulting in even greater social cohesion, the reciprocal acts of touch—those gathered touching Christ and then

Christ touching them—strengthening and adding layer upon layer to those relationships.

The initial touching event also played a role in Christ's introduction of the sacrament and the instruction concerning his church recorded in 3 Nephi 18. After establishing the way the bread of the sacrament would be dispersed and eaten, Christ noted that it should be done "in remembrance of my body, which I have shown unto you" (verse 7). Thus, one element of the new ordinance experience was to remember the experience they had with Christ's body. For those gathered, the sacrament would remind not only of Christ's sacrifice but also his resurrected, tangible body. It would be a reminder that he was there. Therefore, one aspect of the event was to be a specific memory to be used in later spiritual growth.

This aspect of the event, the memory of it, is explicit in Christ's later instruction. Beginning in 3 Nephi 18:22, after noting that the righteous should "meet together oft," Christ teaches that no one should be forbidden from meeting with the congregation: "Ye shall not forbid any man from coming unto you when ye shall meet together; . . . ye shall pray for them, and shall not cast them out" (verses 22–23). Why would one do so? Because Christ himself had set the example: "Ye see that I have commanded that none of you should go away, but rather have commanded that ye should come unto me" (verse 25). This is then followed by a direct reference to the event and an exhortation to do likewise: "That ye should come unto me, that ye might feel and see; even so shall ye do unto the world" (verse 25; emphasis added).

The last clause, "even so shall ye do unto the world," is beautifully ambiguous. What is it exactly that those gathered were to do? On one level, it appears they were to bring people to Christ much as he had brought those gathered to him. In other words, they, having experienced Christ, would now go and invite others to come unto him. Doing so may be reflected in something as simple as a handshake or a pat on the back, a physical act that demonstrates to the one touched that they are being thought of and known, that they belong and are valued. Yet it is equally possible that Christ's request is not alluding to the act of physical touch but instead to an individual making themselves as available, as open, as he had, demonstrating the same willingness to be vulnerable and receptive to others as Christ himself had been.[30] Or perhaps it is both—both a request that invites others to the supernal knowledge that we ourselves know concerning Christ and the willingness to make ourselves as open and vulnerable as Christ himself was.

Conclusion

However we are to understand this commandment, it arises from the powerful experience of touch. It was through touching and being touched that those gathered that day in Bountiful truly knew that Jesus Christ was the fulfillment of centuries of prophecy, that he was the God who died and was resurrected, not just for those present but for all humanity. It was through touch that physiological effects could take place, reinforcing Christ's teachings concerning unity and oneness. It was through the experience of touch that the new ordinance of the sacrament was introduced. It was the memory of touch that led to Christ's supernal, and open-ended, invitation to "do unto the world." Even as we recognize the significance of Christ's spoken teachings, perhaps it is through the unspoken acts of touch that Christ's most significant teaching took place. Certainly its power resonates with us today, his invitation as real now as it was on that day in Bountiful.

DANIEL L. BELNAP *is a professor of ancient scripture at Brigham Young University.*

Notes

1. Though he does not use the term "crucifixion," Nephi$_1$ does appear to be aware of the act in his own prophecies. In 1 Nephi 11:33, Nephi relates that he saw Christ "lifted up upon the cross and slain for the sins of the world." This suggests that Nephi$_1$ saw in vision the crucifixion of Christ, though he did not say he saw that, only that he saw Christ lifted on the cross, not the manner of how Christ was attached to the cross.
2. "And as for those who are at Jerusalem, saith the prophet, they shall be scourged by all the people, because they crucify the God of Israel" (1 Nephi 19:13). The immediate precedent for "the prophet" is Zenos, suggesting it is Zenos's prophecies to which Nephi$_1$ is alluding.
3. Brant A. Gardner, *Second Witness: Analytical and Contextual Commentary on the Book of Mormon* (Salt Lake City: Greg Kofford Books, 2007), 3:302. Gardner suggests that Abinadi's awareness of the crucifixion came from the Nephite records, not Isaiah: "The

crucifixion is stated explicitly in 1 Nephi 19:13, 2 Nephi 6:9, 10:3, 25:13, sources that predate Abinadi and to which he must have had some access. Since it is unlikely that Abinadi had access to the small plates, we may suppose that this information also appeared on the large plates which would have served as Abinadi's source." See also Gardner, *Second Witness*, 1:210–13, in which he notes the possibility of cross imagery in Mesoamerica but not Roman-style crucifixion.

4. Brant A. Gardner, *Second Witness*, 2:185: "I tend to see the inclusion of the specific word 'crucifixion' as a modern artifact rather than accurate rendition of plate text. Even assuming that Jacob understood exactly what crucifixion was, the chance that his audience would be familiar with that form of execution is extremely remote. Those who came from the Old World might possibly know it, but the New World portions of the Nephite population ... would not."

5. Gardner notes the absence of this prophecy in later Nephite tradition, see Gardner, *Second Witness*, 1:224: "These verses prophesy the events recorded in 3 Nephi. Oddly enough, despite its explicitness, this particular prophecy is never referenced close to that time. While the people recognize that the Messiah's death and arrival among them is approaching, it is the predictions of Samuel the Lamanite, not Nephi, that they recall (3 Nephi 8:3). What this silence confirms is that Nephi's personal record on the small plates is essentially lost to the greater tradition. Mormon tells us that he found the small plates only as he searched among the records (Words of Mormon 1:3). He was not only in charge of the records but was also researching the information which to create his own summary text. If Mormon, at the end of the Nephite civilization, was unaware of these small plates, we may assume that earlier keepers of the records were similarly unaware of them." There does appear to be some evidence that at least some of the small plates are known by earlier writers in Alma and Helaman. In Alma 63:12 we learn that Helaman₁ initiated a program in which the existing texts were made more available, presumably via making copies: "All those engravings which were in the possession of Helaman were written and sent forth among the children of men throughout all the land." According to Words of Mormon 1:10, Amaleki delivered all the plates he had, which would have been the small plates of Nephi, to Benjamin, who "put them with the other plates," presumably describing the storage facility for all records, until all the records were received by Mormon. This transfer would have occurred just a few generations before Helaman,'s work. Thus, it is possible that at least until Helaman₁ the material on the small plates was known. Thanks to my colleague John Hilton III for pointing out this connection. With that said, Gardner's point concerning the specificity of this prophecy and its apparent ignorance by those gathered in Bountiful at the time of Christ's appearance is intriguing.

6. See notes 2–3 and the possibility of ignorance to prophetic statements found exclusively on the small plates. With this said, it is possible that there are other texts that Mormon used. The prophecy alluded to by Mormon in 3 Nephi 11:12, "they remembered that it had been prophesied among them that Christ should show himself unto them after his ascension into heaven," is not found anywhere else in the Book of Mormon.

7. The role of Abinadi's teachings in the church's doctrine may be seen in Mosiah 18:1–2 and 19–20 where the church's understanding of the gospel principle of redemption appears to be based on Abinadi's understanding of redemption, provided in Mosiah 14–15. Abinadi's teachings concerning redemption are again mentioned in the Mosiah 26, which provides the regulations of Christ's church, via revelation (see verses 15, 25–27, the latter of which associates redemption with the eschatological judgment like Abinadi's association in Mosiah 15:19–27).

8. Gardner, *Second Witness*, 4:8: "Alma understands that Jesus will live his life in the Old World but does not know if Jesus will come to the New World as a mortal."

9. Heather Hardy, "'Saving Christianity': The Nephite Fulfillment of Jesus's Eschatological Prophecies," in *Journal of Book of Mormon Studies* 23, no. 1 (2014): 22–55: "Although six hundred years prior to the devastation, Book of Mormon prophet Nephi had clearly taught that the resurrected Lord would visit Lehi's posterity, . . . the fact that Samuel the Lamanite, just a generation before, had not mentioned a post resurrection visit may have led the Nephites to forget the earlier prophecy or to interpret it other than literally" (40). Samuel's prophecies, and the narrative of their presentation, is not so clear-cut either. For more on the history and compilation of Samuel's prophecies, see Daniel L. Belnap, "'There was One Samuel': Possible Multiple Sources for the Samuel Narrative," in *Samuel the Lamanite: That Ye May Believe*, ed. Charles Swift (Provo, UT: Religious Studies Center; Salt Lake City: Deseret Book, 2021), 251–92.

10. Hardy, "'Saving Christianity,'" 39–40: "Despite the Father's explicit introduction, the Nephites are genuinely puzzled when the resurrected Lord descends from the skies. . . . It appears that the Nephite survivors are not expecting a divine manifestation beyond Jesus's voice from heaven." This is perhaps even more probable if one considers the survivors to be predominantly Lamanite (see 3 Nephi 6:14).

11. See Gardner, *Second Witness*, 1:214–22, for an excellent introduction to this challenge and his approach to the problem (specifying that "Son of God" has reference to Christ as the son of El Elyon [Most High God], with references to Christ as Father in reference to Christ's role as Father to humankind). While this may resolve some issues, as we'll see, there are several references that simply discuss Christ as "God" or do not identify the title or designation with any specific individual.

12. See Alma 5:50; 6:8; 7:9, 10, 13; 9:26; 11:32, 35, 38; 13:16; 16:19, 20; 33:14, 17, 18, 22; 36:17, 18.

13. Though the following may seem to be referencing the ongoing discussion concerning the depiction of God in the Book of Mormon as a modalist or a trinitarian model, this argument is actually addressing what those in the Book of Mormon may have understood God to be ontologically, or what they thought about God in physical form. For more on the modalist or trinitarian discussion, see Hull and Smoot in this volume. See also David L. Paulsen and Ari D. Bruening, "The Social Model of the Trinity in 3 Nephi," in *Third Nephi: An Incomparable Scripture*, ed. Andrew C. Skinner and Gaye Strathearn (Provo, UT: Neal A. Maxwell Institute for Religious Scholarship; Salt Lake City: Deseret Book, 2012), 191–234.

14. Gardner, *Second Witness*, 4:292, notes the incompatibility and suggests it is a "cultural/religious difference."
15. It is possible that the Jaredite record may contain an interaction with a physical body. In Ether 3:8–13, the brother of Jared interacts with the Lord in such a manner that may have included seeing a body. According to verse 7, when questioned as to why the brother of Jared had fallen to the ground, he states, "I saw the finger of the Lord. . . . I knew not that the Lord had flesh and blood." The Lord's response is that because of his faith, the brother of Jared saw that the Lord would "take upon me flesh and blood" (verse 9). What exactly the brother of Jared saw is unclear. Moroni appears to believe that he saw Christ's spirit form, but which was "after the manner and in the likeness of the same body even as he showed himself unto the Nephites" (verse 17). Elder Jeffrey R. Holland entertained the possibility that in some revelatory manner the brother of Jared actually saw the body of Christ. See Jeffrey R. Holland, *Christ and the New Covenant* (Salt Lake City: Deseret Book, 1997), 22: "Another interpretation of this passage is that the faith of the brother of Jared was so great he saw not only the spirit finger and body of the premortal Jesus . . . but also some distinctly more revealing aspect of Christ's body of flesh, blood, and bone." With that said, Elder Holland's opinion falls on the following interpretation: "A final explanation—and in terms of the brother of Jared's faith the most persuasive one—is that Christ was saying to the brother of Jared, "Never have I showed myself unto man in this manner, without my volition, driven solely by the faith of the beholder." As a rule, prophets are invited into the presence of the Lord, are bidden to enter his presence by him and only with his sanction. The brother of Jared, on the other hand, seems to have thrust himself through the veil, not as an unwelcomed guest but perhaps technically as an uninvited one" (23).
16. Christiane Kiese-Himmel, "Haptic Perception in Infancy and First Acquisition of Object Words: Developmental and Clinical Approach," in *Human Haptic Perception: Basics and Applications*, ed. Martin Grunwald (Birkhäuser Basel, 2008), 321–34: "Altogether, the development starts in sensory modality, i.e, haptic schemas (references are percepts), followed by image-schemas in the second half of the first year (references are mental images), culminating in arbitrary symbols (words)" (328).
17. Helen Keller, *The Story of My Life: Parts I & II by Helen Keller, 1880–1968; Part III from the Letters and Reports of Anne Mansfield Sullivan, ca.1867–1936*, ed. John Albert Macy (New York: Doubleday, Page, 1905), 24.
18. The literature on this is voluminous. For a general overview, see Tiffany Field, *Touch* (Cambridge, MA: MIT, 2001).
19. Toku Takshashi, *Physiology of Love: Role of Oxytocin in Human Relationships, Stress Response, and Health* (New York: Nova Science, 2013).
20. A. Crusco and C. G. Wetzel, "The Midas Touch: The Effects of Interpersonal Touch on Restaurant Tipping," in *Personality and Social Psychology Bulletin* 10 (1984): 512–17.
21. Siri Leknes et al., "Oxytocin Enhances Pupil Dilation and Sensitivity to 'Hidden' Emotional Expressions," in *Social Cognitive and Affective Neuroscience* 8, no. 7 (2013): 741–49.

22. Colin Holbrook, Jennifer Hahn-Holbrook, and Julianne Holt-Lunstad, "Self-Reported Spirituality Correlates with Endogenous Oxytocin," in *Psychology of Religion and Spirituality* 7, no. 1 (2015): 46–50; see also Elena L. Grigorenko, "Closeness of All Kinds: The Role of Oxytocin and Vasopressin in the Physiology of Spiritual and Religious Behavior," in *Thriving and Spirituality Among Youth: Research Perspectives and Future Possibilities*, ed. Amy Eva Alberts Warren, Richard M. Lerner, and Erin Phelps (Hoboken, NJ: John Wiley & Sons, 2012), 33-60.

23. Bryan Lawson, *The Language of Space* (Oxford: Architectural Press, 2001): "Humans normally only allow bodily contact in a number of limited contexts: first, and most obviously, this is between sexual partners whether of the opposite or same gender; secondly, between close relatives, particularly parents and their young children; thirdly, between the very young before the social taboo of contact has been acquired; fourth, in greetings, when momentary contact is allowed as in handshakes, kisses or even nose rubs, depending on your culture; fifth, for the comforting of individuals in exceptional circumstances of distress; and finally, of course, in the highly specialized settings of professional treatment by doctors, dentists and so on. However, for the vast majority of the time in nearly all our relationships we feel uncomfortable if bodily contact is made and usually apologize if we accidently bump into each other" (102).

24. Lawson, *Language of Space*, 110: "Distance is not abstract, since it quite strongly relates to the way we are aware of our fellow human beings. Under normal circumstances, the senses work in the series of nested spatial bubbles rather like 'Russian dolls'. We can see, hear, smell and touch people in that order."

25. Matthias M. Müller and Claire-Marie Giabbiconi, "Attention in Sense of Touch," in *Human Haptic Perception*, 199–26: "Contrary to vision for instance, while visual and auditory stimuli might be miles away from our body, somatosensory stimuli are not. They have an immediate impact on our body surface, which makes somatosensory stimuli very different from auditory or visual ones" (199). See also Stephen Thayer, "Social Touching," in *Tactual Perception: A Sourcebook*, ed. William Schiff and Emerson Foulke (Cambridge: Cambridge University Press, 1982), 263–304: "Touch, like all nonverbal behaviors, rarely has a unitary, unequivocal meaning. Whether it is a tap, a shove, or a caress, the meaning or message can vary profoundly depending upon a host of other factors. Because touching another's body generates an immediate demand for response, as well as a special intimacy or threat unique among communicative behaviors, touch is probably the most carefully guarded and monitored of all social behaviors" (266). Also Lawson, *Language of Space*, 115: "Inside the distance of a half a metre or so, we can touch another person. We may feel body heat and smell body odour, and we may smell breath and perfume. If facing one another, we can see the face in sufficient detail to appreciate emotion accurately unless very skillfully concealed. This then is a distance of trust and intimate activity. It is a distance that we enter normally only with permission. It is socially difficult to ignore someone with this distance, and some form of acknowledgement at the very least is expected. Indeed it may even be hard to ignore some else's presence simply because of the wealth of ways they can be sensed at this distance. Public display of the affection associated with such a distance is

disapproved of in some cultures and many situations. Communication at this distance can be by whispering, and thus can remain private from all other people in the same space."

26. Judith A. Hall, "Gender and Status Patterns in Social Touch," in *The Handbook of Touch: Neuroscience, Behavioral, and Health Perspectives*, ed. Matthew J. Hertenstein and Sandra J. Weiss (New York: Springer, 2011), 329–50, specifically pages 341–46.

27. For the specific studies, see Hall, "Gender and Status Patterns in Social Touch," 343: "The lower-status person was significantly more likely to initiate handshake, whereas the higher-status person was non-significantly more likely to engage in affectionate and hand-to-shoulder and hand-to-arm touch."

28. For more on those similarities, see John W. Welch, *Illuminating the Sermon at the Temple and the Sermon on the Mount* (Provo, UT: FARMS, 1999).

29. This passage has long been recognized as foundational to Nephite prophecy and teachings. For more on its importance, see *Abinadi: He Came Among Them in Disguise*, ed. Shon D. Hopkin (Provo, UT: Religious Studies Center; Salt Lake City: Deseret Book, 2018). See also Dana M. Pike, "'How Beautiful upon the Mountains': The Imagery of Isaiah 52:7–10 and Its Occurrences in the Book of Mormon," in *Isaiah in the Book of Mormon*, ed. Donald W. Parry and John W. Welch (Provo, UT: FARMS, 1998), 242–92. Also, Daniel L. Belnap, "The Bible, The Book of Mormon, and the Concept of Scripture," in *No Weapon Shall Prosper: New Light on Sensitive Issues*, ed. Robert L. Millet (Provo, UT: Religious Studies Center and Deseret Book, 2011), 141–70, specifically 146–51.

30. One intriguing implication is that the invitation connects the event to Christ's teachings concerning becoming like a little child, found in 3 Nephi 11:37–38; 12:9, 45. One cohort of the population that would allow for the touching of their belly as open and trusting and innocently as Christ did would be little children. Thus, it is possible that the event and the nature of Christ's trust were reflected in his call for those gathered to become as a little child, expressing similar characteristics.

12

Mentoring in the Savior's Way
Learning from Jesus Christ's Example in 3 Nephi

CAMEY L. ANDERSEN

Our Heavenly Father and our Savior, Jesus Christ, are our greatest examples of mentoring. Elder Dieter F. Uchtdorf of the Quorum of the Twelve Apostles said, "The most powerful and capable being in the universe has as His greatest purpose to mentor you, His children, and provide a way for them to one day live with Him. . . . Think of the people Jesus ministered to during His mortal life. . . . His teachings centered on assuring ordinary people that God was among them, would answer their prayers, place them on His shoulders, and carry them home."[1]

In the Book of Mormon, the Savior continued his Father's work of mentoring, this time among the Nephites after his resurrection. In 3 Nephi we see how the Savior fulfilled important mentoring roles in his visit to the Nephites. While he was not a traditional mentor in interacting with them over an extended period, the Savior mentored them as individuals and as a group in powerful experiences during his brief time with them. A key feature of mentoring is the transformative growth opportunities it offers for individuals who are mentored.[2] In 3 Nephi we see a society transformed by their visit with the Savior, and the Savior's mentoring during his time with them and what the

Nephites learned from him played an essential role in their becoming "all converted unto the Lord" (4 Nephi 1:2).

This essay will show how the Savior mentored the Nephites through his words, teachings, and actions and will provide the reader with ideas about how to be a better mentor from the Savior's example and teachings. Using an adaptation of foundational mentoring principles by Amaury Nora and Gloria Crisp,[3] this article discusses (1) his emotional support for them, (2) his knowledge support in teaching them, providing learning about specific subject knowledge, and (3) the role model he was for them. These mentoring principles are further applied by examining scriptural examples and by additional mentoring research. His example can strengthen and inspire readers to be effective mentors as they serve in their personal and professional lives and in their Church callings and assignments. Mentoring in the Savior's way can make a difference in the lives of those we work with, minister to, and love.

The Savior Mentors with Emotional Support

First, he provided emotional support for the Nephites. In mentoring, emotional support can be defined as supportive help to identify challenges and provide increased confidence about responsibilities ahead.[4] Nora and Crisp described this aspect of mentoring as "an emotional safety net" that also includes "words of encouragement and support[, providing...] attentiveness and nurturing."[5] The Savior began his ministry to the Nephites with an immediate personal engagement and established a relationship of trust with them, reflecting the mentoring emotional support he would provide during his time with them. In 3 Nephi 11 we read that he invited them to interact with him "one by one."

> And it came to pass that the Lord spake unto them saying:
> Arise and come forth unto me, that ye may thrust your hands into my side, and also that ye may feel the prints of the nails in my hands and in my feet, that ye may know that I am the God of Israel, and the God of the whole earth, and have been slain for the sins of the world.
> And it came to pass that the multitude went forth, and thrust their hands into his side, and did feel the prints of the nails in his hands and in

> his feet; and this they did do, going forth one by one until they had all gone forth, and did see with their eyes and did feel with their hands, and did know of a surety and did bear record, that it was he, of whom it was written by the prophets, that should come.
>
> And when they had all gone forth and had witnessed for themselves, they did cry out with one accord, saying:
>
> Hosanna! Blessed be the name of the Most High God! And they did fall down at the feet of Jesus, and did worship him. (3 Nephi 11:13–17)

Because the Nephites had individual and personal time with him after his appearance, including touching the prints in his hands and feet, they were able to gain a knowledge of his divinity and then give their own witness of him. This interaction created both a trust and knowledge of what they had only believed before. Later in chapter 17 he had the people bring their sick to him one by one, and he healed "every one" (3 Nephi 17:9). "He took their little children, one by one, and blessed them, and prayed unto the Father for them" (3 Nephi 17:21).

In these examples, we see how the Savior prioritized the individual. He provided emotional support not just for a group of Saints but for each Nephite by allowing them to interact with him personally, and he included groups that might be marginalized such as the sick and the little children. He also created trust between him and the Nephites through his caring and personal interaction with each of them. In mentoring research, trust in the mentor determines how positive the mentee felt about the mentoring relationship, and supportive mentors look for opportunities to build trust with mentees.[6] The Savior's inclusion of all shows us how we need to pay particular attention in mentoring individuals who may not reach out for help.

It is noteworthy that the Savior began his ministry to the Nephites with this one-by-one interaction. As we begin our ministries in different callings or look to improve our service, we can learn from his example. Establishing a personal connection with individuals should be a highest priority of mentors.[7] The Nephites "were in number about two thousand and five hundred souls; and they did consist of men, women, and children" (3 Nephi 17:25), and the Savior ministered to them individually. He reminds us of our responsibility to reach out to the one, no matter how small or large our assignments.

The Savior concluded his ministry with one-by-one ministry to the apostles. Third Nephi 28:1 explained, "And it came to pass when Jesus had said these words, he spake unto his disciples, one by one, saying unto them: What is it that ye desire of me, after that I am gone to the Father?" When three of the twelve did not speak, Jesus continued to reach out to them individually.

> And when he had spoken unto them, he turned himself unto the three, and said unto them: What will ye that I should do unto you, when I am gone unto the Father?
>
> And they sorrowed in their hearts, for they durst not speak unto him the thing which they desired.
>
> And he said unto them: Behold, I know your thoughts, and ye have desired the thing which John, my beloved, who was with me in my ministry, before that I was lifted up by the Jews, desired of me.
>
> Therefore, more blessed are ye, for ye shall never taste of death; but ye shall live to behold all the doings of the Father unto the children of men, even until all things shall be fulfilled according to the will of the Father, when I shall come in my glory with the powers of heaven. (3 Nephi 28:4–7)

He knew the needs and desires of each apostle. He did not need to ask them. However, he still showed the value of each apostle and each apostle's feelings, first by asking each individual his desire. Then even when those desires were not verbally shared, he discerned them and helped all these disciples achieve their righteous hopes. Although three of the apostles expressed an unconventional desire—to continue to live and serve beyond their normal life span—the Savior did not discourage them. Instead, he provided the help they needed to achieve their desired goal to serve until he comes again. Without his miraculous help, their desires would have been impossible.

While we do not have the perfect mentoring abilities of the Savior in discerning individual needs, we can ask for and be blessed with the gift of discernment in mentoring and, as worthy members of the Church, have the gift of the Holy Ghost to help identify individual needs. The Savior recognized his apostles as unique individuals with unique capacities to serve him and our Heavenly Father and to minister to others. Through mentoring, we can support others to achieve goals that may seem impossible to them. We help others elevate their vision and confidence to see what they can be and become.[8]

When the Savior first descended from heaven and invited the Nephites to feel his wounded side and the nail prints in his hands and feet, he also promised them a three-part knowledge and blessing from that interaction: they would "know that I am the God of Israel, and the God of the whole earth, and have been slain for the sins of the world" (3 Nephi 11:14). In the same way, our mentoring can help those we serve learn for themselves and develop unshakable testimonies of the Savior as we foster that connection and point them to him.

The Savior Mentors with Knowledge Support

A second important part of mentoring is providing knowledge support, or helping mentees understand information that needs explanation, clarification, or even correction. The Nephites had the unique blessing of having Jesus Christ, the Creator of the universe, with them to share knowledge and understanding for issues they were facing. While the all-knowing Savior could have provided knowledge for them on any or all topics, we see how the specific knowledge he shared with them helped them better understand the doctrine of Christ and being children of the covenant.

One of the first doctrines Christ emphasized was baptism. He explained how it should be done, who is eligible for baptism, and what words should be used for the baptism. In providing these details about baptism, he wanted the Nephites to clearly understand that this is the correct way to baptize and explained, "And there shall be no disputations among you" (3 Nephi 11:22). To help the Nephites comprehend what they needed to know about the gospel, he further emphasized "this is my doctrine" and "this is not my doctrine" (see 3 Nephi 11:30–32, 35, 39–40).

The Savior also mentored by providing additional resources for the Nephites. He referred them to the words of Isaiah in the strongest terms: "Ye ought to search these things. Yea, a commandment I give unto you that ye search these things diligently; for great are the words of Isaiah. For surely he spake as touching all things concerning my people which are of the house of Israel" (3 Nephi 23:1–2). He also counseled them to read the words of other prophets, "Search the prophets, for many there be that testify of these things" (3 Nephi 23:5).

In a poignant moment in 3 Nephi, the Savior provided a mentoring example of kindly correcting when a mistake has been made. He first told the Nephites that they needed to record scriptures they had not recorded. He then asked Nephi to show him their record and asked why they had not preserved the words of Samuel the Lamanite. The Savior said,

> Verily I say unto you, I commanded my servant Samuel, the Lamanite, that he should testify unto this people, that at the day that the Father should glorify his name in me that there were many saints who should arise from the dead, and should appear unto many, and should minister unto them. And he said unto them: Was it not so?
>
> And his disciples answered him and said: Yea, Lord, Samuel did prophesy according to thy words, and they were all fulfilled.
>
> And Jesus said unto them: How be it that ye have not written this thing, that many saints did arise and appear unto many and did minister unto them? . . .
>
> And it came to pass that Jesus commanded that it should be written; therefore it was written according as he commanded. (3 Nephi 23:9–11, 13)

As the Lord and Savior, Jesus could have given them any instruction, but the attentive personal mentoring he had shown them previously likely would have made his correction easier for the Nephites to accept and follow. The Savior's example is instructive for mentors to remember that a foundational personal relationship with those we serve can help them be more receptive when information shared requires change. In 3 Nephi 24, we see the Savior also commanded the Nephites to write the words of the prophet Malachi from the Old Testament, which he also "expounded" (3 Nephi 24:1). These teachings included messages about paying tithes and offerings, the Second Coming, and the return of Elijah the prophet (3 Nephi 24–26).

These examples show how the Savior noticed what knowledge the Nephites were missing. He helped them identify it and add it to the learning they would have. He also took the time to explain principles to them and why they were valuable for their happiness. As mentors, we should take the time to explain concepts. We are patient when information needs to be clarified. We also understand the importance of teaching doctrine and the power in knowledge for mentees. We see that "when Jesus had expounded all the scriptures in one, which they had written, he commanded them that they should teach the things which he had expounded unto them" (3 Nephi 23:14). He taught and mentored the disciples, and then he asked them to teach the people with what they had learned.

The Savior had an eternal perspective that was greater than the Nephites' earthly view, and he tried to expand their knowledge by sharing some of that understanding with them. He said, "These scriptures which ye had not with you, the Father commanded that I should give unto you; for it was wisdom in him that they should be given unto future generations" (3 Nephi 26:2). By offering the Nephites the missing scriptures, not only was the Savior mentoring them and providing spiritual knowledge for them; under the direction of his Father, he was providing support for future generations who would also need that knowledge and counsel.

He also provided clarification with the name of the church, which was causing disagreements among the people (3 Nephi 27:3). The Savior said,

> Verily, verily, I say unto you, why is it that the people should murmur and dispute because of this thing?
> Have they not read the scriptures, which say ye must take upon you the name of Christ, which is my name? For by this name shall ye be called at the last day;
> And whoso taketh upon him my name, and endureth to the end, the same shall be saved at the last day.
> Therefore, whatsoever ye shall do, ye shall do it in my name; therefore ye shall call the church in my name; and ye shall call upon the Father in my name that he will bless the church for my sake.
> And how be it my church save it be called in my name? For if a church be called in Moses' name then it be Moses' church; or if it be called in the name of a man then it be the church of a man; but if it be called in my name then it is my church, if it so be that they are built upon my gospel. (3 Nephi 27:4–8)

Not only did he clarify the correct name of the church but he also explained why the church was called in his name, including an explanation for why they were to take upon themselves his name. Still today, the Savior's teachings help modern Saints understand or explain why the church is called The Church of Jesus Christ of Latter-day Saints.[9]

Just as the Savior clarified the name of the church, he also resolved the disagreements and confusion the Nephites had on uncertainties of doctrine. In 3 Nephi 11:28 he said, "And according as I have commanded you thus shall ye baptize. And there shall be no disputations among you, as there have hitherto been; neither shall there be disputations among you concerning the points of my doctrine as there have hitherto been." The Savior's mentoring dissipated the contention that had been among Nephites, but it required multiple efforts, even by him, to eliminate the disagreements.

The Savior also helped the new apostles better understand their roles and callings when he spoke directly to them. He said, "Remember the words which I have spoken. For behold, ye are they whom I have chosen to minister unto this people. Therefore I say unto you, take no thought for your life, what ye shall eat, or what ye shall drink; nor yet for your body, what ye shall put on. . . . For your heavenly Father knoweth that ye have need of all these things" (3 Nephi 13:25, 32). As we mentor, we can help those we are responsible for understand their roles and responsibilities. We can help them learn how to use their talents. We can encourage them in the journey ahead and reassure them that Heavenly Father will help them, even as they face difficulties.

The Savior Mentors as a Role Model

In 3 Nephi the Savior also provided a perfect example to the Nephites of how to live the gospel. Being a role model is one of the most important responsibilities of a mentor as we show mentees possibilities for their future and provide encouragement and a vision for their potential.[10] As our divine role model, the Savior provided many aspects of gospel living to emulate during his time among the Nephites. He said, "Behold I am the light; I have set an example for you" (3 Nephi 18:16). While his time with the Nephites was not long, his impact was lasting (see 4 Nephi 1). Even for modern role models, it is the quality, not a prescribed quantity, of mentoring interactions that can have the greatest impact on mentoring.[11] Mentors should not minimize the potential impact of their intentional mentoring efforts.

Three examples of role modeling the Savior used are (1) administering the sacrament; (2) teaching prayer; and (3) showing support for his apostles as leaders. First, in chapter 18, Jesus taught the Nephites how to administer the sacrament, as well as its importance: "And it came to pass that Jesus commanded his disciples that they should bring forth some bread and wine unto him" (3 Nephi 18:1). After he asked the disciples to bring the bread and wine for the sacrament, the Savior himself broke and blessed the bread to show how the sacrament should be administered. He oversaw the administration of the sacrament twice in this example—first to the disciples, then to the multitude. Then the Savior took the time to explain what is required for the sacrament—the one administering it must be ordained and the importance of following his example in administering it (3 Nephi 18:5–7). He also explained the meaning and significance of the bread and in later verses the wine (3 Nephi 18: 7, 11) and how both are a representation of him. He promised the Nephites that if they would remember him, they would have his Spirit to be with them: "And this ye shall do in remembrance of my body, which I have shown unto you. And it shall be a testimony unto the Father that ye do always remember me. And if ye do always remember me ye shall have my Spirit to be with you" (3 Nephi 18:7).

Later, in chapter 20, he again provided a model for the sacrament and breaking and blessing the bread. In this example, no one brought the bread or wine for the sacrament. Still, they were able to miraculously witness the Savior administer the sacrament another time. He reiterated the importance of the sacrament ordinances when he said, "He that eateth this bread eateth of my body to his soul; and he that drinketh of this wine drinketh of my blood to his soul; and his soul shall never hunger nor thirst, but shall be filled" (3 Nephi 20:8). The Savior reinforced the principles of the sacrament by administering it to the Nephites twice and by explaining its expected practice and significance. In our roles, our examples will often be the most powerful mentoring, but taking the time to explain principles as the Savior did—even if it requires multiple attempts—can strengthen those we serve.

Second, the Savior is also a role model of prayer and how to pray. In chapter 17 we read how the Savior asked for all the children to be brought around him, and then he prayed. His prayer was an example to the Nephites and to all of us, even though the specific words are not recorded. First, he commanded the multitude to kneel: "he commanded the multitude that they should kneel down upon the ground" (3 Nephi 17:13). Then the Savior began to pray: "he himself also knelt upon the earth; and behold he prayed unto the Father, and the things which he prayed cannot be written, and the multitude did bear record who heard him" (3 Nephi 17:15).

In chapter 19 we see an even more detailed example of the Savior's prayer with and for the Nephites: "And tongue cannot speak the words which he prayed, neither can be written by man the words which he prayed. And the multitude did hear and do bear record; and their hearts were open and they did understand in their hearts the words which he prayed" (3 Nephi 19:32–33). In verses 20–23 we read the words of the Savior's actual prayer:

> Father, I thank thee that thou hast given the Holy Ghost unto these whom I have chosen; and it is because of their belief in me that I have chosen them out of the world.
>
> Father, I pray thee that thou wilt give the Holy Ghost unto all them that shall believe in their words.
>
> Father, thou hast given them the Holy Ghost because they believe in me; and thou seest that they believe in me because thou hearest them, and they pray unto me; and they pray unto me because I am with them.
>
> And now Father, I pray unto thee for them, and also for all those who shall believe on their words, that they may believe in me, that I may be in them as thou, Father, art in me, that we may be one. (3 Nephi 19:20–23)

The Savior was a role model as he invited the Nephites to participate in praying with him. Perhaps to their surprise, they were also invited to receive the miraculous blessings of the prayer. He taught them by example about what a prayer might consist of, including gratitude, a request for the Holy Ghost to be with them, a prayer for others, and a prayer for testimony.

The Savior once again invited the Nephites to participate with him in his prayer—the disciples specifically by praying and the multitude by kneeling and participating (3 Nephi 19:16, 19). Here we see again that the Savior mentored the Nephites by teaching them how to pray by praying with them and not simply telling them to pray or having them watch him pray. As we lead others, this is an important mentoring lesson we learn from the Savior that we need to invite participation and active learning. As we do, those we serve can have their own spiritual experiences as the Nephites did. We read in 3 Nephi 19:24 that as the disciples were following the Savior's example of prayer and prayed "without ceasing, . . . they were filled with desire." The Savior's example of prayer led the Nephites to strengthen their prayers, as well as their personal motivations. As role models, we can motivate those we serve to be filled with desire to live gospel principles with more commitment in their own lives.

In a third example of role modeling, we see the Savior's support for the apostles. He showed the people how they should look to them in how they follow him. In 3 Nephi 12:1 the Savior told the Nephites directly, "Blessed are ye if ye shall give heed unto the words of these twelve whom I have chosen from among you to minister unto you, and to be your servants; and unto them I have given power that they may baptize you with water." In his visit, the Savior was clear about his support for the leaders of his church. He also described them in terms of the service they would give, that they would "minister" and "be your servants" (3 Nephi 12:1).

In mentoring research, mentors positively influenced how mentees viewed the role model's sponsoring organization.[12] As mentors, our support for the prophets and apostles follows the Savior's example and helps those we mentor see that we know where to look for spiritual safety in challenging times. When they come to us with doubts about their faith or with questions in personal times of struggle and uncertainty, they will see us as trusted, faithful sources[13] to reassure them of the Savior's love for them and of the truthfulness of the gospel. In his ministry to the Nephites, the Savior showed his support for the apostles by publicly presenting them in a united ministry with him. We can also see the Savior's support of the Nephite apostles as a model for us today of following his living prophets and standing with them. He gave us a personal and a leadership example for the importance of sustaining his living prophets in our personal lives and as mentors to others.

Conclusion

The Savior's numerous examples of mentoring can strengthen and inspire disciples of Christ to be more effective mentors as they minister to others and serve in their own Church callings and assignments. We can consider how to provide more empathetic emotional connection to those we mentor, how we can be more helpful in conveying knowledge, even in difficult situations, and how we can be role models who emulate the Savior's example. In our professional relationships, we can consider how we might more effectively mentor a colleague, especially if correction needs to be given. In our family relationships, we can remember the importance of one-on-one time together as we hope to create eternal influence for good. We can also remember the Savior's relatively brief time with the Nephites as we keep in mind the perspective that our love, commitment, and service will be the key to effective mentoring more than an arbitrary length of interaction.

While there will be challenges trying to follow the Savior's perfect example of mentoring, we can take courage in our commitment to be better mentors from the Savior's words to the Nephites. He said we could ask for gifts we need from our Heavenly Father:

> Ask, and it shall be given unto you; seek, and ye shall find; knock, and it shall be opened unto you.
>
> For every one that asketh, receiveth; and he that seeketh, findeth; and to him that knocketh, it shall be opened.
>
> Or what man is there of you, who, if his son ask bread, will give him a stone?
>
> Or if he ask a fish, will he give him a serpent?
>
> If ye then, being evil, know how to give good gifts unto your children, how much more shall your Father who is in heaven give good things to them that ask him? (3 Nephi 14:7–11)

We can ask for the gift of mentoring in the Savior's way and have faith that he and our Heavenly Father will help us mentor like they do. The Savior also said to his disciples, "Hold up your light that it may shine unto the world. Behold I am the light which ye shall hold up—that which ye have seen me do" (3 Nephi 18:24). The Savior has counseled us to hold up our light to the world. Mentoring gives us opportunities to share our light in gospel and secular contexts. We can study the Savior's example of mentoring and know that he will help us magnify our light as we share his light of mentoring with others.

At the end of the record of his ministry in 3 Nephi, his final recorded words are "And the Holy Ghost beareth record of the Father and me; and the Father giveth the Holy Ghost unto the children of men, because of me" (3 Nephi 28:11). Mentoring will be individual and will require unique skills and creative insights for individual mentoring opportunities across the world. As we assist our Heavenly Father in his eternal plan of bringing his children home, we can have confidence that the Holy Ghost will help us in our efforts to encourage them forward on the covenant path. We can develop the gifts we need to share the Savior's light as we follow Heavenly Father's and Jesus Christ's examples of mentoring. We can learn to mentor as the Savior did.

CAMEY L. ANDERSEN *is a manager of Education Support with the Succeed in School program in Seminaries and Institutes of Religion. She is an adjunct instructor of Religious Education at Brigham Young University.*

Notes

1. Dieter F. Uchtdorf, "Young Adult Area Devotional with Elder Uchtdorf," January 9, 2022. See also Neal A. Maxwell, "Jesus, the Perfect Mentor" (Church Educational System fireside at Brigham Young University, February 6, 2000).
2. Camey L. Andersen and Richard E. West, "Improving Mentoring in Higher Education in Undergraduate Education and Exploring Implications for Online Learning," *Revista de Educación a Distancia* 20, no. 64 (2020). This article is a literature review of ten years (2008–18) of mentoring and higher education research. While research referenced mentoring and higher education, principles cited are applicable to general mentoring.
3. Amaury Nora and Gloria Crisp, "Mentoring Students: Conceptualizing and Validating the Multi-dimensions of a Support System," *Journal of College Student Retention: Research, Theory & Practice* 9, no. 3 (2007): 337–56. Their mentoring principles are based on a literature review of mentoring studies and are differentiated by their functional roles as opposed to definitions of mentors.
4. Nora and Crisp, "Mentoring Students," 342–43.
5. Nora and Crisp, "Mentoring Students," 349–50.
6. Stephen Bear and Gwen Jones, "Students as Protégés: Factors that Lead to Success," *Journal of Management Education* 41, no. 1 (2017): 146–68.

7. Kathy Luckett and Thembi Luckett, "The Development of Agency in First Generation Learners in Higher Education: A Social Realist Analysis," *Teaching in Higher Education* 14, no. 5 (2009): 469–81.
8. Camey L. Andersen and Richard E. West, "'We Overwhelm Them with Hope': How Online Mentors Can Support Online Learners," *Online Learning* 25, no. 4 (2021). This research studied online mentoring in a global higher education initiative (BYU-Pathway Worldwide). Many mentoring principles are applicable to general mentoring. See also Cara Poor and Shane Brown, "Increasing Retention of Women in Engineering at WSU: A Model for a Women's Mentoring Program," *College Student Journal* 47, no. 3 (2013): 421–28; Teresa Smith-Ruig, "Exploring the Links between Mentoring and Work-Integrated Learning," *Higher Education Research & Development* 33, no. 4 (2014): 769–82.
9. Russell M. Nelson, "The Correct Name of the Church," *Liahona*, October 2018, 87–89. See also Neil L. Andersen, "The Name of the Church Is Not Negotiable," *Liahona*, October 2021, 116–19.
10. Andersen and West, "We Overwhelm Them with Hope."
11. Shouping Hu and Yanli Ma. "Mentoring and Student Persistence in College: A Study of the Washington State Achievers Program," *Innovative Higher Education* 35, no. 5 (2010): 329–41.
12. Ivan H. Allen and Samuel M. Lester Jr., "The Impact of a College Survival Skills Course and a Success Coach on Retention and Academic Performance," *Journal of Career and Technical Education* 27, no. 1 (2012): 8–14; Jeanett Castellanos et al., "Mentoring Matters: Racial Ethnic Minority Undergraduates' Cultural Fit, Mentorship, and College and Life Satisfaction," *Journal of College Reading and Learning* 46, no. 2 (2016): 81–98.
13. Russell M. Nelson, "Christ Is Risen; Faith in Him Will Move Mountains," *Liahona*, April 2021, 103.

13

Jesus Christ as a Revealer of Ordinances in the Book of Mormon

David Calabro

The Book of Mormon records that the resurrected Savior, during his personal ministry among the Nephites, gave directions for the regular performance in the Nephite church of at least four ritual acts: baptism (3 Nephi 11:21–41; 12:1–2), the bestowal of the gift of the Holy Ghost (3 Nephi 11:35–36; 12:1–2, 6; 18:36–37; 19:13–14, 20–22), formal communal prayer, or praying together as a group or congregation in a prescribed way (3 Nephi 13:5–15; 17:11–17; 18:15–25; 19:16–36), and the sacrament (3 Nephi 18:1–14, 26–34; 20:3–9). The voice of Jesus was heard by all the Nephites immediately after his crucifixion and the destruction of Nephite cities, and he gave directions concerning ritual: the Nephites were to do away with the animal sacrifices of the law of Moses and were to offer instead "a broken heart and a contrite spirit," which would qualify them to receive the baptism of fire and the Holy Ghost (3 Nephi 9:19–22). He addressed all four rituals during his first visit to the temple in Bountiful (3 Nephi 11–18), beginning with baptism, concerning which he gave specific directions. Further, a large part of the Book of Mormon record of Jesus's ministry is occupied with these ritual matters, even though some of the description is abbreviated and only later expanded on by Moroni (Moroni 2–5). In short, it is clear that the Book of Mormon portrays the Savior as deeply involved in ritual matters.

In this study, I will explore the specifics of this portrayal of Jesus through a close reading of the texts in 3 Nephi and Moroni that quote his words regarding baptism, the bestowal of the gift of the Holy Ghost, communal prayer, and the sacrament. I will argue that Christ's extensive focus on ritual in these chapters reveals his character—not just as one who cares about ritual but as one who delights in blessing his people through these means. Each ritual is fundamentally rooted in the narrative context of Christ's visit to the Nephites; Christ institutes each one and expounds its meaning, and each is performed in the narrative with Christ himself playing a central role. Given this narrative context, the rituals themselves become ways of approaching the living Christ as did the Nephites. Thus, the ritual directions are among the ways in which the Book of Mormon leads its readers to an experiential witness of Christ. This study has special relevance to our modern ordinances because the baptismal words in 3 Nephi 11 and the sacramental words in Moroni 4–5 are the model for the corresponding ordinances performed in the modern church.

Christ as a Revealer of Ordinances: A Distinctive Portrayal

Jesus's attitude toward ritual is characterized in different ways by scholars of the New Testament. James Charlesworth's dictum represents a widespread view: "It is improbable that Jesus established the institution of the Eucharist as described in the synoptics [the books of Matthew, Mark, and Luke]. The liturgies in early Judaism and in the Palestinian Jesus Movement certainly helped shape this account."[1] According to this view, the historical Jesus was not concerned about ritual—it was his followers who would develop the rituals of the church after his departure and would insert ritual elements into the gospel narrative after the fact.[2] Gerd Thiessen and Annette Merz review various approaches to the origins of the Eucharist, some of which attribute the liturgical character of its observance to Christ. They suggest, in line with another widespread view, that baptism and the Eucharist were both originally forms of existing practices adapted to anticipate the end-time, when Jesus's disciples would stand purified and partake of a meal in the newly established kingdom of God; but after Jesus's crucifixion, these practices became distinct rituals charged with significance relating to his death and resurrection.[3] Bruce Chilton posits a more complex development including six different "types" of the Eucharist, the first two of which were those of Jesus during his ministry: first, meals were observed as "an enacted parable of the feast in the kingdom that was to come"; then, after Jesus's cleansing of the temple failed to permanently change the practices of the temple authorities, Jesus reinterpreted the bread and wine as the flesh and blood that his followers should offer in place of the temple sacrifices—a polemical act intended to challenge the temple cult.[4]

Some of these approaches, particularly that of Chilton, ascribe to Jesus some measure of interest in the power of ritual as a means of supporting his message. But none of them comes close to the picture of Jesus in the Book of Mormon. In the latter, Jesus presents a fully developed liturgy, specifying the actions and the very words to be uttered by the officiator and discoursing at length on the doctrinal meaning of these rites. From the standpoint of the Nephite record, the portions of the New Testament that relate to ritual appear reserved, as if they disclose only hints of what Jesus might have said to his disciples.

Not only does the Book of Mormon give us a quantitative sense of Jesus's concern about ritual matters, but also the specifics of his teachings reveal a distinctive portrayal of Christ as a revealer of ordinances. His ritual teachings are not particularly eschatological, nor are they polemically oriented with respect to the sacrificial cult.[5] Instead, they focus explicitly on the blessing of his people. This is apparent in his repeated use of the phrase "blessed are ye" and variations of this phrase in reference to the performance of ordinances. At the beginning of 3 Nephi 12, Jesus uses this phrase to refer to those who are baptized, providing a ritual-focused context for the Beatitudes that follow (compare Matthew 5:3–12):

> *Blessed are ye* if ye shall give heed unto the words of these twelve whom I have chosen from among you to minister unto you, and to be your servants; and unto them I have given power that they may baptize you with

> water; and after that ye are baptized with water, behold, I will baptize you with fire and with the Holy Ghost; therefore *blessed are ye* if ye shall believe in me and be baptized, after that ye have seen me and know that I am.
>
> And again, *more blessed are they* who shall believe in your words because that ye shall testify that ye have seen me, and that ye know that I am. Yea, *blessed are they* who shall believe in your words, and come down into the depths of humility and be baptized, for they shall be visited with fire and with the Holy Ghost, and shall receive a remission of their sins.
>
> Yea, *blessed are the poor in spirit* who come unto me, for theirs is the kingdom of heaven. (3 Nephi 12:1–3; emphasis added)

The connector *yea* implies that the declaration "blessed are the poor in spirit who come unto me" is a restatement of the preceding declaration, which refers to those who "come down into the depths of humility" and are baptized. The blessedness which Jesus pronounces on those who are baptized is framed here in terms of receiving the gift of the Holy Ghost, remission of sins, and ultimately salvation.[6] The rest of the Beatitudes follow, continuing with "blessed are all they that mourn, for they shall be comforted." In the Nephite context, the comfort of which Jesus speaks would take on added meaning from Alma's teachings that those who are baptized into the covenant community are expected "to mourn with those that mourn; yea, and comfort those that stand in need of comfort" (Mosiah 18:9). As the subsequent narrative of Alma's people shows, God himself participates in giving comfort and lifting the burdens of those who enter into the covenant (Mosiah 24:13–15).[7] The Book of Mormon reading of the fourth beatitude, "for they shall be filled *with the Holy Ghost*" confirms that these verses point to a promised state of blessedness predicated on baptism and the reception of the Holy Ghost (3 Nephi 12:6; compare the shorter reading in Matthew 5:6).

Jesus also repeatedly uses the phrase "blessed are ye" when he prays among the people and when he introduces the sacrament:

> And they arose from the earth, and he said unto them: *Blessed are ye* because of your faith. And now behold, my joy is full. (3 Nephi 17:20; emphasis added)

> And when the disciples had done this [i.e., had drunk of the sacramental wine], Jesus said unto them: *Blessed are ye* for this thing which ye have done,

for this is fulfilling my commandments, and this doth witness unto the Father that ye are willing to do that which I have commanded you.

And this shall ye always do to those who repent and are baptized in my name; and ye shall do it in remembrance of my blood, which I have shed for you, that ye may witness unto the Father that ye do always remember me. And if ye do always remember me ye shall have my Spirit to be with you.

And I give unto you a commandment that ye shall do these things. And if ye shall always do these things *blessed are ye*, for ye are built upon my rock....

Therefore *blessed are ye* if ye shall keep my commandments, which the Father hath commanded me that I should give unto you. (3 Nephi 18:10–12, 14; emphasis added)

Here, as with baptism in 3 Nephi 12, the blessing is linked to the reception of the Holy Ghost (here called "my Spirit") through the performance of the ordinance. In both cases, too, there is emphasis on the importance of performing the ordinance in a right state of mind: humility in the case of baptism and remembrance of Christ in the case of the sacrament.

Christ's words as reported in 3 Nephi lay out clear doctrinal explanations of the meanings of the ordinances. In each case the ritual is fundamentally situated in the context of Christ's visits. It is as if the ritual extends his personal ministry at the Bountiful temple across time and space. It allows people to participate vicariously, to be like those who were actually there. In the following sections, I will show how this is the case, addressing each ritual in turn.

Baptism

In the Savior's first visit to the Nephites in 3 Nephi 11, one of the first things he addressed was regulation of the ordinance of baptism, which had apparently been a topic of controversy before his visit (see 3 Nephi 11:28). He began by giving Nephi and others authority to baptize; this was done in front of the multitude so there would be no doubt about where the authority lay (3 Nephi 11:18–22). Then he described the physical procedure and the spoken words of the ordinance (3 Nephi 11:22–27). After this, he turned to the topic of his doctrine. He stated that his doctrine is not to generate contention; then he said, "I will declare unto you my doctrine" (3 Nephi 11:28–31). In 3 Nephi 11:32–38, Jesus's words transition seamlessly from a description of the role of the Father, the Son, and the Holy Ghost in bearing record of his doctrine to the declaration of what constitutes his doctrine. It is difficult to tell where one leaves off and the other begins; indeed, it seems that the divine record-bearing process is an integral part of his doctrine. The core of his doctrine is repentance, belief in Christ, and baptism: "And I bear record that the Father commandeth all men, everywhere, to repent and believe in me. And whoso believeth in me, and is baptized, the same shall be saved; and they are they who shall inherit the kingdom of God. And whoso believeth not in me, and is not baptized, shall be damned" (3 Nephi 11:32–34).

Christ then reiterates the divine record-bearing process, in which the believer is visited "with fire and with the Holy Ghost" (3 Nephi 11:35–36). Finally, Christ restates the process of repentance, belief, and baptism, possibly here referring to two different baptismal events: "And again I say unto you, ye must repent, and become as a little child, and be baptized in my name, or ye can in nowise receive these things. And again I say unto you, ye must repent, and be baptized in my name, and become as a little child, or ye can in nowise inherit the kingdom of God" (3 Nephi 11:37–38).

This passage has clear thematic links with John 3:1–6, where Jesus speaks of being "born again" to "see the kingdom of God" and to "enter into the kingdom of God" (again, possibly referring to two different events).[8] However, in the Nephite context, Jesus's words would resonate with the words of the angel quoted by King Benjamin, in which the putting off of the natural man is equated with becoming "as little children" or "as a child" (Mosiah 3:18–19).[9]

Noel Reynolds has discussed the significance of Christ's doctrine as laid out in 3 Nephi 11:32–39 in a broader Book of Mormon context by putting it in comparison with "the doctrine of Christ" as expounded by Nephi in 2 Nephi 31–32 and with Christ's "gospel" in 3 Nephi 27:13–21. Reynolds shows how these three expositions "all say essentially the same things"; he points to the presence of six elements in all three passages: repentance, baptism, the reception of the Holy Ghost, faith in Christ, endurance to the end, and eternal life.[10] While all three passages are consistent in setting forth these elements, it is important to note how these passages function differently in the

Nephite record. Nephi's exposition is longer than the other two; it unfolds gradually as Nephi reveals words spoken to him by the Father and the Son and then reflects on them. At some points, Nephi enters into dialogue with the reader, even expressing sorrow at the reader's lack of understanding (2 Nephi 32:1–2, 4, 7–8).[11] Nephi anticipates the future revelation of "more doctrine" at the time "when [Christ] shall manifest himself unto you in the flesh," and he exhorts the reader to do what Christ reveals at that time, implying that that doctrine will be different in some way (2 Nephi 32:6). Indeed, Christ's concise declaration of his "doctrine" in 3 Nephi 11 includes new elements, such as the record-bearing roles of the Father, the Son, and the Holy Ghost and the requirement of becoming like little children. Christ's "gospel" in 3 Nephi 27 is unlike both these passages in that it is framed as an announcement of two key events: the crucifixion in which Christ was "lifted up by men" and the final judgment in which men will be "lifted up by the Father" (3 Nephi 27:14). The "gospel" in 3 Nephi 27 may have been a paraphrase of Christ's teachings, including his "doctrine" in 3 Nephi 11. Believers are to "build upon" both of them (3 Nephi 11:39; 27:8), but only in the case of his "doctrine" is there a specific commandment regarding how the words are to be used (see below).

One way to interpret Jesus's declaration of his doctrine in 3 Nephi 11:32–39 is to understand these words as part of the baptismal liturgy as laid down by Jesus. Immediately following these words, Jesus stated, "Whoso shall declare more or less than this, and establish it for my doctrine, the same cometh of evil, and is not built upon my rock" (3 Nephi 11:40). Just as he had introduced his words with the statement, "I will *declare* unto you my doctrine" (3 Nephi 11:31; emphasis added), he commanded the twelve disciples to "go forth unto this people, and *declare* the words which I have spoken, unto the ends of the earth" (3 Nephi 11:41; emphasis added). Jesus next turned to the multitude and exhorted them to heed the words that the twelve would teach them, after which they should be baptized and receive the Holy Ghost, precisely as outlined in Christ's doctrine (3 Nephi 12:1).[12] That the twelve interpreted literally the injunction to declare nothing more or less than "the words which I have spoken" is possible in light of their teaching of the multitude on the following day, when they "ministered those same words which Jesus had spoken—nothing varying from the words which Jesus had spoken" (3 Nephi 19:8).[13] The disciples then prayed for "that which they most desired," which was the Holy Ghost, and went down to the water's edge to baptize each other (3 Nephi 19:8–12).

If Christ's doctrine in 3 Nephi 11:32–39 is indeed intended as a liturgy to be recited word for word, it might imply that the liturgy had the character of a ritual drama. Nearly every sentence of the passage uses first-person pronouns referring to Christ, who is speaking the words; thus, if a disciple spoke the words without alteration, he would be taking on the role of Christ as if in a dramatic performance. For instance, he would say, "And whoso believeth in me, and is baptized, the same shall be saved." This would be an especially poignant way of reinvoking Christ's personal ministry whenever baptism was administered to those who were not there at the temple in Bountiful (for such instances, see 3 Nephi 26:17; 27:1).

Jesus's sermon in 3 Nephi 12–14, which parallels the Sermon on the Mount in Matthew 5–7, may constitute a second set of teachings that were to be imparted to candidates for baptism. Here, unlike Jesus's words to the twelve disciples in 3 Nephi 11:22–41, his words are addressed to the entire multitude gathered at the temple. John Welch has argued extensively for the sacred, temple-related nature of this sermon; according to him, this sermon was used to instruct baptismal candidates to prepare them to enter into a covenant with Christ.[14] This larger sermon ends with the metaphor of building on a rock rather than on the sand, very much like the metaphor at the end of Christ's doctrine in 3 Nephi 11. The same metaphor also appears at the end of Christ's teachings about the sacrament (3 Nephi 18:12–13). This could mean that all three sets of teachings are related to one another as sacred teachings accompanying the administration of ordinances in the temple.

The ordinance of baptism stands out from the other ordinances introduced by Christ at the temple in Bountiful, since Christ does not model the performance of the ordinance itself.[15] Like the other ordinances, Christ gives instructions for the performance of baptism, and the ordinance is to be performed in his name (3 Nephi 11:23, 25, 27, 37–38); however, he does not actually perform the ordinance in these chapters of 3 Nephi. This contrasts with his role in the bestowal of the Holy Ghost, which I will now discuss.

Bestowal of the Gift of the Holy Ghost

Many of Christ's teachings to the Nephites relate to the gift of the Holy Ghost, which he typically refers to as baptism by fire and the Holy Ghost, using language similar to Matthew 3:11 and Luke 3:16 (3 Nephi 9:19–22; 11:35–36; 12:1–2, 6; 27:20).[16] The accounts attributed in the Book of Mormon to the multitude and to the disciples describe Christ's institution of a ritual that would perpetuate the effects of his personal ministry. He presented this ritual as a complement to baptism by water, promising that he would play a direct role in performing the baptism by fire and the Holy Ghost.

In his words heard by the Nephites immediately after his crucifixion, Christ promised those who would come unto him "with a broken heart and a contrite spirit" that he would baptize them "with fire and with the Holy Ghost, even as the Lamanites, because of their faith in me at the time of their conversion, were baptized with fire and with the Holy Ghost, and they knew it not" (3 Nephi 9:20). The event referred to here is described in Helaman 5:43–48. According to this account, a group of Lamanites, having imprisoned the prophets Nephi and Lehi, were led to repent. They were encircled by fire and filled with the Holy Ghost, and they heard the voice of the Father testifying of Christ. After this, "angels came down out of heaven and ministered unto them."

Very similar to the account in Helaman 5 is the description of what happened on the morning after Christ's first visit to the Nephites. As the multitude looked on, the disciples who had just baptized each other "were filled with the Holy Ghost and with fire" and "were encircled about as if it were by fire" (3 Nephi 19:13–14). Here too, "angels did come down out of heaven and did minister unto them," although in this instance the Savior himself also came and stood amid the disciples (3 Nephi 19:14–15).

Since it was only the twelve disciples who were filled with the Holy Ghost in 3 Nephi 19, this event can be regarded only as a partial fulfillment of Christ's promise in 3 Nephi 9:20. The twelve on this occasion experienced for themselves the doctrine of Christ they had heard on the previous day (3 Nephi 11:32–39). From the perspective of the multitude at the temple, who witnessed the miraculous baptism of the disciples and bore record of it (3 Nephi 19:14), the event provided a personal experience corresponding to the verbal promise they had heard months previously (3 Nephi 9:20) as well as the promise Christ had given them as he stood in their midst on the previous day (3 Nephi 12:1).[17] Those in the multitude who would eventually receive the Holy Ghost could regard that gift as a likeness of what they had witnessed at the temple in Bountiful. Further, those who would receive the multitude's witness (3 Nephi 12:2) could likewise view their own experience in the context of the Savior's words and their partial fulfillment at the Bountiful temple.

According to Mormon's account, the twelve disciples bore record of the Savior's instructions concerning the ritual by which the Holy Ghost was to be bestowed (3 Nephi 18:36–37). These instructions, which were not heard by the multitude, are conveyed by Moroni near the end of the Book of Mormon: Christ laid his hands on the disciples and charged them to give others the Holy Ghost "in my name" (Moroni 2:1–2). Just as Christ laid his hands on the disciples to give them this charge (an aspect also witnessed by the multitude), the disciples were to lay their hands on those to whom they would give the Holy Ghost. Thus, whenever the ordinance would be performed, even the gesture of the officiator would invoke Christ's actions as he instituted the ordinance at the temple in Bountiful.

Jesus's teachings consistently portray the gift of the Holy Ghost in a complementary relationship to baptism. Once Jesus introduces baptism in 3 Nephi 11, the ordinance of bestowing the gift of the Holy Ghost is always described in conjunction with baptism. For instance, speaking of the twelve, Jesus says to the multitude, "And unto them I have given power that they may baptize you with water; and after that ye are baptized with water, behold, I will baptize you with fire and with the Holy Ghost" (3 Nephi 12:1). The same pattern is evident in the baptism of the twelve: after they baptized each other, the Holy Ghost immediately "did fall upon them, and they were filled with the Holy Ghost and with fire" (3 Nephi 19:11–13).

In terms of participant format, Jesus's role in the bestowal of the Holy Ghost was to be more direct than his role in baptism. The baptism with water was to be performed by his disciples in his name (3 Nephi 11:23, 27, 37–38).[18] The giving of the Holy Ghost by the laying on of hands was also performed in Jesus's name (Moroni 2:2); however, he himself promised to carry out the actual baptism with fire and the Holy Ghost (3 Nephi 9:20; 12:1).[19]

Christ's institution of the bestowal of the Holy Ghost in 3 Nephi points to his character as one who cares deeply for his people. Throughout the pericopes describing Christ's institution of this ordinance, the focus is on what Christ and his Father will do for their people, who are conceived of both as individuals (3 Nephi 11:35–36) and as a group (3 Nephi 12:1–2; 19:13–14). These people will be born record to (3 Nephi 11:35–36), visited (3 Nephi 11:35; 12:2), "baptized" (with fire, 3 Nephi 12:1), comforted (3 Nephi 12:4), filled (3 Nephi 12:6; 19:13), and encircled about (3 Nephi 19:14). The emphasis is consistently on the recipients of these blessings; there is no indication of a worldly agenda in the ordinance. We can conclude from this that Christ's character is generous—in his institution of ordinances, he is preoccupied with blessing his people.

Formal Communal Prayer

Like the Sermon on the Mount, Jesus's sermon at the Bountiful temple includes the Lord's Prayer with accompanying instructions (3 Nephi 13:5–15). The Book of Mormon account also includes two additional prayers (3 Nephi 17:11–17; 19:15–36) and further instruction on prayer (3 Nephi 18:15–25).

The two additional prayers recorded in 3 Nephi are mutually similar. In the first instance, Jesus commanded the multitude to bring their little children and then to kneel, and he stood "in the midst" of the children and prayed, using words that could not be repeated (3 Nephi 17:11–17). In the second instance, he came and stood "in the midst" of the disciples, who had just been baptized and received the Holy Ghost, and commanded the surrounding multitude to kneel while he prayed three times, ending with words that could not be repeated (3 Nephi 19:15–36).[20] Both instances are alike except for the people immediately surrounding Jesus: the children in one instance and the recently baptized disciples in the other. As Jesus had just taught that those who are baptized become "as a little child" (3 Nephi 11:37–38), it seems likely that the two instances are complementary in some way.

There are at least two things to note regarding Jesus's role in these two prayers. First, his position in the event was central: he was "in the midst" of the praying multitude; even though he departs "out of the midst of them" in 3 Nephi 19:19, he is still the one to whom they are praying as he prays to the Father. In both prayers, there is a smaller group that is closer to Christ than the general multitude, giving the impression of concentric groups with Christ as the focal point. Second, Jesus gives attention to the postures of prayer. He commands the multitude and the disciples to kneel (3 Nephi 17:13–14; 19:16–17), and he models three postures for them: standing (3 Nephi 17:13), kneeling (3 Nephi 17:15), and finally "bow[ing] himself to the earth" (3 Nephi 19:19, 27). Jesus's directions and example may have served a didactic purpose. According to Donald Parry, on these occasions "Jesus provided instructions regarding the posture of prayer, and then showed the Nephite Saints at Bountiful how to pray."[21]

As with the other ritual actions which he introduced to the Nephites, Christ instituted prayer as a permanent practice for the church: "And as I have prayed among you even so shall ye pray in my church, among my people who do repent and are baptized in my name. Behold I am the light; I have set an example for you" (3 Nephi 18:16).

It is possible that this ritual was regularly performed with converts as part of a sequence including baptism, the bestowal of the Holy Ghost, and the sacrament. This combination of rites would be modeled on Christ's personal ministry among the Nephites. During both his first and his second visit, his prayer amid the children or his recently baptized disciples occurred just before an administration of the sacrament. Similarly, the apocryphal book known as the *Acts of John* mentions that Christ led the Apostles in a prayer as they gathered in a circle in the upper room on the night of his arrest—the same occasion on which he administered the sacrament, although the text does not mention the sacrament.[22] One can therefore imagine a ritual in which recently baptized converts, who had become "as a little child," participated in a communal prayer and partook of the sacrament, all of this being modeled after Christ's personal ministry at the temple in Bountiful.

As with the bestowal of the Holy Ghost, Jesus's teachings about prayer point overwhelmingly to his concern for his people. He prays for the people using words too "great and marvelous" to be written, after which he blesses the children, they are encircled about with fire, and angels minister to them (3 Nephi 17:17, 21, 24). Later, Jesus prays for people to be one with him and with his Father and to be purified, and he again uses words too "great and marvelous" to be written (3 Nephi 19:23, 28–29, 34). He exhorts his people to pray in their families for the blessing of their wives and children and to pray in their congregations for others (3 Nephi 18:21–23). The picture of a generous Christ who delights in blessing others is consistent with what we have seen in the case of the bestowal of the Holy Ghost.

Administration of the Sacrament

The sacrament is perhaps the clearest example of an ordinance designed to recall Christ's visit at the temple in Bountiful, thus allowing those who receive the ordinance to relive the experience of that event. Christ administered the sacrament to the Nephites on two occasions: once in his first visit and again in his second visit (3 Nephi 18:1–14; 20:3–9). On the second occasion, he miraculously provided the bread and wine, recalling the miraculous feeding of multitudes in his mortal ministry (3 Nephi 20:6–7; Matthew 14:15–21; 15:32–38). In both instances in 3 Nephi, Christ gave the bread and wine first to the disciples and then commanded the disciples to distribute them to the multitude; Christ thus plays a central role in both events, providing bread and wine symbolic of his own body and blood to a widening circle of recipients.

Moroni records the words of the sacrament prayers used by the Nephites (Moroni 4; 5); the words echo the language Christ uses in his explanation of the ordinance in 3 Nephi 18, which means that the Nephites would "commemorate this extraordinary day [when Christ first administered the sacrament] by ceremoniously remembering and religiously repeating the words they heard Jesus speak on that occasion."[23] Both Christ's explanation and the prayers themselves emphasize the ritual's commemorative character:

O God, the Eternal Father, we ask thee in the name of thy Son, Jesus Christ, to bless and sanctify this bread to the souls of all those who partake of it; that they may eat *in remembrance of the body of thy Son*, and witness unto thee, O God, the Eternal Father, that they are willing to take upon them the name of thy Son, and *always remember him*, and keep his commandments which he hath given them, that they may always have his Spirit to be with them. Amen. (Moroni 4:3; emphasis added)	And this shall ye do *in remembrance of my body, which I have shown unto you.* And it shall be a testimony unto the Father that ye do *always remember me.* And if ye do always remember me ye shall have my Spirit to be with you. (3 Nephi 18:7; emphasis added)
O God, the Eternal Father, we ask thee, in the name of thy Son, Jesus Christ, to bless and sanctify this wine to the souls of all those who drink of it, that they may do it *in remembrance of the blood of thy Son, which was shed for them*; that they may *witness unto thee, O God, the Eternal Father, that they do always remember him*, that they may have his Spirit to be with them. Amen. (Moroni 5:2; emphasis added)	And ye shall do it *in remembrance of my blood, which I have shed for you*, that ye may *witness unto the Father that ye do always remember me.* And if ye do always remember me ye shall have my Spirit to be with you. (3 Nephi 18:11; emphasis added)

As John Welch has noted, the words of the prayers and of Jesus's explanations echo the covenantal language of king Benjamin's sermon in Mosiah 5, so the words would resonate deeply for Nephite believers, like the words associated with baptism as noted above.[24]

The connection to Christ's personal ministry is clearest in his explanation of the sacramental bread: "in remembrance of my body, which I have shown unto you." The relative clause is absent from the prayer on the bread, perhaps because it would not necessarily apply to those who would use the prayer in the generations following Christ's visit to Bountiful. Even so, this explanation shows that the ordinance as presented to the Nephites is ultimately rooted in his personal ministry among them. The corresponding relative clause "which

I have shed for you" is preserved (with a shift to the passive) in the prayer on the wine because this would apply universally to those who would carry out the ordinance. But in the Nephite context, these words would recall the multitude's one-by-one encounter with Jesus, in which they witnessed by sight and touch that he had been "slain for the sins of the world" (3 Nephi 11:13–15).

Once again, we get a clear picture of Christ as one who seeks to provide for his people through the ordinances of the church. The providing of bread and wine is both a concrete indicator of his generosity and a symbol of the spiritual blessings he wishes to give. Christ's explanations of the sacrament emblems end with the promise "Ye shall have my Spirit to be with you," which points to the purpose of this ordinance (3 Nephi 18:7, 11). After partaking of the bread and wine, the people were "filled"—the text leaves ambiguity as to whether this was physical, spiritual, or both (3 Nephi 18:5, 9). Jesus's promise in 3 Nephi 20 more clearly portrays being filled as a spiritual blessing of the sacrament: "And he said unto them: He that eateth this bread eateth of my body to his soul; and he that drinketh of this wine drinketh of my blood to his soul; and his soul shall never hunger nor thirst, but shall be filled" (3 Nephi 20:8).

The imagery of not hungering or thirsting and of being filled echoes Jesus's language in the Beatitudes referring to the Holy Ghost (3 Nephi 12:6). The teachings on the sacrament also include a warning not to allow people to partake of it unworthily; this warning reflects Christ's concern for the spiritual welfare of his people (3 Nephi 18:27–29).

Conclusion

On a basic level, the preoccupation of Christ's ministry in 3 Nephi with matters of ritual suggests that Christ places importance on the physical, formal acts of the gospel as means of discipleship. But in contrast to many modern approaches to Christ's involvement with ritual, the Book of Mormon portrays Christ as a revealer of ordinances with the primary purpose of blessing his people through the reception of the Holy Ghost (compare 3 Nephi 27:20–22). The record of how these ordinances were instituted gives us extensive insight into Christ's character as a generous giver of blessings. Each of the practices he prescribed in 3 Nephi is rooted in the context of his personal ministry among the Nephites so that one may participate vicariously in the events of his ministry through the ritual. To receive Christ's teachings concerning baptism, delivered without alteration as he commanded, would be like receiving them from Christ himself. After being baptized like the twelve disciples on the morning of Christ's second visit, a person would receive the baptism of fire by Christ himself as the twelve disciples did. The ritual action by which the gift of the Holy Ghost was administered was the laying on of hands, the same gesture by which Jesus gave his twelve disciples authority to bestow the gift. By participating in communal prayer as Jesus directed, people could imagine themselves in place of the disciples as Jesus offered prayer in their midst. Finally, as people partook of the sacrament, they would remember Christ showing his body to the Nephites and allowing them to witness for themselves, one by one, that his blood had been shed for them.

We can see glimpses of the impact of these ordinances among the Nephites. After Christ's second visit, the disciples "began from that time forth to baptize and to teach as many as did come unto them." Those who were baptized "were filled with the Holy Ghost" and "saw and heard unspeakable things, which are not lawful to be written" (3 Nephi 26:17–18). This last description recalls the prayers Jesus had uttered among the Nephites at Bountiful, which included words that could not be repeated. Moroni also describes some of the ordinances performed in the church in his day (Moroni 2–6).

The ordinances of baptism and the sacrament as performed in The Church of Jesus Christ of Latter-day Saints are also modeled on those described in the Book of Mormon, using the same procedures and prayers (Doctrine and Covenants 20:37, 72–79).[25] Thus, members of the church today may vicariously experience Christ's personal ministry, as did the Nephites, through the ordinances he revealed. In doing so, we gain a more intimate understanding of our Savior, who is eager to bless us.

DAVID CALABRO *is a visiting assistant professor of ancient scripture at Brigham Young University.*

Notes

1. James Charlesworth, "The Historical Jesus: How to Ask Questions and Remain Inquisitive," in *Handbook for the Study of the Historical Jesus*, ed. Tom Holmén and Stanley E. Porter (Leiden: Brill, 2011), 1:114. Charlesworth clarifies in his further remarks on pages 121–22 that the original Last Supper stressed "the dawning of God's Rule and the importance of the Twelve within it" and included a plea to remember Jesus (not the crucified figure of Christ, which did not yet exist).
2. Thus, Paul's description in 1 Corinthians 11:23–29 would be "important as the earliest attestation of the way Jesus instituted the Eucharist"; yet even this description, which includes some ritual elements, is understood as "a formulation composed some time after the event and dependent on a liturgical tradition." See Joseph A. Fitzmyer, *First Corinthians: A New Translation with Introduction and Commentary*, The Anchor Yale Bible (New Haven: Yale University Press, 2008), 431. A similar explanation would apply to the institution of the Lord's Prayer in Matthew 6:9–13. New Testament references to Jesus participating in baptism and individual prayer are frequent, but he is not portrayed as instituting these practices, and the New Testament is silent on the degree of formality involved in them.
3. Gerd Theissen and Annette Merz, *The Historical Jesus: A Comprehensive Guide* (Minneapolis: Fortress Press, 1998), 405–39.
4. Bruce D. Chilton, "Method in a Critical Study of Jesus," in *Handbook for the Study of the Historical Jesus*, 132–42. The other four types are associated with Peter and his circle, James, Paul and the Synoptic Gospels, and finally John.
5. The abolishment of blood sacrifice in favor of the offering of "a broken heart and a contrite spirit" in 3 Nephi 9:19–22 may at first seem like a move similar to what Chilton suggests happened in Jerusalem in the latter part of Jesus's ministry. However, it is not framed here in polemical terms. Jesus claims both the old practice and the new one as his: "And ye shall offer up *unto me* no more the shedding of blood; . . . for *I will accept* none of your sacrifices and your burnt offerings. And ye shall offer for a sacrifice *unto me* a broken heart and a contrite spirit" (3 Nephi 9:19–20; emphasis added). It is thus framed as a mandated change from the top down. Note that the cessation of animal sacrifice was new, but the requirement to offer "a broken heart and a contrite spirit" was a renewal of an expectation that had existed previously (Psalms 34:18; 51:16–17; 2 Nephi 2:7; 4:32). See Dana M. Pike, "3 Nephi 9:19–20: The Offering of a Broken Heart," in *Third Nephi, An Incomparable Scripture*, ed. Andrew C. Skinner and Gaye Strathearn (Provo, UT: Neal A. Maxwell Institute for Religious Scholarship, 2012), 35–56. Christ later reiterated this latter requirement during his personal appearance to the Nephites (3 Nephi 12:19).
6. Based on 3 Nephi 11:33, it seems that the inheriting of the kingdom is understood as equivalent to receiving personal salvation: "And whoso believeth in me, and is baptized, the same shall be saved; and they are they who shall inherit the kingdom of God."

7. One can accordingly understand "they shall be comforted" (Greek *paraklēthēsontai*) in Matthew 5:4 to imply divine aid, just as Jesus promised to send the Holy Ghost as a "Comforter" (*paraklētos*) in John 14:26.
8. Interpretation of this passage in John is varied; according to Jerome H. Neyrey, Jesus refers in verse 3 to being born "from above," which Nicodemus misinterprets as being born "again" (the Greek word *anōthen* has both meanings); see *The New Oxford Annotated Bible*, Fully Revised Fourth Edition, ed. Michael D. Coogan (Oxford: Oxford University Press, 2010), 1886. Since the births mentioned in verses 3 and 5 lead to different results ("seeing" and "entering" the kingdom of God), it is reasonable to suppose that Jesus is referring to different events or types of rebirth, possibly aligning with those in 3 Nephi 11:37–38.
9. Compare John W. Welch, *Illuminating the Sermon at the Temple and the Sermon on the Mount* (Provo, UT: FARMS, 1999), 29–30.
10. Noel B. Reynolds, "The Gospel of Jesus Christ as Taught by the Nephite Prophets," *BYU Studies* 31, no. 3 (1991): 31–50.
11. The fact that Nephi's expressions of sorrow are in written form poses an interesting paradox, for any reader, no matter how spiritually prepared, receives the same sorrowful judgment. This implies that Nephi knows his words are difficult, despite his statement that they are "as plain as word can be" (2 Nephi 32:7).
12. In 3 Nephi 12:1–2, Jesus seems to make a distinction between "the words of these twelve" and "your words." Jesus's doctrine in 3 Nephi 11:32–39 was addressed to the twelve and not the multitude, so "your words" must refer to something other than that passage.
13. It is not certain that this refers exclusively to the words in 3 Nephi 11:32–39, but this seems a reasonable possibility. Joseph Fielding McConkie, Robert L. Millet, and Brent L. Top likewise connect 3 Nephi 19:8 with Jesus's injunction in 3 Nephi 11:39–40 in *Doctrinal Commentary on the Book of Mormon*, vol. 4 (Salt Lake City: Bookcraft, 1992), 132.
14. Welch, *Illuminating the Sermon*, 11, 28–30.
15. By contrast, the Synoptic Gospels describe the baptism of Jesus (Matthew 3:13–17; Mark 1:9–11; Luke 3:21–22), and the Gospel of John indicates that Jesus performed some baptisms during his mortal ministry (John 3:22; Joseph Smith Translation, John 4:1–2). The baptism of Jesus does feature prominently in Nephi's exposition of the doctrine of Christ (2 Nephi 31:4–7, 17).
16. Compare also Mark 1:8; John 1:33; Acts 1:5; 11:16, which mention baptism by the Holy Ghost without adding the word *fire*. In John 1:33, some early manuscript witnesses (including a third-century papyrus, a fifth-century Greek majuscule codex, and the Sahidic Coptic version) include the word *fire*, but otherwise the reading without *fire* in these latter passages is constant. See Barbara and Kurt Aland, Johannes Karavidopoulos, Carlo M. Martini, and Bruce M. Metzger, eds., *Novum Testamentum Graece*, 28th revised edition (Stuttgart: Deutsche Bibelgesellschaft, 2012), 294. In 3 Nephi 27:20, Christ uses different language in his words to the twelve Nephite disciples, referring to the gift of the Holy Ghost as being "sanctified by the reception of the Holy Ghost."
17. For the space of time between these two promises, see 3 Nephi 8:5; 9:1; 10:18.

18. I understand the phrase "in my name" to be equivalent to "having authority given me of Jesus Christ" in the baptismal prayer (3 Nephi 11:25).
19. Although Jesus claims the role of baptizing with fire and the Holy Ghost (3 Nephi 12:1), it is the Father who is said to "visit [the baptized person] with fire and with the Holy Ghost" (3 Nephi 11:35). Thus, all three members of the Godhead, in whose name the baptism with water is explicitly performed (3 Nephi 11:25), are more closely involved in the second stage of the ritual.
20. In the second prayer, there are clear resonances with Jesus's intercessory prayer in John 17 and with his prayer in the garden of Gethsemane in Matthew 26:36–46; Mark 14:32–42; Luke 22:39–46. See Jeffrey R. Holland, *Christ and the New Covenant* (Salt Lake City: Deseret Book, 2006), 265–67. Whereas Jesus prays three times in Gethsemane and each time finds the apostles asleep rather than watching and praying, in 3 Nephi 19 he prays three times and finds the multitude praying "steadfastly, without ceasing" (3 Nephi 19:30). The contrast may be what causes Jesus to remark in verses 35–36 that because of the Nephites' great faith, they were able to see and hear more than those in Jerusalem.
21. Donald W. Parry, "'Pray Always': Learning to Pray as Jesus Prayed," in *The Book of Mormon: 3 Nephi 9–30, This Is My Gospel*, ed. Monte S. Nyman and Charles D. Tate Jr. (Provo, UT: Religious Studies Center, 1993), 139.
22. *Acts of John*, 94–95; See J. K. Elliott, *The Apocryphal New Testament* (Oxford: Clarendon Press, 1993), 318.
23. John W. Welch, "From Presence to Practice: Jesus, the Sacrament Prayers, the Priesthood, and Church Discipline in 3 Nephi 18 and Moroni 2–6," *Journal of Book of Mormon Studies* 5, no. 1 (1996): 122. On the relationship between 3 Nephi 18 and the sacrament prayers recorded in Moroni 4–5, and the temple-related nature of these texts on the sacrament, see Welch, *Illuminating the Sermon*, 99–100; Welch, "From Presence to Practice," 123–26.
24. John W. Welch, "Our Nephite Sacrament Prayers," in *Reexploring the Book of Mormon*, ed. John W. Welch (Provo, UT: FARMS, 1992), 286–89.
25. Welch, "From Presence to Practice," 120–21.

14

The Way, the Truth, and the Way to Truth

Harmony in Pursuit of Orthodoxy

Jared M. Halverson

President Ezra Taft Benson kept a plaque on his desk that read, "Be right, and then be easy to live with, if possible—but in that order."[1] To those who knew his forthright personality, the plaque captures him perfectly, but to those striving to navigate our fractured social environment, difficult questions arise. What does it mean to be right when taking a position is neither simple, clear, nor uncontested? How can we "be easy to live with" when it seems that only the argumentative and unbending prevail? Is it possible to maintain conviction *and* extend compassion simultaneously, when one so often succumbs to the other? If not, which of the two stands first in order of importance? Or if so, in which order should they be pursued? When the two seem mutually exclusive, surely some principle exists to determine which to choose.

With such questions compelling us, we shift President Benson's mantra from plaque to paperweight, grounding the pages that follow under the weight of its words. Each element will demand our attention: being right (which this paper will label *orthodoxy*[2]), being "easy to live with" (here labeled *harmony*), their occasional incompatibility ("if possible"), and the proper order in which they should be valued and pursued. We will first reframe the problem in religious terms, after which we will turn to the Book of Mormon for possible solutions, primarily in the Lord's postmortal ministry among the Nephites. Specifically, we will study how Jesus dealt with three instances of orthodoxy being pursued at harmony's expense, interactions he uniformly condemned in favor of a better, more balanced way. That way will confirm the cogency of President Benson's desktop reminder, affirm the compatibility of orthodoxy and harmony, and nuance the thorny issue of *order*—distinguishing between their *order of importance* and their *order of implementation*. Based on the Savior's approach, this paper will argue that conviction and compassion *can* coexist, that orthodoxy must remain the ultimate end, and that harmony in pursuit of orthodoxy is more likely to achieve its aim than orthodoxy in pursuit of harmony. By seeing how the Savior steered his disciples between a kind but indiscriminate relativism at one extreme (harmony at the expense of orthodoxy) and a well-meaning but confrontational dogmatism at the other (orthodoxy at the expense of harmony), we will learn how we might inch across similar tightropes. The way to "be right" and simultaneously "easy to live with" is to follow the example of Jesus Christ.

"If Possible"

Orthodoxy and harmony can form a notoriously unstable compound, as anyone caught in conflict or compromise can attest. Orthodoxy tends to privilege a single correct way of believing or behaving, while harmony, by nature, involves blending multiple notes simultaneously. Orthodoxy can be broad enough to include multiple perspectives, of course, and harmonies can include dissonance as well as well as consonance, but the notes must be in a particular relationship to one another lest cacophony result. Abraham Lincoln seemed to have this in mind when he chose the perfect metaphor with which to conclude his fraught first inaugural address: "the mystic *chords* of memory" would have to replace sectional disharmony if the "chorus of the Union" were again to "swell," and such notes would have to come from North and South alike.[3]

The same is true of the issues that currently divide our society. As President Dallin H. Oaks has recently urged, we must "work for a better way—a way to resolve differences without compromising core values."[4] Rival camps must each provide notes to form a common chord, aiming to harmonize despite deep and seemingly intractable differences.

The challenge, of course, is that "resolv[ing] differences without compromising core values" is painstaking and precarious work, with each half of President Oaks's statement causing concern at opposite extremes. For staunch proponents of a position, the phrase "resolv[ing] differences" with one's opponents sounds like capitulation, and for those same opponents, the phrase "without compromising core values" makes proponents seem unbending from the start. Thus, friction arises not only *between* parties but *within* them, as clashes over compromise erupt between moderates and "extremists" (as moderates call the uncompromising) or between purists and "sellouts" (as purists call the compromisers). Even in language, neutrality is hard to find.

Diversity is thus fraught with difficulty, requiring each of us to learn when, if, and (most importantly) how to compromise. In the face of conflict, creating harmonious chords typically requires one orthodoxy to bow to another, or both to bow together. In music theory—and we could add political theory—the term is "resolution," and it occurs only when one or more notes in a dissonant chord finally change their pitch. Even then harmony may only last a measure, especially when culture keeps changing its key. Even at its most stable, orthodoxy is seldom a permanently settled, universally recognized, or uniformly applied standard, especially in diverse societies that strain the elasticity of orthodoxy and harmony alike.

Whether it is orthodoxy that should acquiesce or harmony that ought to surrender is thus as debatable as which should yield first ("in that order") or whether either could even hope to produce its opposite ("if possible"). This leaves these two elements either locked in a game of chicken or stuck in a chicken-and-egg dilemma, made all the more intractable precisely because of their seeming incompatibility. Here, chickens don't want to lay and eggs don't want to hatch, for neither wants to admit that they are related, let alone make way for its alternate. But lay and hatch they must, for the survival of the species depends on it.

The same is true of humans, for feathers or not we unavoidably flock together. Thus, one need not master the intricacies of Hobbes, Locke, and Rousseau to wrestle with social contract theory.[5] Experience with social *contact* theory will do, for we debate issues of orthodoxy—with or without the academic jargon—in myriad interactions across the political aisle, the religious wall, and even the backyard fence.[6] And somehow we remain amicable neighbors (more or less), whether through uncomfortable compromises or a mutual tolerance often closer to awkward avoidance or benign neglect. Unfortunately, our interactions typically come at the expense of either orthodoxy or harmony, and our imbalances seem to be widening. Against a backdrop of hyperpartisan politics, economic inequality, racial discord, and social schism ("civil wars" no less divisive than that of Lincoln's day), we seem to be deficient in both consensus and compassion, and we long to do better. We hope to coexist *and* cooperate, the first facilitated by shared fellow feeling (the realm of harmony), and the second catalyzed by shared vision and common goals (the domain of orthodoxy). The former wants to *do* right by those with whom it associates; the latter wants to *be* right by a standard suspicious of debate. Whence cometh compromise? That is the pressing question.

The challenge maps nicely over Robert Putnam and David Campbell's *American Grace*, a sociological study that tries to make sense of the current state of religion in the United States, which somehow combines both deepening polarization (the bad news) and increasing pluralism (the good news). The authors describe the potential conflict between diversity, which prizes harmony, and devotion, which prizes orthodoxy, and identify as most potentially volatile those societies with high levels of both. If a society is diverse but not devout, then differences of opinion do not lead to conflict because people do not feel deeply enough about them to care. Conversely, in a society that is devout but not diverse, opinions are deeply held—to the point that they may not be considered opinions—but because people agree upon those issues they can pursue them fairly uniformly. Friction arises when differences exist that are passionately debated, in which case either the difference of opinion or the depth of one's emotion must be sacrificed somewhat. How have we handled this religiously? Putnam and Campbell argue that it is our religious fluidity that facilitates peaceful coexistence, which in turn has enabled interreligious relationships to develop. It is these relationships that defuse the potential powder keg, since "it is difficult to damn those you know and love."[7]

Love wins the day, then—more proof that "charity never faileth" (1 Corinthians 13:8). But is it love of neighbor at the expense of love of God? A sacrifice of religious orthodoxy on the altar of social harmony? The very fluidity Putnam and Campbell identify as the oil that reduces religious friction would suggest that devotion is acquiescing to diversity as horizontal relationships with others trump one's vertical relationship with God. Examples in the book abound: a prominent megachurch pastor carrying a Bible during his self-help sermons but not opening it to quote the potentially divisive word of God; the avoidance of denominational labels in favor of a generic Christianity that avoids drawing lines in the ecclesial sand; a preference among parishioners for a "flexible theology" some have labelled "Christianity Lite." As an Episcopal priest admitted, "The church is experiencing a moment of theological crisis right now" due to a lack of clear conviction (that is, an established orthodoxy). "Our greatest strength is that we don't come down hard on a lot of issues. But it's also our greatest weakness."[8]

Thankfully, Jesus Christ has a way of turning weaknesses into strengths (see Ether 12:27). In fact, as he told Philip near the end of his mortal ministry, he *is* "the way" (John 14:6), meaning his message, ministry, and mission provide the answers to the kinds of questions we are wrestling with here. Furthermore, in the same breath Jesus affirmed that he was also "the truth" and "the life," titles suggestive of the dual demands we are striving to balance. As the truth, Jesus is the embodiment of orthodoxy: "No man cometh unto the Father, but by me" (John 14:6). But as the life, Jesus also personifies the traits that smooth the rough edges of our lived interpersonal experiences, the attributes that allow diverse individuals to "live together in love" (Doctrine and Covenants 42:45). The Savior's way perfectly balances truth and life, orthodoxy and harmony, justice and mercy, law and love. He who said, "If ye love me, keep my commandments" (John 14:15), also commanded that we "love one another" as he did (John 13:34; 15:12, 17), which involved the constant interaction of the first and second "great commandments." On the proper balancing of these opposites "hang all the law and the prophets" (Matthew 22:37–40). More dramatically given our current context, on the interplay of orthodoxy and harmony hangs the future of society itself.

Condemning Contention: The Doctrine of Christ

In searching for the proper balance between orthodoxy and harmony, it is worth noting that Jesus, during his postmortal ministry among the Nephites, first emphasized what *not* to do, clearly identifying which of the two elements, in absence, presented the greater sin. Once that boundary was firmly established, he could then help his disciples practice walking the tightrope in relative safety. Notice the order of events in 3 Nephi 11. After descending amid the multitudes, the risen Lord first introduces himself as the fulfillment of prophecy, the light and life of the world, and the submissive Son and Savior. Next, he invites the multitudes to come and feel the wounds in his hands and feet, to confirm for themselves his divine identity. He then confirms upon Nephi and the other disciples the authority to baptize but prefaces his explanation of the ordinance with the caution, "On this wise shall ye baptize [a call for orthodoxy]; and there shall be no disputations among you [a call for harmony]" (3 Nephi 11:22). Essential instructions then follow—the need for sincere desire and honest repentance, the proper liturgical language, and the requirement of ritual immersion—after which Jesus repeats his initial admonition: "and according as I have commanded you thus shall ye baptize [orthodoxy]. And there shall be no disputations among you, as there have hitherto been; neither shall there be disputations among you concerning the points of my doctrine, as there have hitherto been [harmony]" (3 Nephi 11:28). In the first commandment he gives the gathered multitude, Jesus establishes orthodoxy but prohibits the lack of harmony in its pursuit.

In condemning contention, Jesus is not speaking theoretically but concretely and historically: disputations *had* occurred in the past, no doubt in pursuit of orthodoxy,[9] but this contentious approach had to stop. Establishing liturgical orthodoxy concerning baptism—an essential ordinance without which none can enter the kingdom of heaven (see John 3:5)—is thus bookended by clear calls for harmony, which are immediately reconfirmed by

Christ's explanation of what we might call the "doctrine" of harmony because of the way he presented it: "For verily, verily I say unto you, he that hath the spirit of contention is not of me, but is of the devil, who is the father of contention, and he stirreth up the hearts of men to contend with anger, one with another. Behold, this is not my *doctrine*, to stir up the hearts of men with anger, one against another; but this is my *doctrine*, that such things should be done away" (3 Nephi 11:29–30; emphasis added).

Significantly, Christ presents the need for harmony not as mere caution while clarifying the more central doctrine of baptism but as a recognizable *doctrine* of its own. The word *doctrine* appears nine times in 3 Nephi 11, foregrounding orthodoxy in the Lord's postmortal ministry (etymologically, the "doc" of doctrine equals the "dox" of orthodoxy). The fundamental orthodoxy Jesus is establishing is the "doctrine of Christ," the essentials of which are captured in the "first principles and ordinances of the Gospel" enumerated in the fourth article of faith. But he couches that doctrine in the doctrine of harmony, suggesting that while orthodoxy is the goal, harmony must be the means whereby we pursue it. As the Savior concludes the discussion, "And whoso shall declare more or less than this, and establish it for my doctrine, the same cometh of evil, and is not built upon my rock" (3 Nephi 11:40). Here Jesus explicitly reconfirms the importance of orthodoxy but implicitly reaffirms the need for harmony, since "declar[ing] more or less" than his established doctrine (a sin against orthodoxy) would likely lead to renewed disputation (a sin against harmony).

The Savior's categorical condemnation of contention, presented as a doctrine tasked with policing the conflicts between other, more contestable doctrines, gives harmony an orthodoxy of its own. Disharmony, that is, is unorthodox. Seen in this light, those Nephite antagonists for whom unorthodoxy was the greater sin would be constrained by their own convictions to maintain harmony at all costs. Otherwise, their pursuit of orthodoxy would itself be unorthodox, a fascinating example of reframing the problem so that one's strength could combat a related weakness.

But again, as the Savior framed it, among these Nephite disciples in active pursuit of orthodoxy, unorthodoxy was *not* the greater sin; contention was, for he explicitly condemns their disputations, not the fact that they had not yet arrived at unanimity in true doctrine. These were righteous people pursuing righteous aims, but they were going about it in an unrighteous way. And rather than excusing their regrettable means in deference to their noble ends, as they might have done, Jesus refused such justification. He did not consider contention in pursuit of consensus a necessary evil. It was simply an evil, inspired by "the father of contention" himself, and as such, it was decidedly *not* necessary. In fact, in the spirit of "no power or influence *can* or *ought* to be maintained" by anything compulsory or un-Christlike (and contention is both), such approaches are not only unrighteous (the "ought"), they are downright ineffective (the "can") (Doctrine and Covenants 121:41; emphasis added). Sinning against harmony does not lead others to stop sinning against orthodoxy, at least not willingly or permanently, which is what Jesus wants. Consequently, he did not prioritize orthodoxy in hopes that harmony would follow (a version of "if you build it, they will come"). Rather, he prioritized harmony, confident that orthodoxy could be reached if fellow feeling ensured mutual cooperation, compromise, and commitment over time. Order was everything, and he outlawed disharmony first.

But a word lest we overcorrect. In identifying a lack of harmony (i.e., disputation and contention) as the principal sin Christ condemns in 3 Nephi 11, it must not be forgotten that a lack of orthodoxy—or more accurately, orthopraxy (right behavior as defined by right belief)—was the principal sin leading up to the Savior's appearance. I say this to emphasize the fact that social harmony did not outweigh religious orthodoxy or obedience in the eyes of Jesus. Third Nephi 8–10 makes it painfully clear that it was the wickedness of the people, both their sins against obedience (orthopraxy) and their silencing of the prophets (the guardians of orthodoxy), that brought about their destruction. Suggesting that obedience is negotiable so long as harmony prevails is overswinging the pendulum; in fact, it is succumbing to the kind of moral relativism espoused by such anti-Christs as Nehor and Korihor (see Alma 1:4; Alma 30:17), and Jesus refused to countenance that.

He it was, after all, who placed the two great commandments in their proper order. The "first and great commandment" was love of God, which ensures orthodoxy; love of neighbor, which embraces harmony, was a second-place finisher—though not a distant one. The "second is like unto" the first

(Matthew 22:37–40), Jesus taught, meaning orthodoxy and harmony must remain inseparably connected. They form, respectively, the vertical and horizontal components of the cross, the post (love of God) firmly planted so that the crossbeam (love of neighbor) can be firmly attached. Love of neighbor then extends our love of God outward, while love of God lifts love of neighbor upward, raising its recipients to a higher, holier plane.

Elder D. Todd Christofferson discussed the tandem nature of the two great commandments in a 2022 message to young adults, the group most likely to reverse their order of importance. "The second commandment is a brilliant guide for human interaction," he affirmed, but it must not be allowed to trump the first commandment as our "overarching priority."[10] The first is "foundation," making the second, well, secondary. Elder Christofferson made it clear, however, that these rankings were not intended to diminish the "wonderful and essential" nature of what we have been calling harmony, only to keep it in proper perspective. The difference is one of priority, which, ironically, might best be pursued by reversing their chronology, as Jesus is doing in 3 Nephi 11. We speak of "means" and "ends," with the means preceding the ends chronologically but the ends superseding the means hierarchically. Similarly, orthodoxy can be prioritized as the ends, but with harmony as the catalyzing means. Or to state the matter differently, orthodoxy is the final destination, but harmony must pave the path.

Jesus hints at these nuances (order of priority as opposed to order of implementation) during his Sermon at the Temple, reminiscent of his Old-World Sermon on the Mount. Nothing he was about to teach was meant to "destroy the law," which would be a sin against orthodoxy; rather, his aim was that the purposes of the law would be "fulfilled" (3 Nephi 12:17–18). However, fulfillment in the vertical sense would never come without harmony in the horizontal sense. To emphasize this point, Jesus affirms "the law and the commandments of [his] Father" and states that "except ye shall keep my commandments, . . . ye shall in no case enter into the kingdom of heaven" (3 Nephi 12:19–20). But he follows this clear confirmation of orthodoxy with a clarion call to harmony in orthodoxy's pursuit. First, he passes judgment on "whosoever is angry with his brother" (3 Nephi 12:22)—devoid of the mitigating clause in Matthew, "without a cause" (Matthew 5:22)—suggesting that even unorthodoxy is not a justifiable "cause" for anger toward others (Jesus's point in 3 Nephi 11). "Therefore," he explains, "if ye shall come unto me [which assumes orthodoxy], or shall desire to come unto me [which at least maintains orthodoxy's pursuit], and rememberest that thy brother hath aught against thee [a lack of harmony]—go thy way unto thy brother, and *first* be reconciled to thy brother, and *then* come unto me with full purpose of heart, and I will receive you" (3 Nephi 12:23–24; emphasis added).

Notice the Savior's clear ordering of these two elements. First, orthodoxy remains the ultimate aim throughout. In fact, where Matthew's version replaces "com[ing] unto me" with "bring[ing] thy gift to the altar," Jesus even recommends "leav[ing] there thy gift before the altar" before going thy way to be reconciled (Matthew 5:23–24). Thus, the original goal is preserved, keeping us from forgetting the first great commandment as we turn to fulfill the second. Brotherly reconciliation does not excuse us from giving God the gifts intended; it merely pauses the process so it can be correctly pursued. Orthodoxy—whether in keeping commandments, coming unto Christ, or giving God our best offerings—remains the higher objective (first in order of priority), but if contention is present to mar the process, then horizontal harmony must *first* be achieved (first in order of implementation). Only *then* can we continue our shared upward journey.

This explains the potentially confusing next passage, in which the Savior commands, "Agree with thine adversary quickly while thou art in the way with him, lest at any time he shall get thee, and thou shalt be cast into prison. Verily, verily, I say unto thee, thou shalt by no means come out thence until thou has paid the uttermost senine. And while ye are in prison can ye pay even one senine? Verily, verily, I say unto you, Nay" (3 Nephi 12:25–26). What seems like a sin against orthodoxy through capitulating compromise (agree with thine adversary?) becomes instead a foregrounding of harmony in hopes of ultimately achieving the orthodoxy desired. We simply cannot arrive there *together* if we are "in the way" with each other, or to put it differently, if we are in each other's way. If my neighbor casts me into a prison of animosity, policed by disagreement and mutual mistrust, what good does my unbending orthodoxy do him? Can it make even a senine's worth of difference? Even worse, that "adversary" feels justified in being adversarial, since I acted as an enemy as well.

Note that agreeing here does not mean denying our own orthodoxy; rather, the Greek behind the word in Matthew's version suggests thinking kindly of the other person, of being favorably disposed toward them as a fellow human being. Jesus is commanding his disciples to avoid becoming disagreeable, even in important disagreements. That is refusing to lose hold on harmony, even during orthodoxy's pursuit.

Looking through the lens of these passages in 3 Nephi 12, we can return to 3 Nephi 8–11 and see the destruction of the wicked (enforcing orthodoxy) and the wickedness of disputation (requiring harmony) as a delicate balancing act. Contention was a problem, but blanket amnesty for wrongdoing was not the solution, no matter how soft-sounding or well-meaning it seemed. The Nephites knew this, which may be why a caution against unorthodoxy was slightly less explicit in Christ's message than his caution against disharmony. After the devastation they had endured, the people needed very little convincing that obedience to divine standards was required. Unlike the doctrine of harmony, that is, the doctrine of orthodoxy was clear, and they only awaited the Lord's explanation of what his specific orthodoxies entailed. Once he declared the essentials concerning his doctrine, his disciples were ready to fulfill his command to "go forth unto this people, and declare the words which [he had] spoken, unto the ends of the earth" (3 Nephi 11:41). Still, the *manner* of that declaration required additional practice, for disputations continued to arise.

Establishing Orthodoxy: The Name of the Church

A second instance of contention over orthodoxy arose soon after the first, but because the Savior's response on that occasion will require our closest attention, we will first address in brief the third example of the problem, which occurred shortly before the Lord ascended to heaven. In 3 Nephi 27 as the disciples were journeying about "preaching the things which they had both heard and seen [the orthodox doctrine of Christ], and were baptizing in the name of Jesus [no doubt in the orthodox manner]," they paused their preaching, "gathered together," and "united in mighty prayer and fasting" (3 Nephi 27:1). In response to this display of true harmony, the Lord reappeared and asked the disciples what they desired of him, to which they responded, "Lord, we will that thou wouldst tell us the name whereby we shall call this church." In addition to their question, however, came an important confession: "For there are disputations among the people concerning this matter" (3 Nephi 27:3). The present tense of that verb must have been concerning to them, for not only did it evince an absence of orthodoxy on a point that had not yet been established, but worse, it revealed that they (or the people at least) had not yet overcome their tendency to descend into disharmony over their differences of opinion.

Jesus was quick to establish orthodoxy in this area (see 3 Nephi 27:5–8) but even quicker to chasten them for their contentious approach. "Why is it that the people should murmur and dispute because of this thing?" (3 Nephi 27:4). To resolve the conflict, he pointed them to the scriptures and grounded his answer in what was written there, implying that they could have found the answer to their question in the word. Still, recognizing that scripture is not always interpreted easily or uniformly, Jesus then applied the scripture to their question and provided a clear answer. Orthodoxy was thereby established, with harmony not only reached by conversation's end but directly reaffirmed along the way. For Jesus, the approach was as important as the outcome.

This clarification of orthodoxy regarding the name of the Lord's church, introduced by a confirmation of the need for harmony in deciding it, is particularly relevant considering its repetition nearly two thousand years later within The Church of Jesus Christ of Latter-day Saints. In an official statement published in August 2018, in an address giving in the subsequent general conference, and in repeated reminders in the years since, President Russell M. Nelson has reiterated the need for orthodoxy in this area.[11] "The Lord has impressed upon my mind the importance of the name He has revealed for His Church," his official statement read, a name that "is not negotiable," as he affirmed in general conference. This nonnegotiability lies at the heart of orthodoxy, but making anything sacrosanct also makes harmony more difficult to achieve or maintain. As President Nelson admitted, "Responses to this statement ... have been mixed," just "as you would expect." Still, he declared, "It *is* the command of the Lord."[12]

This modern episode, which so clearly echoes the ancient one, illustrates how difficult it can be to balance orthodoxy and harmony. As one scholar of

Latter-day Saint culture observed, emphasizing orthodoxy in this area "has driven a new wedge of judgment, giving members a convenient shibboleth by which to measure whether someone else truly belongs."[13] It has also given outsiders and former members a convenient issue to dispute. As a student of faith loss myself, I noticed a significant amount of pushback to these pronouncements—some satirical, but much of it openly contentious—in online forums among disaffiliated or dissatisfied members of the Church. As just mentioned, President Nelson had expected such mixed responses but was quick to counsel Church members not to allow orthodoxy to eclipse the harmony that ought to prevail, urging instead to "be courteous and patient in our efforts to correct these errors."[14] Unfortunately, in certain circles on both sides of the issue, the same tendency to "murmur and dispute" that Jesus noted in his day (3 Nephi 27:4) remains present in our own.

Finding the Balance: Administering the Sacrament

Of the three instances in which Jesus condemned the Nephites' disharmonious approach to establishing orthodoxy, the second instance is the most useful, as it provides a key to unlock all three. Here Jesus is administering the sacrament and explaining its sacred nature, clarifying that it is an ordinance that, like baptism, requires proper priesthood authority on the part of the administrator and the requisite preparation on the part of the recipient (see 3 Nephi 18:5). He explains its symbolism and then, as with his explanation of the doctrine of Christ, warns the disciples against "do[ing] more or less" than what he had taught them (3 Nephi 18:13). Orthodoxy meant "buil[ding] upon my rock" and anything beyond or beneath—anything out of balance, that is—was "buil[ding] upon a sandy foundation" (3 Nephi 18:12–13).

Jesus explains what might constitute the "more or less" of the sacrament later in his discourse, a concept we will visit in a later section. But first he warns against "the gates of hell," the "tempt[ations of] the devil," and Satan's desire to "sift you as wheat" (3 Nephi 18:13, 15, 18). Then, as if to acknowledge the difficulty of navigating that path without error, Jesus commands them to "meet together oft" (3 Nephi 18:22), presumably to "fast and to pray, and to speak one with another concerning the welfare of their souls," as well as "to partake of bread and wine, in remembrance of the Lord Jesus," to borrow Moroni's later echo and explanation of the phrase (Moroni 6:5–6). Moroni's reliance on Christ's teachings in 3 Nephi 18 continues in what he says next: "And they were strict to observe that there should be no iniquity among them," ensuring orthodoxy by blotting out the names of the unrepentant. Among the repentant, meanwhile, harmony could prevail, as it promised that "as oft as they repented and sought forgiveness, with real intent, they were forgiven" (Moroni 6:7–8).[15]

In the case that serves as Moroni's precedent, Jesus has warned his disciples that in the frequent meetings which he was commanding, "Ye shall *not forbid* any man from coming unto you when ye shall meet together, but suffer them that they may come unto you and *forbid them not*" (3 Nephi 18:22; emphasis added). Having twice forbidden them from forbidding others, Jesus then repeats himself a third time: "Ye . . . shall not cast them out" (verse 23)—affirming an "all comers" policy among the people of God. That way, he suggests, the faithful could "pray for [others]" in person (verse 23), in hopes that the gospel message and the accompanying power of God might have their intended effect. This too Jesus repeats in quick succession, reaffirming that the purpose of gathering together was to invite all to come unto him. Christ had allowed them that opportunity, after all, and so he reminded them: "Ye see that I have commanded that none of you should go away, but rather have commanded that ye should come unto me, that ye might feel and see" (verse 25). His was an example of invitation and inclusivity that he wanted his disciples to reflect "unto the world." If they denied this openness they might themselves be closed off, for "whosoever breaketh this commandment suffereth himself to be led into temptation" (verse 25).

This affirmation of nonjudgmental inclusivity (harmony), however, is balanced by the instructions Jesus then gives to the disciples, which constitute a clear confirmation of orthodoxy: "Ye shall not suffer any one knowingly to partake of my flesh and blood unworthily, when ye shall minister it" (verse 28). In fact, this is the one instance of "forbidding" others that Jesus not only allows but requires: "If ye know that a man is unworthy to eat and drink of my flesh and blood ye shall forbid him" from partaking of it (verse 29). Lowering the standard of righteousness for participation in the sacrament would be as damning as raising the standard of admittance to the meetings in which the sacrament was administered. The former would make repentance seem unnecessary and the latter would make repentance seem unattainable. Either way, by lowering the likelihood that people would come unto Christ, an imbalance between orthodoxy and harmony would defeat the purpose of Christ's coming unto them.

The rival pulls between a high standard of worthiness and a low standard of admittance play out in the three verses that follow, as Jesus goes back and forth confirming *both* orthodoxy *and* harmony. One can sense his striving for a precarious balance through the conjunctions and conjunctive adverbs that open each verse, words that shift the center of gravity alternately from one side to the other, like a tightrope walker constantly shifting their weight. You must forbid the unworthy from partaking of the sacrament, the Savior commands, but then adds,

> *Nevertheless*, ye shall not cast him out from among you, but ye shall minister unto him and shall pray for him unto the Father, in my name; and if it so be that he repenteth and is baptized in my name, then shall ye receive him, and shall minister unto him of my flesh and blood.
>
> *But* if he repent not he shall not be numbered among my people, that he may not destroy my people, for behold I know my sheep, and they are numbered.
>
> *Nevertheless*, ye shall not cast him out of your synagogues, or your places of worship, for unto such shall ye continue to minister; for ye know not but what they will return and repent, and come unto me with full purpose of heart, and I shall heal them; and ye shall be the means of bringing salvation unto them. (3 Nephi 18:30–32; emphasis added)

In Christ's extended discussion of the sacrament in 3 Nephi 18, his emphasis alternates between orthodoxy and harmony repeatedly, as the following graphic makes clear:

Orthodoxy	Harmony
verses 15–21	
	verses 22–25
verses 26–29	
	verse 30
verse 31	
	verse 32

Jesus then reminds, "Keep these sayings which I have commanded you that ye come not under condemnation," and closes with a gentle note of condemnation of his own: "And I give you these commandments because of the disputations which have been among you. And blessed are ye if ye have no disputations among you" (verses 33–34). As with Christ's explanation of baptism earlier and his clarification of the name of the Church yet to come, this discussion was also an effort to end disputation, contention being the inadmissible common denominator each time.

Echoes of Imbalance

One more parallel between these three accounts is worth noting, and that is the fact that orthodoxy, once reached, does not necessarily stay settled, making the need for harmony a constant through periods of conflict and change. As already mentioned, the controversy over the name of Christ's church has been repeated in our day, and subsequent controversies echoing the arguments in 3 Nephi over baptism and the sacrament have been ongoing as well. Nearly four centuries after Jesus settled the matter of baptism, for example, Mormon learned that "there [had] been disputations among [his people] concerning the baptism of [their] little children." In response he urged his son Moroni to put an end to the "gross error" of infant baptism and to reestablish doctrinal orthodoxy. He did so in a scathing epistle that was eminently clear and unapologetically bold, hallmarks of orthodoxy's enforcement. But Mormon's condemnation of heterodoxy also reflected regret over disharmony, "for it grieveth me that there should disputations rise among you" (Moroni 8:4–6). Like Jesus before him, Mormon lamented the loss of true doctrine but also grieved over the way his people were attempting to correct it.

More recent disputations over baptism have colored much of Christian history, from the arguments between Pelagius and Augustine in the fifth century to the rejection of both Catholic and Lutheran baptisms by the Anabaptists during the Reformation. Contention continued in Joseph Smith's day, with rival restorationist Alexander Campbell writing a massive treatise on baptism in 1852[16] and the Lord himself confirming the need for an orthodox and authorized baptism in Doctrine and Covenants 22. But perhaps even more reflective of what we are discussing here is the repetition of controversy regarding admission to church meetings and to the sacrament during the Restoration's earliest days. This too reflects the need to maintain harmony while pursuing orthodoxy and draws directly upon the Savior's way of settling these difficulties during his Book of Mormon ministry.

With the restored Church less than a year old, the early saints began wrestling with their previously held beliefs about the standards for church admittance and attendance, much as the Nephite disciples were doing in 3 Nephi 18. The early Puritans had aspired to create a gathered community of what they termed "visible saints," believers who were granted admission into the congregation only upon giving satisfactory evidence of saving grace.[17] The infant "Church of Christ," as it was then called, began leaning in a similar direction, raising the standard of admittance for its meetings despite the Book of Mormon's warnings to the contrary.

Oliver Cowdery included those cautions in his 1829 "Articles of the Church of Christ," which drew heavily upon the Book of Mormon and, consequently, ended up addressing all three of the controversies Jesus settled in 3 Nephi. In Cowdery's words we see the same attempt to balance orthodoxy and harmony exemplified by Christ, usually in identical language. In Church meetings, for example, the saints were to "preach the truth in soberness [orthodoxy] casting out none from among you but rather invite them to come [harmony]." The sacrament was to be administered frequently, but

> if ye know that a man is unworthy to eat & drink of my flesh & blood ye shall forbid him [orthodoxy] nevertheless ye shall not cast him out from among you but ye shall minister unto him & shall pray for him unto the Father in my name & if it so be that he repenteth & is baptized in my name then shall ye receive him & shall minister unto him of my flesh & blood [harmony] but if he repenteth not he shall not be numbered among my people that he may not destroy my people For behold I know my Sheep & they are numbered [orthodoxy] nevertheless ye shall not cast him out of your Synagogues or your places of worship [harmony] ... And the church shall meet together oft for prayer & suplication casting out none from your places of worship but rather invite them to come [harmony] ... And there shall be no pride nor envying nor strifes nor malice nor idoletry nor witchcrafts nor whoredoms nor fornications nor coveteousness nor lying nor

deceits nor no manner of iniquity & if any one is guilty of any or the least of these & doth not repent & shew fruits meats for repentance they shall not be numbered among my people that they may not destroy my people [orthodoxy].[18]

These countervailing cautions notwithstanding, in their own imperfect attempts to strike a balance the early saints seemed to prefer a closed communion rooted in orthodoxy to an open community focused on harmony. To those familiar with 3 Nephi, this came as a surprise. As John Whitmer observed, "In the beginning of the church, while yet in her infancy, the disciples used to exclude unbelievers, which caused some to marvel, and converse about this matter because of the things that were written in the Book of Mormon."[19] (Based on how such issues were discussed within the Book of Mormon, one wonders how much disputing and contending accompanied this marveling and conversing!) In response, the Lord revealed what now appears as Doctrine and Covenants 46, which gives additional canonical shape to the balancing act illustrated in 3 Nephi 18 and in Cowdery's Church Articles.

In the revelation, the Lord allows the elders to "conduct all meetings as they are directed and guided by the Holy Spirit" (Doctrine and Covenants 46:2) but then clarifies a position he would not want a mistaken impression to overturn, complete with the counterbalancing conjunctive adverbs we saw in 3 Nephi 18: "*Nevertheless* ye are commanded never to cast any one out from your public meetings, which are held before the world. Ye are also commanded not to cast any one who belongeth to the church out of your sacrament meetings [harmony]; *nevertheless*, if any have trespassed, let him not partake until he makes reconciliation [orthodoxy]" (verses 2–4; emphasis added). Here again we see the Lord combining a harmonious openness to outsiders (and even unworthy insiders) with an orthodox affirmation of standards of worthiness.

Further commandments to "not cast any out" of the Church's sacrament meetings and confirmation meetings appear in the next two verses, after which the revelation shifts to its more recognized focus on the gifts of the Spirit. But even that discussion should be viewed in light of the Lord's effort to balance order (orthodoxy) and openness (harmony). On the one hand, orthodoxy discerns the "diversities of operations" (verse 16) and demands that true spiritual gifts be distinguished from "evil spirits, or doctrines of devils, or the commandments of men" (verse 7). But on the other hand, harmony honors the reality that "to every man"—including the curious onlookers, unworthy adherents, and earnest investigators mentioned at the beginning of the revelation—"is given a gift by the Spirit of God" (verse 11). No wonder "Visitors Welcome" signs grace the outside of our chapels. In the spirit of Doctrine and Covenants 46, it is a recognition that visitors of all kinds have spiritual gifts to offer those more orthodox members assembled inside. Still, in the spirit of 3 Nephi 18 and Moroni 6, that harmony within the chapel is meant to help true disciples minister to those who have entered that open door, preparing them to enter other doors that do not open quite so unconditionally. A different message graces the outside of our temples, and it is to these temple signs that those chapel signs are pointing and preparing: from the harmony of "Visitors Welcome" toward the orthodoxy of "Holiness to the Lord."

The Way toward Balance

From discussions of personal worthiness to matters of Church discipline, what texts like 3 Nephi 18 and Doctrine and Covenants 46 are striving to balance is the sanctity of the sacraments and the worth of souls. The first honors orthodoxy and the second prizes harmony, but both are "great in the sight of God" (Doctrine and Covenants 18:10). The same God who "cannot look upon sin with the least degree of allowance" made the ultimate allowance in the gift of his Only Begotten Son, making it possible for that stern warning against sin to be balanced by the merciful promise that immediately follows: "*Nevertheless*, he that repents and does the commandments of the Lord shall be forgiven" (Doctrine and Covenants 1:31–32; emphasis added). Seen in this light, our efforts to balance orthodoxy and harmony, which we pursue imperfectly, are reflective of the Lord's balance of justice and mercy, which he achieves perfectly.

Our challenge is to move in the direction of the Lord's perfect balance, to follow his "way" of honoring both the orthodox "truth" and the harmonious "life." This is the type of balance he exemplified in his interactions with the woman taken in adultery (see John 8:1–11), in which he neither condoned sin (orthodoxy) nor condemned the sinner (harmony) but instead allowed law and love to remain in active tension as he "let patience have her perfect work" (James 1:4). Granted that time and given that trust, "the woman glorified God from that hour, and believed on his name" (Joseph Smith Translation, John 8:11). She arrived at orthodoxy, that is, because harmony allowed and enabled it.

This is the same type of balance the Lord was commending in his interactions with the Nephite disciples during their three rounds of contentious disputation (and, in a similar way, the same balance the "voice of the Lord" recommended to Alma as he was pondering the role of discipline within the church [see Mosiah 26:14, 28–32]). With balance being the principal objective, it seems fitting that Christ would include the warning against declaring "more or less" than what he had established as his doctrine. He did this explicitly in his discussion of the doctrine of Christ as well as in his explanation of the sacrament (see 3 Nephi 11:40; 18:13), and it would have been equally appropriate in his clarification of the name of the church. By forbidding "more or less" Jesus is drawing his disciples away from extremes at either end of the spectrum, keeping orthodoxy from becoming a dogmatism that damns all who disagree (the "more"), and keeping harmony from becoming a relativism that eliminates even the possibility of absolute truth (the "less"). Thus, a safe center is established, a "Goldilocks Zone" where "too hot" and "too cold" are avoided in favor of a balanced, even a blended, middle ground.

Admittedly, this delicate balancing act makes the strait and narrow path seem more like a razor's edge, and sometimes it is, especially when the tension we are striving to hold is between things of infinite worth, like souls and sacraments. G. K. Chesterton captured the challenge well when he said that some things are "only a matter of an inch; but an inch is everything when you are balancing." What Chesterton was trying to balance were the rival orthodoxies at the heart of Christianity—its own set of "crosses," each of which "has at its heart a collision and a contradiction," like the two great commandments already discussed. Justice and mercy, agency and inspiration, mind and heart, individuality and community, male and female—the list is almost endless. As Chesterton wisely surmised, the key to navigating these paradoxes was not to hold to one at the expense of the other but somehow to hold onto both. In his eloquent description of the feat, "The Church could not afford to swerve a hair's breadth on some things if she was to continue her great and daring experiment of the irregular equilibrium. Once let one idea become less powerful and some other idea would become too powerful. It was no flock of sheep the Christian shepherd was leading, but a herd of bulls and tigers, of terrible ideals and devouring doctrines, each one of them strong enough to turn to a false religion and lay waste the world."[20]

Such was the flock that the Good Shepherd tended. He kept orthodoxy's lion from devouring harmony's lamb but also kept the lamb from enfeebling the lion. Jesus, himself both lamb of God and lion of the tribe of Judah, understood that both were but halves of one great whole and prized equally the truth he taught *and* the souls to whom he taught it. More importantly, his teachings and example provide his disciples—past and present—with the model to follow.

Conclusion

In a statement that fires the imagination, Joseph Smith observed, "By proving contraries, truth is made manifest."[21] At the time, he may simply have been encouraging the exploration of differing viewpoints (itself a healthy exercise in harmony seeking orthodoxy), but his words are suggestive of deeper realities. They hint at the "collisions and contradictions" that Chesterton saw in the cross; they evoke what Emerson called the "balanced antagonisms" by which "the world stands."[22] These "contraries," paradoxes, or "positive polarities," as we might call them, require the coexistence and cooperation of elements—both desirable—that may seem mutually exclusive, but end up being mutually beneficial instead. The contradictory become complementary as they fuse into what Chesterton called "some more startling synthesis."[23]

This study has wrestled with one such contrary, that of orthodoxy and harmony, or in the words of President Benson's desk plaque, the need to "be right" *and* to "be easy to live with." The plaque wondered if such a fusion of attributes was possible, but as we have seen, Christ's teachings attest that we must achieve this balance, just as his example confirms that we can. This is the "convicted civility" of evangelical leader Richard Mouw[24] and the "Christian courage" of Elder Robert D. Hales.[25] It is the "love and law" and the "truth and tolerance" of President Dallin H. Oaks,[26] or the "speaking the truth in love" of the apostle Paul (Ephesians 4:15). It is what Hans Frei described as a "generous orthodoxy,"[27] what a group of Latter-day Saint scholars labeled a "radical orthodoxy,"[28] and what this paper has portrayed as a harmonious orthodoxy-in-the-making.

What would Jesus call it? *Discipleship*. And he exemplified it in both its vertical and horizontal dimensions: its upward reach and its outward grasp, its valiant conviction and heartfelt compassion, its relentless pursuit of truth and its patience in letting others arrive there. For this reason he condemned contention in pursuit of consensus and instead recommended harmony in pursuit of orthodoxy.

That these elements can and must coexist has been the argument of this paper, but its deeper contention (offered as noncontentiously as possible!) is that when proving contraries, *order* does matter. Balancing ostensible opposites is difficult, and errors will unavoidably be made. But this begs the question: on which side should we err? The common refrain is to "err on the side of mercy," and this contrary seems to lend credence to that choice. However, as we have wrestled with the difference between order of importance and order of implementation, a more nuanced expression is better: err on whichever side best allows for ongoing adjustments, the determination of which will always be situation specific and therefore must always be Spirit directed.[29] Put simply, in choosing between opposite goods, the goal is to choose both, by starting with the one most likely to draw in the other.

Ultimately it is Christ's orthodoxy that will prevail, as every knee bows and every tongue confesses that he is the Christ (see Philippians 2:10–11). But it is his charity—the highest form of harmony—that will draw us there, a charity that "suffereth long" (1 Corinthians 13:4) as the process slowly unfolds. This was the central message of President Russell M. Nelson's general conference address in April 2023, in which he defended orthodoxy but denounced any kind of contention in its pursuit. "As disciples of Jesus Christ," he explained, "we are to be examples of how to interact with others—*especially* when we have differences of opinion." We are to "build, lift, encourage, persuade, and inspire—no matter how difficult the situation." In short, we are to be peacemakers, even as we stand valiantly for the doctrines of the Prince of Peace.[30]

Harmony is our best hope to progress toward orthodoxy as a society. It invites patience, empathy, understanding, and humility, and ensures that consensus will be reached in the Savior's way.[31] That way is truth at its clearest and life at its kindest, and it centers on him. "Therefore, what manner of men ought ye to be?" Especially when striving to balance orthodoxy and harmony, the Lord's answer is clear: "Verily I say unto you, even as I am" (3 Nephi 27:27).

Jared M. Halverson is an associate professor of ancient scripture at Brigham Young University.

Notes

1. Boyd K. Packer, "We Honor Now His Journey," *Ensign*, July 1994, 32; see also Ezra Taft Benson, "In His Steps," devotional address at Brigham Young University, March 4, 1979.
2. *Orthodoxy* is "authorized or generally accepted theory, doctrine, or practice." *Merriam-Webster's Online Dictionary*, s.v. "orthodoxy."
3. Abraham Lincoln, First Inaugural Address, March 4, 1861 (emphasis added); available online at https://avalon.law.yale.edu/19th_century/lincoln1.asp.
4. Dallin H. Oaks, "Going Forward with Religious Freedom and Nondiscrimination," 2021 Joseph Smith Lecture at the University of Virginia, November 12, 2021.
5. On social contract theory, see Christopher W. Morris, ed., *The Social Contract Theorists: Critical Essays on Hobbes, Locke, and Rousseau* (Lanham, MD: Rowman & Littlefield, 1999).
6. On social contact theory, see, for example, Loris Vezzali and Sofia Stathi, eds., *Intergroup Contact Theory: Recent Developments and Future Directions* (London: Routledge, 2017).
7. Robert D. Putnam and David E. Campbell, *American Grace: How Religion Divides and Unites Us* (New York: Simon & Schuster, 2010), 4–6, 516–50.
8. Putnam and Campbell, *American Grace*, 53–68.
9. For a fascinating discussion of what these disputations may have entailed, see Joseph M. Spencer, *An Other Testament: On Typology*, 2nd ed. (Provo, UT: Neal A. Maxwell Institute for Religious Scholarship, 2016), 106–9.
10. D. Todd Christofferson, "The First Commandment First," BYU devotional address, March 22, 2022, https://speeches.byu.edu/talks/d-todd-christofferson/the-first-commandment-first/.
11. See Russell M. Nelson, "The Name of the Church," official statement, August 16, 2018, https://newsroom.churchofjesuschrist.org/article/name-of-the-church; "The Correct Name of the Church," *Ensign*, November 2018, 87–89.
12. Nelson, "The Correct Name of the Church," 87.
13. Jana Riess, "Oh, now I get it: Purging the word 'Mormon' is a bid for the mainstream," *Religion News Service*, July 14, 2022, https://religionnews.com/2022/07/14/oh-now-i-get-it-purging-the-word-mormon-is-a-bid-for-the-mainstream/.

14. Nelson, "The Correct Name of the Church," 89.
15. On Moroni's reliance on Christ's teachings in 3 Nephi 18, see John W. Welch, "From Presence to Practice: Jesus, the Sacrament Prayers, the Priesthood, and Church Discipline in 3 Nephi 18 and Moroni 2–6," *Journal of Book of Mormon Studies* 5, no. 1 (1996): 119–39.
16. Alexander Campbell, *Christian Baptism: with its Antecedents and Consequents* (Bethany, VA: Alexander Campbell, 1852).
17. See Edmund S. Morgan, *Visible Saints: The History of a Puritan Idea* (Ithaca, NY: Cornell University Press, 1963).
18. Appendix 3: "Articles of the Church of Christ, June 1829," pp. [1–2], The Joseph Smith Papers.
19. John Whitmer, "History, 1831–circa 1847," p. 23, The Joseph Smith Papers, https://www.josephsmithpapers.org/paper-summary/john-whitmer-history-1831-circa-1847/27.
20. G. K. Chesterton, *Orthodoxy* (New York: John Lane, 1908; reprint, 1914), 184, 50.
21. Joseph Smith, *History of the Church of Jesus Christ of Latter-day Saints* (Salt Lake City: Deseret Book, 1980): 6:428; "Letter to Israel Daniel Rupp, 5 June 1844," p. [1], The Joseph Smith Papers.
22. Ralph Waldo Emerson, "The Natural History of Intellect," in *The Complete Works of Ralph Waldo Emerson*, vol. 12 (Boston: Houghton Mifflin, 1904), 53.
23. Chesterton, *Orthodoxy*, 272.
24. Richard J. Mouw, *Uncommon Decency: Christian Civility in an Uncivil World*, rev. ed. (Downers Grove, IL: InterVarsity Press, 2010), 11.
25. Robert D. Hales, "Christian Courage: The Price of Discipleship," *Ensign*, November 2008, 72–75.
26. Dallin H. Oaks, "Love and Law," *Ensign*, November 2009, 26–29; "Truth and Tolerance," Church Educational System devotional address, September 11, 2011.
27. See Jason A. Springs, *Toward a Generous Orthodoxy: Prospects for Hans Frei's Postliberal Theology* (New York: Oxford University Press, 2010).
28. See https://latterdayorthodoxy.org/.
29. In terms of the contrary we have been investigating in this paper, erring on the side of harmony would mean postponing orthodoxy (or at least its enforcement on others) in the short term if it threatens to obliterate harmony in the long term. An example of this might be parenting a wayward child (the father of the prodigal son surrenders orthodoxy to harmoniously honor the agency of his son, who eventually returns). Erring on the side of orthodoxy, meanwhile, would mean surrendering harmony in the short term if the results of unorthodoxy might prove irrecoverable in the long term. An example of this would be when someone threatens physical or spiritual suicide, in which case erring on the side of harmony/agency/mercy might prove fatal. Returning to the example of Abraham Lincoln, whom we quoted earlier, this was essentially the choice he made in refusing to allow the Confederacy to secede from the United States.
30. Russell M. Nelson, "Peacemakers Needed," April 2023 general conference address; President Nelson's entire talk is a powerful example of the kind of harmony in pursuit of orthodoxy this paper attempts to describe.
31. See Doctrine and Covenants 121:41–46 and 107:27–31.

15

Ascended into Heaven
The Book of Mormon's Witness of Jesus Christ's Ascension

WILLIAM PEREZ

If you were to outline the moments that constitute what members of The Church of Jesus Christ of Latter-day Saints recognize as the atonement of Jesus Christ, what would be on your list? While most Latter-day Saints would include and focus on the Savior's suffering in the garden, his death on the cross, and his resurrection from the tomb, few would think to mention Christ's ascension into heaven as part of God's marvelous gift to humanity.[1] However, several prophets *do* include the Savior's ascension in their overview of Christ's redemptive work, indicating that this final act may have more importance than our current culture realizes. Several of these references are found in the Book of Mormon, emphasizing the Lord's ascension into heaven as a crucial part of its messianic message. As "Another Testament of Jesus Christ," how does the Book of Mormon contribute to our understanding of his ascension? Additionally, how does this understanding foster new insight into interrelated principles found throughout the text? By analyzing both the explicit and implicit references to Christ's ascension found in the Book of Mormon, this chapter presents a framework for understanding the ascension's salvific role and appreciating its implications for Jesus's followers. As a result, readers are invited to consider the "essential ascension"[2] as an important aspect of the Savior's atonement.[3]

The meaning of "ascension" as discussed here is twofold. First, ascension refers to the literal entrance of Christ "into heaven itself, now to appear in the presence of God for us" (Hebrews 9:24). This occurred after his resurrection from the dead but before his general appearances to the apostles, the Nephites, and others (see John 20:17; 3 Nephi 10:18). This ascension was a symbolic and literal victory over spiritual death as Jesus, in the flesh, vicariously reintroduced humanity into the presence of the Father. After this initial return to the Father, others were privileged to witness subsequent instances where Jesus was "carried up into heaven" (Luke 24:51) as a testimony of his atoning work and as a reminder that "when [Christ] ascended up on high, he led captivity captive, and gave gifts unto men" (Ephesians 4:8). Secondly, ascension refers to the moment when disciples of Christ will be caught up "to meet the Lord in the air" (1 Thessalonians 4:17) at his second coming (see Doctrine and Covenants 88:96–98). This ascension is preceded by internal and symbolic moments of descent and ascent scattered throughout a lifetime of discipleship.[4] To lose sight of the literal and symbolic significance of Christ's ascension is to risk narrowing our insights into his complete atonement and into our personal trajectories along his covenant path.

Patrick Henry Reardon, a Christian leader and author, proclaimed, "The Lord's ascension . . . is essential to the work of atonement. . . . In Christ's ascension, God eradicates every vestige of our alienation from Him."[5] Despite its prominence in Latter-day Saint scripture and theology,[6] the ascension is often inappropriately relegated to a chronological event in the New Testament rather than celebrated as an indispensable part of Christ's atonement. The fact that Book of Mormon prophets such as Abinadi, Alma, and Mormon specifically mention Christ's ascension suggests that it merits deeper consideration within the modern-day gospel paradigm. The ascension was also emphasized in the early days of the Restoration when the Prophet Joseph Smith included ascension in a list of Christ's atoning acts. He taught, "The fundamental principles of our religion is the testimony of the apostles and prophets concerning Jesus Christ, 'that he died, was buried, and rose again the third day, *and ascended up into heaven;*' and all other things are only appendages to these, which pertain to our religion."[7] Over one hundred years after Joseph Smith's declaration, President Hugh B. Brown stated, "We believe that the greatest story ever told in all the annals of history, is the story of the atonement of Christ. The record of his resurrection and ascension, without which the atonement would not have been complete, is the climax to that story, and now, two thousand years after the event, it is still central and pivotal in all true Christian thought."[8] The writers of the *New Testament Student Manual* described "the Ascension as the culmination of the Atonement of Jesus Christ."[9]

Such mentions of the ascension within the context of Christ's atonement emphasize its importance.[10] With this encouragement we can better investigate instances throughout scripture that directly mention or allude to the Savior's ascension. This chapter explores the direct and indirect principles connected to the Lord's ascension that are illuminated throughout the Book of Mormon.

The Book of Mormon provides readers with straightforward references to the ascension of Jesus Christ as well as a foundation from which to draw additional connections to it. Sometimes the Book of Mormon distinctly uses the words *ascension* or *ascended*, such as when Alma the Younger taught, "The souls and the bodies are reunited, of the righteous, at the resurrection of Christ, *and his ascension into heaven*" (Alma 40:20; emphasis added). Other times, *ascension* is implicit, underscored by the foregrounding of complementary concepts such as *condescension* or being *raised* unto exaltation. We turn first to verses in the Book of Mormon that directly describe the ascension of Jesus Christ. We will then review how the truths found in these prophetic pronouncements shed light on other major themes in the Book of Mormon: namely, Jesus Christ's descent below all things, his promise of exaltation for his followers, and his ascending to prepare a place for them. Lastly, we will explore how an understanding of the Book of Mormon's stated and implied teachings relating to Christ's ascension empower believers in accessing "the lifting power of the Lord."[11]

The Redemption of the People: Scriptural Mentions of Ascension

The ascension of Jesus Christ was on Book of Mormon prophets' minds at least one hundred years before it occurred and certainly for centuries thereafter. Specific references to this monumental moment are first found in the teachings of the prophet Abinadi and bookended in a sermon by Mormon, the narrative's primary compiler. In addition, a group of Nephites was privileged to experience the Lord's ascension firsthand during his personal ministry among them. All these accounts taken together set the stage for extended reflection on the importance of the ascension as a redeeming event with ongoing effects. These conscious prophetic insertions reveal a unique element of why Book of Mormon authors talked of Christ, rejoiced in Christ, preached of Christ, and prophesied of Christ (see 2 Nephi 25:26).

Mosiah 15:8–9

While testifying that "salvation doth not come by the law alone" but by the literal sacrifice of "God himself" (see Mosiah 13:28), Abinadi detailed how Christ's ascension was to be part of humankind's redemption. After a miraculous ministry that would culminate in his being crucified and slain, Abinadi declared that the Son's will would be completely "swallowed up in the will of the father" (Mosiah 15:7). Through this infinite offering, "God breaketh the bands of death, having gained the victory over death; giving the Son power to make intercession for the children of men" (Mosiah 15:8). Abinadi then highlighted this endowment of power through his subsequent description of the process: "*Having ascended into heaven*, having the bowels of mercy; being filled with compassion towards the children of men; . . . having redeemed them, and satisfied the demands of justice" (Mosiah 15:9; emphasis added). In this explanation, the ascension of Jesus Christ into heaven is positioned as a link between—or at least a part of—breaking the bands of death and receiving power to make intercession for God's children.

Mosiah 18:1–2

Abinadi's description of Christ's atonement was later adopted and streamlined by his convert, Alma. Their inclusion of Christ's ascension as a key component became standard enough that the prophet-historian Mormon cemented it in his summary of Alma's teachings. He wrote that Alma "went about privately among the people, and began to teach the words of Abinadi— yea, concerning that which was to come, and also concerning the resurrection of the dead, and the redemption of the people, which was to be brought to pass through the power, and sufferings, and death of Christ, and his resurrection *and ascension* into heaven" (Mosiah 18:1–2; emphasis added). Once again, the ascension is listed as a unique factor in redeeming the human family. Abinadi and Alma both stressed that the Savior would undergo agony and death as part of redeeming all people from "their lost and fallen state" (Mosiah 16:4). However, their synopsis also makes clear that just as Christ's suffering and humiliation were necessary for redemption, his resurrection and subsequent ascension into heaven finalized his victory on our behalf. Furthermore, *all* aspects of the Lord's atoning work as described by these prophets would be attested during his ministry in the Americas.

3 Nephi

Christ's ascension into heaven was recorded by his followers on both continents as a noteworthy landmark in the unfolding events of his postmortal ministry. Following a period of destruction and darkness, the Nephites were gathered at the temple when Jesus descended into their midst. As they recognized him, "they remembered that it had been prophesied among them that Christ should show himself unto them after his ascension into heaven" (3 Nephi 11:12). Inviting them to come unto him, Jesus commenced a personal ministry among the people. At the conclusion of his initial visit, and paralleling New Testament authors who described how Jesus "was taken up; and a cloud received him out of their sight" (Acts 1:9), the Nephite record then reads: "It came to pass that . . . there came a cloud and overshadowed the multitude that they could not see Jesus. And while they were overshadowed he departed from them, and ascended into heaven. And the disciples saw and did bear record that he ascended again into heaven" (3 Nephi 18:38–39). Just like the Savior's disciples in the Holy Land (see Luke 24:50–53; Acts 2:32–35), his flock in the New World also affirmed the resurrected Lord's ascension into heaven.

Although not directly referenced, the Nephite account is reminiscent of the description given in Mosiah 18:2 of redemption being brought about through Christ's power, sufferings, death, resurrection, and ascension. It is significant that throughout this experience the Nephites received the opportunity to bear record of each facet of the Savior's atonement. Jesus descended among the Nephites in power. He invited the multitude one by one to experience his sufferings and death by allowing them to thrust their hands into his side and to feel the nail prints in his hands, "that ye may know that I . . . have been slain for the sins of the world" (3 Nephi 11:14). He later healed and made whole all who were present. In addition to meeting the resurrected Lord himself and witnessing the miracles that accompanied his resurrection (see 3 Nephi 23:9–10), the Nephite disciples ultimately bore record that he had ascended (see 3 Nephi 18:38–39). This account of the resurrected Lord personally appearing to the Nephites, sharing with them the marks of his sacrifice and death, powerfully healing them, and then being lifted up out of their sight agrees with Abinadi and Alma's summary of how redemption was to be realized.

Moroni 7

Toward the end of the Nephite record, Moroni included an address given by his father, Mormon, that encouraged "the peaceable followers of Christ" (Moroni 7:3) to exercise faith in their ascended Lord. Urging them to believe Christ's words and hope for miracles, Mormon asked his audience this question: "Wherefore, my beloved brethren, have miracles ceased because Christ hath ascended into heaven, and hath sat down on the right hand of God, to claim of the Father his rights of mercy which he hath upon the children of men?" (Moroni 7:27). Mormon rhetorically described the Savior's ascension into heaven as the culmination of Christ's atoning work and dealings with humanity, underscoring its significance as a redemptive event. However, the true purpose of his question is to convince his listeners that the ascension does not merely represent a conclusion, but a continuation of Christ's redemptive work.

Just as Abinadi paired Jesus's ascension with his ability to intercede on our behalf (see Mosiah 15:8–9), Mormon makes clear that Christ's ascension was a precursor to his making a full claim on the ability to extend the Father's mercy and serve as an advocate for his children.[12] After the initial question, Mormon declared: "For he hath answered the ends of the law, and he claimeth all those who have faith in him; and they who have faith in him will cleave unto every good thing; wherefore he advocateth the cause of the children of men; and he dwelleth eternally in the heavens" (Moroni 7:28). Having ascended to the right hand of God, Jesus takes an active role in the affairs of his kingdom and makes possible our own return into the Father's presence.

Ascended Above All Things: Implicit Connections to Ascension

The Book of Mormon's rich doctrinal commentary goes beyond simply asserting that Jesus Christ's ascension played a part in bringing about "the redemption of the people" (Mosiah 18:2). From the vantage points it provides regarding this miraculous occurrence, we can further flesh out the significance of analogous truths found across its pages. Such principles include the Savior's condescension—which encompasses his descending below all things—and the subtle but significant ways in which the text differentiates between resurrection and exaltation. Although the following examples do not contain exact references to the Savior's post-resurrection ascension, examining them as working in harmony with what the Book of Mormon does say about the ascension of Jesus Christ can help us better connect the dots in a gospel plan described as being "one eternal round" (1 Nephi 10:19; Doctrine and Covenants 3:2).

The condescension of God

Because of an important connection between descending and ascending, the Book of Mormon's emphasis on Christ's descent is one of the major ways it testifies of his ascent. Just as certain as is the text's indictment that "all are fallen and are lost" (Alma 34:9) is its declaration that "the Messiah cometh in the fulness of time, that he may redeem the children of men from the fall" (2 Nephi 2:26). Elder Jeffrey R. Holland, in speaking of the Savior's power to end Adam and Eve's "spiritual banishment," recognized that "fortunately, there was going to be a way out and a way *up*."[13] In order to provide a way up, the Savior was willing to come *down*. While the Book of Mormon describes Christ's bodily descent on several occasions (see 1 Nephi 1:9; Mosiah 3:5; 3 Nephi 11:8), it more often speaks to a broader theme of descent embodied in the concept of condescension—a word defined by President Ezra Taft Benson as meaning "to descend or come down from an exalted position to a place of inferior status."[14]

In the Book of Mormon, Nephi became a witness of the Savior's condescension[15] as manifested through Jesus's mortal birth, baptism, and crucifixion (see 1 Nephi 11:14–33; 2 Nephi 31:4–7). These acts of humility and alignment with the Father's will served as symbols of descent and as necessary precursors to Christ's ascension. Of the Savior's baptism in the lowest body of fresh water on the planet, President Russell M. Nelson asked, "Could [Jesus] have selected a better place to symbolize the humble depths to which He went and from which He rose?"[16] In what Elder Neal A. Maxwell described as the "grand and glad irony of Christ's great mission,"[17] Nephi saw the Lamb of God "lifted up upon the cross and slain for the sins of the world" (1 Nephi 11:33) so that, as Jesus himself would later explain, the Savior would have power to lift all men up to stand before him (see 3 Nephi 27:13–15). Christ's condescension can be read as a paradoxical foreshadowing of his ascension, which materialized his ability to "succor his people according to their infirmities" and secured "the power of his deliverance" (Alma 7:12–13). The latter could not have happened without the former. Nephi came to understand that through this process, the Savior brought about redemption for all of God's children.

The Book of Mormon's recounting of Christ's condescension complements the teachings of early and modern-day church leaders who have also noted the link between the glory of Jesus's ascension and the necessity of his descent below all things. Irenaeus, a second-century church leader, described how after descending to "those things which are of the earth beneath" in search of lost sheep, Jesus "ascend[ed] to the height above, offering and commending to His Father that human nature (hominem) which had been found."[18] The Doctrine and Covenants describes the Savior as "he that ascended up on high, as also he descended below all things" (Doctrine and Covenants 88:6). President Nelson has reiterated that Christ "literally descended beneath all things to rise above all things."[19] Lastly, Elder D. Todd Christofferson offered this assurance: "The atoning power of Jesus Christ—who descended below all things and then ascended on high and who possesses all power in heaven and in earth—ensures that God can and will fulfill His promises."[20] Understanding Christ's complete descent allows us to better comprehend the magnitude of his overcoming all things and ascending to "[sit] on the right hand of [the Father's] power" (Moroni 9:26).

Counterfeit ascension

The Book of Mormon also helps us appreciate the value of Christ's condescension and ascension by illustrating a series of contrasting counterfeit ascensions. In the iconic vision of the tree of life, the symbol opposite to God's love and condescension is the great and spacious building. This building "stood as it were in the air, high above the earth" (1 Nephi 8:26). Its ascension was fueled by the pride of the world, its inhabitants having chosen loftiness over lowliness of heart. Ultimately, the structure fell, "and the fall thereof was exceedingly great" (1 Nephi 11:36). In like manner, in Nephi's inclusion of Isaiah's writings, we learn of Lucifer's corrupt desires: "I will ascend into heaven, I will exalt my throne above the stars of God; . . . I will ascend above the heights of the clouds; I will be like the Most High" (2 Nephi 24:13–14). However, because Lucifer seeks to force his own ascension without humbly condescending, he is ultimately forced to descend: "Yet thou shalt be brought down to hell, to the sides of the pit" (2 Nephi 24:15). Only the Savior Jesus Christ could merit for himself and for those who lay hold on him an ascent into the kingdom of heaven. Jesus promises that the righteous who endure and humbly fall and partake of his love (see 1 Nephi 8:30) "shall be lifted up at the last day" (1 Nephi 13:37), while those who elevate themselves[21] and fight against him will fall into the pit (see 1 Nephi 22:14).

Lifted up at the last day

Acknowledging the efficacy of Christ's ascension allows us to expand our reading of Book of Mormon passages that discuss promised blessings to the faithful. In a powerful explanation of his gospel, the Savior explained that because he was lifted upon the cross, "even so should men be lifted up by the Father, to stand before me, to be judged of their works" (3 Nephi 27:14). In this sense, Christ's death and resurrection unlock a resurrection and judgment for all the Father's children in which they, at least momentarily, are brought back into his presence. The Savior continued his discourse by reiterating invitations to repent, pursue a covenant path, and be washed in his blood (see 3 Nephi 27:16, 19–20). He concluded with a promise: "Therefore, if ye do these things blessed are ye, for ye shall be lifted up at the last day" (3 Nephi 27:22). While resurrection and judgment bring an end to our estrangement from God to a limited extent, it is Christ's gospel, covenant path, atoning blood,[22] *and* his ascension[23] that yield a permanent *lifting up* into the presence of God, a complete defeat of spiritual death.[24]

In the same vein, the prophet Jacob taught that after being reconciled unto Christ, "ye may obtain a resurrection, according to the power of the resurrection which is in Christ, *and* be presented as the first-fruits of Christ unto God" (Jacob 4:11; emphasis added). Two blessings of reconciliation to Christ are at play here: one is obtaining a resurrection and the other is to be presented as the first fruits of Christ unto God. Both can be viewed as distinct blessings made possible by the totality of the Savior's atonement. In light of additional scripture stating that the "first fruits" are those who ascend, or are "caught up to meet [Christ]" (Doctrine and Covenants 88:96–98) and inherit his kingdom (see Doctrine and Covenants 76:62–65), Jacob's wording reminds readers that each aspect of Christ's atonement, including his ascension, has direct implications on what is possible for those who avail themselves of the Savior's power. Such a reading of passages like Jacob 4:11 are often hindered by a tendency to fuse resurrection and ascension.

One of the reasons why the ascension of Jesus Christ is often overshadowed by his resurrection is that at first glance, many scriptural promises seem to point us to resurrection as the ultimate gift and goal. A careful reading, however, reveals otherwise.[25] For example, during Nephi's visionary experience, the Savior blesses those who seek to build his kingdom with the power of the Holy Ghost. He then states, "*If* they endure unto the end they shall be lifted up at the last day, and shall be saved in the everlasting kingdom of the Lamb" (1 Nephi 13:37; emphasis added). Although being "lifted up" or "raised up" at the last day is sometimes viewed as synonymous with resurrection, the *if* in this statement makes being lifted up a conditional promise, even a metaphor for ascension unto exaltation. The conditionality of the passage indicates that it cannot be referring merely to the promise of resurrection because, as Elder Dale G. Renlund and Sister Ruth Lybbert Renlund have reiterated, "Resurrection is universally and unconditionally given."[26]

Because resurrection is unconditional, it becomes clear that the many scriptural instances of conditionally being raised up refer to a literal or symbolic ascent into the kingdom of God.[27] In a written First Presidency message, President Gordon B. Hinckley expressed gratitude for the gift of resurrection and then added, "But there is a goal beyond Resurrection. That is exaltation in our Father's kingdom."[28] Factoring in the redemptive power of Jesus Christ's ascension within the plan of salvation allows readers to notice these important distinctions that are repeated throughout the Book of Mormon—preventing a shortsighted conflation[29]—and keep the ultimate goal of ascension unto exaltation in mind.

Raised unto exaltation

A powerful image for the exaltation of the righteous is found in the Book of Mormon's interweaving of ascending and sitting down. As part of being assured a seat in the Father's kingdom, three Nephites in the Book of Mormon temporarily ascended in a foretaste of the day when "they were to receive a greater change, and to be received into the kingdom of the Father to go no more out, but to dwell with God eternally in the heavens" (3 Nephi 28:40). In her article "Sitting Enthroned: A Scriptural Perspective," Jennifer C. Lane establishes that the imagery of "sitting down" found throughout scripture is a metaphor for exaltation in God's kingdom. Her analysis includes a reference to the three Nephites who were "caught up into heaven, and saw and heard unspeakable things" (3 Nephi 28:13). Lane points out that these men were promised by Jesus that "ye shall have fulness of joy; *and ye shall sit down in the kingdom of my Father;* . . . and ye shall be even as I am, and I am even as the Father" (3 Nephi 28:10; emphasis added). She writes that the promise of becoming as the Father and Son—given to amplify the promise of their eventual sitting down in God's kingdom—"is the fullest possible sense of being exalted, or lifted up, to a new status."[30] It was the Savior who first "ascended into heaven, and hath sat down on the right hand of God" (Moroni 7:27). By laying hold upon him, all of creation can be "raised to dwell at the right hand of God" (Alma 28:12) and "*to sit down* with Abraham, and Isaac, and with Jacob, and with all our holy fathers, to go no more out" (Helaman 3:30; emphasis added). To be "lifted up" and allowed to "sit down" is to follow in the footsteps of the ascended Lord who prepared the way for all humanity.

Preparing a place

Jesus Christ's ascent into heaven is a necessary part of his preparing heaven for those who will follow. The Book of Mormon's vivid descriptions of the Redeemer's ascension help us better understand not only what he has done for his followers through his sufferings, death, and resurrection, but also what he is preparing for them through his ascension. Just as Jesus ascended "and hath sat down on the right hand of God" (Moroni 7:27), the Book of Mormon assures that "whoso believeth in God might with surety hope for a better world, yea, even a place at the right hand of God" (Ether 12:4). Having ascended into heaven, Christ is engaged in readying the kingdom for those who will yet inherit it. In the Book of Mormon, he himself promises an eventual ascent to this prepared abode: "And blessed is he that is found faithful unto my name at the last day, for he shall be lifted up to dwell in the kingdom prepared for him from the foundation of the world" (Ether 4:19). This promise is also consistent with a latter-day revelation in which Christ reminded the saints that he is "prepar[ing] all things before he taketh you; for ye are the church of the Firstborn, and he will take you up in a cloud, and appoint every man his portion" (Doctrine and Covenants 78:20–21).[31] Keeping the Lord's promised provisions in mind, Moroni beautifully encapsulated Christ's atoning work when he testified that "thou [Jesus Christ] hast loved the world, even unto the laying down of thy life for the world [sufferings and death], that thou mightest take it again [resurrection] to prepare a place for the children of men [ascension]" (Ether 12:33).

May Christ Lift Thee Up

The Book of Mormon showcases that the Savior's covenant path leads us through a paradoxical descending discipleship[32] that progressively ascends into our receiving his image in our countenances (see Alma 5:14) and "see[ing] Christ] as he is" (Moroni 7:48). This descent—requiring a broken heart and a contrite spirit (see 3 Nephi 9:19–20)—occurs as we humbly take Jesus's name upon us and pursue a lifetime of service and worship (see Mosiah 18:8–10). President Russell M. Nelson observed that following Christ into the depths of a baptismal font symbolizes how "we, too, can come from the depths to ascend to lofty heights of our own destiny."[33] For Latter-day Saints, this process of descending and ascending includes receiving the ordinances and covenants of the temple, which represent "a step-by-step ascent into the Eternal Presence."[34] Overtime, consecrated efforts propel us upwards towards Christ until we too "may be lifted up at the last day and enter into his rest" (Alma 13:29).

Despite difficulties throughout the disciple's journey, the Savior's ascension can serve as a source of strength that lifts weary spirits from "sin's dark prison" into "a holier state."[35] In this manner, scattered moments of spiritual ascent provide comfort in this life and hope for the next. During a time of trial, Moroni's faith was strengthened by his father directing him toward the ascended Savior. Mormon's counsel to his son is just as relevant for the lives of modern disciples. He writes:

> My son, be faithful in Christ; and may not the things which I have written grieve thee, to weigh thee down unto death; but may Christ lift thee up, and may his sufferings and death, and the showing his body unto our fathers, and his mercy and long-suffering, and the hope of his glory and of eternal life, rest in your mind forever. And may the grace of God the

Father, whose throne is high in the heavens, and our Lord Jesus Christ, who sitteth on the right hand of his power, until all things shall become subject unto him, be, and abide with you forever. (Moroni 9:25–26)

Like Mormon, President Nelson has testified that because Christ overcame the world and has risen—or ascended—above it, as we descend with him, "the Savior *lifts* us above the pull of this fallen world by blessing us with greater charity, humility, generosity, kindness, self-discipline, peace, and *rest*."[36]

A Fundamental Principle

Both overtly and between the lines, the Book of Mormon points us upward, toward an ascended Christ who has made heaven accessible to his people. President Nelson declared, "The Book of Mormon provides the fullest and most authoritative understanding of the Atonement of Jesus Christ to be found anywhere."[37] A key part of this understanding includes an acknowledgment of the Savior's ascension as part of his redemptive work. The Book of Mormon testifies of the ascension as an indispensable part of the Savior's postmortal ministry, as a complementary conclusion to Christ's condescension, and as a promised possibility for all of humanity. These principles provide a powerful perspective that affords hope in this life and optimism for the life to come. To ignore the ascension is to reduce the totality of Christ's salvific journey and to dull the landscape of the covenant path and its accompanying rewards.

As we contemplate the moments that constitute what members of The Church of Jesus Christ of Latter-day Saints recognize as the atonement of Jesus Christ, may we remember the Book of Mormon's testimony of a Redeemer who took upon himself infirmity, suffering, and death (see Alma 7:11–12); a Savior who "bringeth to pass the resurrection of the dead (Mosiah 15:20); *and* a Risen Lord who has "ascended into heaven, and hath sat down on the right hand of God" (Moroni 7:27). The testimony of holy prophets makes clear that "the redemption of the people . . . was to be brought to pass through the power, and sufferings, and death of Christ, and his resurrection *and* ascension into heaven" (Mosiah 18:2; emphasis added). President Joseph Fielding Smith's hymn "Does the Journey Seem Long?" captures the pinnacle of this redemption as taught throughout the Book of Mormon:

> Let your heart be not faint
> Now the journey's begun;
> There is One who still beckons to you.
> So look upward in joy
> And take hold of his hand;
> He will lead you to heights that are new—
>
> A land holy and pure,
> Where all trouble doth end,
> And your life shall be free from all sin,
> Where no tears shall be shed,
> For no sorrows remain.
> Take his hand and with him enter in.[38]

Truly, "the ascension of Christ is our elevation"[39] as much as it is one of "the fundamental principles of our religion."[40]

WILLIAM PEREZ *is a PhD candidate in American religious history at Florida State University.*

Notes

1. In the April 2019 general conference, Tad R. Callister described the atonement of Jesus Christ as "a series of events that commenced in the Garden of Gethsemane, continued on the cross, and culminated with the Savior's Resurrection from the tomb." That same year, Brigham Young University professor John Hilton summarized an informal survey in which students answered the question "Where did the atonement take place?" All student answers indicated that the atonement either took place in Gethsemane or in Gethsemane and on the cross. See Tad R. Callister, "The Atonement of Jesus Christ," *Liahona*, May 2019, 85, and John Hilton, "Teaching the Scriptural Emphasis on the Crucifixion of Jesus Christ," *Religious Educator* 20, no. 3 (2019): 134.
2. Patrick Henry Reardon, "The Essential Ascension," *Touchstone*, May/June 2014, 48.
3. In doing so, I want to be clear that I am not dismissing Gethsemane, the cross, or the resurrection as essential elements of Christ's atonement. My focus on the ascension in this chapter should not diminish our study or emphasis of any aspect of the atonement but enrich our overall appreciation for Christ's salvific gift. As a precedent for this caveat, see Gaye Strathearn, "Christ's Crucifixion: Reclamation of the Cross," in *With Healing in His*

Wings, ed. Camille Fronk Olson and Thomas A. Wayment (Provo, UT: BYU Religious Studies Center, 2013), 56.
4. See William Perez, "The Principle of Ascension in the Revelations of the Restoration," *Religious Educator* 22, no. 1 (2021): 59–77.
5. Reardon, "Essential Ascension," 48.
6. For a more complete examination of a Latter-day Saint theology of ascension, see William Perez, "The Ascension of Jesus Christ: Its Role in Redemption from a Latter-day Saint Theological Perspective" (master's thesis, Brigham Young University, 2019).
7. "Elders' Journal, July 1838," 44, emphasis added, The Joseph Smith Papers.
8. Hugh B. Brown, *Continuing the Quest* (Salt Lake City: Deseret Book, 1961), 74.
9. *New Testament Student Manual, Religion 211–212* (Salt Lake City: The Church of Jesus Christ of Latter-day Saints, 2018), chapter 14.
10. Similarly, at a worldwide Face to Face event for youth in 2017, Elder Jeffrey R. Holland talked about the gift of the Holy Ghost being an extension of the Savior's atonement: "You remember in the New Testament when [Christ] said, 'Unless I go away, the Holy Ghost can't come.' I wondered about that for thirty years. Well, I think what he means is 'Unless I fulfill my Atonement—that requires my death and resurrection, and absence, my ascension—the Holy Ghost can't come, and that's what you're really going to need to get through, once I've provided my Atonement.'" See "Face to Face with President and Elder Holland," The Church of Jesus Christ of Latter-day Saints, March 4, 2017.
11. Russell M. Nelson, "Endure and Be Lifted Up," *Ensign*, May 1997, 70.
12. When our best efforts feel insufficient, we can find encouragement in a Savior who, having ascended, advocates for us. Elder Bruce C. Hafen and Sister Marie K. Hafen wrote, "And when the merits of our case are not strong enough by themselves to return us to the highest place of all, he, having arrived there ahead of us, will plead our case before God." Bruce C. Hafen and Marie K. Hafen, *The Belonging Heart: The Atonement and Relationships with God and Family* (Salt Lake City: Deseret Book, 1994), 60.
13. Jeffrey R. Holland, "Behold the Lamb of God," *Ensign*, April 2019, 44; emphasis added.
14. Ezra Taft Benson, "Five Marks of the Divinity of Jesus Christ," *Ensign*, December 2001, 10.
15. Bishop Richard C. Edgley noted that the angel who was teaching Nephi "may have been speaking of two condescensions—one of God the Father and one of the Son Jesus Christ." Bishop Edgley wrote that "While God the Father's condescension reflects His great love for all mankind by permitting His Only Begotten to be sacrificed for even the humblest and lowliest of His children, Christ's condescension was more personal and visible—for He was the sacrifice. His condescension was manifest by who He was and the way He lived. His condescension can be seen in almost every recorded act of His 33 years of mortality." Richard C. Edgley, "The Condescension of God," *Ensign*, December 2001, 18.
16. Russell M. Nelson, "Why This Holy Land?," *Ensign*, December 1989, 15.
17. Neal A. Maxwell, "Irony: The Crust on the Bread of Adversity," *Ensign*, May 1989, 64.
18. *The Writings of Irenaeus: Volume 1*, trans. Alexander Roberts and W. H. Rambaut (Edinburgh: T&T Clark: 1868), 346.

19. Nelson, "Why This Holy Land?," 15.
20. D. Todd Christofferson, "Our Relationship with God," *Liahona*, May 2022, 78.
21. Consider the apostate Zoramites whose place of prayer was "high above the head; and the top thereof would only admit one person" (Alma 31:13). We read that "their hearts were *lifted up* unto great boasting, in their pride" (Alma 31:25; emphasis added).
22. The Book of Mormon makes clear that there could be no redemption without the atonement of Christ's blood (see Mosiah 3:11, 15-16; Alma 21:9). It also reminds us that "all things . . . are the typifying of [Christ]" (2 Nephi 11:4; see also Alma 13:2). Literature dealing with ancient sacrifice, such as instructions and commentary pertaining to the observance of the Day of Atonement, indicate that a valid sacrifice included the proper presentation of blood unto God (see Leviticus 16; Hebrews 9–10). A comprehensive atonement required the high priest to ascend into the holy of holies and therefore took place beyond the initial shedding of blood. The Savior's ascension can thus be imagined as a final presentation of his sacrifice before God the Father himself. Jesus Christ, the "high priest of good things to come" (Hebrews 9:11), ascended into the heavenly holy of holies, or the presence of God, "once for all" (Hebrews 10:10) to complete an atonement for humanity. Through his "great and last sacrifice" (Alma 34:10), we too can "enter into the holiest by the blood of Jesus" (Hebrews 10:19).
23. Theologians outside of the Latter-day Saint tradition have often commented on the implications of Christ's ascension for his followers. Saint Bede, an English monk during the Middle Ages, wrote about the significance of Christ ascending in the flesh: "[Jesus] was now returning to the throne of his Father's glory with the conquered mortal nature that he had taken. How sweet were the tears that they [his apostles] poured out when they were burning with lively hope and gladness over the prospect of their own entry into the heavenly fatherland! They knew that their God and Lord was now bringing there part of their own nature! Such a sight rightly restored them!" *Ancient Christian Commentary on Scripture: New Testament III (Luke)*, ed. Arthur A. Just Jr, (Downers Grove, IL: InterVarsity Press: 2003), 393.
24. In his classic work *The Infinite Atonement*, Tad R. Callister describes two types of spiritual death. The first is the universal consequence of Adam's transgression in which "all men are born in a setting outside God's physical presence." The second spiritual death is "a separation from God because of our individual sins." The atonement of Jesus Christ corrects both conditions. See Tad R. Callister, *The Infinite Atonement* (Salt Lake City: Deseret Book: 2000), 45.
25. For example, Doctrine and Covenants 14:7 clearly states that "eternal life . . . is the greatest of all the gifts of God."
26. Dale G. Renlund and Ruth Lybbert Renlund, *The Melchizedek Priesthood: Understanding the Doctrine, Living the Principles* (Salt Lake City: Deseret Book: 2018), 52.
27. Examples in the Book of Mormon include 2 Nephi 10:25; Mosiah 23:22; Alma 26:7; 36:28; 37:37; 38:5; 3 Nephi 15:1; and Ether 4:19.
28. Gordon B. Hinckley, "Temples and Temple Work," *Ensign*, February 1982, 3.

29. Douglas Farrow, a Christian professor and theologian, warned that "to cut short the journey of Jesus by conflating resurrection and ascension, however, is to alter the goal of salvation history." Douglas Farrow, *Ascension and Ecclesia* (Edinburgh: T&T Clark: 1999), 28.
30. Jennifer C. Lane, "Sitting Enthroned: A Scriptural Perspective," *Religious Educator* 19, no. 1 (2018): 114.
31. The first Latter-day Saint hymnal also makes several references to the ascension of Jesus Christ. One of the hymns included by Emma Smith describes a reminiscence of the Savior's ascension as well as a joyful anticipation of what it makes possible for his followers. Verse 5 reads: "Thence he arose, ascending high, And show'd our feet the way: Up to the Lord our flesh shall fly, At the great rising day." "Collection of Sacred Hymns, 1835," p. 119, The Joseph Smith Papers.
32. President Russell M. Nelson taught, "As Jesus descended below all things in order to rise above all things, He expects us to follow His example." Russell M. Nelson, "The Peace and Joy of Knowing the Savior Lives," *Ensign*, December 2011, 21.
33. Nelson, "Why This Holy Land?," 15.
34. Truman G. Madsen, *The Temple: Where Heaven Meets Earth* (Salt Lake City: Deseret Book, 2008), 11. This quote is attributed to President David O. McKay and was also referenced in a footnote to President Nelson's October 2022 general conference address "Overcome the World and Find Rest."
35. Cecil Frances Alexander, "He Is Risen," *Hymns* (Salt Lake City: The Church of Jesus Christ of Latter-day Saints, 1985), no. 199.
36. Russell M. Nelson, "Overcome the World and Find Rest," *Liahona*, November 2020, 97.
37. Russell M. Nelson, "The Book of Mormon: What Would Your Life Be Like without It?," *Ensign*, November 2017, 62.
38. Joseph Fielding Smith, "Does the Journey Seem Long?," *Hymns* (Salt Lake City: The Church of Jesus Christ of Latter-day Saints, 1985), no. 127.
39. *Ancient Christian Commentary on Scripture: New Testament III (Luke)*, ed. Arthur A. Just Jr., (Downers Grove, IL: InterVarsity Press: 2003), 392.
40. "Elders' Journal, July 1838," 44, emphasis added, The Joseph Smith Papers.

Index

A

Aaron, 220
Aaron, serpent of, 103n5
Abinadi
    awareness of crucifixion, 229n3
    hears voice of Lord, 113–14
    teachings on ascension, 296
    teachings on Godhead, 187–88
    teachings on Jesus and Mosaic law, 155–58, 164n4, 167n37, 167n42
    teachings on redemption, 176–77, 231n7
Abrahamic covenant, 20–22, 32
accountability, 77–79
accusations, false, 133
Adam and Eve, 20, 90, 162
adultery, woman taken in, 287–88
affliction, and remembering, 79–81

agency
    in applying Atonement of Jesus Christ, 182, 183, 184
    in following Jesus, 100
    and remembering, 77–79
Alma the Elder, 113–14, 158, 167n42, 297
Alma the Younger
    connects Jesus Christ with brazen serpent, 93–94
    exposes leadership's lack of moral authority, 132–36
    hears voice of Lord, 114
    overcomes evil by allowing evil to destroy itself, 136–40
    prophesies of Christ's post-Resurrection ministry, 215
    responds peacefully to persecution, 128–32
    teachings on Redeemer, 178, 180
    as type of Christ, 127

Amaleki, 153
Ammon, 114, 194–95, 219–20
Ammonihah, 114, 126–40, 179
Amulek
    debate with Zeezrom, 218–19
    exposes leadership's lack of moral authority, 132–36
    overcomes evil by allowing evil to destroy itself, 136–40
    responds peacefully to persecution, 128–32
    teachings on nature of God and Jesus, 218–19
    teachings on Redeemer, 179–80
    as type of Christ, 127
Amun-Re-Ptah, 192, 193–94, 205n24
ancient Near East
    symbolism of serpent in, 87, 96–99
    triads in, 190–94, 205n24, 206n27
Andersen, Neil L., 129
angel, appears to Benjamin, 154–55
anger, 277–78
animal sacrifice, 150, 154, 160–61, 249, 265n5
Anti-Nephi-Lehies, 159
aphesin (release from bondage), 172
Apis Bull, 193
Apophis, 97–98
apostles
    Jesus's ministry to, 109–11, 238, 242
    Jesus's support for, 245
    priesthood authority conferred upon, 109–10, 274
"Articles of the Church of Christ" (1829), 285–86
Asay, Carlos E., 94
ascension of Jesus Christ
    Atonement and, 293–95, 296, 302, 309n22
    in Book of Mormon, 296–99, 306–7
    connection to other Book of Mormon themes, 299–305
    as fundamental principle, 294–95, 306–7
    meaning of term, 294
    and resurrection, 310n29
    significance of, 309n23
ascensions, counterfeit, 301
Assmann, Jan, 192–93
Atonement
    agency in applying, 182, 183, 184
    Amulek's teachings on, 179–80
    ascension and, 293–95, 296, 302, 309n22
    events of, 307n1
    as fulfillment of law of Moses, 155, 162
    gift of Holy Ghost as extension of, 308n10
    Jacob's teachings on, 150
    redemption through, 12–13, 181–82
Atum, 97, 193

B

Ball, David, 39
bands of death, 139, 296
baptism
    and bestowal of Holy Ghost, 257, 258
    covenants of, 252
    disputations over, 284–85
    establishing liturgical orthodoxy concerning, 274–75
    following Christ's crucifixion, 251–52
    of Jesus, 266n15, 300, 305
    in modern Church, 264
    symbolism of, 305
    taught to Nephites, 239, 249–50, 253–56, 264
Beatitudes, 251–52
Bede, Saint, 309n23
Benjamin, King, 153–55, 166n29
Benson, Ezra Taft, 7–8, 269, 300
Benson, RoseAnn, 119

Berlin, Heinrich, 195–96
Bible, dual symbolism of serpent in, 88–91. *See also* New Testament; Old Testament
"blessed are ye," 251–53
blessing(s)
    in Abrahamic covenant, 20
    action required for, 92
    asking for, 246
    of obedience, 10, 32
blood of the Lamb, 169–70, 171–72, 182, 184
blot out, 171
Book of Mormon. *See also* Book of Mormon, latter-day relevance of
    as central to gathering of Israel, 33–34
    geography of, 204n8
    inspired authorship of, 121n2
    key message of, 185n3
    minor prophets in, 121n2
    promises made in, 10–13
    small plates, 152–53, 154, 213, 230n5
Book of Mormon, latter-day relevance of, 1–2
    and Book of Mormon Experiment, 4
    and declaration of humans' divine identity, 13–14
    and desire in learning, 3
    finding, 5–7
    and fulfillment of covenant with Israel, 15
    and intended audience of Book of Mormon, 7–9
    and promises made in Book of Mormon, 10–13
    and scriptures as written in retrospective, 9
    and teaching gospel, 2–3
Book of Mormon Experiment, 4
Brandt, Edward J., 145

brazen serpent, 87–88. *See also* serpent(s)
    and dual roles of Jesus Christ, 99–102
    dual symbolism of, in Bible, 88–90
    dual symbolism of, in Book of Mormon, 91–92
broken heart and contrite spirit, 149, 160–61, 175, 249, 257, 265n5, 305
brother of Jared, 111–12, 115, 232n15
Brown, Hugh B., 295
building, great and spacious, 301

C

Callister, Tad R., 307n1, 309n24
Campbell, David, 272–73
charity, 290
Charlesworth, James, 250, 265n1
chastisement, 101
Chesterton, G. K., 288–89
child development, touch in, 221–22
Chilton, Bruce, 251
Christ, meaning of title, 150, 172. *See also* Jesus Christ
Christofferson, D. Todd, 43, 121n3, 277, 301
church meetings
    admittance standards for, 282–83, 285–87
    to partake of sacrament, 281–82
Church of Jesus-Christ of Latter-day Saints, The
    authority of prophets and apostles of, 120
    and gathering of Israel, 27
    name of, 241–42, 280–81
    ordinances performed in, 250
    position on Book of Mormon geographical setting, 204n8
    relevance of Mosaic law to, 162–63
    terminology for deity, 203n6
Coffin Texts, 191–92

commandments
  to love God and neighbor, 276–78
  remembering and obeying, 74–77
compassion. See orthodoxy, harmony in pursuit of
compromise, 271, 278. See also orthodoxy, harmony in pursuit of
condescension of God / Jesus Christ, 174, 176–77, 299–301, 308n15, 310n32
consequences, allowed by God, 140
contention, 226, 242, 274–79. See also disagreement; orthodoxy, harmony in pursuit of
contrite spirit, 95, 99–100, 102, 149, 160–61, 175, 249, 257, 265n5, 305
conviction. See orthodoxy, harmony in pursuit of
Cook, Quentin L., 10
corruption, exposed by Alma and Amulek and Jesus, 132–36
counterfeit ascensions, 301
covenants, 20. See also Abrahamic covenant
Cowdery, Oliver, 285
Crisp, Gloria, 236
crucifixion, 128, 135–36, 137–38, 213–14, 222, 229n1, 229n3, 230n4

D

Dan, 90–91
death
  bands of, 139, 296
  spiritual, 294, 296, 302, 309n24
deities
  ancient Near Eastern, in form of serpent, 96–99, 104n28
  triads of ancient Egyptian, 190–94, 205n24, 206n27
  triads of Mesoamerican, 194–98, 199–200

de Jonge, Marinus, 48
Demotic Chronicle, 193
devotion, and diversity, 272
disagreement, 278–79. See also contention; orthopraxy
discernment, in mentoring, 238
discipleship, 289–90, 305–6. See also orthodoxy, harmony in pursuit of
diversity, 271, 272
divine identity, 13–14
doctrine of Christ, 102, 121n2, 226, 254–55, 274–79. See also orthodoxy, harmony in pursuit of
Duhm, Bernhard, 129–30

E

easy to live with, being, 269–70. See also orthodoxy, harmony in pursuit of
Edgley, Richard C., 308n15
Egypt, triads in ancient, 190–94, 205n24, 206n27
Elohim, God as, 203n6
Emerson, Ralph Waldo, 289
emotional support, mentoring with, 236–39
enemy, loving, 125–26, 226
Enos, 113, 121n7, 152
Eshmun, 99, 105n50
Esplin, Scott, 119
Ether, 115
evil, overcoming, 125–26, 140–41
  by allowing evil to destroy itself, 136–40
  and establishing types of Christ, 126–27
  by exposing leadership's lack of moral authority, 132–36
  by responding to persecution with peace, 128–32
exaltation, 31, 303–4
example, mentoring and serving as, 242
Exodus, 169–70
Eyring, Henry B., 120

F

fallen state, and need for redemption, 172–73, 175–76, 181, 182–83
Farrow, Douglas, 310n29
fathers, remembering, 81–82
Faust, James E., 121n7
fiery serpents, 88–89, 103n1
first fruits, 302
fluidity, religious, peaceful coexistence through, 272–73
foundation, metaphor of, 256
Frei, Hans, 290

G

Gale, Aaron M., 54–55
Gardiner, Alan H., 192
Gardner, Brant, 135, 200, 229n3, 230n4, 230n5
Gentiles, 29–30
Giabbiconi, Claire-Marie, 233n25
gifts. See blessing(s); spiritual gifts
God. *See also* trinitarianism
  condescension of, 174, 176–77, 299–301, 308n15
  consequences allowed by, 140
  distinction between Jehovah and, 188–89
  as Elohim, 203n6
  fulfillment of covenant between Israel and, 15
  "I am God" statement, 47
  Jesus Christ as, 218–19
  Jesus Christ as Son of, 53–55, 189, 217–18, 219
  kingdom of, 254, 265n6, 303–5
  love for, 276–78
  presence of, 183
  unity between Jesus and, 202n2, 209n71

Godhead, Nephite understanding of, 188–90, 199, 201, 217–21. *See also* trinitarianism
gospel
  of Christ, 102, 121n2, 226, 254–55, 274–79. *See also* orthodoxy, harmony in pursuit of
  fulness of, taken from Gentiles, 29–30
  knowledge of, promised in Book of Mormon, 11
  restoration of, 21–22, 35n3, 110
  teaching, 2–3, 72
great and spacious building, 301
Great Spirit, 194–95, 219–20
Griffiths, J. Gwyn, 190–91, 193, 206n30

H

Hafen, Bruce C. and Marie K., 308n12
Hales, Robert D., 126, 141, 289
Hansen, Richard D., 196
Hardy, Grant, 156
Hardy, Heather, 231n9, 231n10
harm, allowed by God, 140
harmony. See orthodoxy, harmony in pursuit of
Hays, Richard, 126
healing(s)
  performed by Jesus, 227–28
  serpent as symbol of, 99, 101
heart
  broken, and contrite spirit, 149, 160–61, 175, 249, 257, 265n5, 305
  change of, 13
Helaman, 167n31, 230n5
Hezekiah, King, 89, 103n8
Hill, Andrew E., 44–45
Hilton, John III, 128, 166n29, 307n1
Hinckley, Gordon B., 184, 303
Holland, Jeffrey R., 55, 140, 232n15, 300, 308n10

Holy Ghost. *See also* trinitarianism
　bestowal of gift of, 252, 253, 257–59, 264, 266n16
　gift of, as extension of Atonement, 308n10
　in Jesus's prayer for Nephites, 118
　and mentoring, 247
home, as center of gospel learning, 72
Hopkin, Shon, 121n2
hormones, and touch, 223–24
Horus, 191
Houston, Stephen, 197

I

"I am able to do my own work," 43
"I am a God of miracles," 43–44
"I am" statements, 37–38
　absolute, 39, 40, 45–49, 53–55
　in Book of Mormon, 39–55
　and coming to know Christ, 55–56
　by Jesus Christ in Book of Mormon, 57–60
　metaphorical, 39, 40, 41–45, 49–52
　New Testament categories for studying, 38–39
"I am the same yesterday, today, and forever," 44–45
if, indirectly exposing evil through use of term, 133–35
individual, Jesus's focus on, 237–38
infant baptism, 284
innocent, wrongful conviction of, 133
inspiration, recognizing, 121n7. *See also* revelation
Irenaeus, 300–301
Isaiah, 239
Isis, 191
Israel. *See also* Israel, gathering of
　fulfillment of covenant with, 15
　law of Moses given to, 146–47, 162
　redemption of, 169–71
　scattering of, 22–24
　and symbolism of serpent in Bible, 88–89
　and symbolism of serpent in Book of Mormon, 91–92
Israel, gathering of, 19–20, 33–34
　and Abrahamic covenant, 20–22
　accomplishment of, 24
　Book of Mormon as central to, 33–34
　Book of Mormon teachings on, 24–28
　final phase of, 31
　Jesus's teachings on, 29–30
　as primary responsibility of Christ, 52
　Russell M. Nelson on, 32–33
　salvation and, 52
　and scattering of Israel, 22–24
　stages of, 35n4

J

Jacob
　as doctrinal source of Benjamin, 166n29
　hears voice of Lord, 113
　ordained as priest, 150
　and understanding coming of Messiah through Mosaic law, 151–52
Jared, brother of, 111–12, 115, 232n15
Jaredites, serpents among, 96
Jarom, 152
Jehovah. *See also* Jesus Christ; Messiah
　and Abrahamic covenant, 20–21
　absolute "I am" statements by premortal, 45–49
　Book of Mormon teachings on, 40
　connection between Lamb of God and, 173–74
　distinction between God and, 188–89
　Jesus Christ as, 203n6, 204n7
　metaphorical "I am" statements by premortal, 41–45

as Redeemer, 169
unchanging nature of, 44–45
Jesus Christ. *See also* crucifixion; "I am" statements; Jehovah; mentoring; Messiah; prophets, Jesus Christ's communication to and about; redemption; touch, in Jesus's post-Resurrection ministry; trinitarianism
   Abinadi's teachings on Mosaic law and, 155–58, 164n4, 167n37
   as advocate, 308n12
   agency in following, 100
   ascension of, 293–307
   baptism of, 266n15, 300, 305
   Benjamin's teachings on Mosaic law and, 153–55
   brazen serpent as symbol of, 87, 91–95
   brother of Jared sees, 111–12, 232n15
   character of, 68
   coming to know, 55–56
   condescension of, 174, 176–77, 299–301, 308n15, 310n32
   connection between law of Moses and, 145–46, 162–63
   connection between remembering and, 63–66
   doctrine / gospel of, 102, 121n2, 226, 254–55, 274–79. *See also* orthodoxy, harmony in pursuit of
   dual roles of, 99–102
   early Book of Mormon teaching on, as Redeemer, 172–76
   establishing types of, 126–27
   as God, 218–19
   healings performed by, 227–28
   innocence of, 133
   introduced by name to Nephites, 145–46, 158–59, 165n16
   as Jehovah, 203n6, 204n7
   as judge, 93–94, 100–101
   Lehite knowledge concerning Mosaic law and, 147–49
   looking unto, 95, 100
   and meaning of *Christ* title, 150
   ministry to Nephites, 109–11, 116–19, 160–61, 297–98
   name of church of, 241–42, 279–81
   names of, 37
   Nephite knowledge concerning Mosaic law and, 150–53
   Nephite uncertainty regarding identity of, 217–21
   overcomes evil by allowing evil to destroy itself, 136–40
   persecution suffered by Alma and Amulek and, 128
   presence of, 51–52
   prophecies concerning coming of, 214–17
   reconciliation to, 302
   as Redeemer, 169, 171
   and relevance of Mosaic law to modern Church, 162–63
   remembering, 66–69, 82–83
   remembers, 72–74
   responses to persecution and distress, 127, 131
   as revealer of ordinances in Book of Mormon, 249–64
   as role model, 242
   salvation through, 92–93, 102, 155, 167n31, 183–84
   as Son of God, 53–55, 189, 217–18, 219
   as suffering servant, 129–30, 170, 178
   teachings on gathering of Israel, 29–30
   teachings on Godhead, 188
   and themes related to remembering, 66–82, 85n10
   as truth and life, 273

Jesus Christ (*continued*)
    unity between Father and, 202n2, 209n71
    witnesses of redeeming sacrifice of, 180–81
Judah, gathering of, 26
judgment
    accountability at, 79
    and allowing evil, 137–38
    brass serpent as representing, 93–94, 101
    and exposure of leadership's lack of moral authority, 136
    unlocked by resurrection, 302
Junajpu, 198
Jun Junajpu, 198

K

Keller, Helen, 222
Kimball, Spencer W., 63, 120
King, Martin Luther, Jr., 125, 141
kingdom of God, 254, 265n6, 303–5
knowledge
    acquired through touch, 212–13, 221–23
    and mentoring, 239–42
    promised in Book of Mormon, 11
Komatsu, Adney Y., 112–13

L

Lamanites, religious beliefs of, 194–95, 219–20
Lamb of God, 173–75. *See also* blood of the Lamb
Lamoni, 194–95, 219–20
Lamoni, father of, 220
Lane, Jennifer C., 303–4
latter days. See Book of Mormon, latter-day relevance of
law of Moses
    Abinadi's teachings on Jesus Christ and, 155–58, 164n4, 167n37
    Atonement as fulfillment of, 155, 162
    Benjamin's teachings on Jesus Christ and, 153–55
    connection between Jesus and, 145–46, 162–63
    given to Israel, 146–47, 162
    and Jesus's ministry to Nephites, 160–61
    Lehites' knowledge concerning Jesus Christ and, 147–49
    Nephites' knowledge concerning Jesus Christ and, 150–53
    Paul and, 147, 165n13
    relevance to modern Church, 162–63
    staying power of, among Nephites, 158–60, 166n25
Lawson, Bryan, 233n23, 233n24, 233n25
Lee, Harold B., 76
Lehi
    and Abrahamic covenant, 21
    hears voice of Lord, 113
    prophesies of coming Messiah, 148–49, 172–73, 174, 175–76, 200
Lehites, knowledge of, regarding Jesus Christ and Mosaic law, 147–49
Liahona, 94, 104n21
light, sharing, 246–47
Lincoln, Abraham, 270, 292n29
Lord, "I am the," 47–48
love
    commandments concerning, 276–78
    for enemy, 125–26, 226
    peaceful coexistence through, 273
    redemption as act of, 171, 185n5

M

Malachi, 240
marriage, and exaltation, 31
Martin, Simon, 195

Maxwell, Neal A., 43, 300
Mayan triadic deity complexes, 195–98
McConkie, Bruce R., 26, 33
meetings
    admittance standards for, 282–83, 285–87
    to partake of sacrament, 281–82
mentoring, 235–36, 246–47
    with emotional support, 236–39
    with knowledge support, 239–42
    as role model, 242–45
Merz, Annette, 250
Messiah. *See also* Jehovah; Jesus Christ
    Christ versus, 150
    coming of, 95
    gathering to, 24–25, 26
    meaning of term, 172
    miracles and, 43–44
    Nephite belief in, 150
    prophecies concerning coming of, 148–49, 172–76, 200, 214–17
Midgley, Louis C., 74
Millennium, 27, 91, 102
miracles, "I am a God of," 43–44. *See also* healing(s)
mistakes, correcting, 240–41
Monson, Thomas S., 51
moral authority, lack of, exposed by Alma and Amulek and Jesus, 132–36
Mormon
    counsel to Moroni, 305–6
    hears voice of Lord, 115
    knowledge of small plates, 230n5
    sources used by, 230n6
    teachings on Anti-Nephi-Lehies, 159
    as witness of Jesus Christ, 112
Moroni
    hears voice of Lord, 115
    Mormon's counsel to, 305–6
    as witness of Jesus Christ, 112
Mosiah, sons of, 114, 159
mourning, 252

Mouw, Richard, 289
Müller, Matthias M., 233n25

N

natural man, 80
Near East, ancient, symbolism of serpent in, 87, 96–99
Nehorites, 160
Nehushtan, 89, 103n8
neighbor, love for, 276–78
Nelson, Russell M.
    on baptism, 305
    on being lifted by Savior, 306
    on Book of Mormon, 107, 306
    on condescension of Christ, 301, 310n32
    on continuing revelation, 120
    on exaltation, 31
    on gathering of Israel, 32–34, 52
    on harmony, 290
    on hearing Lord's voice, 116
    on Jesus's baptism, 300
    on latter days, 2
    on name of Church, 280, 281
    on power of Book of Mormon truths, 2
    on remembering Jesus Christ, 82
    on teaching gospel in home, 72
Nephi (son of Helaman), 95, 109, 114–15
Nephi (son of Lehi)
    commanded to build ship, 91–92
    hears voice of Lord, 113
    prophesies of Christ's post-Resurrection ministry, 215, 231n9
    prophesies of coming Messiah, 173–75
    prophesies of crucifixion, 229n1
    references to brazen serpent, 92–93
    teachings on Godhead, 187
    temple built by, 150
    and understanding coming of Messiah through Mosaic law, 149–51, 166n25

Nephites
    anticipate Christ's coming, 146
    Jesus Christ as mentor to, 235–36. *See also* mentoring
    Jesus Christ introduced by name to, 145–46, 158–59, 165n16
    Jesus's ministry to, 109–11, 116–19, 160–61, 297–98. *See also* touch, in Jesus's post-Resurrection ministry
    knowledge of small plates, 230n5
    knowledge regarding crucifixion, 230n4
    knowledge regarding Jesus Christ and Mosaic law, 150–53
    ordinances taught to, 249–64
    recognize Christ as Jehovah, 204n7
    staying power of Mosaic law among, 158–60, 166n25
    understanding of Godhead, 188–90, 199, 201, 217–21
Nephthys, 191
New Jerusalem, 27, 28
New Kingdom papyrus, 192
New Testament
    categories for studying "I am" statements, 38–39
    "I am" statements in, 49
Nibley, Hugh, 167n36
Noah, 156–58
Nora, Amaury, 236

O

Oaks, Dallin H., 101, 271, 289–90
obedience, 10, 32, 74–77
Ogden, D. Kelly, 49, 52
Old Testament, "I am" statements in, 42–43, 45
Omni, 152–53
order and harmony in pursuit of orthodoxy, 270, 276, 290
ordinances
    in Book of Mormon, 249–64
    prophetic pattern concerning, 109–10

orthodoxy, harmony in pursuit of, 269–70, 289–91, 292n29
    and administration of sacrament, 279–81
    balance in, 287–89
    and condemnation of contention, 274–79
    and name of Church, 279–81
    possibility of, 270–77
    through periods of change, 284–87
orthopraxy, 276
other sheep, 29, 226–27
Otto, Eberhard, 192, 205n24
oxytocin, 223–24

P

Packer, Boyd K., 31
Palenque, 195–96, 197
parallelomania, 126
parenthetical reflections, in Book of Mormon, 8
Parry, Donald, 260
Partridge, Edward, 141
Paul, 147, 165n13
peace and peacemaking, 290
    as Christ's doctrine, 226, 242
    responding to persecution with, 128–32, 140–41, 142n16
    through religious fluidity, 272–73
persecution, responding to, with peace, 128–32, 140–41, 142n16
Piedras Negras, 197–98
Pratt, Parley P., 121n2
prayer(s)
    answers to, 9
    Jesus as role model of, 243–45
    resonances between, in Old and New Worlds, 267n20
    responding to persecution with, 131
    sacrament, 261–63
    taught to Nephites, 259–61
    of Zoramites, 309n21

priesthood, conferred upon Nephite
    apostles, 109–10, 274
prison, destruction of Ammonihah's, 137
prophetic words, remembering, 69–72
prophets, Jesus Christ's communication
    to and about, 107–8, 119–20
  Jesus speaks directly to prophets
    without appearing, 113–16
  Jesus's personal appearances to
    prophets, 108–13
  Jesus's teachings about prophets,
    116–19, 239–40
  means for, 121n3
prosperity, 10
punishment, allowed by God, 140
Putnam, Robert, 272–73
Pyramid Texts, 191

Q

Quiroa, Nestor, 198

R

Rasband, Ronald A., 44
Re, 97–98, 191. *See also* Amun-Re-Ptah
Reardon, Patrick Henry, 294
reconciliation to Christ, 302
redemption, 169–70
  Abinadi's teachings on, 176–77,
    231n7
  as act of lovingkindness, 171, 185n5
  Alma's teachings on, 178, 180
  Amulek's teachings on, 179–80
  ascension and, 296–99
  Christ's witness of, 180–81
  early Book of Mormon teaching on
    Jesus as Redeemer, 172–76
  spiritual reframing of, 170–72
  through Atonement, 12–13, 181–82
  willingness for, 182–84
refinement, 101

religious fluidity, peaceful coexistence
    through, 272–73
remember / remembering, 63–64, 82–84
  affliction and, 79–81
  and agency and accountability, 77–79
  as connected to Jesus Christ, 63,
    64–66
  defining, 83
  done by Jesus Christ, 72–74
  fathers, 81–82
  frequency of term in Book of
    Mormon, 84n2, 84n8
  Jesus Christ, 66–69, 82–83
  obedience and, 74–77
  prophetic words, 69–72
  themes related to, 66–82, 85n10
Renlund, Dale G., 92, 183, 303
Renlund, Ruth Lybbert, 303
repentance, 43, 254
restoration, 21–22, 35n3, 110
resurrection, 135–36, 138–39, 157,
    302–3, 310n29
retaliation, 125–26
revelation
  as bound to culture and language, 200
  continuing, 120
  methods of, 121n3
  pattern for, 111
  recognizing, 121n7
  through personal appearance of Jesus
    Christ, 108–13
  through voice of Jesus, 113–16
revenge, 125–26
Reynolds, Noel, 254
right, being, 269–70. *See also* orthodoxy,
    harmony in pursuit of
righteous, separated from wicked, 23
righteousness, generational impact of,
    13–14
rituals, 250, 251. *See also* ordinances
rod of Aaron, 103n5

S

sacrament
- under "Articles of the Church of Christ," 285–86
- establishment of, 250–51, 265n2
- following Christ's crucifixion, 251–52
- and harmony in pursuit of orthodoxy, 279–81
- and Jesus's name in connection with blood sacrifice, 162–63
- in modern Church, 264
- and remembering Jesus Christ, 68–69, 83
- standard of righteousness for taking, 282–83
- taught to Nephites, 109–10, 243, 252–53, 261–63
- touch and introduction of, 228–29

sacrifice(s)
- animal, 150, 154, 160–61, 249, 265n5
- of broken heart and contrite spirit, 149, 160–61, 175, 249, 257, 265n5
- and Jesus's fulfillment of Mosaic law, 160–61, 249
- under law of Moses, 146–47, 150, 154
- offered by Adam and Eve, 20, 162

salvation
- Abinadi's teachings on, 156–57
- availability of, 43
- and gathering of Israel, 31, 52
- and remembering Jesus Christ, 67–68, 69
- through Jesus Christ, 92–93, 102, 155, 167n31, 183–84

Samuel the Lamanite, 114, 116, 215–16, 230n5, 231n9, 240

Satan
- connection between serpent and, 90, 95–96
- counterfeit ascension of, 301
- subjection to, 138

Schmitt, Jonathan S., 37

scriptures. *See also* Bible; Book of Mormon
- answers in, 280
- as written in retrospective, 9

sealing, and exaltation, 31

seraphim, 91

serpent(s). *See also* brazen serpent
- of Aaron, 103n5
- connection between Satan and, 90, 95–96
- dual symbolism of, in Bible, 88–91
- dual symbolism of, in Book of Mormon, 91–96
- fiery, 88–89, 103n1
- symbolism of, in ancient Near East, 87, 96–99
- winged, 91

Seth, 191

sheep, other, 29, 226–27

Sherem, 151–52

ship, Nephi commanded to build, 91–92

sickness, 178

silence, responding to persecution with, 129

sin
- as bondage, 171, 177, 182, 183
- redemption from, 171–72, 176, 177, 179, 180–81, 182

sitting down imagery, 303–4

Skinner, Andrew C., 49, 52, 89

Skousen, Royal, 165n16

small plates, 152–53, 154, 213, 230n5

Smith, Emma, 310n31

Smith, John H., 111

Smith, Joseph
- and coming forth of Book of Mormon, 1
- on contraries and truth, 289
- foreordination of, 119

on fundamental principles of Church, 294–95
on gathering of Israel, 19, 31
prophecies regarding, 119
and restoration of gospel, 21, 35n3
Smith, Joseph Fielding, 306–7
Son of God, 53–55, 189, 217–18, 219
sons of Mosiah, 114, 159
spiritual death, 294, 296, 302, 309n24
spiritual gifts, 286–87
Stuart, David, 197
suffering servant, 129–30, 170, 178

T

temple(s)
built by Nephi, 150
as dwelling of gods, 200, 209n72
Ten Commandments, 146, 162
Te Velde, Herman, 206n27
Thayer, Stephen, 233n25
theosynthesis, 195, 200
Thiessen, Gerd, 250
three days / third day, 138–39
three Nephites, 110, 303–4
Tiamat, 97
touch, in Jesus's post-Resurrection ministry, 211–12, 229
acquisition of knowledge through, 212–13, 221–23
and healing, 227–28
and institution of sacrament, 228–29
and physiological effects of touch, 223–24
and sacrament prayers, 262–63
and social regulation of touch, 224–26, 233n23, 233n24, 233n25, 234n30
and uncertainty concerning Christ as God, 217–21
and uncertainty concerning Christ's coming, 214–17
and uncertainty concerning death by crucifixion, 213–14, 222
triads
in ancient Egypt, 190–94, 205n24, 206n27
Mesoamerican, 194–98, 199–200
trials, and remembering, 79–81
trinitarianism
and ancient Egyptian triads, 190–94, 205n24, 206n27
in Book of Mormon, 187–90, 198–201, 202n4
and Mesoamerican triads, 194–98, 199–200
type(s)
defined, 127
establishing, of Christ, 126–27

U

Uchtdorf, Dieter F., 235
Unis, 191
unity. *See also* contention; orthodoxy, harmony in pursuit of
as Christ's doctrine, 226, 242
between God and Jesus Christ, 202n2, 209n71

V

vengeance, 125–26
Viñas, Francisco J., 115–16
Vogel, Dan, 202n4

W

Wadjet, 98
Warner, C. Terry, 127
wealth, versus prosperity, 10
Welch, John, 256, 262
Wells, Robert E., 110
Whitmer, John, 286
wicked, separation of righteous from, 23
Wilson, John A., 192

winged serpent, 91
wiping, 171, 185n7
woman taken in adultery, 287–88
work, "I am able to do my own," 43
Wright, Mark Alan, 197, 199, 200
Wright, N. T., 133

Z

Zeezrom, 219
Zeniff, 155–56, 167n37
Zenos, 71, 213, 229n2
Zionism, 26
Zoramites, 159–60, 179–80, 309n21